T0213075

Lecture Notes in Computer Science 10687

Commenced Publication in 1973
Founding and Former Series Editors:
Gerhard Goos, Juris Hartmanis, and Jan van Leeuwen

More information about this series at http://www.springer.com/series/7407

Carlos Martín-Vide · Roman Neruda
Miguel A. Vega-Rodríguez (Eds.)

Theory and Practice of Natural Computing

6th International Conference, TPNC 2017
Prague, Czech Republic, December 18–20, 2017
Proceedings

 Springer

Editors
Carlos Martín-Vide ⓘ
Rovira i Virgili University
Tarragona
Spain

Miguel A. Vega-Rodríguez ⓘ
University of Extremadura
Cáceres
Spain

Roman Neruda ⓘ
Academy of Sciences of the Czech Republic
Prague
Czech Republic

ISSN 0302-9743   ISSN 1611-3349   (electronic)
Lecture Notes in Computer Science
ISBN 978-3-319-71068-6   ISBN 978-3-319-71069-3   (eBook)
https://doi.org/10.1007/978-3-319-71069-3

Library of Congress Control Number: 2017959616

LNCS Sublibrary: SL1 – Theoretical Computer Science and General Issues

Printed on acid-free paper

This Springer imprint is published by Springer Nature
The registered company is Springer International Publishing AG
The registered company address is: Gewerbestrasse 11, 6330 Cham, Switzerland

Preface

These proceedings contain the papers that were presented at the 6th International Conference on the Theory and Practice of Natural Computing (TPNC 2017), held in Prague, Czech Republic, during December 18–20, 2017.

The scope of TPNC is rather broad, including:

- Theoretical contributions to: amorphous computing, ant colonies, artificial chemistry, artificial immune systems, artificial life, bacterial foraging, cellular automata, chaos computing, collision-based computing, complex adaptive systems, computing with DNA, computing with words and perceptions, developmental systems, evolutionary computing, fractal geometry, fuzzy logic, gene assembly in ciliates, granular computing, intelligent systems, in vivo computing, membrane computing, nanocomputing, neural computing, optical computing, physarum machines, quantum computing, quantum information, reaction-diffusion systems, rough sets, self-organizing systems, swarm intelligence, synthetic biology
- Applications of natural computing to: algorithmics, bioinformatics, control, cryptography, design, economics, graphics, hardware, human–computer interaction, knowledge discovery, learning, logistics, medicine, natural language processing, optimization, pattern recognition, planning and scheduling, programming, robotics, telecommunications, Web intelligence

TPNC 2017 received 39 submissions. Papers were reviewed by three Program Committee members. There were also a few external reviewers consulted. After a thorough and vivid discussion phase, the committee decided to accept 23 papers (which represents an acceptance rate of about 59%). The conference program included three invited talks and some poster presentations of work-in-progress as well.

The excellent facilities provided by the EasyChair conference management system allowed us to deal with the submissions successfully and handle the preparation of these proceedings in time.

We would like to thank all invited speakers and authors for their contributions, the Program Committee and the external reviewers for their cooperation, and Springer for its very professional publishing work.

October 2017

Carlos Martín-Vide
Roman Neruda
Miguel A. Vega-Rodríguez

Organization

TPNC 2017 was organized by the Institute of Computer Science, Czech Academy of Sciences, Prague, Czech Republic, the Faculty of Mathematics and Physics, Charles University, Prague, Czech Republic, and the Research Group on Mathematical Linguistics — GRLMC, Rovira i Virgili University, Tarragona, Spain.

Program Committee

Ajith Abraham	Machine Intelligence Research Labs, USA
Uwe Aickelin	University of Nottingham, UK
Robert Babuska	Delft University of Technology, The Netherlands
Thomas Bäck	Leiden University, The Netherlands
Gilles Brassard	University of Montréal, Canada
Erik Cambria	Nanyang Technological University, Singapore
Carlos Coello Coello	CINVESTAV-IPN, Mexico
David W. Corne	Heriot-Watt University, UK
Dipankar Dasgupta	University of Memphis, USA
Kalyanmoy Deb	Michigan State University, USA
Marco Dorigo	Université Libre de Bruxelles, Belgium
Andries Engelbrecht	University of Pretoria, South Africa
Michel Gendreau	Polytechnique Montréal, Canada
Deborah M. Gordon	Stanford University, USA
Lawrence Hall	University of South Florida, USA
Enrique Herrera-Viedma	University of Granada, Spain
Licheng Jiao	Xidian University, China
Janusz Kacprzyk	Polish Academy of Sciences, Poland
Hamid Reza Karimi	Polytechnic University of Milan, Italy
Joshua Knowles	University of Birmingham, UK
Andrew Kusiak	University of Iowa, USA
Vittorio Maniezzo	University of Bologna, Italy
Carlos Martín-Vide	Rovira i Virgili University, Spain (Chair)
Luis Martínez López	University of Jaén, Spain
José M. Merigó Lindahl	University of Chile, Chile
Radko Mesiar	Slovak University of Technology, Slovakia
Risto Miikkulainen	University of Texas, Austin, USA
Christos Ouzounis	Centre for Research and Technology Hellas, Greece
Henri Prade	Paul Sabatier University, France
Patrick Siarry	University of Paris-Est, France
Andrzej Skowron	University of Warsaw, Poland
John A. Smolin	IBM Thomas J. Watson Research Center, USA
Thomas Stützle	Université Libre de Bruxelles, Belgium

Ponnuthurai N. Suganthan	Nanyang Technological University, Singapore
Johan Suykens	KU Leuven, Belgium
Guy Theraulaz	Paul Sabatier University, France
Jon Timmis	University of York, UK
Xin-She Yang	Middlesex University, UK
Yiyu Yao	University of Regina, Canada
Lotfi A. Zadeh	University of California, Berkeley, USA
Anton Zeilinger	University of Vienna, Austria

Additional Reviewers

Rahul Paul
Thuy Pham Xuan
Jianbin Qiu
Josep M. Rossell

Dong Wang
Yanling Wei
Anton Zeilinger

Organizing Committee

Carlos Martín-Vide, Tarragona (Co-chair)
Roman Neruda, Prague (Co-chair)
Manuel J. Parra Royón, Granada
Martin Pilat, Prague
David Silva, London
Miguel A. Vega-Rodríguez, Cáceres

Contents

Molecular Computation

Neural Networks

Quantum Computing

Invited Talk

Recent Results and Open Problems
in Evolutionary Multiobjective Optimization

Carlos A. Coello Coello[✉]

Evolutionary Computation Group, Departamento de Computación, CINVESTAV,
Av. IPN No. 2508, Col. San Pedro Zacatenco, Mexico D.F. 07360, Mexico
ccoello@cs.cinvestav.mx

Abstract. Evolutionary algorithms (as well as a number of other meta-heuristics) have become a popular choice for solving problems having two or more (often conflicting) objectives (the so-called multi-objective optimization problems). This area, known as EMOO (Evolutionary Multi-Objective Optimization) has had an important growth in the last 20 years, and several people (particularly newcomers) get the impression that it is now very difficult to make contributions of sufficient value to justify, for example, a PhD thesis. However, a lot of interesting research is still under way. In this paper, we will briefly review some of the research topics on evolutionary multi-objective optimization that are currently attracting a lot of interest (e.g., indicator-based selection, many-objective optimization and use of surrogates) and which represent good opportunities for doing research. Some of the challenges currently faced by this discipline will also be delineated.

Keywords: Evolutionary computing · Optimization

1 Introduction

The solution of problems having two or more (normally conflicting) objectives has attracted a considerable attention in the last few years. The solution of these so-called *multi-objective optimization problems* (MOPs) gives rise to a set of solutions representing the best possible trade-offs among the objectives. Such solutions, defined in decision variable space constitute the so-called *Pareto optimal set*, and their corresponding objective function values form the so-called *Pareto front*.

Although a number of mathematical programming techniques have been developed since the 1970s to solve MOPs [81], such techniques present several limitations, from which two of the most relevant are that these algorithms are normally very susceptible to the shape or continuity of the Pareto front and that they tend to generate a single element of the Pareto optimal set per run. Additionally, in some real-world MOPs, the objective functions are not provided in algebraic form, but are the output of a black box software (which, for example, runs a simulation to obtain an objective function value), thus limiting the

C. Martín-Vide et al. (Eds.): TPNC 2017, LNCS 10687, pp. 3–21, 2017.
https://doi.org/10.1007/978-3-319-71069-3_1

applicability of mathematical programming techniques. Such limitations have motivated the development of alternative approaches from which metaheuristics[1] have been, with no doubt, the most popular and effective choice available so far (see for example [24]).

From the many metaheuristics in current use, Evolutionary Algorithms (EAs) are, clearly, the most popular in today's specialized literature. EAs are inspired on the "survival of the fittest" principle from Darwin's evolutionary theory [43], and simulate the evolutionary process in a computer, as a way to solve problems. EAs have become very popular as multi-objective optimizers because of their ease of use (and implementation) and generality (e.g., they are less sensitive than mathematical programming techniques to the initial points used for the search and to the specific features of a MOP). EAs have also an additional advantage: since they are population-based techniques, it is possible for them to manage a set of solutions at a time, instead of only one, as normally done by traditional mathematical programming techniques. This allows EAs to generate several elements from the Pareto optimal set in a single run.

The first Multi-Objective Evolutionary Algorithm (MOEA) was proposed in the mid-1980s by David Schaffer [103]. However, it was until the mid-1990s that MOEAs started to attract serious attention from researchers. Nowadays, it is possible to find applications of MOEAs in practically all domains.[2]

The remainder of this paper is organized as follows. In Sect. 2, we provide some basic multi-objective optimization concepts required to make this paper self-contained. Section 3 briefly describes some relevant research topics that are worth currently being explored by EMOO researchers. In Sect. 4, we present other challenges in the field that have been only scarcely explored. Finally, the main conclusions of this paper are provided in Sect. 5.

2   Basic Concepts

We are interested in solving problems of the type[3]:

$$\text{minimize } \boldsymbol{f}(\boldsymbol{x}) := [f_1(\boldsymbol{x}), f_2(\boldsymbol{x}), \ldots, f_k(\boldsymbol{x})] \tag{1}$$

subject to:

$$g_i(\boldsymbol{x}) \leq 0 \quad i = 1, 2, \ldots, m \tag{2}$$

$$h_i(\boldsymbol{x}) = 0 \quad i = 1, 2, \ldots, p \tag{3}$$

---

[1] A **metaheuristic** is a high level strategy for exploring search spaces by using different methods [14]. Metaheuristics have both a diversification (i.e., exploration of the search space) and an intensification (i.e., exploitation of the accumulated search experience) procedure.

[2] The author maintains the EMOO repository, which currently contains over 10,850 bibliographic references related to evolutionary multi-objective optimization. The EMOO repository is located at: https://emoo.cs.cinvestav.mx.

[3] Without loss of generality, we will assume only minimization problems.

where $x = [x_1, x_2, \ldots, x_n]^T$ is the vector of decision variables, $f_i : \mathbb{R}^n \to \mathbb{R}$, $i = 1, \ldots, k$ are the objective functions and $g_i, h_j : \mathbb{R}^n \to \mathbb{R}$, $i = 1, \ldots, m$, $j = 1, \ldots, p$ are the constraint functions of the problem.

To describe the concept of optimality in which we are interested, we will introduce next a few definitions.

Definition 1. Given two vectors $x, y \in \mathbb{R}^k$, we say that $x \leq y$ if $x_i \leq y_i$ for $i = 1, \ldots, k$, and that x **dominates** y (denoted by $x \prec y$) if $x \leq y$ and $x \neq y$.

Definition 2. We say that a vector of decision variables $x \in \mathcal{X} \subset \mathbb{R}^n$ is **non-dominated** with respect to $\mathcal{X}$, if there does not exist another $x' \in \mathcal{X}$ such that $f(x') \prec f(x)$.

Definition 3. We say that a vector of decision variables $x^* \in \mathcal{F} \subset \mathbb{R}^n$ ($\mathcal{F}$ is the feasible region) is **Pareto-optimal** if it is nondominated with respect to $\mathcal{F}$.

Definition 4. The **Pareto Optimal Set** $\mathcal{P}^*$ is defined by:

$$\mathcal{P}^* = \{x \in \mathcal{F} | x \text{ is Pareto-optimal}\}$$

Definition 5. The **Pareto Front** $\mathcal{PF}^*$ is defined by:

$$\mathcal{PF}^* = \{f(x) \in \mathbb{R}^k | x \in \mathcal{P}^*\}$$

We thus wish to determine the Pareto optimal set from the set $\mathcal{F}$ of all the decision variable vectors that satisfy (2) and (3). Note however that in practice, not all the Pareto optimal set is normally desirable (e.g., it may not be desirable to have different solutions that map to the same values in objective function space) or achievable.

3   Some Open Research Topics that Are Worth Exploring

In spite of the significant development that MOEAs have experienced since their inception, there are still some research topics that are worth exploring in the next few years. From them, we will discuss three in this paper:

1. Algorithmic design
2. Scalability
3. Dealing with expensive objective functions

Next, we briefly discuss some of the most representative research that has been conducted on these topics.

3.1   Algorithmic Design

In the early days of MOEAs, the approaches that were adopted were very simple and naive. For example, it was relatively common to use linear aggregating functions that combined all the objective functions into a single scalar value [48]. However, by the mid-1990s, several MOEAs started to adopt mechanisms such as *Pareto ranking* [43] and *nondominated sorting* [109]. In these mechanisms, the idea is to rank solutions based on Pareto optimality, such that nondominated individuals obtain the highest (best) possible rank. Since diversity is an important issue in MOEAs, in order to avoid convergence to a single solution, an additional mechanism was integrated to them: the so-called density estimator. Since the mid-1990s, a number of density estimators have been adopted, including: fitness sharing [44], clustering [129], adaptive grids [67], crowding [30], entropy [88] and parallel coordinates [54].

By the end of the 1990s, another mechanism was incorporated into MOEAs: elitism. The intuition behind the concept of *elitism* is that we need to retain the solutions that remain nondominated with respect to the new individuals that are being generated by our MOEA (otherwise, such solutions could be lost). Elitism is important not only from a practical point of view, but also for theoretical reasons, since this mechanism is required to guarantee convergence [99].

In spite of the large number of MOEAs that were proposed in the 1990s, few of them were widely used. From them, clearly the **Nondominated Sorting Genetic Algorithm II** (NSGA-II) [30] was the most popular (and is still being used today).

However, a few years after NSGA-II, another interesting MOEA was proposed: the **Multi-Objective Evolutionary Algorithm based on Decomposition** (MOEA/D) [124]. The idea of using decomposition was originally proposed in mathematical programming and it consists in transforming a multiobjective problem into several single-objective optimization problems which, in the case of MOEA/D are simultaneously solved, using neighborhood search. Decomposition-based methods would eventually become very popular research trend in algorithmic design (see for example [101]) and would influence the design of the **Nondominated Sorting Genetic Algorithm III** (NSGA-III) [29] which adopts decomposition and reference points.

Nevertheless, since 2004, a different type of algorithmic design has increasingly attracted interest from researchers: indicator-based selection. The idea of this sort of MOEA was introduced in the **Indicator-Based Evolutionary Algorithm** (IBEA) [126] which consists of an algorithmic framework that allows the incorporation of any performance indicator into the selection mechanism of a MOEA. IBEA was originally tested with the hypervolume [128] and the binary ϵ indicator [127]. Indicator-based selection has attracted a lot of interest, mainly because this sort of mechanism is known to work properly in many-objective optimization (i.e., MOPs having four or more objectives).

Over the years, a number of indicator-based MOEAs have been proposed, but probably the most representative approach within this family has been the **S Metric Selection Evolutionary Multiobjective Algorithm**

(SMS-EMOA) [36]. SMS-EMOA randomly generates an initial population and then produces a single solution per iteration (i.e., it uses steady state selection) using the crossover and mutation operators from NSGA-II. Then, it applies nondominated sorting (as in NSGA-II). When the last nondominated front has more than one solution, SMS-EMOA uses hypervolume to decide which solution should be removed. Beume et al. [11] proposed a new version of SMS-EMOA in which the hypervolume contribution is not used when, in the nondominated sorting process, we obtain more than one front. In this case, they use the number of solutions that dominate to a certain individual (i.e., the solution that is dominated by the largest number of solutions is removed).

After the introduction of SMS-EMOA, most indicator-based MOEAs that have been proposed adopt a performance indicator in their density estimator,[4] and not in their selection mechanism (see for example [59]). The actual use of a "pure" indicator-based selection mechanism has been very rare (see for example [78]).

So, at this point, one obvious question is: why is that the *hypervolume* is such an attractive choice for indicator-based selection?

The hypervolume (also known as the S metric or the Lebesgue Measure) of a set of solutions measures the size of the portion of objective space that is dominated by those solutions collectively. One of its main advantages are its mathematical properties, since it has been proved that the maximization of this performance measure is equivalent to finding the Pareto optimal set [39]. Additionally, empirical studies have shown that (for a certain number of points previously determined) the maximization of the hypervolume does indeed produce subsets of the Pareto front which are well-distributed [36,65]. Also, the hypervolume assesses both convergence and, to a certain extent, also the spread of solutions along the Pareto front (although without enforcing uniform distribution of solutions).

However, there are several issues regarding the use of the hypervolume. First, the computation of this performance measure depends of a reference point, which can influence the results in a significant manner. Some people have proposed to use the worst objective function values in the current population, but this requires scaling of the objectives. Nevertheless, the most serious limitation of the hypervolume is its high computational cost. The best algorithms known to compute hypervolume have a polynomial complexity on the number of points used, but such complexity grows exponentially on the number of objectives [12]. This has triggered a significant amount of research regarding algorithms that can reduce the computational cost of computing the hypervolume[5] (see for example [15,57,120,121]).

---

[4] In fact, the earliest use of the hypervolume into a MOEA is as a density estimator in a secondary population (see [65]).

[5] See also:
http://ls11-www.cs.uni-dortmund.de/rudolph/hypervolume/start
http://people.mpi-inf.mpg.de/~tfried/HYP/
http://iridia.ulb.ac.be/~manuel/hypervolume.

An alternative to deal with this problem is to approximate the actual hypervolume contributions. This is the approach adopted by the **Hypervolume Estimation Algorithm for Multi-Objective Optimization** (HyPE) [3] in which Monte Carlo simulations are used to approximate exact hypervolume values. Although this is certainly a very interesting idea, in practice HyPE does not produce results as competitive as when using exact hypervolume computations.

Another possibility is to use another performance indicator, but the fact that the hypervolume is the only unary indicator which is known to be Pareto compliant [130] has made this alternative less attractive to researchers. Nevertheless, the use of a few other performance indicators has been reported to be successful in practice. Examples of these alternative indicator that have been used within MOEAs are: $R2$ [16,17,33,46,51,52], Δ_p [79,98,105] and Inverted Generational Distance plus ($IGD+$) [60,74]. Also, the use of other mechanisms such as the maximin fitness function, which seems to be related to the ϵ indicator are very promising (see for example [77]). All of these MOEAs are computationally inexpensive and perform quite well in many-objective problems, however, their use in practice is still very limited.

It is worth indicating that while some researchers debate if decomposition-based MOEAs or indicator-based MOEAs will become the new algorithmic trend in the next few years, other alternatives to the use of Pareto-based selection have been proposed. For example, Molinet Berenguer and Coello Coello [7], proposed an approach that transforms a multi-objective optimization problem into a linear assignment problem using a set of weight vectors uniformly scattered. Uniform design is adopted to obtain the set of weights, and the Kuhn-Munkres (Hungarian) algorithm [68] is used to solve the resulting assignment problem. This approach was found to perform quite well (and at a low computational cost) in many-objective optimization problems.

3.2   Scalability

In their early days, MOEAs were mainly used to solve problems having only two or three objectives. However, once Pareto-based MOEAs became popular, the need for solving problems having more objectives was very evident. At this point, problems started to arise, since it was soon evident that Pareto-based MOEAs tend to perform poorly in many-objective optimization problems [56].

Experimental [89,117] and analytical studies [26,66] have identified the following limitations of Pareto-based MOEAs in many-objective problems:

1. *Deterioration of the Search Ability:* The proportion of nondominated solutions in a population increases rapidly with the number of objectives [37]. According to Bentley *et al.* [5] the number of nondominated k-dimensional vectors on a set of size n is $O(\ln^{k-1} n)$. This implies that in problems with a large number objectives, the selection of solutions is carried out almost at random or guided by diversity criteria. In fact, Mostaghim and Schmeck [85] have shown that a random search optimizer achieves better results than NSGA-II [30] in a problem with 10 objectives.

2. *Dimensionality of the Pareto front:* Due to the 'curse of dimensionality' the number of points required to represent accurately a Pareto front increases exponentially with the number of objectives. The number of points necessary to represent a k-dimensional Pareto front with resolution r is given by $O(kr^{k-1})$ (*e.g.*, see [106]). This poses a challenge both to the data structures to efficiently manage that number of points and to the density estimators to achieve an even distribution of the solutions along the Pareto front.

3. *Visualization of the Pareto front:* Clearly, with more than three objectives is not possible to plot the Pareto front as usual. This is a serious problem since visualization plays a key role for a proper decision making process. In recent years, a number of visualization techniques have been proposed for many-objective problems (see for example [113]), but this is still an active research area.

In order to properly deal with many-objective optimization problems, three main approaches have been normally adopted [4,70,72]:

1. As indicated before, the use of indicator-based MOEAs has been an important research trend to deal with many-objective optimization problems, in spite of the limitations of some performance indicators such as the hypervolume (see for example [62]).

2. One interesting possibility that was adopted in the early days of many-objective optimization was the use of an optimality relation that yields a solution ordering finer than that yielded by Pareto optimality. Among these alternative relations we can find average ranking [6,40], k-optimality [37], preference order ranking [32], favour relation [110], and a method that controls the dominance area [102], among others. Besides providing a richer ordering of the solutions, these relations obtain an optimal set that it is usually a subset of the Pareto optimal set.

3. Another interesting approach which is now rarely used is to reduce the number of objectives of the problem during the search process or in an *a posteriori* manner, during the decision making process [18,31,71]. The main goal of this kind of reduction techniques is to identify redundant objectives (or redundant to some degree) in order to discard them. A redundant objective is one that can be removed without changing the dominance relation induced by the original objective set.

In contrast with the significant interest that many-objective optimization has attracted in recent years, scalability in decision variable space has been only recently studied in the context of multi-objective optimization (see for example [73,82,83,125]). This is remarkable if we consider that large-scale multi-objective optimization problems (i.e., problems having more than 100 decision variables) are not rare in real-world applications (see for example [119]). In this area, the use of cooperative coevolutionary approaches (which have been very successful in single-objective large-scale optimization) is the most common research trend. It is worth indicating, however, that no current benchmark exists that includes large-scale multi-objective optimization problems.

A more challenging problem would consist in solving many-objective large-scale problems, but no work in this direction has been reported yet, to the best of the author's knowledge.

3.3 Dealing with Expensive Objective Functions

In spite of the current popularity of MOEAs, one of their limitations is that, since they are stochastic search techniques, they normally require a significant number of objective function evaluations in order to generate a proper sampling that allows a reasonably good approximation of the Pareto front, even when dealing with problems of low dimensionality. This is, indeed, a serious limitation when dealing with real-world problems, because in many cases, the cost of a MOEA becomes prohibitive.

In general, MOEAs can be unaffordable for an application when:

- The evaluation of the fitness functions is computationally expensive (i.e., it takes from minutes to hours).
- The fitness functions cannot be defined in an algebraic form (e.g., when the fitness functions are generated by a simulator).
- The total number of evaluations of the fitness functions is limited by financial constraints (i.e., there is a financial cost involved in computing the fitness functions).

In recent years, a significant amount of research has been conducted to allow MOEAs to properly deal with computationally expensive problems [100]. The main approaches that have been developed in this area can be roughly divided into three main groups:

1. **Use of parallelism:** This is clearly the most obvious approach given the current access to cheap parallel architectures (e.g., GPUs [8, 28, 107]). It is worth noting, however, that in spite of the existence of interesting proposals in this area (see for example [1, 84, 111]), the basic research in this area has remained scarce, since most publications involving parallel MOEAs focus on specific applications or on parallel extensions of specific MOEAs.
2. **Surrogates:** In this case, knowledge of past evaluations of a MOEA is used to build an empirical model that approximates the fitness functions to be optimized. This approximation can then be used to predict promising new solutions at a smaller evaluation cost than that of the original problem [63, 64]. Current functional approximation models include Polynomials (response surface methodologies [41, 92]), neural networks (e.g., multi-layer perceptrons (MLPs) [55, 58, 87]), radial-basis function (RBF) networks [86, 114, 122], support vector machines (SVMs) [13, 104], Gaussian processes [20, 115], and Kriging [35, 93] models. Although frequently used in engineering applications, surrogate methods can normally be adopted only in problems of low dimensionality, which is an important limitation when dealing with real-world MOPs.

3. **Fitness inheritance:** This technique was introduced by Smith et al. [108], and its main motivation is to reduce the total number of fitness function evaluations performed by a (single-objective) evolutionary algorithm. The mechanism works as follows: when assigning the fitness to an individual, some times we evaluate the objective function as usual, but the rest of the time, we assign fitness as an average of the fitness of the parents. This saves one fitness function evaluation, and is based on the assumption of similarity of an offspring to its parents. Fitness inheritance must not be always applied, since the algorithm needs to use the true fitness function several times, in order to obtain enough information to guide the search. The percentage of time in which fitness inheritance is applied is called *inheritance proportion*. If this inheritance proportion is 1, the algorithm is most likely to prematurely converge [23]. Extending fitness inheritance involves several issues, mainly related to its apparent limitation for dealing with non-convex Pareto fronts [34]. However, some researchers have managed to successfully adapt fitness inheritance to MOEAs [94], reporting important savings on the total number of objective function evaluations performed.

Other approaches are also possible. For example, some researchers have adopted cultural algorithms [9,10,25,95], which obtain knowledge during the evolutionary process and use it to perform a more efficient search at the expense of a significantly large memory usage. Cultural algorithms were proposed by Reynolds [96,97], as an approach that tries to add domain knowledge to an evolutionary algorithm during the search process, avoiding the need to add it *a priori*. This approach uses, in addition to the population space commonly adopted in evolutionary algorithms, a belief space, which encodes the knowledge obtained from the search points and their evaluation, in order to influence the evolutionary operators that guide the search. However, the belief space is commonly designed based on the group of problems that is to be solved. At each generation, the cultural algorithm selects some exemplar individuals from the population, in order to extract information from them that can be useful during the search. Such an information is used to update the belief space. The belief space will then influence the operators of the evolutionary algorithm, to transform them in informed operators and enhance the search process. Cultural algorithms can be an effective means of saving objective function evaluations, but since a map of decision variable space must be kept at all times, their cost will soon become prohibitive even for problems of moderate dimensionality.

4   Other Challenges

Several other topics remain scarcely explored in evolutionary multi-objective optimization. For example:

1. **Dynamic problems:** In the real world, there are problems in which the objective function values may vary over time (e.g., because of the presence of noise), depending on certain events. The solution of such problems requires

algorithms that are able to quickly "adapt" to these changes in the environment. There are relatively few MOEAs that have been designed to deal with dynamic MOPs and the current research in this area remains relatively scarce [21,27,49,91,118]. It is worth noting that dynamic problems require different types of benchmarks (see for example [38]) and performance measures (see for example [50]).

2. **Hyper-heuristics:** In spite of the fact that multi-objective memetic algorithms (i.e., MOEAs that are hybridized with a local search engine, which could be, for example, a gradient-based method [69] or a direct search method [123]) have gained popularity in recent years (see for example [42,61,75]), hyper-heuristics have been only scarcely explored in the context of multi-objective optimization, particularly for dealing with continuous optimization problems (see for example [45,53]). Hyper-heuristics [22] are approaches that combine several types of heuristics, with the aim of combining their advantages in a wide class of problems. Their main motivation is to have a more general search engine that can solve a wider variety of hard optimization problems. Hyper-heuristics have been mostly developed for discrete search spaces and have been used to solve mainly single-objective optimization problems. However, their use in continuous multi-objective optimization problems, although possible, has been scarcely explored (see for example [76]). The use of other (similar) approaches that combine operators and different MOEAs into a common framework are also promising research venues (see for example [47,116]).

3. **Automatic parameter configuration:** Although some relevant work has been conducted on parameter fine-tuning for MOEAs (see for example [2, 19,112]), it has been only recently that researchers in evolutionary multi-objective optimization have considered the use of tools to do an automatic calibration of MOEAs (see for example [80]). One limitation for the use of such tools is that a scalar measure is required, but some researchers have relied on the use of hypervolume (see for example [90]) for that sake.

5   Conclusions

In this paper, a few research trends in evolutionary multi-objective optimization have been briefly described with the aim of encouraging more research in such areas.

The main goal of this paper is to illustrate that, in spite of its 32 years of existence, evolutionary multi-objective optimization still has several research opportunities to offer to newcomers. The contents of this paper is just a small sample of the several topics that are still available for starting a research career in this area.

Acknowledgements. The author gratefully acknowledges support from CONACyT grant no. 221551.

References

1. Alba, E., Luque, G., Nesmachnow, S.: Parallel metaheuristics: recent advances and new trends. Int. Trans. Oper. Res. **20**(1), 1–48 (2013)
2. Andersson, M., Bandaru, S., Ng, A.H.: Tuning of multiple parameter sets in evolutionary algorithms. In: 2016 Genetic and Evolutionary Computation Conference (GECCO 2016), Denver, Colorado, USA, 20–24 July 2016, pp. 533–540. ACM Press (2016). ISBN 978-1-4503-4206-3
3. Bader, J., Zitzler, E.: HypE: an algorithm for fast hypervolume-based many-objective optimization. Evol. Comput. **19**(1), 45–76 (2011). Spring
4. Bechikh, S., Elarbi, M., Ben Said, L.: Many-objective optimization using evolutionary algorithms: a survey. In: Bechikh, S., Datta, R., Gupta, A. (eds.) Recent Advances in Evolutionary Multi-objective Optimization. ALO, vol. 20, pp. 105–137. Springer, Cham (2017). https://doi.org/10.1007/978-3-319-42978-6_4
5. Bentley, J., Kung, H., Schkolnick, M., Thompson, C.: On the average number of maxima in a set of vectors and applications. J. Assoc. Comput. Mach. **25**(4), 536–543 (1978)
6. Bentley, P.J., Wakefield, J.P.: Finding acceptable solutions in the pareto-optimal range using multiobjective genetic algorithms. In: Chawdhry, P.K., Roy, R., Pant, R.K. (eds.) Soft Computing in Engineering Design and Manufacturing, Part 5, pp. 231–240. Springer, London (1997). https://doi.org/10.1007/978-1-4471-0427-8_25. Presented at the 2nd On-line World Conference on Soft Computing in Design and Manufacturing (WSC2)
7. Molinet Berenguer, J.A., Coello Coello, C.A.: Evolutionary many-objective optimization based on kuhn-munkres' algorithm. In: Gaspar-Cunha, A., Henggeler Antunes, C., Coello, C.C. (eds.) EMO 2015. LNCS, vol. 9019, pp. 3–17. Springer, Cham (2015). https://doi.org/10.1007/978-3-319-15892-1_1
8. de Oliveira, F.B., Davendra, D., Guimarães, F.G.: Multi-objective differential evolution on the GPU with C-CUDA. In: Snášel, V., Abraham, A., Corchado, E.S. (eds.) SOCO 2012. AISC, vol. 188, pp. 123–132. Springer, Heidelberg (2013). https://doi.org/10.1007/978-3-642-32922-7_13
9. Best, C.: Multi-Objective Cultural Algorithms. Master's thesis, Wayne State University, Detroit, Michigan, USA (2009)
10. Best, C., Che, X., Reynolds, R.G., Liu, D.: Multi-objective cultural algorithms. In: 2010 IEEE Congress on Evolutionary Computation (CEC 2010), Barcelona, Spain, 18–23 July 2010, pp. 3330–3338. IEEE Press (2010)
11. Beume, N., Naujoks, B., Emmerich, M.: SMS-EMOA: multiobjective selection based on dominated hypervolume. Europ. J. Oper. Res. **181**(3), 1653–1669 (2007)
12. Beume, N., Naujoks, B., Preuss, M., Rudolph, G., Wagner, T.: Effects of 1-Greedy S-metric-selection on innumerably large pareto fronts. In: Ehrgott, M., Fonseca, C.M., Gandibleux, X., Hao, J.-K., Sevaux, M. (eds.) EMO 2009. LNCS, vol. 5467, pp. 21–35. Springer, Heidelberg (2009). https://doi.org/10.1007/978-3-642-01020-0_7
13. Bhattacharya, M., Lu, G.: A dynamic approximate fitness based hybrid ea for optimization problems. In: Proceedings of IEEE Congress on Evolutionary Computation. pp. 1879–1886 (2003)
14. Blum, C., Roli, A.: Metaheuristics in combinatorial optimization: overview and conceptual comparison. ACM Comput. Surv. **35**(3), 268–308 (2003)

15. Bringmann, K., Friedrich, T.: The maximum hypervolume set yields near-optimal approximation. In: Proceedings of the 12th Annual Conference on Genetic and Evolutionary Computation (GECCO 2010), Portland, Oregon, USA, 7–11 July 2010, pp. 511–518. ACM Press (2010). ISBN 978-1-4503-0072-8

16. Brockhoff, D.: A bug in the multiobjective optimizer IBEA: salutary lessons for code release and a performance re-assessment. In: Gaspar-Cunha, A., Henggeler Antunes, C., Coello, C.C. (eds.) EMO 2015. LNCS, vol. 9018, pp. 187–201. Springer, Cham (2015). https://doi.org/10.1007/978-3-319-15934-8_13

17. Brockhoff, D., Wagner, T., Trautmann, H.: On the properties of the $R2$ indicator. In: 2012 Genetic and Evolutionary Computation Conference (GECCO 2012), Philadelphia, USA, pp. 465–472. ACM Press, July 2012. ISBN: 978-1-4503-1177-9

18. Brockhoff, D., Zitzler, E.: Are all objectives necessary? on dimensionality reduction in evolutionary multiobjective optimization. In: Runarsson, T.P., Beyer, H.-G., Burke, E., Merelo-Guervós, J.J., Whitley, L.D., Yao, X. (eds.) PPSN 2006. LNCS, vol. 4193, pp. 533–542. Springer, Heidelberg (2006). https://doi.org/10.1007/11844297_54

19. Büche, D., Milano, M., Koumoutsakos, P.: Self-organizing maps for multi-objective optimization. In: Barry, A.M. (ed.) GECCO 2002: Proceedings of the Bird of a Feather Workshops, Genetic and Evolutionary Computation Conference, pp. 152–155. AAAI, New York (2002)

20. Bueche, D., Schraudolph, N., Koumoutsakos, P.: Accelerating evolutionary algorithms with gaussian process fitness function models. IEEE Trans. Syst. Man Cybern. Part C $35(2)$, 183–194 (2005)

21. Bui, L.T., Nguyen, M.H., Branke, J., Abbass, H.A.: Tackling dynamic problems with multiobjective evolutionary algorithms. In: Knowles, J., Corne, D., Deb, K. (eds.) Multi-Objective Problem Solving from Nature: From Concepts to Applications, pp. 77–91. Springer, Berlin (2008). https://doi.org/10.1007/978-3-540-72964-8_4

22. Burke, E.K., Gendreau, M., Hyde, M., Kendall, G., Ochoa, G., Özcan, E., Qu, R.: Hyper-heuristics: a survey of the state of the art. J. Oper. Res. Soc. $64(12)$, 1695–1724 (2013)

23. Chen, J.H., Goldberg, D.E., Ho, S.Y., Sastry, K.: Fitness inheritance in multi-objective optimization. In: Langdon, W., Cantú-Paz, E., Mathias, K., Roy, R., Davis, D., Poli, R., Balakrishnan, K., Honavar, V., Rudolph, G., Wegener, J., Bull, L., Potter, M., Schultz, A., Miller, J., Burke, E., Jonoska, N. (eds.) Proceedings of the Genetic and Evolutionary Computation Conference (GECCO 2002), San Francisco, California, pp. 319–326. Morgan Kaufmann Publishers, July 2002

24. Coello Coello, C.A., Lamont, G.B., Van Veldhuizen, D.A.: Evolutionary Algorithms for Solving Multi-Objective Problems, 2nd edn. Springer, New York (2007). ISBN 978-0-387-33254-3

25. Coello Coello, C.A., Landa Becerra, R.: Evolutionary multiobjective optimization using a cultural algorithm. In: 2003 IEEE Swarm Intelligence Symposium Proceedings, Indianapolis, Indiana, USA, pp. 6–13. IEEE Service Center, April 2003

26. Corne, D., Knowles, J.: Techniques for highly multiobjective optimisation: some nondominated points are better than others. In: Thierens, D. (ed.) 2007 Genetic and Evolutionary Computation Conference (GECCO 2007), vol. 1, pp. 773–780. ACM Press, London (2007)

27. Cruz, C., Gonzalez, J.R., Pelta, D.A.: Optimization in dynamic environments: a survey on problems, methods and measures. Soft. Comput. $15(7)$, 1427–1448 (2011)

28. Cserti, P., Szondi, S., Gaál, B., Kozmann, G., Vassányi, I.: GPU based parallel genetic algorithm library. In: Filipič, B., Šilc, J. (eds.) Bioinspired Optimization Methods and Their Applications, Proceedings of the Fifth International Conference on Bioinspired Optimization Methods and their Applications, BIOMA 2012, Bohinj, Slovenia, 24–25 May 2012, pp. 231–244. Jožef Stefan Institute (2012). ISBN 978-961-264-043-9

29. Deb, K., Jain, H.: An evolutionary many-objective optimization algorithm using reference-point-based nondominated sorting approach, Part I: solving problems with box constraints. IEEE Trans. Evol. Comput. 18(4), 577–601 (2014)

30. Deb, K., Pratap, A., Agarwal, S., Meyarivan, T.: A fast and elitist multiobjective genetic algorithm: NSGA-II. IEEE Trans. Evol. Comput. 6(2), 182–197 (2002)

31. Deb, K., Sinha, A., Kukkonen, S.: Multi-objective test problems, linkages, and evolutionary methodologies. In: Keijzer, M. et al. (eds.) 2006 Genetic and Evolutionary Computation Conference (GECCO 2006), Seattle, Washington, USA, vol. 2, pp. 1141–1148. ACM Press, July 2006. ISBN 1-59593-186-4

32. di Pierro, F.: Many-objective evolutionary algorithms and applications to water resources engineering. Ph.D. thesis, School of Engineering, Computer Science and Mathematics, UK, August 2006

33. Díaz-Manríquez, A., Toscano-Pulido, G., Landa-Becerra, R.: A hybrid local search operator for multiobjective optimization. In: 2013 IEEE Congress on Evolutionary Computation (CEC 2013), Cancún, México, 20–23 June 2013, pp. 173–180. IEEE Press (2013). ISBN 978-1-4799-0454-9

34. Ducheyne, E., De Baets, B., De Wulf, R.: Is fitness inheritance useful for real-world applications? In: Fonseca, C.M., Fleming, P.J., Zitzler, E., Thiele, L., Deb, K. (eds.) EMO 2003. LNCS, vol. 2632, pp. 31–42. Springer, Heidelberg (2003). https://doi.org/10.1007/3-540-36970-8_3

35. Emmerich, M., Giotis, A., Özdemir, M., Bäck, T., Giannakoglou, K.: Metamodel—assisted evolution strategies. In: Guervós, J.J.M., Adamidis, P., Beyer, H.-G., Schwefel, H.-P., Fernández-Villacañas, J.-L. (eds.) PPSN 2002. LNCS, vol. 2439, pp. 361–370. Springer, Heidelberg (2002). https://doi.org/10.1007/3-540-45712-7_35

36. Emmerich, M., Beume, N., Naujoks, B.: An EMO algorithm using the hypervolume measure as selection criterion. In: Coello Coello, C.A., Hernández Aguirre, A., Zitzler, E. (eds.) EMO 2005. LNCS, vol. 3410, pp. 62–76. Springer, Heidelberg (2005). https://doi.org/10.1007/978-3-540-31880-4_5

37. Farina, M.: A neural network based generalized response surface multiobjective evolutionary algorithm. In: Congress on Evolutionary Computation (CEC 2002), Piscataway, New Jersey, vol. 1, pp. 956–961. IEEE Service Center, May 2002

38. Farina, M., Deb, K., Amato, P.: dynamic multiobjective optimization problems: test cases, approximations, and applications. IEEE Trans. Evol. Comput. 8(5), 425–442 (2004)

39. Fleischer, M.: The measure of pareto optima applications to multi-objective metaheuristics. In: Fonseca, C.M., Fleming, P.J., Zitzler, E., Thiele, L., Deb, K. (eds.) EMO 2003. LNCS, vol. 2632, pp. 519–533. Springer, Heidelberg (2003). https://doi.org/10.1007/3-540-36970-8_37

40. Garza-Fabre, M., Pulido, G.T., Coello, C.A.C.: Ranking methods for many-objective optimization. In: Aguirre, A.H., Borja, R.M., Garciá, C.A.R. (eds.) MICAI 2009. LNCS (LNAI), vol. 5845, pp. 633–645. Springer, Heidelberg (2009). https://doi.org/10.1007/978-3-642-05258-3_56

41. Goel, T., Vaidyanathan, R., Haftka, R., Shyy, W., Queipo, N., Tucker, K.: Response surface approximation of pareto optimal front in multiobjective optimization. Technical report 2004–4501, AIAA (2004)
42. Goh, C.K., Ong, Y.S., Tan, K.C. (eds.): Multi-Objective Memetic Algorithms. Springer, Berlin (2009). ISBN 978-3-540-88050-9
43. Goldberg, D.E.: Genetic Algorithms in Search. Optimization and Machine Learning. Addison-Wesley Publishing Company, Reading (1989)
44. Goldberg, D.E., Richardson, J.: Genetic algorithms with sharing for multimodal function optimization. In: Genetic Algorithms and their Applications: Proceedings of the Second International Conference on Genetic Algorithms, Massachusetts, USA, pp. 41–49. Lawrence Erlbaum, July 1987. ISBN 0-8058-0158-8
45. Gonçalves, R.A., Kuk, J.N., Almeida, C.P., Venske, S.M.: MOEA/D-HH: a hyperheuristic for multi-objective problems. In: Gaspar-Cunha, A., Henggeler Antunes, C., Coello, C.C. (eds.) EMO 2015. LNCS, vol. 9018, pp. 94–108. Springer, Cham (2015). https://doi.org/10.1007/978-3-319-15934-8_7
46. Phan, D.H., Suzuki, J.: R2-IBEA: R2 indicator based evolutionary algorithm for multiobjective optimization. In: 2013 IEEE Congress on Evolutionary Computation (CEC 2013), Cancún, México, 20–23 June 2013, pp. 1836–1845. IEEE Press (2013). ISBN 978-1-4799-0454-9
47. Hadka, D., Reed, P.: Borg: an auto-adaptive many-objective evolutionary computing framework. Evol. Comput. 21(2), 231–259 (2013). Summer
48. Hajela, P., Lin, C.Y.: Genetic search strategies in multicriterion optimal design. Struct. Optim. 4, 99–107 (1992)
49. Helbig, M., Engelbrecht, A.P.: Dynamic multi-objective optimization using PSO. In: Alba, E., Nakib, A., Siarry, P. (eds.) Metaheuristics for Dynamic Optimization, chap. 8, pp. 147–188. Springer, Berlin (2013). ISBN 978-3-642-30664-8
50. Helbig, M., Engelbrecht, A.P.: Performance measures for dynamic multi-objective optimisation algorithms. Inform. Sci. 250, 61–81 (2013)
51. Hernández Gómez, R., Coello Coello, C.A.: MOMBI: a new metaheuristic for many-objective optimization based on the R2 indicator. In: 2013 IEEE Congress on Evolutionary Computation (CEC 2013), Cancún, México, 20–23 June, pp. 2488–2495. IEEE Press (2013). ISBN 978-1-4799-0454-9
52. Hernández Gómez, R., Coello Coello, C.A.: Improved metaheuristic based on the R2 indicator for many-objective optimization. In: 2015 Genetic and Evolutionary Computation Conference (GECCO 2015), Madrid, Spain, July 11–15 2015, pp. 679–686. ACM Press (2015). ISBN 978-1-4503-3472-3
53. Hernández Gómez, R., Coello Coello, C.A.: A hyper-heuristic of scalarizing functions. In: 2017 Genetic and Evolutionary Computation Conference (GECCO 2017), Berlin, Germany, 15–19 July 2017, pp. 577–584. ACM Press (2017). ISBN 978-1-4503-4920-8
54. Hernández Gómez, R., Coello Coello, C.A., Alba Torres, E.: A multi-objective evolutionary algorithm based on parallel coordinates. In: 2016 Genetic and Evolutionary Computation Conference (GECCO 2016), Denver, Colorado, USA, 20–24 July 2016, pp. 565–572. ACM Press (2016). ISBN 978-1-4503-4206-3
55. Hong, Y.S., Lee, H.: Tahk, M.J.: Acceleration of the convergence speed of evolutionary algorithms using multi-layer neural networks. Eng. Optim. 35(1), 91–102 (2003)
56. Hughes, E.J.: Evolutionary many-objective optimisation: many once or one many? In: 2005 IEEE Congress on Evolutionary Computation (CEC 2005), Edinburgh, Scotland, vol. 1, pp. 222–227. IEEE Service Center, September 2005

57. Hupkens, I., Deutz, A., Yang, K., Emmerich, M.: Faster exact algorithms for computing expected hypervolume improvement. In: Gaspar-Cunha, A., Henggeler Antunes, C., Coello, C.C. (eds.) EMO 2015. LNCS, vol. 9019, pp. 65–79. Springer, Cham (2015). https://doi.org/10.1007/978-3-319-15892-1_5

58. Hüscken, M., Jin, Y., Sendhoff, B.: Structure optimization of neural networks for aerodynamic optimization. Soft. Comput. 9(1), 21–28 (2005)

59. Igel, C., Hansen, N., Roth, S.: Covariance matrix adaptation for multi-objective optimization. Evol. Comput. 15(1), 1–28 (2007). Spring

60. Ishibuchi, H., Masuda, H., Tanigaki, Y., Nojima, Y.: Modified distance calculation in generational distance and inverted generational distance. In: Gaspar-Cunha, A., Henggeler Antunes, C., Coello, C.C. (eds.) EMO 2015. LNCS, vol. 9019, pp. 110–125. Springer, Cham (2015). https://doi.org/10.1007/978-3-319-15892-1_8

61. Jaszkiewicz, A., Ishibuchi, H., Zhang, Q.: Multiobjective memetic algorithms. In: Neri, F., Cotta, C., Moscato, P. (eds.) Handbook of Memetic Algorithms, chap. 13, pp. 201–217. Springer, Berlin (2012). ISBN 978-3-642-23246-6

62. Jiang, S., Zhang, J., Ong, Y.S., Zhang, A.N., Tan, P.S.: A simple and fast hypervolume indicator-based multiobjective evolutionary algorithm. IEEE Trans. Cybern. 45(10), 2202–2213 (2015)

63. Jin, Y., Sendhoff, B., Körner, E.: Evolutionary multi-objective optimization for simultaneous generation of signal-type and symbol-type representations. In: Coello Coello, C.A., Hernández Aguirre, A., Zitzler, E. (eds.) EMO 2005. LNCS, vol. 3410, pp. 752–766. Springer, Heidelberg (2005). https://doi.org/10.1007/978-3-540-31880-4_52

64. Knowles, J.: ParEGO: a hybrid algorithm with on-line landscape approximation for expensive multiobjective optimization problems. IEEE Trans. Evol. Comput. 10(1), 50–66 (2006)

65. Knowles, J., Corne, D.: Properties of an adaptive archiving algorithm for storing nondominated vectors. IEEE Trans. Evol. Comput. 7(2), 100–116 (2003)

66. Knowles, J., Corne, D.: Quantifying the effects of objective space dimension in evolutionary multiobjective optimization. In: Obayashi, S., Deb, K., Poloni, C., Hiroyasu, T., Murata, T. (eds.) EMO 2007. LNCS, vol. 4403, pp. 757–771. Springer, Heidelberg (2007). https://doi.org/10.1007/978-3-540-70928-2_57

67. Knowles, J.D., Corne, D.W.: Approximating the nondominated front using the pareto archived evolution strategy. Evol. Comput. 8(2), 149–172 (2000)

68. Kuhn, H.W.: The Hungarian method for the assignment problem. Naval Res. Logistics Q. 2(1–2), 83–97 (1955). http://dx.doi.org/10.1002/nav.3800020109

69. Lara, A., Sanchez, G., Coello Coello, C.A., Schütze, O.: HCS: a new local search strategy for memetic multi-objective evolutionary algorithms. IEEE Trans. Evol. Comput. 14(1), 112–132 (2010)

70. Li, B., Li, J., Tang, K., Yao, X.: Many-objective evolutionary algorithms: a survey. ACM Comput. Surv. 48(1), 1–35 (2015)

71. López Jaimes, A., Coello Coello, C.A., Chakraborty, D.: Objective reduction using a feature selection technique. In: 2008 Genetic and Evolutionary Computation Conference (GECCO 2008), Atlanta, USA, pp. 674–680. ACM Press, July 2008. ISBN 978-1-60558-131-6

72. von Lücken, C., Baran, B., Brizuela, C.: A survey on multi-objective evolutionary algorithms for many-objective problems. Comput. Optim. Appl. 58(3), 707–756 (2014)

73. Ma, X., Liu, F., Qi, Y., Wang, X., Li, L., Jiao, L., Yin, M., Gong, M.: A multiobjective evolutionary algorithm based on decision variable analyses for multiobjective optimization problems with large-scale variables. IEEE Trans. Evol. Comput. **20**(2), 275–298 (2016)
74. Manoatl Lopez, E., Coello Coello, C.A.: IGD^+-EMOA: A multi-objective evolutionary algorithm based on IGD^+. In: 2016 IEEE Congress on Evolutionary Computation (CEC 2016), Vancouver, Canada, 24–29 July 2016, pp. 999–1006. IEEE Press (2016). ISBN 978-1-5090-0623-9
75. Mashwani, W.K., Salhi, A.: Multiobjective memetic algorithm based on decomposition. Appl. Soft Comput. **21**, 221–243 (2014)
76. McClymont, K., Keedwell, E.C.: Markov Chain hyper-Heuristic (MCHH): an online selective hyper-heuristic for multi-objective continuous problems. In: 2011 Genetic and Evolutionary Computation Conference (GECCO 2011), Dublin, Ireland, 12–16 July 2011, pp. 2003–2010. ACM Press (2011)
77. Menchaca-Mendez, A., Coello Coello, C.A.: Selection mechanisms based on the maximin fitness function to solve multi-objective optimization problems. Inform. Sci. **332**, 131–152 (2016)
78. Menchaca-Mendez, A., Coello Coello, C.A.: An alternative hypervolume-based selection mechanism for multi-objective evolutionary algorithms. Soft. Comput. **21**(4), 861–884 (2017)
79. Menchaca-Mendez, A., Hernández, C., Coello Coello, C.A.: Δ_p-MOEA: a new multi-objective evolutionary algorithm based on the Δ_p indicator. In: 2016 IEEE Congress on Evolutionary Computation (CEC 2016), Vancouver, Canada, 24–29 July 2016, pp. 3753–3760. IEEE Press (2016). ISBN 978-1-5090-0623-9
80. Menchaca-Mendez, A., Montero, E., Riff, M.-C., Coello, C.A.C.: A more efficient selection scheme in iSMS-EMOA. In: Bazzan, A.L.C., Pichara, K. (eds.) IBERAMIA 2014. LNCS (LNAI), vol. 8864, pp. 371–380. Springer, Cham (2014). https://doi.org/10.1007/978-3-319-12027-0_30
81. Miettinen, K.M.: Nonlinear Multiobjective Optimization. Kluwer Academic Publishers, Boston (1999)
82. Miguel Antonio, L., Coello Coello, C.A.: Use of cooperative coevolution for solving large scale multiobjective optimization problems. In: 2013 IEEE Congress on Evolutionary Computation (CEC 2013), Cancún, México, 20–23 June 2013, pp. 2758–2765. IEEE Press (2013). ISBN 978-1-4799-0454-9
83. Miguel Antonio, L., Coello Coello, C.A.: Indicator-based cooperative coevolution for multi-objective optimization. In: 2016 IEEE Congress on Evolutionary Computation (CEC 2016), Vancouver, Canada, 24–29 July 2016, pp. 991–998. IEEE Press (2016). ISBN 978-1-5090-0623-9
84. Mishra, B., Dehuri, S., Mall, R., Ghosh, A.: Parallel single and multiple objectives genetic algorithms: a survey. Int. J. Appl. Evol. Comput. **2**(2), 21–57 (2011)
85. Mostaghim, S., Schmeck, H.: Distance based ranking in many-objective particle swarm optimization. In: Rudolph, G., Jansen, T., Beume, N., Lucas, S., Poloni, C. (eds.) PPSN 2008. LNCS, vol. 5199, pp. 753–762. Springer, Heidelberg (2008). https://doi.org/10.1007/978-3-540-87700-4_75
86. Ong, Y.S., Nair, P.B., Keane, A.J., Wong, K.W.: Surrogate-assisted evolutionary optimization frameworks for high-fidelity engineering design problems. In: Jin, Y. (ed.) Knowledge Incorporation in Evolutionary Computation. STUDFUZZ, pp. 307–332. Springer, Heidelberg (2004). https://doi.org/10.1007/978-3-540-44511-1_15
87. Pierret, S.: Turbomachinery blade design using a Navier-Stokes solver and artificial neural network. ASME J. Turbomach. **121**(3), 326–332 (1999)

88. Pires, E.J.S., Machado, J.A.T., de Moura Oliveira, P.B.: Entropy diversity in multi-objective particle swarm optimization. Entropy 15(12), 5475–5491 (2013)
89. Praditwong, K., Yao, X.: How well do multi-objective evolutionary algorithms scale to large problems. In: 2007 IEEE Congress on Evolutionary Computation (CEC 2007), pp. 3959–3966. IEEE Press, Singapore, September 2007
90. López-Ibáñez, M., Stützle, T.: Automatic configuration of multi-objective ACO algorithms. In: Dorigo, M., et al. (eds.) ANTS 2010. LNCS, vol. 6234, pp. 95–106. Springer, Heidelberg (2010). https://doi.org/10.1007/978-3-642-15461-4_9
91. Raquel, C., Yao, X.: Dynamic multi-objective optimization: a survey of the state-of-the-art. In: Yang, S., Yao, X. (eds.) Evolutionary Computation for Dynamic Optimization Problems, chap. 4, pp. 85–106. Springer, Berlin (2013). ISBN 978-3-642-38415-8
92. Rasheed, K., Ni, X., Vattam, S.: Comparison of methods for developing dynamic reduced models for design optimization. Soft. Comput. 9(1), 29–37 (2005)
93. Ratle, A.: Accelerating the convergence of evolutionary algorithms by fitness landscape approximation. In: Eiben, A., Bäck, T., Schoenauer, M., Schwefel, H.P. (eds.) Parallel Problem Solving from Nature, vol. V, pp. 87–96 (1998)
94. Reyes Sierra, M., Coello Coello, C.A.: Fitness Inheritance in Multi-Objective Particle Swarm Optimization. In: 2005 IEEE Swarm Intelligence Symposium (SIS 2005), Pasadena, California, USA, pp. 116–123. IEEE Press, June 2005
95. Reynolds, R., Liu, D.: Multi-objective cultural algorithms. In: 2011 IEEE Congress on Evolutionary Computation (CEC 2011), New Orleans, Louisiana, USA, 5–8 June 2011, pp. 1233–1241. IEEE Service Center (2011)
96. Reynolds, R.G.: An Introduction to Cultural Algorithms. In: Sebald, A.V., Fogel, L.J. (eds.) Proceedings of the Third Annual Conference on Evolutionary Programming, pp. 131–139. World Scientific, River Edge (1994)
97. Reynolds, R.G., Michalewicz, Z., Cavaretta, M.: Using cultural algorithms for constraint handling in GENOCOP. In: McDonnell, J.R., Reynolds, R.G., Fogel, D.B. (eds.) Proceedings of the Fourth Annual Conference on Evolutionary Programming, pp. 298–305. MIT Press, Cambridge (1995)
98. Rodríguez Villalobos, C.A., Coello Coello, C.A.: A new multi-objective evolutionary algorithm based on a performance assessment indicator. In: 2012 Genetic and Evolutionary Computation Conference (GECCO 2012), Philadelphia, USA, pp. 505–512. ACM Press, July 2012. ISBN: 978-1-4503-1177-9
99. Rudolph, G., Agapie, A.: Convergence properties of some multi-objective evolutionary algorithms. In: Proceedings of the 2000 Conference on Evolutionary Computation, Piscataway, New Jersey, vol. 2, pp. 1010–1016. IEEE Press, July 2000
100. Santana-Quintero, L.V., Arias Montaño, A., Coello Coello, C.A.: A review of techniques for handling expensive functions in evolutionary multi-objective optimization. In: Tenne, Y., Goh, C.K. (eds.) Computational Intelligence in Expensive Optimization Problems, pp. 29–59. Springer, Berlin (2010). https://doi.org/10.1007/978-3-642-10701-6_2
101. Santiago, A., Huacuja, H.J.F., Dorronsoro, B., Pecero, J.E., Santillan, C.G., Barbosa, J.J.G., Monterrubio, J.C.S.: A survey of decomposition methods for multi-objective optimization. In: Castillo, O., Melin, P., Pedrycz, W., Kacprzyk, J. (eds.) Recent Advances on Hybrid Approaches for Designing Intelligent Systems. SCI, vol. 547, pp. 453–465. Springer, Cham (2014). https://doi.org/10.1007/978-3-319-05170-3_31

102. Sato, H., Aguirre, H.E., Tanaka, K.: Controlling dominance area of solutions and its impact on the performance of MOEAs. In: Obayashi, S., Deb, K., Poloni, C., Hiroyasu, T., Murata, T. (eds.) EMO 2007. LNCS, vol. 4403, pp. 5–20. Springer, Heidelberg (2007). https://doi.org/10.1007/978-3-540-70928-2_5

103. Schaffer, J.D.: Multiple objective optimization with vector evaluated genetic algorithms. In: Genetic Algorithms and their Applications: Proceedings of the First International Conference on Genetic Algorithms, pp. 93–100. Lawrence Erlbaum (1985)

104. Abboud, K., Schoenauer, M.: Surrogate deterministic mutation: preliminary results. In: Collet, P., Fonlupt, C., Hao, J.-K., Lutton, E., Schoenauer, M. (eds.) EA 2001. LNCS, vol. 2310, pp. 104–116. Springer, Heidelberg (2002). https://doi.org/10.1007/3-540-46033-0_9

105. Schütze, O., Esquivel, X., Lara, A., Coello Coello, C.A.: Using the averaged hausdorff distance as a performance measure in evolutionary multiobjective optimization. IEEE Trans. Evol. Comput. **16**(4), 504–522 (2012)

106. Sen, P., Yang, J.B.: Multiple Criteria Decision Support in Engineering Design. Springer, London (1998)

107. Sharma, D., Collet, P.: Implementation techniques for massively parallel multiobjective optimization. In: Tsutsui, S., Collet, P. (eds.) Massively Parallel Evolutionary Computation on GPGPUs. NCS, pp. 267–286. Springer, Heidelberg (2013). https://doi.org/10.1007/978-3-642-37959-8_13

108. Smith, R.E., Dike, B.A., Stegmann, S.A.: Fitness inheritance in genetic algorithms. In: SAC 1995: Proceedings of the 1995 ACM Symposium on Applied Computing, pp. 345–350. ACM Press, New York (1995).

109. Srinivas, N., Deb, K.: Multiobjective optimization using nondominated sorting in genetic algorithms. Evol. Comput. **2**(3), 221–248 (1994). Fall

110. Sülflow, A., Drechsler, N., Drechsler, R.: Robust multi-objective optimization in high dimensional spaces. In: Obayashi, S., Deb, K., Poloni, C., Hiroyasu, T., Murata, T. (eds.) EMO 2007. LNCS, vol. 4403, pp. 715–726. Springer, Heidelberg (2007). https://doi.org/10.1007/978-3-540-70928-2_54

111. Talbi, E.-G., Mostaghim, S., Okabe, T., Ishibuchi, H., Rudolph, G., Coello Coello, C.A.: Parallel approaches for multiobjective optimization. In: Branke, J., Deb, K., Miettinen, K., Słowiński, R. (eds.) Multiobjective Optimization. LNCS, vol. 5252, pp. 349–372. Springer, Heidelberg (2008). https://doi.org/10.1007/978-3-540-88908-3_13

112. Toscano Pulido, G., Coello Coello, C.A.: The micro genetic algorithm 2: towards online adaptation in evolutionary multiobjective optimization. In: Fonseca, C.M., Fleming, P.J., Zitzler, E., Thiele, L., Deb, K. (eds.) EMO 2003. LNCS, vol. 2632, pp. 252–266. Springer, Heidelberg (2003). https://doi.org/10.1007/3-540-36970-8_18

113. Tušar, T., Filipič, B.: Visualization of pareto front approximations in evolutionary multiobjective optimization: a critical review and the prosection method. IEEE Trans. Evol. Comput. **19**(2), 225–245 (2015)

114. Ulmer, H., Streichert, F., Zell, A.: Model-assisted steady-state evolution strategies. In: Cantú-Paz, E., et al. (eds.) GECCO 2003. LNCS, vol. 2723, pp. 610–621. Springer, Heidelberg (2003). https://doi.org/10.1007/3-540-45105-6_72

115. Ulmer, H., Streichert, F., Zell, A.: Evolution startegies assisted by Gaussian processes with improved pre-selection criterion. In: Proceedings of IEEE Congress on Evolutionary Computation, pp. 692–699 (2003)

116. Vrugt, J.A., Robinson, B.A.: Improved evolutionary optimization from genetically adaptive multimethod search. Proc. Nat. Acad. Sci. U.S.A. **104**(3), 708–711 (2007)

117. Wagner, T., Beume, N., Naujoks, B.: Pareto-, aggregation-, and indicator-based methods in many-objective optimization. In: Obayashi, S., Deb, K., Poloni, C., Hiroyasu, T., Murata, T. (eds.) EMO 2007. LNCS, vol. 4403, pp. 742–756. Springer, Heidelberg (2007). https://doi.org/10.1007/978-3-540-70928-2_56

118. Wang, Y., Dang, C.: An evolutionary algorithm for dynamic multi-objective optimization. Appl. Math. Comput. **205**(1), 6–18 (2008)

119. Watanabe, S., Ito, M., Sakakibara, K.: A proposal on a decomposition-based evolutionary multiobjective optimization for large scale vehicle routing problems. In: 2015 IEEE Congress on Evolutionary Computation (CEC 2015), Sendai, Japan, 25–28 May 2015, pp. 2581–2588. IEEE Press, ISBN 978-1-4799-7492-4

120. While, L., Bradstreet, L., Barone, L.: A fast way of calculating exact hypervolumes. IEEE Trans. Evol. Comput. **16**(1), 86–95 (2012)

121. While, L., Hingston, P., Barone, L., Huband, S.: A faster algorithm for calculating hypervolume. IEEE Trans. Evol. Comput. **10**(1), 29–38 (2006)

122. Won, K.S., Ray, T.: Performance of kriging and cokriging based surrogate models within the unified framework for surrogate assisted optimization. In: 2004 Congress on Evolutionary Computation (CEC 2004), Portland, Oregon, USA, vol. 2, pp. 1577–1585. IEEE Service Center, June 2004

123. Zapotecas Martínez, S., Arias Montaño, A., Coello Coello, C.A.: A nonlinear simplex search approach for multi-objective optimization. In: 2011 IEEE Congress on Evolutionary Computation (CEC 2011), New Orleans, Louisiana, USA, 5–8 June 2011, pp. 2367–2374. IEEE Service Center (2011)

124. Zhang, Q., Li, H.: MOEA/D: a multiobjective evolutionary algorithm based on decomposition. IEEE Trans. Evol. Comput. **11**(6), 712–731 (2007)

125. Zille, H., Ishibuchi, H., Mostaghim, S., Nojima, Y.: Mutation operators based on variable grouping for multi-objective large-scale optimization. In: 2016 IEEE Symposium Series on Computational Intelligence (SSCI 2016), Athens, Greece, 6–9 December 2016. IEEE Press (2016). ISBN 978-1-5090-4240-1

126. Zitzler, E., Künzli, S.: Indicator-based selection in multiobjective search. In: Yao, X., et al. (eds.) PPSN 2004. LNCS, vol. 3242, pp. 832–842. Springer, Heidelberg (2004). https://doi.org/10.1007/978-3-540-30217-9_84

127. Zitzler, E., Laumanns, M., Bleuler, S.: A tutorial on evolutionary multiobjective optimization. In: Gandibleux, X., Sevaux, M., Sörensen, K., T'kindt, V. (eds.) Metaheuristics for Multiobjective Optimisation. Lecture Notes in Economics and Mathematical Systems, vol. 535, pp. 3–37. Springer, Berlin (2004). https://doi.org/10.1007/978-3-642-17144-4_1

128. Zitzler, E., Thiele, L.: Multiobjective optimization using evolutionary algorithms-a comparative study. In: Eiben, A.E. (ed.) Parallel Problem Solving from Nature V, pp. 292–301. Springer, Amsterdam (1998)

129. Zitzler, E., Thiele, L.: Multiobjective evolutionary algorithms: a comparative case study and the strength pareto approach. IEEE Trans. Evol. Comput. **3**(4), 257–271 (1999)

130. Zitzler, E., Thiele, L., Laumanns, M., Fonseca, C.M., da Fonseca, V.G.: Performance assessment of multiobjective optimizers: an analysis and review. IEEE Trans. Evol. Comput. **7**(2), 117–132 (2003)

Applications of Natural Computing

A Formal Framework for Composing Qualitative Models of Biological Systems

Hanadi Alkhudhayr[1,2] and Jason Steggles[1(✉)]

[1] School of Computing, Newcastle University, Newcastle upon Tyne, UK
jason.steggles@ncl.ac.uk
[2] Faculty of Computing and Information Technology,
King Abdulaziz University, Rabigh, Saudi Arabia
h.alkhudhayr1@ncl.ac.uk

Abstract. Boolean networks are a widely used qualitative modelling approach which allows the abstract description of a biological system. One issue with the application of Boolean networks is the state space explosion problem which limits the applicability of the approach to large realistic systems. In this paper we investigate developing a compositional framework for Boolean networks to facilitate the construction and analysis of large scale models. The compositional approach we present is based on merging entities between Boolean networks using conjunction and we introduce the notion of compatibility which formalises the preservation of behaviour under composition. We investigate characterising compatibility and develop a notion of trace alignment which is sufficient to ensure compatibility. The compositional framework developed is supported by a prototype tool that automates composition and analysis.

Keywords: Qualitative models · Boolean network · Model composition

1 Introduction

In order to study and synthesize complex biological systems a range of qualitative modelling techniques have emerged [3,4]. *Boolean networks* [8,9] are one such approach which are based on abstractly representing the state of a regulatory entity as a Boolean value, where 1 represents the entity is active and 0 inactive. The state of each entity is then regulated by other entities based on a defined next–state function and their dynamic behaviour results in attractor cycles that can then be associated with biological phenomena. Entities can either be updated *synchronously*, where the state of all entities is updated simultaneously, or *asynchronously*, where entities update their state independently.

Despite their simplicity, Boolean networks have been shown to allow a range of interesting biological analysis to be performed and have been widely considered in the literature (for example, see [1,3,10,11,13]). Indeed, it can be seen that they have an important role to play in advancing our understanding and engineering capability of complex biological systems. However, one important

© Springer International Publishing AG 2017
C. Martín-Vide et al. (Eds.): TPNC 2017, LNCS 10687, pp. 25–36, 2017.
https://doi.org/10.1007/978-3-319-71069-3_2

issue that limits the scalable application of Boolean networks is the well–known state space explosion problem.

In this paper we investigate developing a formal framework for the composition of Boolean networks to facilitate the construction and analysis of large scale models. The compositional approach we present is based on merging entities in Boolean networks using conjunction (though the results presented hold for other logical connectives). We introduce the notion of compatibility which formalises the idea of preserving the underlying behaviour of models that are composed. The compatibility property is problematic as it references the composed model and so we develop a notion of trace alignment which we show is sufficient to ensure compatibility. We illustrate the alignment property by presenting results about the compatibility of composing duplicate copies of a Boolean network. The compositional framework developed is supported by a prototype tool that automates the composition process and associated analysis.

This paper is organized as follows. In Sect. 2 we provide a brief introduction to Boolean networks. In Sect. 3 we develop a compositional framework for Boolean networks and consider the preservation of behaviour under composition which we formalise by a notion of compatibility. In Sect. 4 we investigate characterising compatibility and introduce the property of alignment which avoids directly considering the composed model. Finally, in Sect. 5 we present some concluding remarks and discuss future work.

2   Boolean Networks

Boolean networks [8,9] are a widely used qualitative modelling approach for biological control systems (see for example [1,3,10,11,13]). In this section we introduce the basic definitions for Boolean networks needed in the sequel and provide illustrative examples.

A Boolean network consists of a set of regulatory entities $G = \{g_1, \ldots, g_n\}$ which can be in one of two possible states, either 1 representing the entity is active (e.g. a gene is expressed or a protein is present) or 0 representing the entity is inactive (e.g. a gene is not expressed or a protein is absent). The state of each entity is regulated by a subset of entities in the Boolean network and we refer to this subset as the *neighbourhood* of an entity (an entity may or may not be in its own neighbourhood). An entity updates its state by applying a logical *next–state function* to the current states of the entities in its neighbourhood.

We can define a Boolean network more formally as follows.

Definition 1. *A Boolean Network $\mathcal{BN}$ is a tuple $\mathcal{BN} = (G, N, F)$ where:*

(i) $G = \{g_1, \ldots, g_k\}$ *is a non-empty, finite set of entities;*

(ii) $N = (N(g_1), \ldots, N(g_k))$ *is a tuple of neighbourhoods, such that $N(g_i) \subseteq G$ is the neighbourhood of g_i; and*

(iii) $F = (F(g_1), \ldots, F(g_n))$ *is a tuple of next-state functions, such that the function $F(g_i) : \mathbb{B}^{|N(g_i)|} \to \mathbb{B}$ defines the next state of g_i.*

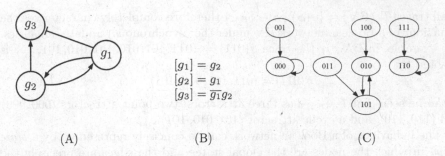

$$[g_1] = g_2$$
$$[g_2] = g_1$$
$$[g_3] = \overline{g_1}g_2$$

(A)   (B)   (C)

Fig. 1. Example of a Boolean network $\mathcal{BN}_{Ex1}$ consisting of: (A) Wiring diagram; (B) Equational definition of next–state functions for $\mathcal{BN}_{Ex1}$; (C) Synchronous state graph

As an example, consider the Boolean network $\mathcal{BN}_{Ex1} = (G_{Ex1}, N_{Ex1}, F_{Ex1})$ defined in Fig. 1. It consists of three entities $G_{Ex1} = \{g_1, g_2, g_3\}$ with neighbourhoods $N_{Ex1}(g_1) = \{g_2\}$, $N_{Ex1}(g_2) = \{g_1\}$, and $N_{Ex1}(g_3) = \{g_1, g_2\}$. The next-state functions F_{Ex1} are defined equational in Fig. 1(B), where we use $[g_i]$ to represent the next state of an entity g_i.

A *global state* of a Boolean network $\mathcal{BN}$ with n entities is represented by a tuple of Boolean states $(s_1, \ldots, s_n)$, where $s_i \in \mathbb{B}$ represents the state of entity $g_i \in \mathcal{BN}$. Note as a notational convenience we often use $s_1 \ldots s_n$ to represent a global state $(s_1, \ldots, s_n)$. When the current state of a Boolean network is clear from the context we allow g_i to denote both the name of an entity and its corresponding current state. The state space of a Boolean network $\mathcal{BN}$, denoted $S_{\mathcal{BN}}$, is therefore the set of all possible global states $S_{\mathcal{BN}} = \mathbb{B}^{|G|}$.

The state of a Boolean network can be updated either *synchronously* [9,16], where the state of all entities is updated simultaneously in a single update step, or *asynchronously* [6], where entities update their state independently. In the following we focus on the synchronous update semantics which has received considerable attention in the literature (see for example [1,2,8,9,12,16]). Given two states $S_1, S_2 \in S_{\mathcal{BN}}$, let $S_1 \rightarrow S_2$ represent a *(synchronous) update step* such that S_2 is the state that results from simultaneously updating the state of each entity g_i using its associated update function $F(g_i)$ and the appropriate neighbourhood of states from S_1. As an example, consider the global state 011 for $\mathcal{BN}_{Ex1}$ (see Fig. 1), where entity $g_1 = 0$, $g_2 = 1$, and $g_3 = 1$. Then $011 \rightarrow 101$ is an update step in $\mathcal{BN}_{Ex1}$.

The sequence of global states through $S_{\mathcal{BN}}$ from some initial state is called a *trace*. Note that in the case of the synchronous update semantics such traces are deterministic and infinite. However, given that the global state space is finite, this implies that a trace must eventually enter a cycle, known formally as an *attractor cycle* [9,14]. Attractor cycles are very important biologically where they are seen as representing different biological states or functions (e.g. different cellular types such as proliferation, apoptosis and differentiation [7]). We define a finite canonical representation for synchronous traces $\sigma(S)$, for $S \in S_{\mathcal{BN}}$, which specifies the infinite behaviour of a trace up to the first repeated state. The set of all traces $Tr(\mathcal{BN}) = \{\sigma(S) \mid S \in S_{\mathcal{BN}}\}$ therefore completely characterizes the behaviour of a Boolean network $\mathcal{BN}$ under the (synchronous) update semantics. For example, in $\mathcal{BN}_{Ex1}$ the trace $\sigma(011) = \langle 011, 101, 010, 101, 010, 101, \ldots \rangle$ is denoted by

$$\sigma(011) = \langle 011, 101, 010, 101 \rangle$$

It can be seen that $\mathcal{BN}_{Ex1}$ has three attractors: two point attractors $\langle 000, 000 \rangle$ and $\langle 110, 110 \rangle$; and a cyclic attractor $\langle 101, 010, 101 \rangle$.

The behaviour of a Boolean network can be concisely represented by a *state graph* in which the nodes are the global states and the edges are precisely the synchronous update steps allowed. We let $SG(\mathcal{BN}) = (S_{\mathcal{BN}}, \rightarrow)$ denote the state graph for a Boolean network $\mathcal{BN}$ under the synchronous trace semantics. As an example, consider the synchronous state graph $SG(\mathcal{BN}_{Ex1})$ for $\mathcal{BN}_{Ex1}$ presented in Fig. 1(C).

3   Compositional Framework

In this section we introduce definitions for composing two Boolean networks by merging entities and prove some simple results such as commutativity. We then consider what it means for the behaviour of an individual Boolean network in a composed model to be preserved and formulate a notion of *compatibility*.

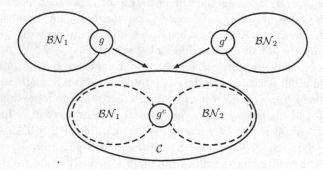

Fig. 2. Pictorial representation of composing $\mathcal{BN}_1$ and $\mathcal{BN}_2$ to form a new Boolean network $\mathcal{C}$ by merging entities $g \in \mathcal{BN}_1$ and $g' \in \mathcal{BN}_2$ into a new entity g^c

In the sequel, let $\mathcal{BN}_1 = (G_1, N_1, F_1)$ and $\mathcal{BN}_2 = (G_2, N_2, F_2)$ be two Boolean networks such that $G_1 = \{g, g_1, \ldots, g_n\}$ and $G_2 = \{g', g'_1, \ldots, g'_m\}$ are disjoint sets, for some $n, m \in \mathbb{N}$.

We formally define the composition of two Boolean networks $\mathcal{BN}_1$ and $\mathcal{BN}_2$ based on using conjunction (see Fig. 2). (Note all results presented also hold using disjunction.)

Definition 2. *(Composition) Let $\mathcal{C}(\mathcal{BN}_1, \mathcal{BN}_2, g, g')$ denote the Boolean network constructed by merging $\mathcal{BN}_1$ and $\mathcal{BN}_2$ on entities g and g' defined as follows:*

1. **Entities:** *the finite set of entities* $G = (G_1/\{g\}) \cup (G_2/\{g'\}) \cup \{g^c\}$, *where* g^c *denotes the new entity created by merging* g *and* g'.
2. **Neighbourhood:** *for any entity* $h_i \in G$, *the neighbourhood* $N(h_i)$ *is defined as follows:*

$$N(h_i) = \begin{cases} N_1(h_i)[g/g^c], & if\ h_i \in G_1 \\ N_2(h_i)[g'/g^c], & if\ h_i \in G_2 \\ N_1(g)[g/g^c] \cup N_2(g')[g'/g^c], & if\ h_i = g^c \end{cases}$$

where $S[f/e]$ *represents set* S *with all occurrences of element* f *replaced by* e.

3. **Functions:** *for any* $h_i \in G$, *the next-state function* $F(h_i)$ *is defined:*

$$F(h_i) = \begin{cases} F_1(h_i), & if\ h_i \in G_1 \\ F_2(h_i), & if\ h_i \in G_2 \\ \mathcal{F}, & if\ h_i = g^c \end{cases}$$

where $\mathcal{F} : \mathbb{B}^{|N(g^c)|} \to \mathbb{B}$ *is defined using four cases as follows:*

(i) *If* $g \notin N_1(g)$ *and* $g' \notin N_2(g')$, *where* $N_1(g) = \{l_1, ..., l_p\}$ *and* $N_2(g') = \{l'_1, ..., l'_q\}$, *then* $\mathcal{F}(l_1, ..., l_p, l'_1, ..., l'_q) = F_1(g)(l_1, ..., l_p) \wedge F_2(g')(l'_1, ..., l'_q)$;

(ii) *If* $g \in N_1(g)$ *and* $g' \notin N_2(g')$, *where* $N_1(g) = \{g, l_1, ..., l_p\}$ *and* $N_2(g') = \{l'_1, ..., l'_q\}$, *then* $\mathcal{F}(g^c, l_1, ..., l_p, l'_1, ..., l'_q) = F_1(g)(g^c, l_1, ..., l_p) \wedge F_2(g')(l'_1, ..., l'_q)$;

(iii) *If* $g \notin N_1(g)$ *and* $g' \in N_2(g')$, *where* $N_1(g) = \{l_1, ..., l_p\}$ *and* $N_2(g') = \{g', l'_1, ..., l'_q\}$, *then* $\mathcal{F}(g^c, l_1, ..., l_p, l'_1, ..., l'_q) = F_1(g)(l_1, ..., l_p) \wedge F_2(g')(g^c, l'_1, ..., l'_q)$;

(iv) *If* $g \in N_1(g)$ *and* $g' \in N_2(g')$, *where* $N_1(g) = \{g, l_1, ..., l_p\}$ *and* $N_2(g') = \{g', l'_1, ..., l'_q\}$, *then*

$$\mathcal{F}(g^c, l_1, ..., l_p, l'_1, ..., l'_q) = F_1(g)(g^c, l_1, ..., l_p) \wedge F_2(g')(g^c, l'_1, ..., l'_q).$$

In the sequel, we let g^c denote the new entity created by merging g and g' and assume that $\mathcal{C}(\mathcal{BN}_1, \mathcal{BN}_2, g, g')$ has global states $(g^c\ g_1\ ...\ g_n\ g'_1\ ...\ g'_m) \in \mathcal{S}_C$.

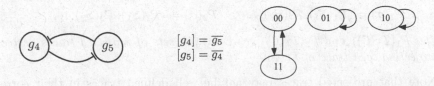

$$[g_4] = \overline{g_5}$$
$$[g_5] = \overline{g_4}$$

Fig. 3. A second Boolean network example $\mathcal{BN}_{Ex2}$ containing the wiring diagram, next–state equations, and state graph

As an example, consider composing $\mathcal{BN}_{Ex1}$ (Fig. 1) and $\mathcal{BN}_{Ex2}$ (Fig. 3) on entities g_1 and g_4. The resulting Boolean network $\mathcal{C}(\mathcal{BN}_{Ex1}, \mathcal{BN}_{Ex2}, g_1, g_4)$ is depicted in Fig. 4.

The following results shows that composition is commutative.

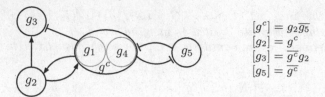

$$[g^c] = g_2\overline{g_5}$$
$$[g_2] = g^c$$
$$[g_3] = \overline{g^c}g_2$$
$$[g_5] = \overline{g^c}$$

Fig. 4. Boolean network $\mathcal{C}(\mathcal{BN}_{Ex1}, \mathcal{BN}_{Ex2}, g_1, g_4)$ resulting from the composition of $\mathcal{BN}_{Ex1}$ and $\mathcal{BN}_{Ex2}$ on entities g_1 and g_4

Lemma 3. *For any Boolean networks $\mathcal{BN}_1$ and $\mathcal{BN}_2$ and entities $g \in \mathcal{BN}_1$ and $g' \in \mathcal{BN}_2$ we have $\mathcal{C}(\mathcal{BN}_1, \mathcal{BN}_2, g, g') = \mathcal{C}(\mathcal{BN}_2, \mathcal{BN}_1, g', g)$.*

Proof. Straightforward based on the commutativity of conjunction.   □

Composition gives a means of constructing new Boolean networks from well–understood and analysed Boolean networks. In particular, we would like to be able to infer properties and behaviour of a composed system from the underlying Boolean networks that have been composed. Being able to do this would allow us to construct large Boolean models with known properties without the limitations imposed by the state space explosion problem. The following definitions formalize the idea that the original behaviour of the underlying Boolean networks can be preserved in their composition.

We begin by defining *projection operators* which are able to extract states and traces from a composed system.

Definition 4. *(Projections) Let $\mathcal{C} = \mathcal{C}(\mathcal{BN}_1, \mathcal{BN}_2, g, g')$ be the new Boolean network constructed by composing $\mathcal{BN}_1$ and $\mathcal{BN}_2$ on entities g and g'. Let $S = (g^c\ g_1 \cdots g_n\ g'_1 \cdots g'_m) \in \mathcal{S}_\mathcal{C}$ be a global state in the composed system. Then we define the left $\mathcal{P}_1 : \mathcal{S}_\mathcal{C} \to \mathcal{S}_{\mathcal{BN}_1}$ and right $\mathcal{P}_2 : \mathcal{S}_\mathcal{C} \to \mathcal{S}_{\mathcal{BN}_2}$ projection operators by*

$$\mathcal{P}_1(S) = (g^c\ g_1 \cdots g_n), \quad \mathcal{P}_2(S) = (g^c\ g'_1 \cdots g'_m)$$

We can extend the projection operators to traces $\sigma = \langle S_1, S_2, \ldots \rangle \in Tr(\mathcal{C})$ by

$$\mathcal{P}_1(\sigma) = \langle \mathcal{P}_1(S_1), \mathcal{P}_1(S_2), \ldots \rangle, \quad \mathcal{P}_2(\sigma) = \langle \mathcal{P}_2(S_1), \mathcal{P}_2(S_2), \ldots \rangle$$

and let $\mathcal{P}_1(Tr(\mathcal{C}))$ and $\mathcal{P}_2(Tr(\mathcal{C}))$ represent the sets of projected traces derived by projecting each trace in $Tr(\mathcal{C})$.

Note that projected traces may not be well–defined traces in their corresponding Boolean network, i.e. $\mathcal{P}_j(Tr(\mathcal{C})) \nsubseteq Tr(\mathcal{BN}_j)$ may hold, for $j \in \{1, 2\}$.

We are interested in situations where composing two Boolean networks preserves their behaviour and define a notion of *compatibility*.

Definition 5. *(Compatibility) Let $\mathcal{C} = \mathcal{C}(\mathcal{BN}_1, \mathcal{BN}_2, g, g')$ be the Boolean network resulting from composing $\mathcal{BN}_1$ and $\mathcal{BN}_2$ on entities g and g'. Then we say that $\mathcal{BN}_1$ and $\mathcal{BN}_2$ are compatible on g and g' iff $Tr(\mathcal{BN}_1) \subseteq \mathcal{P}_1(Tr(\mathcal{C}))$ and $Tr(\mathcal{BN}_2) \subseteq \mathcal{P}_2(Tr(\mathcal{C}))$.*

To illustrate the definition of compatibility consider composing $\mathcal{BN}_{Ex1}$ and $\mathcal{BN}_{Ex2}$ to produce $\mathcal{C} = \mathcal{C}(\mathcal{BN}_{Ex1}, \mathcal{BN}_{Ex2}, g_1, g_4)$ (see Fig. 4). Then examples of projected traces in $\mathcal{P}_2(Tr(\mathcal{C}))$ (assuming state order (g^c g_2 g_3 g_5)) will be

$$\mathcal{P}_2(\langle 0100, 1011, 0100 \rangle) = \langle 00, 11, 00 \rangle \qquad \mathcal{P}_2(\langle 0001, 0001 \rangle) = \langle 01, 01 \rangle$$
$$\mathcal{P}_2(\langle 1001, 0100, 1011, 0100 \rangle) = \langle 11, 00, 11 \rangle \qquad \mathcal{P}_2(\langle 1100, 1100 \rangle) = \langle 10, 10 \rangle$$

It can be seen that $Tr(\mathcal{BN}_{Ex2}) \subseteq \mathcal{P}_2(Tr(\mathcal{C}))$ and so since we can also show $Tr(\mathcal{BN}_{Ex1}) \subseteq \mathcal{P}_1(Tr(\mathcal{C}))$ we know $\mathcal{BN}_{Ex1}$ and $\mathcal{BN}_{Ex2}$ are compatible on g_1 and g_4.

The following results show that composition is associative and so given Lemma 3 (commutativity) this means that the order in which multiple Boolean networks are composed does not affect the resulting model.

Lemma 6. *Let $\mathcal{BN}_1$, $\mathcal{BN}_2$ and $\mathcal{BN}_3$ be three Boolean networks, and let $g_1 \in \mathcal{BN}_1$, $g_2, g_3 \in \mathcal{BN}_2$, $g_2 \neq g_3$, and $g_4 \in \mathcal{BN}_3$. Then we have*

$$\mathcal{C}(\mathcal{C}(\mathcal{BN}_1, \mathcal{BN}_2, g_1, g_2), \mathcal{BN}_3, g_3, g_4) = \mathcal{C}(\mathcal{BN}_1, \mathcal{C}(\mathcal{BN}_2, \mathcal{BN}_3, g_3, g_4), g_1, g_2)$$

Proof. Let $\mathcal{C}_2 = \mathcal{C}(\mathcal{BN}_1, \mathcal{BN}_2, g_1, g_2)$, $\mathcal{C}_3 = \mathcal{C}(\mathcal{C}_2, \mathcal{BN}_3, g_3, g_4)$, and let $\mathcal{C}_4 = \mathcal{C}(\mathcal{BN}_2, \mathcal{BN}_3, g_3, g_4)$, $\mathcal{C}_5 = \mathcal{C}(\mathcal{BN}_1, \mathcal{C}_4, g_1, g_2)$. Let g_2^c be the entity representing the merge of g_1 and g_2, and g_4^c the merge of g_3 and g_4. Then by Definition 2 it suffices to show: (1) $F_{\mathcal{C}_3}(g_2^c) = F_{\mathcal{C}_5}(g_2^c)$; and (2) $F_{\mathcal{C}_3}(g_4^c) = F_{\mathcal{C}_5}(g_4^c)$.

We prove (1) as follows. By Definition 2 we know

$$F_{\mathcal{C}_3}(g_2^c) = F_{\mathcal{C}_2}(g_2^c), \quad \text{and} \quad F_{\mathcal{C}_2}(g_2^c) = F_1(g_1) \wedge F_2(g_2)$$

where $F_1(g_1) \wedge F_2(g_2)$ represents the function formed by the conjunction of the results of the two subfunctions $F_1(g_1)$ and $F_2(g_2)$. Then it follows from above that

$$F_{\mathcal{C}_3}(g_2^c) = F_1(g_1) \wedge F_2(g_2) \tag{I}$$

Again, by Definition 2 we know

$$F_{c_4}(g_2) = F_2(g_2), \quad \text{and} \quad F_{c_5}(g_2^c) = F_1(g_1) \wedge F_{c_4}(g_2)$$

and so it follows that

$$F_{c_5}(g_2^c) = F_1(g_1) \wedge F_2(g_2) \tag{II}$$

The result therefore follows by (I) and (II). The proof of (2) follows along similar lines to above. □

Lemma 7. *Let $\mathcal{BN}_1$, $\mathcal{BN}_2$ and $\mathcal{BN}_3$ be three Boolean networks, and let $g_1 \in \mathcal{BN}_1$, $g_2 \in \mathcal{BN}_2$, and $g_4 \in \mathcal{BN}_3$. Then we have*

$$\mathcal{C}(\mathcal{C}(\mathcal{BN}_1, \mathcal{BN}_2, g_1, g_2), \mathcal{BN}_3, g_2^c, g_4) = \mathcal{C}(\mathcal{BN}_1, \mathcal{C}(\mathcal{BN}_2, \mathcal{BN}_3, g_2, g_4), g_1, g_4^c)$$

where g_2^c is the entity representing the merge of g_1 and g_2, and g_4^c the merge of g_2 and g_4.

Proof. Let $\mathcal{C}_2 = \mathcal{C}(\mathcal{BN}_1, \mathcal{BN}_2, g_1, g_2)$, $\mathcal{C}_3 = \mathcal{C}(\mathcal{C}_2, \mathcal{BN}_3, g_2^c, g_4)$, and g_3^c be the entity representing the merge of g_2^c and g_4. Let $\mathcal{C}_4 = \mathcal{C}(\mathcal{BN}_2, \mathcal{BN}_3, g_2, g_4)$, $\mathcal{C}_5 = \mathcal{C}(\mathcal{BN}_1, \mathcal{C}_4, g_1, g_4^c)$, and g_5^c be the entity representing the merge of g_1 and g_4^c. To show that $\mathcal{C}_3 = \mathcal{C}_5$ we need to show that $F_{c_3}(g_3^c) = F_{c_5}(g_5^c)$. By Definition 2 we know

$$F_{c_3}(g_3^c) = F_{c_2}(g_2^c) \wedge F_3(g_4), \quad \text{and} \quad F_{c_2}(g_2^c) = F_1(g_1) \wedge F_2(g_2)$$

and so it follows that

$$F_{c_3}(g_3^c) = (F_1(g_1) \wedge F_2(g_2)) \wedge F_3(g_4) \tag{III}$$

Again, by Definition 2 we know

$$F_{c_5}(g_5^c) = F_1(g_1) \wedge F_{c_4}(g_4^c), \quad \text{and} \quad F_{c_4}(g_4^c) = F_2(g_2) \wedge F_3(g_4)$$

and so it follows that

$$F_{c_5}(g_5^c) = F_1(g_1) \wedge (F_2(g_2) \wedge F_3(g_4)) \tag{IV}$$

Then the result follows by (III), (IV) and the associativity of $\wedge$. $\square$

4   Compatibility and Alignment

In this section we investigate how to infer compatibility without using the composed model. We formalise the property of *alignment* which we show is sufficient for obtaining compatibility. We use this result to show that duplicate Boolean networks are compatible under composition of corresponding entities.

For any Boolean network $\mathcal{BN}$ with entities $G = \{g_1, \ldots, g_n\}$, global state $S = (s_1 \ldots s_n) \in S_{\mathcal{BN}}$ and any entity $g_i \in \mathcal{BN}$ we define $\rho_{g_i}(S) = s_i$. Then $\rho_{g_i}(\sigma)$ denotes the *projected trace* of entity $g_i \in \mathcal{BN}$ on trace $\sigma = \langle S_1, S_2, \ldots \rangle \in Tr(\mathcal{BN})$ defined by $\rho_{g_i}(\sigma) = \langle \rho_{g_i}(S_1), \rho_{g_i}(S_2), \ldots \rangle$. We let $\rho_{g_i}(Tr(\mathcal{BN})) = \{\rho_{g_i}(\sigma) \mid \sigma \in Tr(\mathcal{BN})\}$. As an example, consider projecting the traces of $\mathcal{BN}_{Ex2}$ (Fig. 3) on g_4 which gives $\rho_{g_4}(Tr(\mathcal{BN}_{Ex2})) = \{\langle 0, 1, 0 \rangle, \langle 0, 0 \rangle, \langle 1, 1 \rangle, \langle 1, 0, 1 \rangle\}$.

We can now define the property of *alignment* as follows.

Definition 8. *(Alignment) Let $\mathcal{BN}_1$ and $\mathcal{BN}_2$ be two Boolean networks and let $g \in \mathcal{BN}_1$ and $g' \in \mathcal{BN}_2$. Then we say that $\mathcal{BN}_1$ and $\mathcal{BN}_2$ are aligned on g and g' iff $\rho_g(Tr(\mathcal{BN}_1)) = \rho_{g'}(Tr(\mathcal{BN}_2))$.*

Let $\mathcal{C} = \mathcal{C}(\mathcal{BN}_1, \mathcal{BN}_2, g, g')$, and $S^1 = (g \ g_1 \ \cdots \ g_n) \in S_{\mathcal{BN}_1}$ and $S^2 = (g' \ g_1' \ \cdots \ g_m') \in S_{\mathcal{BN}_2}$. Then we define $S^1 \wedge S^2 \in S_{\mathcal{C}}$ by merging the state of g with g', that is $S^1 \wedge S^2 = (g \wedge g' \ g_1 \ \cdots \ g_n \ g_1' \ \cdots \ g_m')$. Let $\sigma_1 = \langle S_1^1, S_2^1, \ldots \rangle \in Tr(\mathcal{BN}_1)$ and $\sigma_2 = \langle S_1^2, S_2^2, \ldots \rangle \in Tr(\mathcal{BN}_2)$ be two traces. Then we define $\sigma_1 \wedge \sigma_2 = \langle S_1^1 \wedge S_1^2, S_2^1 \wedge S_2^2, \ldots \rangle$. Note that for any $\sigma_1 \in Tr(\mathcal{BN}_1)$ and $\sigma_2 \in Tr(\mathcal{BN}_2)$ we may have that $\sigma_1 \wedge \sigma_2 \notin Tr(\mathcal{C})$.

We now prove some useful results about merging aligned traces.

Lemma 9. *Let $\mathcal{BN}_1$ and $\mathcal{BN}_2$ be Boolean networks with $G_1 = \{g, g_1, \ldots, g_n\}$ and $G_2 = \{g', g_1', \ldots, g_m'\}$. Let $\mathcal{C} = \mathcal{C}(\mathcal{BN}_1, \mathcal{BN}_2, g, g')$, and let $\sigma^1 \in Tr(\mathcal{BN}_1)$ and $\sigma^2 \in Tr(\mathcal{BN}_2)$ such that $\rho_g(\sigma^1) = \rho_{g'}(\sigma^2)$. Then we have:*

(i) $\sigma^1 \wedge \sigma^2 \in Tr(\mathcal{C})$; and
(ii) $\mathcal{P}_1(\sigma^1 \wedge \sigma^2) = \sigma^1$ and $\mathcal{P}_2(\sigma^1 \wedge \sigma^2) = \sigma^2$.

Proof. Let $\sigma^1 = \langle S_1, S_2, ... \rangle \in Tr(\mathcal{BN}_1)$ and $\sigma^2 = \langle T_1, T_2, ... \rangle \in Tr(\mathcal{BN}_2)$ such that $\rho_g(\sigma^1) = \rho_{g'}(\sigma^2)$. In the following we consider an arbitrary synchronous update step in the above traces: $S_i \rightarrow S_{i+1}$ and $T_i \rightarrow T_{i+1}$, where $S_i = (s^i \, s_1^i \, ... \, s_n^i)$, $S_{i+1} = (s^{i+1} \, s_1^{i+1} \, ... \, s_n^{i+1})$, $T_i = (t^i \, t_1^i \, ... \, t_m^i)$, and $T_{i+1} = (t^{i+1} \, t_1^{i+1} \, ... \, t_m^{i+1})$. Note that by our assumption $\rho_g(\sigma^1) = \rho_{g'}(\sigma^2)$ we know $s^i = t^i$ and so by idempotency of $\wedge$ we have

$$s^i \wedge t^i = s^i = t^i \tag{V}$$

(i) To show $\sigma^1 \wedge \sigma^2 \in Tr(\mathcal{C})$, it suffices to show

$$(s^i \, s_1^i \, ... \, s_n^i) \wedge (t^i \, t_1^i \, ... \, t_m^i) \rightarrow (s^{i+1} \, s_1^{i+1} \, ... \, s_n^{i+1}) \wedge (t^{i+1} \, t_1^{i+1} \, ... \, t_m^{i+1})$$

is a synchronous update step in $\mathcal{C}$. We do this in three stages by considering each possible entity $h \in \mathcal{C}$. (Note to simplify the proof we assume $N_1(h^1) = G_1$ and $N_2(h^2) = G_2$, for any $h^1 \in G_1$ and $h^2 \in G_2$.)

(1) Suppose $h = g_j \in \mathcal{BN}_1$, for some $j \in \{1, ..., n\}$. Then by the definition of merging states and (V) above we have

$$F(g_j)(s^i \wedge t^i, s_1^i, ..., s_n^i) = F_1(g_j)(s^i, s_1^i, ..., s_n^i)$$

By definition of σ^1 we know $F_1(g_j)(s^i, s_1^i, ..., s_n^i) = s_j^{i+1}$ and so it follows that

$$F(g_j)(s^i \wedge t^i, s_1^i, ..., s_n^i) = s_j^{i+1}$$

as required.

(2) Suppose $h = g_j' \in \mathcal{BN}_2$, for some $j \in \{1, ..., m\}$. Then we can prove

$$F(g_j')(s^i \wedge t^i, t_1^i, ..., t_m^i) = t_j^{i+1}$$

using a similar approach to (1) above.

(3) Suppose $h = g^c \in \mathcal{C}$. Then by Definition 2 and (I) above we have

$$F(g^c)(s^i \wedge t^i, s_1^i, ..., s_n^i, t_1^i, ..., t_m^i) = F_1(g)(s^i, s_1^i, ..., s_n^i) \wedge F_2(g')(t^i, t_1^i, ..., t_m^i)$$

Then by our assumptions on σ^1 and σ^2 we have

$$F_1(g)(s^i, s_1^i, ..., s_n^i) \wedge F_2(g')(t^i, t_1^i, ..., t_m^i) = s^{i+1} \wedge t^{i+1}$$

and so the result follows as required.

(ii) By definition of merging traces it suffices to show that

$$\mathcal{P}_1(S_i \wedge T_i) = S_i \text{ and } \mathcal{P}_2(S_i \wedge T_i) = T_i$$

for any $i \in \mathbb{N}$. By definition of merging states we have

$$\mathcal{P}_1(S_i \wedge T_i) = (s^i \wedge t^i \, s_1^i \, ... \, s_n^i) \text{ and } \mathcal{P}_2(S_i \wedge T_i) = (s^i \wedge t^i \, t_1^i \, ... \, t_m^i)$$

Then the result follows by (V) above. $\qquad\qquad\qquad\qquad\qquad\qquad\qquad$ □

We can now prove that *alignment* is a sufficient property for *compatibility*.

Theorem 10. *Let $\mathcal{BN}_1$ and $\mathcal{BN}_2$ be two BNs with $g \in \mathcal{BN}_1$ and $g' \in \mathcal{BN}_2$. Then if $\mathcal{BN}_1$ and $\mathcal{BN}_2$ are aligned on g and g' then $\mathcal{BN}_1$ and $\mathcal{BN}_2$ are compatible on g and g'.*

Proof. Let $\mathcal{C} = \mathcal{C}(\mathcal{BN}_1, \mathcal{BN}_2, g, g')$. By Definition 5 we need to show the following: (i) $Tr(\mathcal{BN}_1) \subseteq \mathcal{P}_1(Tr(\mathcal{C}))$; and (ii) $Tr(\mathcal{BN}_2) \subseteq \mathcal{P}_2(Tr(\mathcal{C}))$.

(i) Since g *aligns* with g' we know that for each trace $\sigma^1 \in Tr(\mathcal{BN}_1)$ there exists $\sigma^2 \in Tr(\mathcal{BN}_2)$ such that $\rho_g(\sigma^1) = \rho_{g'}(\sigma^2)$. Then we need to show that $\sigma^1 \in \mathcal{P}_1(Tr(\mathcal{C}))$. By our assumption above on σ^1 and σ^2 and Lemma 9. (i) we know that $\sigma^1 \wedge \sigma^2 \in Tr(\mathcal{C})$ must hold. Then by Lemma 9. (ii) we have $\mathcal{P}_1(\sigma^1 \wedge \sigma^2) = \sigma^1$ and so $\sigma^1 \in \mathcal{P}_1(Tr(\mathcal{C}))$ as required.

(ii) The proof follows along similar lines to (i) above.   □

The above result provides a means of ensuring compatibility holds without requiring the composed system to be considered. This is important since a composed model will be larger and so more affected by the state space explosion problem. Note that while alignment is a sufficient condition for compatibility it can be shown that it is not a necessary property for it. In future work we intend to investigate strengthening alignment so that it completely characterises compatibility (see Sect. 5).

We say that $\mathcal{BN}_1$ and $\mathcal{BN}_2$ are *duplicates* if they are the same Boolean network up to the renaming of entities (i.e. they are isomorphic). It is interesting to consider what happens when duplicate Boolean networks are merged on corresponding entities (where *corresponding* is defined in the obvious way based on the underlying isomorphism). As an illustration, consider the example presented in Fig. 5 based on composing two duplicate copies of $\mathcal{BN}_{Ex1}$ (Fig. 1).

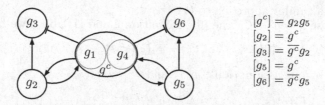

Fig. 5. Composing two duplicate copies of $\mathcal{BN}_{Ex1}$ on corresponding entities g_1 and g_4

We now use the alignment property to show that duplicate Boolean networks are compatible when composed on corresponding entities.

Theorem 11. *Let $\mathcal{BN}_1$ and $\mathcal{BN}_2$ be two duplicate Boolean networks and let $g \in \mathcal{BN}_1$ and $g' \in \mathcal{BN}_2$ be corresponding entities. Then $\mathcal{BN}_1$ and $\mathcal{BN}_2$ are compatible on g and g'.*

Proof. Since $\mathcal{BN}_1$ and $\mathcal{BN}_2$ are duplicates it follows (assuming a corresponding state order) that $Tr(\mathcal{BN}_1) = Tr(\mathcal{BN}_2)$. Thus by Definition 8 we know that $\mathcal{BN}_1$ and $\mathcal{BN}_2$ are aligned on corresponding entities g and g', and so by Theorem 10 we have that $\mathcal{BN}_1$ and $\mathcal{BN}_2$ are *compatible* on g and g' as required.   □

5   Conclusions

In this paper we set out to develop a compositional framework for Boolean networks in order to facilitate the construction and analysis of large scale models. This work was motivated by interesting interactions with the synthetic biology group at Newcastle[1] and their search for formal tools and techniques to support their work on engineering biological systems. We have formally defined our compositional approach and introduced the notion of compatibility to formalize the preservation of a Boolean network's behaviour within a composed model. We formulated the alignment property which we showed was a sufficient condition for ensuring compatibility and used it to investigate the composition of duplicate models. Importantly, the alignment property makes no reference to the composed model and so helps avoid potentially limiting state space explosion issues. The compositional framework developed is supported by a prototype tool that automates the composition process and associated analysis.

A range of related work on composing Boolean networks can be found in the literature. For example, the properties of composing random Boolean network by computing the attractors compositionally is considered in [5]. Other work includes [15] in which a compositional approach is used to study a large-scale network. Our approach based on merging entities and characterising the preservation of model behaviour appears to be new.

In future work we intend to extend the alignment property to provide a complete characterisation of compatibility. Initial work in this area has focused on using a state graph to model the interference that can occur between Boolean networks in a composed model. We are also interested in using our compositional framework as the basis for decomposing large Boolean network models to aid analysis. Further, we intend to undertake a series of large case studies to investigate the applicability of the techniques and tools we have developed.

Acknowledgments. We would like to thank Will Peckham for his work on developing tool support for our framework. We also acknowledge the financial support provided by Faculty of Computing and Information Technology, King Abdulaziz University.

---

[1] www.ncl.ac.uk/csbb/.

References

1. Akutsu, T., Miyano, S., Kuhara, S., et al.: Identification of genetic networks from a small number of gene expression patterns under the boolean network model. Pacific Symp. Biocomputing **4**, 17–28 (1999)
2. Banks, R., Steggles, L.J.: An abstraction theory for qualitative models of biological systems. Theoret. Comput. Sci. **431**, 207–218 (2012)
3. Bartocci, E., Lió, P.: Computational modeling, formal analysis, and tools for systems biology. PLoS Comput. Biol. **12**(1), e1004591 (2016)
4. De Jong, H.: Modeling and simulation of genetic regulatory systems: a literature review. J. Comput. Biol. **9**(1), 67–103 (2002)
5. Dubrova, E., Teslenko, M.: Compositional properties of random boolean networks. Phys. Rev. E **71**, 056116 (2005). http://link.aps.org/doi/10.1103/PhysRevE.71.056116
6. Harvey, I., Bossomaier, T.: Time out of joint: attractors in asynchronous random boolean networks. In: Proceedings of the Fourth European Conference on Artificial Life, pp. 67–75. MIT Press, Cambridge (1997)
7. Huang, S., Ingber, D.E.: Shape-dependent control of cell growth, differentiation, and apoptosis: switching between attractors in cell regulatory networks. Exp. Cell Res. **261**(1), 91–103 (2000)
8. Kauffman, S.A.: Metabolic stability and epigenesis in randomly constructed genetic nets. J. Theor. Biol. **22**(3), 437–467 (1969)
9. Kauffman, S.A.: The Origins of OIrder: Self Organization and Selection in Evolution. Oxford University Press, USA (1993)
10. Rosenblueth, D.A., Muñoz, S., Carrillo, M., Azpeitia, E.: Inference of boolean networks from gene interaction graphs using a SAT solver. In: Dediu, A.-H., Martín-Vide, C., Truthe, B. (eds.) AlCoB 2014. LNCS, vol. 8542, pp. 235–246. Springer, Cham (2014). https://doi.org/10.1007/978-3-319-07953-0_19
11. Saadatpour, A., Albert, R.: Boolean modeling of biological regulatory networks: a methodology tutorial. Methods **62**(1), 3–12 (2013)
12. Schaub, M.A., Henzinger, T.A., Fisher, J.: Qualitative networks: a symbolic approach to analyze biological signaling networks. BMC Syst. Biol. **1**(4) (2007)
13. Steggles, L.J., Banks, R., Shaw, O., Wipat, A.: Qualitatively modelling and analysing genetic regulatory networks: a petri net approach. Bioinformatics **23**(3), 336–343 (2007). http://bioinformatics.oxfordjournals.org/content/23/3/336
14. Thieffry, D., Thomas, R.: Dynamical behaviour of biological regulatory networks-II. Immunity control in bacteriophage lambda. Bull. Math. Biol. **57**(2), 277–297 (1995)
15. Tournier, L., Chaves, M.: Interconnection of asynchronous boolean networks, asymptotic and transient dynamics. Automatica **49**(4), 884–893 (2013)
16. Wuensche, A.: Basins of attraction in network dynamics: a conceptual framework for biomolecular networks. In: Schlosser, G., Wagner, G.P. (eds.) Modularity in Development and Evolution, chap. 13, pp. 288–311. University of Chicago Press, Chicago (2004)

A Statistical Approach to the Identification of Diploid Cellular Automata

Witold Bołt[1(✉)] ⓘ, Aleksander Bołt[2] ⓘ, Barbara Wolnik[2], Jan M. Baetens[3] ⓘ, and Bernard De Baets[3] ⓘ

[1] Systems Research Institute, Polish Academy of Sciences, 01-447 Warsaw, Poland
witold.bolt@ibspan.waw.pl
[2] Institute of Mathematics, Faculty of Mathematics, Physics and Informatics, University of Gdańsk, 80-308 Gdańsk, Poland
[3] KERMIT, Department of Mathematical Modelling, Statistics and Bioinformatics, Ghent University, 9000 Ghent, Belgium

Abstract. In this paper, the identification problem of diploid Cellular Automata is considered, in which, based on a series of observations, the underlying cellular automaton rules are to be uncovered. A solution algorithm based on a statistical parameter estimation method using a normal distribution approximation is proposed. The accuracy of this method is verified in a series of computational experiments.

Keywords: Stochastic cellular automata · Diploid Cellular Automata Parameter estimation · Systems identification

1 Introduction

Cellular Automata (CAs) are commonly used modelling constructs for addressing a variety of practical and theoretical problems [5]. In order to use CAs for a modelling task, one needs to understand the underlying mechanisms of the phenomenon at stake, and translate them into CA rules. This hampers the use of CAs, since there are problems for which it is hard to manually design such rules. Many efforts have been made in the direction of developing automated methods for constructing CAs based on observed space-time diagrams (see [1] for a review of the key methods). Yet, in practice the problem is still not fully solved as most of the methods are only well suited for special classes of problems, or impose strong requirements on the observations.

In this paper we focus on the identification of a class of Stochastic CAs (SCAs), called diploid CAs. Such SCAs recently gained a lot of attention in the research community (see [6] for some recent results). The identification method presented in this paper is an extension of the method presented in [3], where the identification of α-asynchronous CAs was discussed. The presented results form the first step towards establishing a general identification method for SCAs.

The paper is organized as follows. In Sect. 2 we present the key definitions. The identification problem and the description of the identification algorithm are

© Springer International Publishing AG 2017
C. Martín-Vide et al. (Eds.): TPNC 2017, LNCS 10687, pp. 37–48, 2017.
https://doi.org/10.1007/978-3-319-71069-3_3

given in Sect. 3. Section 4 contains the results of our computational experiments. The paper is concluded by Sect. 5, where the results are summarized.

2   Preliminaries

In this paper, we consider 1D CAs in which the cells are arranged in a circular array, and we denote the number of cells by N. We focus on binary CAs with a symmetric neighborhood whose radius is denoted by r. A *configuration* of a given CA A is an element $x = (x_0, x_1, \ldots, x_{N-1})$ of $\{0,1\}^N$, and A is identified with its *global rule* $F \colon \{0,1\}^N \to \{0,1\}^N$, given by the formula $F(x) = (x'_0, x'_1, \ldots, x'_{N-1})$, where $x'_i = f(x_{i-r}, \ldots, x_{i-1}, x_i, x_{i+1}, \ldots, x_{i+r})$ and all operations on the indices are performed modulo N. Here, the function $f \colon \{0,1\}^{2r+1} \to \{0,1\}$, called the *local rule*, is an update function, which may be deterministic or not. For the sake of readability, we number the elements of $\{0,1\}^{2r+1}$ as follows: $N_0 = (0, \ldots, 0, 0)$, $N_1 = (0, \ldots, 0, 1)$, $\ldots$, $N_{s-1} = (1, \ldots, 1, 0)$, $N_s = (1, \ldots, 1, 1)$, where $s = 2^{2r+1} - 1$. Further, x_i^t will be used to denote the value of the i-th cell after the t-th application of F starting from the configuration x.

CAs with a unit neighborhood radius and a deterministic f are known as Elementary CAs (ECAs) [9]. The local rule f of an ECA is a function of three variables: $f \colon \{0,1\}^3 \to \{0,1\}$ as the set $\{0,1\}^3$ has only eight elements: $N_0 = (0,0,0)$, $N_1 = (0,0,1)$, $\ldots$, $N_7 = (1,1,1)$, and the local rule f can be defined by setting the values $\ell_k = f(N_k) \in \{0,1\}$. These values can be presented as a lookup table (LUT) (see Table 1). Note that the order of the neighborhood configurations is fixed, so a given LUT can be stored using its last row, *i.e.* the vector (ℓ_i).

Table 1. General form of the LUT of the local rule of an ECA.

N_0	N_1	N_2	N_3	N_4	N_5	N_6	N_7
(0, 0, 0)	(0, 0, 1)	(0, 1, 0)	(0, 1, 1)	(1, 0, 0)	(1, 0, 1)	(1, 1, 0)	(1, 1, 1)
ℓ_0	ℓ_1	ℓ_2	ℓ_3	ℓ_4	ℓ_5	ℓ_6	ℓ_7

The number $C = \sum_{k=0}^{7} f(N_k) \cdot 2^k$ is called its rule number. We will write ECAC to denote an ECA with rule number C (for example ECA204 denotes the identity CA).

If the local rule of a CA is not deterministic, we are dealing with an SCA. Here, we consider SCAs where the local rule can be expressed as:

$$x_i^{t+1} = X_{t,i}\left(x_{i-r}^t, \ldots, x_{i-1}^t, x_i^t, x_{i+1}^t, \ldots, x_{i+r}^t\right), \tag{1}$$

where $X_{t,i}(N_k)$ are independent Boolean random variables satisfying:

$$\Pr\left(X_{t,i}(N_k) = 1\right) = p_k, \tag{2}$$

i.e. the probability of turning the state of a cell to 1 in the next time step depends only on the states of the cells in its neighborhood and is independent of the time step t and the cell number i. As a consequence of the binary nature of the state set, it holds that:

$$\Pr\left(X_{t,i}(\boldsymbol{N}_k) = 0\right) = 1 - p_k, \tag{3}$$

which means that an SCA can be fully described by the sequence of probabilities $(p_0, p_1, \ldots, p_s)$, usually presented in a tabular form (pLUT). The general form of a pLUT of an SCA with $r = 1$ is given in Table 2.

Table 2. General form of the pLUT of an SCA with unit radius.

$\boldsymbol{N}_0$	$\boldsymbol{N}_1$	$\boldsymbol{N}_2$	$\boldsymbol{N}_3$	$\boldsymbol{N}_4$	$\boldsymbol{N}_5$	$\boldsymbol{N}_6$	$\boldsymbol{N}_7$
(0, 0, 0)	(0, 0, 1)	(0, 1, 0)	(0, 1, 1)	(1, 0, 0)	(1, 0, 1)	(1, 1, 0)	(1, 1, 1)
p_0	p_1	p_2	p_3	p_4	p_5	p_6	p_7

Although Table 2 does not look different from Table 1, its entries p_k are numbers from $[0, 1]$, while each ℓ_k in Table 1 belongs to $\{0, 1\}$.

It is known that every SCA can be expressed as a stochastic mixture of a finite number of deterministic CAs [2], *i.e.* for every SCA A, there exists a finite sequence of deterministic CAs $(A_1, \ldots, A_m)$ and a vector of probabilities $(\lambda_1, \ldots, \lambda_m)$ satisfying $\sum_{i=1}^{m} \lambda_i = 1$, such that A is equivalent to independently selecting A_i for every cell, at every time step, with probability λ_i. In this paper we focus on a special class of SCAs, the so-called *diploid* CAs, which can be expressed as stochastic mixtures consisting of only two deterministic CAs. Such SCAs have been studied earlier by many authors, (*e.g.* [6,8]). Note that a special class of diploid CAs is the class of α-asynchronous CAs [7], where one of the two deterministic CAs is the identity CA.

Definition 1 (Diploid CA). *Let A_1 and A_2 be two different deterministic CAs with the same neighborhood radius r and with f_1 and f_2 as their local rules, respectively. For any mixing rate $\lambda \in]0, 1[$, we define the diploid CA $(A_1, A_2)_\lambda$ as an SCA with the following probabilities:*

$$p_k = \lambda f_1(\boldsymbol{N}_k) + (1 - \lambda) f_2(\boldsymbol{N}_k), \tag{4}$$

for any $k \in \{0, 1, \ldots, s\}$.

Note that any two CAs may be considered as having the same neighborhood radius, since a CA with radius r can be considered as a CA with radius r' for any $r' > r$. For the sake of convenience, we will also use $(A_1, A_2)_\lambda$ for the cases $\lambda \in \{0, 1\}$. According to (4) it holds that $(A_1, A_2)_0 = A_2$ and $(A_1, A_2)_1 = A_1$, meaning that these are deterministic CAs and not diploid CAs. Moreover, it is easy to see that (4) gives:

$$p_k = \begin{cases} 0 & \text{, if } f_1(N_k) = f_2(N_k) = 0 \,, \\ \lambda & \text{, if } f_1(N_k) = 1 \text{ and } f_2(N_k) = 0 \,, \\ 1 - \lambda & \text{, if } f_1(N_k) = 0 \text{ and } f_2(N_k) = 1 \,, \\ 1 & \text{, if } f_1(N_k) = f_2(N_k) = 1 \,. \end{cases} \tag{5}$$

Example 2. Let $A_1 = \text{ECA57}$ and $A_2 = \text{ECA120}$. The general form of the pLUT of $(A_1, A_2)_\lambda$ is shown in Table 3. Some space-time diagrams of $(A_1, A_2)_\lambda$ evolved from the same initial configuration for different values of λ are shown in Fig. 1.

In general, the decomposition of an SCA as a stochastic mixture of CAs is not unique [2], yet the following proposition [6] gives a full characterization of diploid CAs, as well as the conditions for the existence of a unique representation.

Table 3. The LUTs of ECAs 57 and 120 and the pLUT of the diploid $(\text{ECA57}, \text{ECA120})_\lambda$.

	N_0 (0, 0, 0)	N_1 (0, 0, 1)	N_2 (0, 1, 0)	N_3 (0, 1, 1)	N_4 (1, 0, 0)	N_5 (1, 0, 1)	N_6 (1, 1, 0)	N_7 (1, 1, 1)
ECA120	1	0	0	1	1	1	0	0
ECA57	0	0	0	1	1	1	1	0
diploid CA	λ	0	0	1	1	1	$1-\lambda$	0

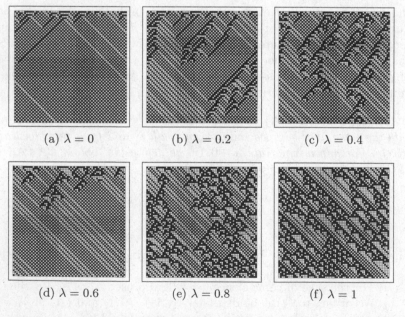

(a) $\lambda = 0$ (b) $\lambda = 0.2$ (c) $\lambda = 0.4$

(d) $\lambda = 0.6$ (e) $\lambda = 0.8$ (f) $\lambda = 1$

Fig. 1. Space-time diagrams of $(\text{ECA57}, \text{ECA120})_\lambda$ for six different mixing rates λ, evolved from the same initial configuration.

Proposition 3. *Let $(p_0, p_1, \ldots, p_s)$ be the pLUT of an SCA A. Then A is a diploid CA if and only if there exists a $\lambda \in]0, 0.5]$ such that $p_k \in \{0, \lambda, 1 - \lambda, 1\}$ for each $k \in \{0, 1, \ldots, s\}$, but $(p_0, p_1, \ldots, p_s) \notin \{0, 1\}^{s+1}$. Moreover, if $\lambda \neq 0.5$, then there exists a unique couple (A_1, A_2) satisfying $A = (A_1, A_2)_\lambda$. Otherwise, if $\lambda = 0.5$, then there are 2^d such couples, with d being the number of p_k equal to 0.5, for $k = 0, 1, \ldots, s$.*

3 Identification

We start with defining the identification problem. Our formulation is based on the concept of an observation of a space-time diagram, which is assumed to originate from some unknown diploid CA $(A_1, A_2)_\lambda$. Solving the identification problem requires finding both CAs A_1 and A_2 and establishing a good estimation of λ. More formally, let $I_1, I_2, \ldots, I_M$ be $N \times T$ arrays with binary entries. Each array I_m, for $m \in \{1, 2, \ldots, M\}$, will be referred to as an observation. The set of all observations will be denoted by $\mathcal{I}$. We assume that each observation $I \in \mathcal{I}$ is a space-time diagram of the same diploid CA $(A_1, A_2)_\lambda$. We choose a small $\alpha \in]0, 1[$ and we take $1 - \alpha$ as a confidence level. Based on the set of observations $\mathcal{I}$, we construct candidates for A_1 and A_2, and we estimate λ by building a confidence interval $[\lambda_L, \lambda_U]$. The probability that both CAs A_1 and A_2 are correctly identified and the true λ belongs to $[\lambda_L, \lambda_U]$ is at least $1 - 2\alpha$.

Below we propose an algorithm for solving the identification problem. Following Proposition 3, it is obvious that it should be assumed that $\lambda \neq 0.5$, but to obtain the required confidence level, we additionally assume that λ is bounded between known bounds a and b, i.e. $0 < a \leq \lambda \leq b < 0.5$.

Based on a set of observations $\mathcal{I}$, we create frequency tables $L = (L_0, \ldots, L_s)$ and $K = (K_0, \ldots, K_s)$, where L_k denotes the number of occurrence of the neighborhood configuration N_k in among the observations $I \in \mathcal{I}$, where the last row of each observation is discarded. To build the table K, we additionally check the state of the central cell in row $t + 1$ for each of the neighborhoods on row t, and we count the number of cases it equals 1. The meaning of the numbers L and K is following. For every $k \in \{0, 1, \ldots, s\}$, the number L_k is the number of occurrences of the neighborhood configuration N_k, while K_k is the number of cases in which the application of the unknown diploid CA to this neighborhood configuration resulted in state 1. Obviously, the number $L_k - K_k$ is the number of cases in which the outcome of the diploid CA's application to N_k was 0. We assume that the set of observations $\mathcal{I}$ is large enough to ensure that each neighborhood configuration was observed at least once (which is always possible if we have control over the initial configurations), so $L_k > 0$ for every k.

Proposition 4. *Assume that the observations in $\mathcal{I}$ are space-time diagrams of a diploid CA $(A_1, A_2)_\lambda$ and f_1 and f_2 are the local rules of A_1 and A_2, respectively. Then for any $k \in \{0, 1, \ldots, s\}$ the proportion $\widehat{p_k} = \frac{K_k}{L_k}$ is a random variable following a binomial distribution with success probability p_k, where p_k is given by (5).*

The first step in the identification is to identify the deterministic CAs A_1 and A_2, *i.e.* to find their corresponding LUTs $\ell_k^{(1)}$ and $\ell_k^{(2)}$, where $(\ell_0^{(1)}, \ell_1^{(1)}, \ldots, \ell_s^{(1)})$ and $(\ell_0^{(2)}, \ell_1^{(2)}, \ldots, \ell_s^{(2)})$ are the LUTs of A_1 and A_2, respectively. For every $k = 0, \ldots, s$ we proceed as follows:

(a) if $K_k = 0$, then we put $\ell_k^{(1)} = \ell_k^{(2)} = 0$,

(b) if $K_k = L_k$, then we put $\ell_k^{(1)} = \ell_k^{(2)} = 1$,

(c) if $\frac{K_k}{L_k} < 0.5$, then we put $\ell_k^{(1)} = 1$ and $\ell_k^{(2)} = 0$,

(d) if $\frac{K_k}{L_k} > 0.5$, then we put $\ell_k^{(1)} = 0$ and $\ell_k^{(2)} = 1$.

Note that if $K_k = 0$, (case (a)), for which we are not sure if both $\ell_k^{(1)}$ and $\ell_k^{(2)}$ are equal to zero, as it is possible that p_k is equal to λ or $1 - \lambda$, while there is no sample in $\mathcal{I}$ with the outcome 1. Fortunately, the probability of this happening equals $(1-\lambda)^{L_k}$ or λ^{L_k}, and thus is less than $(1-a)^{L_k}$. The same considerations apply when $K_k = L_k$ (case (b)), to verify that the probability of mistake is less than $(1-a)^{L_k}$. Hence, to achieve the desired confidence level, we will assume that $(1-a)^{L_k} \leq \frac{\alpha}{2^{s+1}}$. In cases (c) and (d) the situation is a bit more complicated. If $\frac{K_k}{L_k} < 0.5$, then to verify if p_k is really less than 0.5, we can perform a hypothesis test on proportions with alternative hypothesis $H_1 : \ p_k < 0.5$. We use the normal approximation method and a left-tailed test. If the obtained p-value is less than $\frac{\alpha}{2^{s+1}}$, then we may claim that p_k is really less than 0.5. If $\frac{K_k}{L_k} > 0.5$, the alternative hypothesis is $H_1 : \ p_k > 0.5$ and the test is right-tailed. This completes the procedure of finding A_1 and A_2. Given above assumptions, the total probability of picking wrong CAs is less than α.

We now turn to the second step of the algorithm to estimate λ by constructing a relatively small confidence interval $[\lambda_L, \lambda_U]$ that contains the true (unknown) λ with high probability. Let us note that if $\frac{K_k}{L_k} < 0.5$, then we know that the diploid CA $(A_1, A_2)_\lambda$ acted as A_1 K_k times, during L_k independent transitions, while if $\frac{K_k}{L_k} > 0.5$, then this diploid CA acted as A_1 $L_k - K_k$ times within these L_k independent transitions. As a consequence, we get the following proposition.

Proposition 5. *Let* $\Gamma = \{k \in \{0, 1, \ldots, s\} \mid \frac{K_k}{L_k} < 0.5\}$ *and* $\Omega = \{k \in \{0, 1, \ldots, s\} \mid \frac{K_k}{L_k} > 0.5\}$. *Then, the proportion*

$$\widehat{\lambda} = \frac{\sum_{k \in \Gamma} K_k + \sum_{k \in \Omega}(L_k - K_k)}{\sum_{k \in \Gamma} L_k + \sum_{k \in \Omega} L_k}, \tag{6}$$

is a random variable following a binomial distribution with success probability λ.

Following [4] there are various methods for estimating the confidence interval for λ using $\widehat{\lambda}$. Here, we choose the normal distribution approximation, even though the authors of [4] advice against it. This choice is motivated by the fact that this method has reasonable accuracy, while its implementation is straightforward. Assuming that $1 - \alpha$ is the chosen confidence level, then the following holds with probability $1 - \alpha$:

$$\lambda_L := \widehat{\lambda} - z_\alpha \sqrt{\frac{\widehat{\lambda}(1-\widehat{\lambda})}{L^*}} \le \lambda \le \widehat{\lambda} + z_\alpha \sqrt{\frac{\widehat{\lambda}(1-\widehat{\lambda})}{L^*}} =: \lambda_U, \qquad (7)$$

where $L^* = \sum_{k \in \Gamma} L_k + \sum_{k \in \Omega} L_k$, and z_α is the argument at which the cumulative standard normal distribution function takes the value $1 - \frac{\alpha}{2}$. The above holds if L^* is large enough, which in our case means that $L^* \lambda$ and $L^*(1-\lambda)$ are greater than five [4]. Since λ is unknown, due to the assumption $\lambda \ge a$, we can impose a stronger condition $L^* > \frac{5}{a}$, which is easy to verify. With these assumptions, it holds that $\lambda \in [\lambda_L, \lambda_U]$ with probability $1 - \alpha$. Note that $\lambda_U - \lambda_L \le \frac{z_\alpha}{\sqrt{L^*}}$ and for commonly used confidence levels it holds that $z_\alpha < 3$. Thus, if L^* is sufficiently large, we are sure that the interval $[\lambda_L, \lambda_U]$ narrows as the number of observed cells grows.

4 Results

In this section, the results of computational experiments are presented to illustrate the accuracy of the algorithm described in Sect. 3. They involve the identification of diploid CAs consisting of ECAs. More formally, we considered diploid CAs $(A_1, A_2)_\lambda$, with A_1 and A_2 being ECAs and $\lambda = 0.1, 0, 2, 0.3, 0.4$. Since $A_1 \ne A_2$, a total of $256 \times 255 \times 4 = 249900$ diploid CAs were considered. Since $(A_2, A_1)_\lambda$ is identical to $(A_1, A_2)_{1-\lambda}$ all diploid CAs based on ECAs, for $\lambda = 0.1, 0.2, \ldots, 0.9$ were examined, with the exception of $\lambda = 0.5$. The same set of 100 random initial configurations was used for all considered cases. Each of the initial configurations contained 49 cells. Using these initial configurations, 100 observations, each containing 49 times steps, were generated for each $(A_1, A_2)_\lambda$. The identification algorithm was executed based on these observations. The process of constructing the observation set and identifying the CAs was repeated 50 times for each of the considered diploid CAs. Consequently, for each diploid CA $(A_1, A_2)_\lambda$, 50 pairs of candidate CAs $(A_1^{(j)}, A_2^{(j)})$ and 50 confidence intervals $[\lambda_L^{(j)}, \lambda_U^{(j)}]$ for $j = 1, 2, \ldots, 50$ were obtained.

In each run of the algorithm for each diploid CA, the obtained candidate CAs $(A_1^{(j)}, A_2^{(j)})$ were matching the ones building the diploid CA in question. More formally, for every $(A_1, A_2)_\lambda$ it turned out that $A_1 = A_1^{(j)}$ and $A_2 = A_2^{(j)}$ for every j, meaning that the first step of the identification algorithm always resulted in a correct identification of the CAs making up the diploid CAs.

To verify the results of the second step of the algorithm, two error measures were used: the maximal relative error and the maximal distance to the confidence interval. Letting $\widehat{\lambda}^{(j)} = \frac{\lambda_L^{(j)} + \lambda_U^{(j)}}{2}$, the maximal relative error is defined as:

$$E(A_1, A_2, \lambda) = \max_{j=1,\ldots,50} \frac{|\widehat{\lambda}^{(j)} - \lambda|}{\lambda} \times 100\%, \qquad (8)$$

while the maximal distance to the confidence interval is defined as:

$$D(A_1, A_2, \lambda) = \max_{j=1,\ldots,50} d(\lambda, [\lambda_L^{(j)}, \lambda_U^{(j)}]), \qquad (9)$$

where:

$$d(x, [a,b]) = \begin{cases} 0 & \text{, if } x \in [a,b], \\ a - x & \text{, if } x < a, \\ x - b & \text{, if } x > b. \end{cases} \tag{10}$$

A statistical summary containing the minimum, average, 95th-percentile, maximum and the standard deviation of the maximal relative error E is given in Table 4. The maximal error obtained (49.44%) may seem high. Fortunately, as the 95th-percentile values show, in the vast majority of cases the errors are significantly lower.

Table 4. Minimum (min.), average (avg.), 95th-percentile (perc.), maximum (max.) and standard deviation (st. dev.) of the maximal relative error $E(A_1, A_2, \lambda)$ for the different values of λ.

	min.	avg.	95th-perc.	max.	st. dev.
$\lambda = 0.1$	0.89%	3.50%	10.21%	49.44%	3.46%
$\lambda = 0.2$	0.65%	2.42%	7.07%	38.20%	2.33%
$\lambda = 0.3$	0.45%	1.88%	5.49%	26.15%	1.79%
$\lambda = 0.4$	0.33%	1.51%	4.46%	20.58%	1.44%
all λs	0.33%	2.33%	6.68%	49.44%	2.49%

In Fig. 2 the histogram of the maximal relative error E is shown. In Fig. 2(a) the overall histogram from all data points is provided, while in Figs. 2(b)–(i) we show the results grouped by the Hamming distance (dist) between the LUTs of the ECAs A_1 and A_2. As can be seen, the distributions of the relative error for each of the distances are strictly different from each other. Note that each of the histograms has been normalized with respect to the maximal number of occurrences, so that the differences of the number of instances in each class could be ignored.

To further analyze the obtained results, we define the cumulative relative error $C_E(A_1, A_2)$ as:

$$C_E(A_1, A_2) = \sum_{\lambda = 0.1, \ldots, 0.4} E(A_1, A_2, \lambda) + \sum_{\lambda = 0.1, \ldots, 0.4} E(A_2, A_1, \lambda), \tag{11}$$

which for each pair of ECAs combines the results for different values of λ. We assume $C_E(A, A) = 0$ for any ECA A. Obviously, it holds that $C_E(A_1, A_2) = C_E(A_2, A_1)$. The values of this cumulative relative error C_E, normalized with respect to the maximal cumulative error, are shown in Fig. 3. As can be inferred from this graph, there are significant differences between the values of C_E in different areas of the ECA space. Moreover, many of symmetries can be observed, but a more detailed analysis of these is beyond the scope of this paper.

We also grouped the values of C_E according to the Hamming distance between the LUTs of A_1 and A_2 (Fig. 4). As can be seen, the closer the ECAs

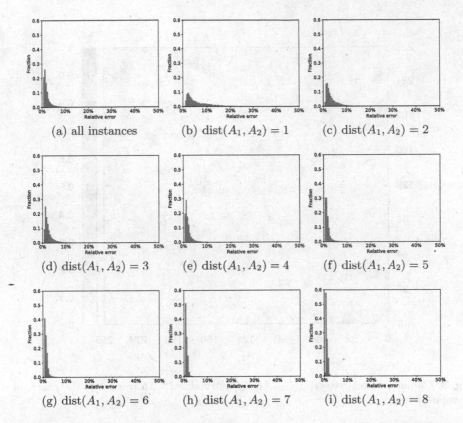

Fig. 2. Histogram of the maximal relative error $E(A_1, A_2, \lambda)$ for all λ with bin size 0.5% (a) for all diploid CAs and (b)–(i) grouped by the Hamming distance of the LUTs of A_1 and A_2.

are to each other in terms of their LUTs, the higher C_E. This can be understood by analyzing (5). The number of positions at which the LUTs of A_1 and A_2 differ determines the number of neighborhoods on which the diploid CA acts non-deterministically, and thus produces transitions that are useful for estimating. This means that CAs that are close to each other will likely produce less samples that can be used for the estimation of λ.

We now turn to the analysis of the maximal distance from the confidence interval $D(A_1, A_2, \lambda)$ (Table 5). In general, the values of D are low, which shows that in most cases the real λ either belongs to the confidence interval or is very close to it. This shows a high accuracy in the estimation of λ, irrespective of λ. For that reason we concentrate our analysis on the cumulative maximal distance to the confidence interval:

$$C_D(A_1, A_2) = \sum_{\lambda=0.1,\ldots,0.4} D(A_1, A_2, \lambda) + \sum_{\lambda=0.1,\ldots,0.4} D(A_2, A_1, \lambda). \qquad (12)$$

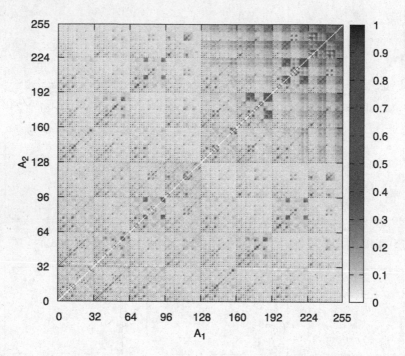

Fig. 3. Cumulative relative error $C_E(A_1, A_2)$ normalized with respect to the maximal cumulative error.

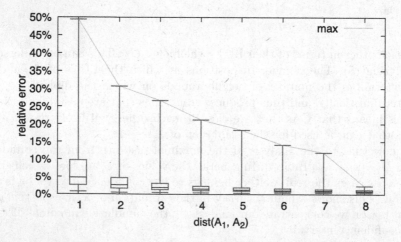

Fig. 4. Relation of the Hamming distance of the LUTs defining A_1 and A_2 to the cumulative relative error C_E.

Table 5. Minimum (min.), average (avg.), 95th-percentile (perc.), maximum (max.) and standard deviation (st. dev.) of the obtained maximal distance from the confidence interval $D(A_1, A_2, \lambda)$ for different values of λ.

	min.	avg.	95th-perc.	max.	st. dev.
$\lambda = 0.1$	0.0	0.0008	0.0024	0.0207	0.0010
$\lambda = 0.2$	0.0	0.0010	0.0034	0.0498	0.0014
$\lambda = 0.3$	0.0	0.0012	0.0040	0.0438	0.0017
$\lambda = 0.4$	0.0	0.0013	0.0044	0.0413	0.0018
all λs	0.0	0.0011	0.0036	0.0498	0.0015

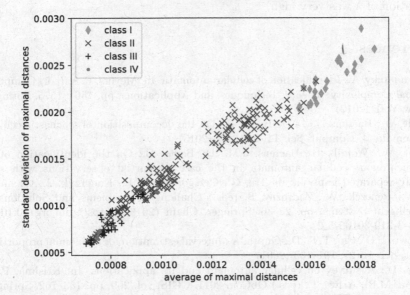

Fig. 5. The relation of the average and the standard deviation of the maximal distance to the confidence interval Δ. The shape and the color of points is assigned according to Wolfram's class of the corresponding ECA. (Color figure online)

These values were then grouped, for each ECA A, as:

$$\Delta(A) = \Big\{ C_D(A, A_2) \mid A_2 \in \{\text{ECA0}, \ldots, \text{ECA255}\} \backslash \{A\} \Big\}. \tag{13}$$

In Fig. 5 the relation between the average and the standard deviation of $\Delta(A)$ is shown for each ECA A. Each point on this plot corresponds to a specific ECA. The shape and the color of each of the points are assigned according to Wolfram's classification [9], where Class I corresponds to simple dynamics resulting in homogenous configurations, Class II — periodic dynamics, Class III — chaotic/random dynamics and Class IV — complex dynamics. As can be seen, there is a strong correlation between the Wolfram class and $\Delta(A)$. In general, the accuracy of the estimation of λ grows with the growing complexity of the ECA in question.

5   Summary

In this paper the identification of a diploid CA from given space-time diagrams has been discussed. A solution method based on a confidence interval estimation method has been presented. The computational experiments showed that the algorithm is very effective. The deterministic CAs constituting the analyzed diploids CAs were always correctly identified. Moreover, the accuracy of the estimation of λ was very high.

References

1. Adamatzky, A.: Identification of cellular automata. In: Meyers, R.A. (ed.) Computational Complexity: Theory, Techniques, and Applications, pp. 1564–1575. Springer, New York (2012)
2. Bołt, W., Baetens, J.M., De Baets, B.: On the decomposition of stochastic cellular automata. J. Comput. Sci. **11**, 245–257 (2015)
3. Bołt, W., Wolnik, B., Baetens, J.M., De Baets, B.: On the identification of α-asynchronous cellular automata in the case of partial observations with spatially separated gaps. In: de Trė, G., Grzegorzewski, P., Kacprzyk, J., Owsiński, J.W., Penczek, W., Zadrożny, S. (eds.) Challenging Problems and Solutions in Intelligent Systems, pp. 23–36. Springer, Cham (2016). https://doi.org/10.1007/978-3-319-30165-5_2
4. Brown, L.D., Cai, T.T., DasGupta, A.: Interval estimation for a binomial proportion. Stat. Sci. **16**(2), 101–133 (2001)
5. Das, D.: A survey on cellular automata and its applications. In: Krishna, P.V., Babu, M.R., Ariwa, E. (eds.) ObCom 2011. CCIS, vol. 269, pp. 753–762. Springer, Heidelberg (2012). https://doi.org/10.1007/978-3-642-29219-4_84
6. Fatès, N.: Diploid cellular automata: first experiments on the random mixtures of two elementary rules. In: Dennunzio, A., Formenti, E., Manzoni, L., Porreca, A.E. (eds.) AUTOMATA 2017. LNCS, vol. 10248, pp. 97–108. Springer, Cham (2017). https://doi.org/10.1007/978-3-319-58631-1_8
7. Fatès, N., Morvan, M.: An experimental study of robustness to asynchronism for elementary cellular automata. Complex Syst. **16**, 1–27 (2005)
8. Mendonça, J., de Oliveira, M.: An extinction-survival-type phase transition in the probabilistic cellular automaton $p182 - q200$. J. Phys. A: Math. Theor. **44** (2011). Article ID 155001
9. Wolfram, S.: Statistical mechanics of cellular automata. Rev. Mod. Phys. **55**, 601–644 (1983)

Modelling Curvature Effects Using L-Systems: From Discrete and Deterministic to Continuous and Stochastic

Julia Pulwicki[✉] and Christophe Godin

Virtual Plants Group, INRIA Montpellier, Montpellier, France
`julia.pulwicki@inria.fr`

Abstract. We present a new computational approach to modelling trajectories on embeddable 2D Riemannian surfaces. By decomposing trajectories into infinitesimal geodesic line segments and rotations, a path through curved space can be represented as a string of basic instructions playing out in curved space. In this way, we can catalog and quantify the fundamental changes a system experiences when expressed in different curvatures. Indeed, we find that curvature can modulate the behaviour of a wide range of trajectories, from discrete and deterministic to continuous and stochastic. Results in constant positive curvature 2-spaces are given for fractals, random walks and diffusion, and we discuss potential applications to biological systems and 4D printing.

Keywords: Fractal geometry · Riemannian geometry · L-systems
Diffusion · Random walk · Curvature · Plant development

1 Introduction

The effect of curvature on physical systems is both profound and non-intuitive. Often, experimental and theoretical approaches to various problems in science and engineering try to eliminate or minimize these effects by studying flat or nearly flat varieties of more general geometries. However, even if a system can be locally approximated as flat, curvature can still produce large-scale effects.

A common example is how we as humans move around on the Earth. Locally, a flat map of our city or local area is completely sufficient to help us navigate by foot, bicycle or car. However, if we start considering larger trips by airplane or boat, then our shortest paths between two points are in fact geodesics of the sphere, known as great circles.

In fact, many physical systems have this fundamental property: at small scales, the system follows flat-space rules, but at large scales experiences the effects of curvature. Formally, we can describe this type of behaviour using the rules of Riemannian geometry, which provides the mathematical tools necessary for incorporating curvature into basic quantities like distance, velocity and force.

Most famously, Einstein's theory of general relativity uses a semi-Riemannian geometry to link the curvature of space-time with gravitational forces. However,

© Springer International Publishing AG 2017
C. Martín-Vide et al. (Eds.): TPNC 2017, LNCS 10687, pp. 49–60, 2017.
https://doi.org/10.1007/978-3-319-71069-3_4

there are many other systems around us like curved plant leaves and meristems (the growing tip of a plant) that are now being observed at new levels of detail, but lack a framework for understanding the geometric aspects central to their development [5,7].

It is for this reason that our goal is to build a computational tool that relies on local rules being interpreted in a curved geometry. Rather than explicitly employing the calculus of curved spaces through geodesic equations or covariant derivatives, we seek to recover these effects by modelling how a multitude of local actions, either deterministic or stochastic, can be altered by the global geometry of the system. By demonstrating how the behaviour of even simple systems is affected by curvature, we can motivate the search for such effects in natural and engineered systems which may utilize curvature to augment processes such as information flow or modulate basic properties like the connectivity of a structure.

An ideal tool for studying the scale-dependent nature of curvature is fractals, which have recursive, scale-free patterns that provide a simple yet effective way to probe curvature effects simultaneously at different length scales. Moreover, the deterministic trajectory of a fractal shape defines a unique topology for each shape which in flat space remains conserved at all length scales. As our preliminary results show, the smallest length scales of a fractal retain their usual flat-space behaviour, but at larger length scales curvature can change both the geometry and topology of the fractal in surprising ways.

Our L-system model can also be pushed to the stochastic limit to study phenomena like random walks and the related phenomenon of diffusion. As will be discussed in detail later, understanding how random walks are affected by curvature is important for many natural systems and has in fact been observed for crystal growth [8] and particle trajectories [10] at μm scales on positively surfaces. Our results on the 2-sphere are consistent with analytical predictions in [4] and [3]. In the last section of this article, we identify potential ways in which curvature effects could influence plant tissue growth as well as applications to materials engineering.

2   Methods

The basic goal of the model developed here is to recreate as closely as possible the notion that local rules of action are being interpreted on a curved surface. Using L-systems, we can specify a trajectory as a string of instructions that are executed following the rules of a curved surface. Such a model allows the dynamics of the system to be specified separately from the space in which they occur, thus allowing one to investigate the role curvature plays in the dynamics of a system.

L-systems are a way to represent geometric shapes in 3D Euclidean space by specifying the motion of a local actor called a turtle [1,9]. The turtle is given a set of instructions in the form of an *lstring* for its trajectory in Euclidean space based on its local frame of reference - what it perceives to be forward, right and up directions (or, equivalently, unit vectors in the (x,y,z) directions).

Those instructions, when displayed graphically, form what we observe to be a geometric shape. In the models below, we use the programming language LPy to generate graphical models of L-systems [2].

A simple example is a square, given by a series of forward steps of unit length $F(1)$ and 90° rotations:

$$\text{lstring} = F(1) + (90)F(1) + (90)F(1) + (90)F(1). \tag{1}$$

More complex shapes can be formed by changing how many forward steps are taken, the length of the forward steps, and the angle of rotation ($+(\beta)$ or $-(\beta)$).

Another way to generate more complex shapes is to provide a *production rule* for $F(x)$. These rules modify an original lstring by specifying how it should be rewritten in a subsequent iteration. For example, a fractal can be generated by applying the following production rule many times:

$$F(x) \rightarrow F(x/3) + (60)F(x/3) - (120)F(x/3) + (60)F(x/3). \tag{2}$$

At each iteration, the lstring is re-written using the production rule for $F(x)$ in the following way:

$$
\begin{aligned}
\text{lstring}_0 &= F(9) \\
\text{lstring}_1 &= F(3) + (60)F(3) - (120)F(3) + (60)F(3) \\
\text{lstring}_2 &= F(1) + (60)F(1) - (120)F(1) + (60)F(1) + (60) \\
&\quad F(1) + (60)F(1) - (120)F(1) + (60)F(1) - (120) \\
&\quad F(1) + (60)F(1) - (120)F(1) + (60)F(1) + (60) \\
&\quad F(1) + (60)F(1) - (120)F(1) + (60)F(1) \\
\text{lstring}_3 &= F(1/3) + (60)...
\end{aligned}
\tag{3}
$$

The result is the Koch curve, shown in Fig. 1.

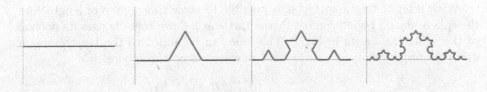

Fig. 1. The first four iterations of the Koch curve as generated by the production rules in Eq. 3. The figures have been created using the LPy programming framework [2].

The next task is to find a way to interpret this set of instructions on a curved surface. Consider the turtle starting its path at the north pole of a sphere. To the turtle, all directions look the same, and locally it seems no different than flat space (i.e. isotropic, homogeneous and locally Euclidean). So it chooses a direction at random and takes a step forward.

An important observation here is that as outside observers (in 3D Euclidean embedding space), we have access to the normal vector perpendicular to the turtle's tangent plane, but the turtle does not. This is pictured in Fig. 2 with one dimension suppressed. Here, the turtle moves along the surface of the sphere from position T1 to T2. Locally, it can follow the vector parallel to the surface of the sphere. In the embedding space, what we can measure for each step on the turtle's path is how much the normal vector rotates and use it to interpret the turtle's motion on the sphere. We denote this kind of motion by the $\wedge$ symbol.

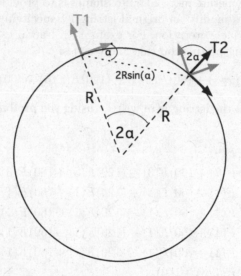

Fig. 2. The geometry of a turtle walking along a geodesic of a curved surface (2-sphere) from position T1 to T2, with one dimension suppressed. The arrows denote the orientation of the turtle's local coordinate system.

With a bit of trigonometry, it is possible to show that a step of length l on the sphere should be interpreted by the turtle as a move that changes its normal to the sphere as shown in Fig. 2. This rule can be added to the L-system as a default interpretation rule for forward movements on the sphere:

$$F(l)_{sphere} \rightarrow {}^{\wedge}(\alpha)F(2R\sin\alpha){}^{\wedge}(\alpha) \tag{4}$$

where $2\alpha = l/R$.

Two properties of Riemannian 2-spheres makes this possible. The first is that any sufficiently small region of a Riemannian metric is locally Euclidean (flat), so our turtle always has a well defined notion of orthogonality, and hence rotation. There is no need to re-interpret rotations for a turtle on the 2-sphere. The second is that the 2-sphere is isotropic and homogeneous, which means that any one step can be understood the same as the 'first' step described above. As long as we can describe the first step correctly, we can describe a string of steps, just like in Euclidean 2-space (the plane).

With $F(l)_{sphere}$ defined in 4 and letting the turtle start from the north pole every time, we can see that the simplest path locally also leads to a geodesic in the curved space. Let us define the simplest path to be a series of forward steps, represented as a string of Fs, which in flat space simply yields a straight line. The analog of a straight line on the 2-sphere is a great circle. Indeed, if we take a series of F_{sphere}, it produces a great circle (Fig. 3).

However, geodesics are only a sub-set of all possible trajectories in a space. Mapping out the geodesics of a Riemannian space is an important step in understanding the structure of the geometry, but we are also interested in the more general case of how any 2D turtle path may look like when expressed in curved space.

Non-geodesic paths can be seen as the turtle experiencing a force. For example, in $F + (\beta)F$, the 'force' enters through the rotation angle β, which can have any value between 0 and 360°. Without this rotation, the turtle continues freely around a great circle; to change this behaviour, 'a force' must be applied regularly to the turtle to keep deflecting it from great circles. With infinitesimal steps and rotations, we can thus generate any trajectory. An example set of trajectories equivalent to the lines of latitude on a globe is shown in Fig. 3.

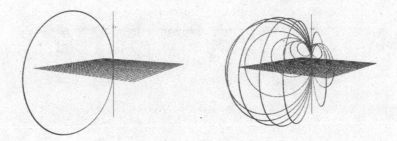

Fig. 3. On the left, a great circle formed by using only forward steps $F(l)_{sphere}$ interpreted as incremental geodesic steps on a sphere. On the right, a set of trajectories formed by varying the 'force' the turtle feels at every step of its path.

3   The 2-Sphere

In this section, we present results on a range of different systems, from discrete and deterministic (closed loops and fractals) to continuous and stochastic (random walks). The examples are intended to illustrate how curvature influences the fundamental properties of each system. In this way, we can catalog and quantify the different effects curvature has and thus motivate the search for curvature effects in both natural and engineered settings.

These models are based on positively curved geometries and, where possible, we compare our results against other analytical or experimental work. The geometries studied here are equivalent to the 2-sphere and provide the simplest system to explore using the L-system scheme.

3.1   A Closed Loop

As a first example, let us go back and look at the trajectory for a square again: lstring $= F + (90)F + (90)F + (90)F$. When expressed on the surface of a sphere, we replace F with F_{sphere}, though in the following we simply use F for clarity.

For a sufficiently small step size, say 1/100th of the radius of curvature of the sphere, the square will look almost identical to the flat-space interpretation. However, we can let the turtle explore more of the curved space by adding more steps between rotations:

$$\text{lstring} = FFF + (90)FFF + (90)FFF + (90)FFF, \tag{5}$$

or even

$$\text{lstring} = F...F + (90)F...F + (90)F...F + (90)F...F \tag{6}$$

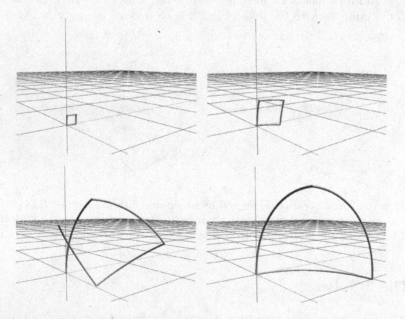

Fig. 4. The lstring $F + (90)F + (90)F + (90)F$ with increasingly longer path lengths interpreted on a 2D spherical geometry. For short path lengths, the shape is approximately a square. At intermediate lengths, the square begins to deform as each path becomes a longer geodesic. Finally, when each side is 1/4 of the circumference of the sphere, the path closes using only 3 geodesics.

where the segment $F...F$ can be many steps forward. Thus, each side of the square becomes an increasingly longer geodesic. A sequence of these paths with successively longer side lengths in shown in Fig. 4.

As each segment of the square becomes longer and longer, the square becomes deformed. When each line segment is 1/4th of the circumference of the sphere, the square appears to become a three-sided shape, thus illustrating the notion that a closed loop in a positively curved space has a smaller perimeter than its flat-space counterpart. This simulation also shows how internal angles of polygons change depending on the curvature of the background space.

3.2 The Koch Curve

Let us now look at the behaviour of our first fractal structure, the Koch curve (Fig. 1). As can be seen, the flat-space Koch curve is an open line segment.

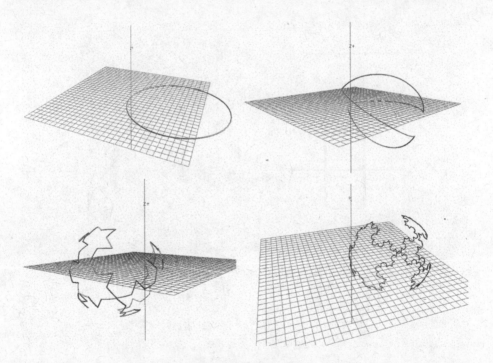

Fig. 5. The first four iterations of a 2-sphere interpretation of a Koch curve.

The Koch curve on a sphere is shown in Fig. 5. The most striking feature of this fractal is that it has formed closed loops when expressed on the sphere, thus changing its topology.

A related physical phenomenon that has been observed to have similar curvature effects is the formation of rigid crystals on a microsphere [8]. Here, the authors were able to show topological defects imposed by the curvature of the sphere that would otherwise not be present in flat space.

3.3 The Sierpinski Carpet

Having seen the effects of curvature on a square as well as simple fractal, we can now investigate a more complex fractal composed of many closed loops at different length scales, the Sierpinski Carpet.

The basic, flat-space structure of this fractal is shown in the left column of Fig. 6. Just as in the closed loop model, we can interpret the line segments as geodesics of the sphere, thus generating the shapes seen in the right column of Fig. 6.

We can see that the curved Sierpinski carpet has behaviours consistent with both the closed-loop and Koch curve models. At small scales, the squares remain relatively unchanged, while the large squares undergo the largest deformations.

Fig. 6. The first four iterations of a Sierpinski carpet. On the left, the flat space interpretation and on the right a curved space interpretation.

Also, line segments previously far apart in flat space may be in direct contact on a sphere.

3.4   Random Walks

Lastly, we model a random walk which can be decomposed into a sequence of forward steps and random rotations in the tangent plane:

$$+ (\beta_{random})F + (\beta_{random})F + (\beta_{random})F... \tag{7}$$

In Fig. 7 we show a sample of what a random walk looks like on a sphere. The step size is kept small and constant relative to the radius of curvature.

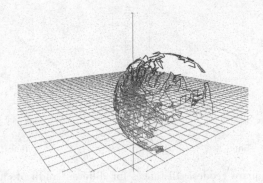

Fig. 7. A set of 20 random walks on a sphere.

A quantity that is often used to characterize a random walk is the mean square distance from the origin. For a curved surface, we must use the mean square geodesic distance (MSGD) as a measure of the distance from the origin along the surface [4]. The MSGD for 800 walkers is shown in Fig. 8 for four different radii of curvature.

In flat space and even small curvatures, the MSGD has a linear behaviour, as expected from standard diffusion theory. However for large positive curvatures, diffusion is no longer linear, with the MSGD becoming smaller than the expected value in flat space. This can be interpreted as diffusion slowing down, an effect predicted in analytical results [3, 4] and confirmed by experiment [10]. The results in Fig. 8 show that our computational approach is valid and, unlike previous analytical results, is not restricted to small curvatures or short times.

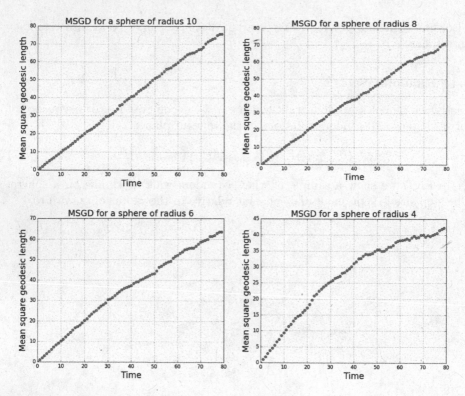

Fig. 8. The mean square geodesic distances for different radii of curvature based on 800 random walks.

4 Discussion

The results of these models show that curvature produces fundamental and quantifiable changes in the behaviour of a wide range of systems. For simple closed-loop shapes, our approach clearly demonstrates how the perimeter, area and internal angles of a closed shape are affected by curvature.

In the case of fractals, the connectivity (topology) of the shapes is significantly altered at scales similar to the radius of curvature of the geometry. However at small scales, the fractals remain relatively unchanged compared to their flat-space counterparts. In these examples of discrete, deterministic systems, one of the fundamental properties that changes when curvature is introduced is that the connectivity of the shape at large scales can no longer be predicted from the behaviour of the shape at small scales.

In the case of random walks, we can begin to see what effects curvature has in the stochastic, continuous limit. Here, the diffusion rate of a system is altered in a non-trivial way when curvature is introduced. Considering how universally utilized the diffusion process is in natural and engineered systems, we can begin to formulate questions about diffusion on curved surfaces. In biology, how has evolution harnessed curvature in processes such as signaling, patterning and development? How could we augment the behaviour of engineered systems using curvature? In the next section, we present possible ways in which curvature effects may present in these two contexts.

5 Biological and Engineering Applications

In future work on modelling the effects of geometry using L-systems, we plan to study more general cases of curvature: non-constant curvatures, negative curvatures as well as dynamically growing geometries. All of these generalizations will help to better elucidate the basic processes at work in chemical, biological and physical systems, which often exhibit complex geometries that may grow or change over time.

One such example is plant tissue growth. At the tip of every growing plant is a meristem, which is a collection of stem cells that differentiate into all the organs of a plant such as leaves and flowers. The geometry of the meristem has regions of dynamically changing positive and negative curvature, and it is known that signaling hormones are transported throughout the meristem to regulate development. Based on the preliminary results here, it is reasonable to hypothesize that the effects of the meristem's geometry may be two-fold.

First is the topology of the cells in the sense of how they are arranged and connected on the meristem. As seen in the Sierpinski carpet model, the smallest scale 'cells' remain relatively unaffected by the curvature of the surface, but the curvature does influence how neighbourhoods of cells develop; for instance, how many neighbours a cell can have. Hence, processes like genetic regulation and cell division could be following flat-space development rules, but more global behaviours like how many cells are in a given piece of tissue or the flux of material into or out of a region of tissue could be affected by curvature. Indeed, the changes in topology seen in crystal growth experiments [8] lend support that a biological equivalent may also exist.

Secondly, as seen in the random walk model, diffusion is directly affected by curvature. In the continuum limit, this effect could be studied by including geometric terms in patterning models such as Turing's reaction-diffusion equations and Wolpert's French Flag model [6]. We expect that including curvature in these equations will reveal an expanded set of dynamics for the transport of chemical substances at scales representing the continuum limit of the system, such as signaling hormones in a multicellular tissue. In future work, we also plan to study how curvature could be an active component in the feedback processes governing growth, rather than merely an end result.

In terms of engineering applications, one can imagine that dynamical geometries may be used as 'switches' between different states of a system. For instance, if a circuit is embedded into a material that can change from positive to negative curvature, then we could regulate which parts of the circuit are connected or disconnected by changing the curvature of the surface, much like the Koch curve becomes connected when described on a spherical surface.

Understanding these types of curvature effects is an important part of many systems in nature and engineering because of the impact on fundamental properties and processes. Building a tool to visualize and quantify the behaviour of systems in curved geometries could aid in discovering new aspects of the systems around us, and help design engineering solutions in emerging fields like 4D printing and soft robotics.

Acknowledgments. J.P. kindly acknowledges the financial support of INRIA for this research.

References

1. Abelson, H., DiSessa, A.: Turtle Geometry: The Computer as a Medium for Exploring Mathematics. MIT press, London (1986)
2. Boudon, F., Pradal, C., Cokelaer, T., Prusinkiewicz, P., Godin, C.: L-py: an l-system simulation framework for modeling plant architecture development based on a dynamic language. Front. Plant Sci., 3 (2012)
3. Castro-Villarreal, P.: Brownian motion meets riemann curvature. J. Stat. Mech: Theor. Exp. **2010**(08), P08006 (2010)
4. Faraudo, J.: Diffusion equation on curved surfaces. i. theory and application to biological membranes. J. Chem. Phys. **116**(13), 5831–5841 (2002)
5. Fernandez, R., Das, P., Mirabet, V., Moscardi, E., Traas, J., Verdeil, J.L., Malandain, G., Godin, C.: Imaging plant growth in 4d: robust tissue reconstruction and lineaging at cell resolution. Nat. Methods **7**(7), 547–553 (2010)
6. Green, J.B., Sharpe, J.: Positional information and reaction-diffusion: two big ideas in developmental biology combine. Development **142**(7), 1203–1211 (2015)
7. Gruel, J., Landrein, B., Tarr, P., Schuster, C., Refahi, Y., Sampathkumar, A., Hamant, O., Meyerowitz, E.M., Jönsson, H.: An epidermis-driven mechanism positions and scales stem cell niches in plants. Sci. Adv. **2**(1), e1500989 (2016)
8. Meng, G., Paulose, J., Nelson, D.R., Manoharan, V.N.: Elastic instability of a crystal growing on a curved surface. Science **343**(6171), 634–637 (2014)
9. Prusinkiewicz, P.: Graphical applications of l-systems. Proc. Graph. Interface **86**, 247–253 (1986)
10. Zhong, Y., Zhao, L., Tyrlik, P.M., Wang, G.: Investigating diffusing on highly curved water-oil interface using three-dimensional single particle tracking. J. Phys. Chem. C **121**(14), 8023–8032 (2017)

Evolutionary Computation

Exploring Target Change Related Fitness Reduction in the Moving Point Dynamic Environment

David Fagan[✉] and Michael O'Neill

Natural Computing Research and Applications Group, School of Business,
University College Dublin, Dublin, Ireland
{david.fagan,m.oneill}@ucd.ie

Abstract. Dynamic Environments present many challenges for Evolutionary Computing. Frequency of change and amplitude of change, all have dramatic effects of how a system will behave. This in conjunction with poor search operators can lead to populations that can't react to change quickly, as they have become converged in the search space. This study presents an overview of some methods to minimize the impact of change, and allow algorithms to better react to change in Dynamic Environments. Through the use of a bare bones tunable dynamic environment, it is shown how the approaches implemented can provide algorithms with faster responses to change. These approaches are also shown to do this without having to redesign the algorithms search operators, and maintaining the same computational effort.

Keywords: Evolutionary computing · Dynamic environments

1 Introduction

Dynamic Environments, while well explored in the literature [1,3,5,6,8,12,13, 15,16] still present and open issue to the evolutionary computing community [10]. What makes these environments so special and challenging is change. There are so many degrees of freedom in an environment subject to possible change that the combination of needed search operators, grammars, and representation can seem daunting.

In a dynamic environment the size, shape, location, frequency of change, amplitude of change, cyclic change patterns, and many more aspects of the environment can be subject to variation. Knowledge of any of these variation aspects presents an opportunity to exploit them. A system can be tuned to compensate for high frequency changes or large amplitude changes for example. Similarly a system designed to be robust to change can offer certain advantages in situations such as high frequency of change or large amplitude changes.

The following study looks to utilises this approach to implement a replacement operator that provides robustness to the system. For this a tunable dynamic

© Springer International Publishing AG 2017
C. Martín-Vide et al. (Eds.): TPNC 2017, LNCS 10687, pp. 63–74, 2017.
https://doi.org/10.1007/978-3-319-71069-3_5

environment will be needed. While others have been previously defined [1,8,14], the recently developed moving point problem environment is selected for its ability to be tuned to specific needs. Taking inspiration from the literature this study presents three approaches to replacement that utilise memory, population reload, and search space sentinels, to provide Grammatical Evolution (GE) [9] with robustness in the environment, by minimizing change related fitness drop-off.

The paper proceeds as follows. Section 2 looks at previous approaches to change in Dynamic Environments. Section 3 introduces the Moving Point Problem, used as the test bed environment in this study. Section 4 outlines the approaches used reload the population during evolution. Section 5 outlines the experimental setup, before the results of the study are presented in Sect. 6. The paper is then concluded with conclusions in Sect. 7, and finally future works are stated in Sect. 8.

2   Target Change in Dynamic Environments

Change is the great unknown in Dynamic Environments. For the majority of cases, when a change will happen, or how large a change to expect is not know a priori. Rohlfshagen et al. [11], set about finding ways to quantify rate of change, and magnitude of change, and to use these to determine how best to deal with change. It was deemed that with a large magnitude of change, the algorithm benefits from a restart as it provides the population with a reset away from the current optimal, and allows for faster adaptation to the new target. Small magnitudes of change benefited more from continuing from the current state of the algorithm, using knowledge already discovered during evolution to help guide the search.

Designing algorithms for dynamic environments has been covered in detail. Branke [1] and Morrison [8] delve into methods to detect change as well as methods to preserve and promote diversity in a population. Morrison explores in detail the idea of detecting change and reacting to change. One of the pivotal ideas put forward is using carefully placed sentinels within the search space to provide algorithms with markers to indicate the state of the environment and detect change, much like buoys on the ocean do. Morrison goes on to provide heuristics for sentinel placement and the difficulties with placing sentinels in higher dimensional spaces.

Branke [1] on the other hand provides an in depth survey of the benefits of reloading the population when change is detected. The benefits being that the algorithm can adapt to change faster. Branke goes further and examines the idea of memory as a tool to aid in performance. Keeping the best previous individuals or a library of previous good populations are examined. These individuals can be used indirectly as sentinels to provide insights into how the environment is changing. Dempsey et al. provide an updated overview in [2]. Branke also covers rate of change and the effects it can have on performance. The idea behind all this work is to be robust to change e.g., to be able to adapt to change quickly whilst not suffering detrimental performance drop-off due to the change experienced.

3   Moving Point Dynamic Environment

Dynamic Environments come in many differing formats, with unique aspects such as frequency of change, size of search space etc. Dempsey et al. [2] makes reference to a spectrum of dynamism, in a very in-depth review of the dynamic problem domain, and examines similar ideas by Branke [1] and DeJong [4]. The spectrum described is one from a problem where the change is predictable and small, to a problem which is completely random.

The Moving Point Problem (MP) was developed as an easy to understand, tunable, dynamic environment. The problem was designed to facilitate easy analysis of the behaviour of search algorithms under varying environmental dynamics, and provide a visualisation of the search algorithms behaviour.

The objective in MP is to track a moving point in three-dimensional space. In its simplest form fitness is the euclidean distance between an individual in the search population and the moving target point. The dynamics of the moving point can be controlled for the frequency or amplitude of change. This allows for the problem to be set up to encompass any point on the dynamism scale [2].

Frequency is determined by how often the target point moves (e.g., each generation vs every 20th generation). Amplitude is the distance the target moves from its current position. Amplitude can be specified in both real numbers, and as a percentage of maximum distance of the search space.

In the default implementation changes occur at random frequency with random amplitude. The range of possible change of frequency and amplitude is a user controlled parameter setting. The frequency and amplitude are controlled by setting a static value for either, whilst varying the other component. It is possible to design a number of variations of the moving point problem, for example, adding multiple target points, moving to higher dimensional space, and allowing the search algorithm limited visibility of the search space to name a few. Each individual of the population is an (x,y,z) co-ordinate that maps to a point in the search space. This is encoded in GE using the grammar below:

```
<xyz>::=<d><d><d><d>  <d><d><d><d>  <d><d><d><d>

<d> ::= 0 | 1 | 2 | 3 | 4 | 5 | 6 | 7 | 8 | 9
```

For the purposes of this study, MP will be constrained to an implementation of the problem where a single target in three-dimensional space is the desired goal. The frequency of change in the environment will be locked, but the amplitude of change will vary. The search population has full visibility of the environment. Example visualisations of the population are provided in Figs. 1 and 2.

4   Approaches for Adapting to a Change in Target in Dynamic Environments

There are many approaches to detecting change and ways to better adapt the population to this change as mentioned in Sect. 2. This study looks specifically

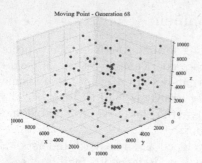

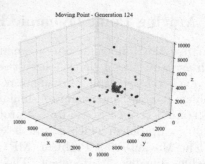

Fig. 1. A visualisation of the moving point problem. The target is displayed in red and the individuals in blue. (Color figure online)

Fig. 2. A visualisation of the moving point problem converged on the target solution. The target within a collection of individuals that are highlighted as green as they are deemed to have direct contact to the target (e.g.; their euclidean distance is within 50. (Color figure online)

at using replacement to enhance a populations reaction to change. This study does not assume the population cannot adapt but looks to minimise the effect of a change on the population to improve response to the change. It is important to adapt quickly to change, as in an unknown environment there is no way to know the frequency of change. This means that adapting quickly to change will provide a better general performance in the environment. The three approaches used in this study are outlined in the sections that follow. The approaches borrow aspect from the approaches outlined in Sect. 2.

4.1 Reload

In reload the initial population is stored in memory along with the fitness of the best initial individual. At each generation the previous generations best individual is compared to the current generations target. If this comparison shows the fitness has gotten worse than the best initial fitness, the population is replaced with the initial population and the best initial population value updated to the reloaded pops best fitness. By doing this we maintain the same number of fitness evaluations in the run, and as variation operations are not performed in reload generations there is a small saving computationally in this method. Reload is dependent on the initial population having good dispersion characteristics in the search space. Having this will provide for faster adaptation as the new target should be closer to an initial population member after reload.

4.2 Percentage Reload

Percentage reload is essentially the same as reload with one small caveat. When a reload is detected a user specified percentage of the initial population is randomly sampled and joined to the top $100 - x\%$, where x is the user specified percentage of the initial population, of the previous generations population. This approach is taken to preserve some of the populations knowledge in case the target oscillates back near its previous state quickly. Again there is no variation operations carried out in this generation.

4.3 Persistent Grid

Persistent Grid takes inspiration from the idea of sentinels mentioned in Sect. 2. In persistent grid a number of individuals (64 or 125 in our case) are evenly distributed across the search space as seen in Fig. 3. The remainder of the population are then randomly placed using initialisation around the search space.

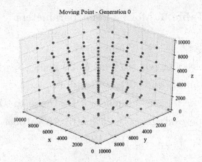

Fig. 3. A visualisation of the persistent grid with 125 individuals, before the remainder of the population is placed in the search space.

Unlike reload, where the fitness is monitored and certain events triggering a reload in the population, in persistent grid the grid individuals are always reloaded during replacement. Assuming there is a population of 500, and a grid of 125 individuals, every generation the top 375 are combined with the grid individuals to form the new population during replacement. The only downside to this grid approach is that trying to locate individuals in this grid setup in higher dimensional spaces would require massive amounts of calculations and require bespoke distance measurements for each search space.

5 Experimental Setup

The aim of the study is to assess the merits of different approaches to allow the algorithm to adapt quickly to a change in environment. Grammatical Evolution [9], specifically a developmental branch of PonyGE [7], was used for all experiments. The common parameters used in PonyGE are listed in Table 1.

Several variations of setups in the MP problem are required for this study. There are the four approaches to change minimisation as discussed in Sect. 4.

Table 1. Experimental setup

Parameter	Value used
Population	500
Generations	500
Number of runs	50
Mutation	Int-Flip Per Codon
Mutation Rate	1/length of genome
Crossover Rate	0.7
Duplicates	Prevented in initialised population
Tournament size	1%
Elitism	1%

Table 2. Moving point parameters

Parameter	Value used
Change frequency	10 gens & 20 gens
Change amplitude	Fixed Random
Fitness	Euclidean Distance to Target
Reload percentages	0% 25% 50% 75% 100%
Grid size	64 & 125

The various settings for these approaches are outlined in Table 2. Certain aspects of the MP problem have been fixed for this study. The amplitude of change, frequency of change, and fitness measure used are also listed in Table 2.

There are three main elements to the study. Firstly what does the reload operator add to the performance of GE in the MP domain. Secondly does the whole population need to be reloaded or will a subset do, thus allowing for retention of some previous knowledge uncovered during evolution. Finally does a sentinel approach as seen in persistent grid provide a performance gain to justify its use owing to the increased overheads of setup it requires.

6   Results

The results are present in the three sections that follow. Firstly a straight comparison between reload and no reload is presented, before moving on to a more in depth look at how much of the population needs reloading. Following this a comparison between reload and grid approaches is performed.

6.1   Reload Versus No Reload

Figure 4 displays the average best fitness over 50 runs of the moving point problem. In the graph the black line represents a standard run of GE on MP. The red line represents GE with reload enabled. What is very apparent is that reload has a significant impact on the fitness drop-off when a change in target is experienced in MP. Standard GE experiences drop-offs in fitness up to above 5000, whilst with reload enabled this drop-off is limited to below 1000 (indicated by the blue line).

The limiting of the drop-off also provides for faster location of the new target as can be seen in Fig. 4. The red line can be seen in most cases to reach the target faster than the black line indicating faster adapting to the environment.

It was evident from the initial runs, with a change frequency of 20 generations, that both approaches were able to adapt to the new target in the time period between changes. To further see the benefits of reload a shorter frequency of change was examined.

Figure 5 shows standard GE against reload averaged over 50 runs with a change frequency of 10. As before the same reduction in drop-off is experienced. However unlike in the previous experiment, where the change frequency was 20, when the frequency is shortened to 10 it is evident that reload enables GE to find the new target faster than standard GE. There is 48 changes in the 500 generations of a run in the experiment, and over the 50 runs conducted, on average reload allows for better final fitness over 80% of the time.

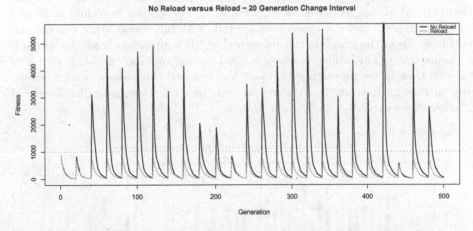

Fig. 4. No Reload versus Reload of initial population over 500 generations. The frequency of change is fixed but the amplitude is random. (Color figure online)

6.2 Reload Versus Percentage Reload

Having established the benefits of reload in the previous section, the next question to be answered was, does a full reload have to take place, or can some of the current population be maintained? The thinking behind this was that there could be some useful information in the current population, or if the target

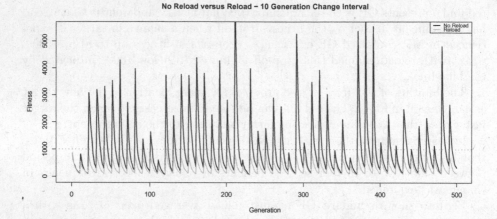

Fig. 5. No Reload versus Reload of initial population over 500 generations. The frequency of change is fixed but the amplitude is random.

was to change positions for a generation or two and then return to its previous location, this would lead to more reloads than might be needed.

To answer this question a range of percentage of reload were examined, the results of which are displayed in Figs. 6 and 7. The graphs have had their line widths increased, and the approaches layered, with full reload being represented by black. From the graph it can be seen that all approaches limit the drop-off to below 1500. This still represents a good saving over no reload. It can also be seen that as the percentage of reload is decreased the drop-off under change also increases. However, the fitness rebounds in all cases to a similar level and in some cases exceeds reloads lower bound.

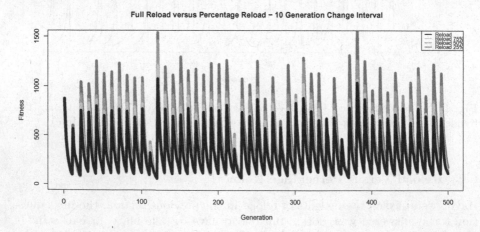

Fig. 6. Reload versus Percentage Reload over 500 generations. Four percentage levels of reload are compared with a change frequency of 10 generations.

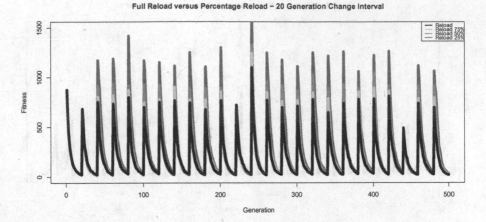

Fig. 7. Reload versus Percentage Reload over 500 generations. Four percentage levels of reload are compared with a change frequency of 20 generations.

Across both cases 75% reload provides comparable performance to full reload. 50% reload appears to be the tipping point for drop-off in performance. It is argued that if users wish to maintain some of the current population, any percentage from 50% to 100% reload would provide all the benefits of full reload, whilst maintaining some of the current population knowledge.

6.3 Reload Versus Persistent Grid

Finally the idea of a persistent grid of individuals was explored. This approach takes inspiration from sentinels and percentage reloads. Figures 8 and 9 display

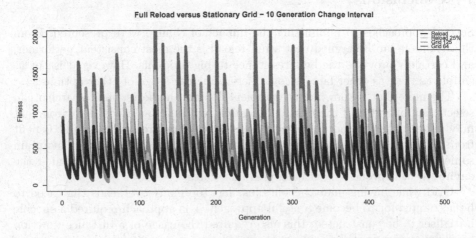

Fig. 8. Grid versus Reload over 500 generations. The frequency of change is fixed at 10 but the amplitude is random.

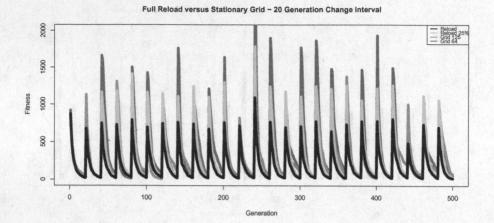

Fig. 9. Grid versus Reload over 500 generations. The frequency of change is fixed at 20 but the amplitude is random.

the results of this study on the two change frequencies. Grid sizes of 64 and 125 were used, and compared to full reload and 25% reload (as 25% reload is similar to 125 grid size in terms of replaced individuals). Again the line widths in the graph have been increased and layer as in the previous section.

From the graphs it is evident that the grid presents mixed results when compared to reload. The drop-off has increased to above 2000, which is a negative, but in some cases in Fig. 8 it can be seen that grid achieves better performance. This indicates that there may be some merit to using a grid approach in a high change frequency environment.

7   Conclusions

Several approaches to minimizing the impact of change were presented. From the results it can be argued that a full reload is the most consistent performer, and certainly provides the best resistance to big drop-offs. However it is not as simple as that, as other factors could determine the usage of other options.

The more that is known of the problem domain the better the researcher can select their operator. If there is no indication of how frequently the environment may change then reload is the way to go. Cyclic environments would benefit from the usage of the percentage reload or the grid approach, as they maintain some memory of the previous environment which may prove beneficial if the environment is prone to revisiting previous states.

Grid while having many benefits just has too many overheads that need to be accounted for to become a useful approach. The approach required a specific initialiser to be constructed, this also required the usage of a distance function to ensure coverage of the grid. As the problem domains dimensionality increase the overhead of this process will become very expensive.

8 Future Work

Having established the merits of reload for the moving point problem, the authors will look to further expand the study to include movement paths, multiple targets, and fight of flight behaviours. By increasing the complexity of the problem it is hoped to gain a firm understanding of the measurements and search operators before tackling higher dimensional real world dynamic problems.

Acknowledgements. This research is based upon works supported by the Science Foundation Ireland under Grant No. 13/IA/1850.

References

1. Branke, J.: Evolutionary Optimization in Dynamic Environments. Kluwer Academic Publishers, Norwell (2001)
2. Dempsey, I., O'Neill, M., Brabazon, A.: Foundations in Grammatical Evolution for Dynamic Environments. Studies in Computational Intelligence. Springer, Berlin (2009). https://doi.org/10.1007/978-3-642-00314-1
3. Farina, M., Deb, K., Amato, P.: Dynamic multiobjective optimization problems: test cases, approximations, and applications. IEEE Trans. Evol. Comput. 8(5), 425–442 (2004)
4. Jong, K.A.D.: Evolving in a changing world. In: ISMIS, pp. 512–519 (1999)
5. Karcz-Duleba, I.: Dynamics of infinite populations evolving in a landscape of uni and bimodal fitness functions. IEEE Trans. Evol. Comput. 5(4), 398–409 (2001)
6. Karcz-Duleba, I.: Dynamics of two-element populations in the space of population states. IEEE Trans. Evol. Comput. 10(2), 199–209 (2006)
7. McDermott, J., Hemberg, E., Byrne, J.: PonyGE. https://github.com/jmmcd/ponyge.git. Accessed 12 Jan 2015
8. Morrison, R.W.: Designing Evolutionary Algorithms for Dynamic Environments. Springer, Verlag (2004). https://doi.org/10.1007/978-3-662-06560-0
9. O'Neill, M., Ryan, C.: Grammatical Evolution: Evolutionary Automatic Programming in a Arbitrary Language. Genetic programming. Kluwer Academic Publishers, Norwell (2003). http://www.wkap.nl/prod/b/1-4020-7444-1
10. O'Neill, M., Vanneschi, L., Gustafson, S., Banzhaf, W.: Open issues in genetic programming. Genet. Program. Evolvable Mach., 11, pp. 339–363 (2010). http://dx.doi.org/10.1007/s10710-010-9113-2
11. Rohlfshagen, P., Lehre, P.K., Yao, X.: Dynamic evolutionary optimisation: an analysis of frequency and magnitude of change. In: GECCO, pp. 1713–1720 (2009)
12. Sternberg, M., Reynolds, R.G.: Using cultural algorithms to support re-engineering of rule-based expert systems in dynamic performance environments: a case study in fraud detection. IEEE Trans. Evol. Comput. 1(4), 225–243 (1997)
13. Ursem, R.K., Krink, T., Jensen, M.T., Michalewicz, Z.: Analysis and modeling of control tasks in dynamic systems. IEEE Trans. Evol. Comput. 6(4), 378–389 (2002)
14. Yang, S.: Non-stationary problem optimization using the primal-dual genetic algorithms. In: Proceedings of the IEEE Congress on Evolutionary Computation, pp. 2246–2253. IEEE Press (2003)

15. Yang, S., Yao, X.: Population-based incremental learning with associative memory for dynamic environments. IEEE Trans. Evol. Comput. **12**(5), 542–561 (2008)
16. Yen, G.G., Lu, H.: Dynamic multiobjective evolutionary algorithm: adaptive cell-based rank and density estimation. IEEE Trans. Evol. Comput. **7**(3), 253–274 (2003)

A Smart Discovery Service in Internet of Things Using Swarm Intelligence

Agostino Forestiero[✉] [ID]

CNR - ICAR, Institute for High Performance Computing and Networking,
National Research Council of Italy, Via Pietro Bucci, 7/11 C, 87036 Rende, CS, Italy
agostino.forestiero@icar.cnr.it

Abstract. The Internet of Things (IoT) has brought to a significant growing of data produced, and therefore, new models and approaches are needed to investigate these "big data" in terms of volume, velocity and variability. IoT services can be considered a dynamic content, including data sources and middleware infrastructures. An effective solution to manage dynamic contents are Content Delivery Networks (CDNs), but, in dynamic and large systems as IoT environment, their limits emerge, therefore, decentralized approaches and algorithms have to be designed and employed. This paper proposes *SmartFinder*, a swarm based algorithm to build a CDN based discovery service in pervasive and dynamic environment as IoT. The CDN servers are represented with metadata obtained through a locality preserving hash function. A swarm of mobile agents move the metadata and, by applying of tailored probability functions, achieve a logical organization of the servers. The outcome is a sorted overlay network that allows content and services discovery operations faster. Experimental results show the effectiveness of the approach.

Keywords: Internet of Things · Content Delivery Networks
Ant-inspired agents · Overlay network

1 Introduction

With the rapid diffusion of the Internet of Things paradigm, the number of objects connected to Internet, and therefore the amount of generated data, is steadily growing. Managing huge quantities of data (big data) brings new issues and challenges, and then traditional approaches, used for performance evaluation and traffic engineering, have to be revised. New solutions are needed to manage the information efficiently, in terms of volume, velocity and variability, and it is necessary the design innovative schemes for contents and services delivery. The applications, in such pervasive environment, have to adapt their behavior based on the environmental context perceived by the smart objects in the Internet of Things. The network raised from the interconnections of IoT objects needs of connectivity and semantic data delivery across middleware services to connect "things" and applications. IoT services can be considered a

© Springer International Publishing AG 2017
C. Martín-Vide et al. (Eds.): TPNC 2017, LNCS 10687, pp. 75–86, 2017.
https://doi.org/10.1007/978-3-319-71069-3_6

dynamic content, including data sources and middleware infrastructures. Devices provide data input and the responses to requests are performed by machine-to-machine applications after middleware processing the requests. Dynamic contents, such as a web 2.0 blog site or IoT services, can be delivered using content distribution networks (CDNs) [15]. Content delivery in IoT environment require realtime transmissions, lower frame loss, tolerable end-to-end delay and jitter. CDN is based on edge servers to store contents and improve web browsing with lower latency ensuring data consistency among them. These networks improve the performance in terms of response time, accessibility and bandwidth. User requests or IoT service requests can be satisfied of the best surrogate server that store copies of the content. Obviously, a centralized mechanism to provide contents and IoT services when requested, is offered. Limited size networks can be acceptably tackled with a centralized approach owing to its poor scalability, but the CDN paradigm shows its limits in large and dynamic systems such as IoT environment. The large variety of the content, services and resources make the management and discovery operations more troublesome. To perform retrieval content or access to IoT services efficiently, centralized approaches that manage the content and/or the IoT services are often inadequate. Low scalability and bottlenecks of centralized mechanisms are intolerable in a dynamic environment such as the Internet of Things networks.

Thanks to their inherent scalability and robustness, peer-to-peer paradigm can be usefully exploited to design algorithm for managing resources in CDNs [10,17]. Main goal of these approaches is to quickly discover CDN servers that stores given contents. Often, content stored in CDN servers can be represented through metadata, that is a syntactical description of contents and/or an ontology description. Metadata are often represented as bit vectors having different meanings. For example, each bit can represent the presence or absence of a given *topic* [5,21]. This approach is particularly useful when the contents are documents, because it is possible to establish the presence of a topic in the document. Differently, the content can be mapped through a hash function into a metadata. If the hash function is locality preserving [3,20], neighbor/similar bit vectors will be assigned to contents with neighbor/similar characteristics. Similarity measure can be the cosine of the angle or the Euclidean distance between the bit vectors.

This paper proposes *SmartFinder*, a swarm based algorithm to build a smart discovery service in IoT environment. *SmartFinder*, thanks to a swarm of ant-inspired agents, is able to logically reorganize the CDN servers and, therefore, to improve the efficiency of discovery operations. Each ant agent executes simple operations autonomously on the network and, at global level, a reorganized overlay emerges. The servers are represented by metadata (bit vectors) obtained through a locality preserving hash function applied to their content. The agents gather, move and deposit the metadata based on tailored probability functions, and an ordered overlay emerges. In the following, Sect. 2 shows an overview of related works in this field, while in Sect. 3 the *SmartFinder* is detailed. Finally, in Sect. 4, some experimental results are reported.

2   Related Works

A wide range of researchers both from academia and industry have conducted several studies to design new approach in Internet of Things environment based on the CDN paradigm. In [15] the platform MobilityFirst, to handle efficiently a content distribution network for IoT services, was presented. This approach start from the assumption that the IoT services tend to be more context sensitive, especially on locations. In [19] a content provisioning cost and the amount of network traffic generated by nodes are derived in the cooperative content delivery model in IoT, was proposed. The effect of varying the cache division ratio and number of nodes to the content provisioning cost and network traffic was analyzed. The advances in mobile communications have enhanced the multimedia IoT scenarios with node mobility. Those scenarios have continuously topology changes due to failure or mobility of nodes, as well as changes in the wireless channel conditions [22]. Paper [24] describes four caching strategies of CDN to serve dynamic content. In order to reduce the operational cost of large amount of data traffic over CDN, Jiang et al. [12] proposes an extension of the CDN infrastructures to the edges of networks. Resources can be utilized through peer-to-peer communications with smart content placement and routing to mitigate the cross-traffic among ISPs.

Several studies has been also conducted to analyze possible hybrid approaches between CDN and P2P technologies. [17] survey CDN-P2P-hybrid architecture technology, including current industry efforts and academic efforts in this field and they make a comparisons between CDN and P2P. The comparison of performances of two main hybrid CDN-P2P architectures, that is CDN-P2P unconnected mesh in which independent P2P mesh networks are constructed under each CDN node, and CDN-P2P connected mesh in which CDN nodes and peers participate in construction of a single P2P mesh network, was achieved in [23]. A novel methodology for mapping the topologies of CDN networks using two real-world traces: a video-on-demand trace and a large-scale software update trace, has been proposed in [11]. [2] proposes a hybrid CDN/P2P solution, that guaranteeing an optimal quality of service, reduces the costs of infrastructure by exploiting local caching and P2P. A multi-layer hybrid approach was proposed in [13,26]. The system, namely LiveSky, tries to balance the shortcomings of P2P systems by leveraging on CDN redirections. The aim is to make peer to peer transfers network-friendly. The system has been commercially deployed by ChinaCache and the architecture showed promising results. To limit the radius of the delivery graph of a P2P video streaming, in [4], a solution that exploits CDN servers is proposed. A group-based CDN-P2P hybrid architecture (G-CP2P), which is a location/content-aware peer selection, was proposed in [14] to reduce service disruption latency.

Some agent systems which aims to solve very complex problems by imitating the behavior of some in species of ants have been inspired by [1]. The idea to reorganize the services so that the metadata descriptors of services that are often used together are placed in neighbor peers, was introduced in [7]. This helps a single query to find multiple basic services, which decreases the number of necessary queries and, consequently, lowers the search time and the network load. In [8,9], the performance of discovery operations are improved through the creation of regions of the network specialized in a particular class of resources. Whereas [25] proposes a decentralized scheme to tune the activity of a single agent. These systems are positioned along a research avenue whose objective is to devise possible applications of ant algorithms [1,6]. A tree-based ant colony algorithm to support large-scale Internet-based live video streaming broadcast in CDNs, was proposed in [16]. In this paper, differently from the traditional solution to find paths, an algorithm to optimize the multicast tree directly and integrate them into a multicast tree, was exploited.

3   *SmartFinder* Algorithm

SmartFinder aims to build an overlay network that allows discovery operations faster. The CDN servers are represented through metadata – bit vectors with N_b bits – obtained through a locality preserving hash function applied to the content to guarantee that similar contents are indexed with similar metadata. Ant-inspired agents are exploited to reorganize such metadata and build a distributed information system. The agents move among servers performing simple operations on the basis of their state: (i) when it is unloaded, it decides whether to gather one or more metadata from the current server; (ii) if it is loaded, it decides whether to release one or more metadata in the local server. Two tailored probability functions, P_g and P_d, drive the agents' decision. The probability functions are based on a similarity function introduced in [18]. Formula (1) reports the function that measures the similarity of a metadata d with all the metadata located in the region R.

$$S(\bar{d}, R) = \frac{1}{N_d} \sum_{d \in R} 1 - \frac{H(d, \bar{d})}{\alpha} \tag{1}$$

The region R for each server s, is represented by s and of all server reachable from s with a given number of hops. Here the number of hops is set to 1. N_d is the overall number of metadata located in R, while $H(d, \bar{d})$ is the Hamming distance between d and $\bar{d}$. The similarity parameter α is set to 2. The value of S ranges from -1 to 1, but negative values are septated to 0 [18].

Intuitively, the probability function to gather metadata from a server has to be inversely proportional to the value of S, while, the probability function of deposit metadata has to be directly proportional to S. The probability functions to gather a metadata P_g and the probability function to deposit a metadata P_d, are reported in formulas (2) and (3), respectively.

$$P_g = \left(\frac{k_g}{k_g + S(\bar{d}, R)} \right)^2 ; \tag{2}$$

$$P_d = \left(\frac{S(\bar{d}, R)}{k_d + S(\bar{d}, R)} \right)^2 \tag{3}$$

The degree of similarity among metadata are tuned through the parameter k_g and k_d with values comprised between 0 and 1 [1].

The steps of the algorithm performed by the mobile agents are reported in Algorithm 1. Cyclically, the agents perform a given number of hops among servers, and when they get to a new server decide which probability function compute based on their condition (loaded or unloaded). In particular, if the agent does not carries metadata, it computes P_g, otherwise, if the agent carries metadata, P_d is computed.

---

while a new server is reached **do**
　if *it is unloaded* **then**
　　foreach *metadata* d *stored in the server* **do**
　　　compute P_g probability;
　　　if P_g *is satisfied* **then**
　　　　| gather d from the server
　　　end
　　end
　else
　　foreach *carried metadata* d **do**
　　　compute P_d probability;
　　　if P_d *is satisfied* **then**
　　　　| deposit d in the server
　　　end
　　end
　end
　make n hops towards a random neighbor
end

Algorithm 1. Steps performed by the mobile agents

The processing load, Pl, that is the average number of agents per second that are processed by a server, is reported in formula (4). It does not depend neither on the network size nor on the churn rate. The value of the processing load only depends on the number of agents and the frequency of their movements.

$$Pl = \frac{N_a}{N_s \cdot T_m} = \frac{F_g}{T_m} \qquad (4)$$

where N_a and N_s represent the number of agents and the number of servers, respectively; T_m represents the average time between two successive movement of an agent and F_g represents the frequency with which agents are generated by a server.

To locate resources with given characteristics, generally, in distributed systems, each search operation collects a number of resources and the users can choose the resources that best fit their needs. In this system, a query message is issued by a server, on behalf of a user, to collect a set of metadata as similar as possible to the "target metadata". The target metadata is the metadata representing the content requested by the user. Thanks to the spatial sorting achieved by the agents, the discovery procedure can be simply performed by forwarding the request, at each step, towards the "best neighbor server". The selected neighbor server is the server that maximizes the similarity value between the target metadata and the *mean metadata* calculates by each server. The *mean metadata* is a bit vector composed of real numbers where the value of element is calculated by averaging the values of the each bits, in the same position, of all the metadata stored by the server. For example, the *mean metadata* of a server having the three metadata: [0, 1, 1], [1, 0, 1] and [0, 1, 1] will be equal to [0.33, 0.67, 1].

The cosine measure, as reported in formula (5), is exploited to compute the similarity between the target metadata and the mean metadata. Here $\overrightarrow{u} \cdot \overrightarrow{v}$ indicates the *dot-product* between the vectors $\overrightarrow{u}$ and $\overrightarrow{v}$.

$$cos(\overrightarrow{u}, \overrightarrow{v}) = \frac{\overrightarrow{u} \cdot \overrightarrow{v}}{|\overrightarrow{u}|_2 \times |\overrightarrow{v}|_2} \tag{5}$$

The search operation terminates whenever the best neighbor server is not better than the server where the query has arrived so far. A reply message with all metadata collected is forwarded to the server that has issued the request.

4   Experimental Results

An event-based simulator was implemented to evaluate the performance of the algorithm. In our experiments, each server manages about 15 metadata representing the contents and it is linked to 8 server on average. A graphical description of the logical reorganization is reported in Fig. 1. To each metadata is associated a gray-scale color and the server is represented with the color of the metadata managed with the maximum number of element. A portion of the network is photographed: (a) at $Time = 0$ time units, when the process is starting and the metadata are randomly distributed and (b) at $Time = 50,000$ time units, when the process is in steady situation. Notice that similar metadata are located in the same region and among near regions the color change gradually, which proves the spatial sorting on the cyber layer.

The processing load, that is the number of agents that go through a server per unit time, was calculated as in formula (4) and shown in Fig. 2. In the simulated scenario, T_m is equals to 60 s and F_g is equals to 0.5, so that each server processes about one agent every 120 s, which can be considered acceptable. Notice that the processing load does not depend on other system parameters such as the average number of metadata handled by a server or the number of server, that confirms the scalability properties of the algorithm. The value of processing load changes according to the maximum number of hops performed within a single agent movement.

It was noted experimentally that the reorganization of metadata is accelerated if agent movements are longer, because they can explore the network more quickly. In order to select the right number of hops is necessary individuate a compromise between the processing load tolerable and the rapidity and efficiency of the reorganization process.

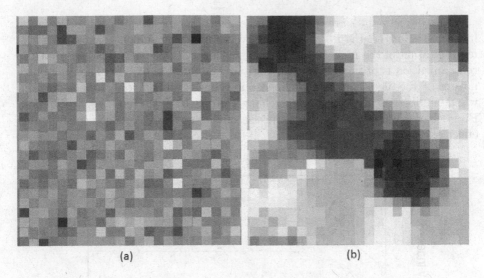

(a)   (b)

Fig. 1. Snapshots of a portion of the network when the process is starting (a), and when the process is in steady situation (b).

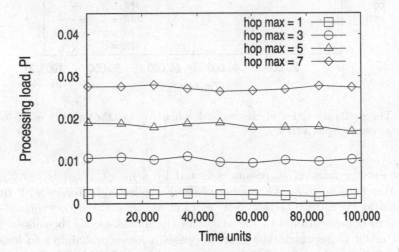

Fig. 2. The processing load generated by the algorithm when the number of hops performed within a single agent movement ranges from 1 to 7.

The effectiveness of the algorithm was evaluated by defining of a similarity index, SI, as reported in formula 6. The similarity index over the whole network is obtained averaging the similarity indexes of all servers. The similarity index of a single server s, is obtained by averaging the Hamming distance between every couple of metadata contained in the region R related to the server s.

$$SI = N_b - Average_{d,\bar{d} \epsilon R}(H(d,\bar{d})) \qquad (6)$$

If similar metadata are collected in the same region, the value of the similarity index SI increases. Figure 3 shows the overall similarity index when N_b, i.e. the number of bit of the metadata describing each service, is varied. Notice that the reorganization is obtained independently of the number of bits. The scalability nature of the algorithm is confirmed observing the behavior of the algorithm when number of involved servers changes from 1000 to 7000, as reported in Fig. 4. It is possible to note that the size of the network, N_s, has no detectable effect on the performance.

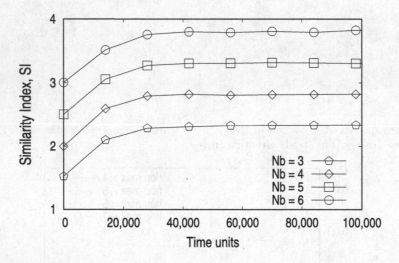

Fig. 3. The similarity index of the network when N_b, i.e. the number of bit of the metadata, ranges from 3 to 6.

The average number of results collected by a query, N_{res}, is reported in Fig. 5. We can note that, the number of results collected increases with time – the discovery operations become more efficient as metadata are organized – and it is inversely proportional to the length of the metadata N_d, because a large number of bit to represent the content causes a lower probability to locate a target metadata. The value of N_d has to be tuned for each application field taking into account that a wide classification can facilitate the discovery operations.

The resolution of "range queries" is a fundamental requirement in distributed and large scale systems as IoT environments. A simple query is issued to find a given metadata, while, a range query is a query in which the target metadata contains one or more "star" bits. These bits can assume either the 0 or the 1 value.

If the target metadata contains b^* star bits, the range query can return 2^{b^*} possible metadata. The discovery algorithm was modified to handle the range queries. The neighbor selected to forward the query, is chosen by calculating the cosine similarity between the target metadata and the *mean metadata* of the neighbor server and omitting the star bits. As the simple queries, a range query

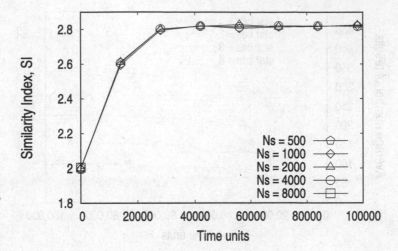

Fig. 4. The similarity index, vs. time, for different values of N_s, i.e. the number of servers.

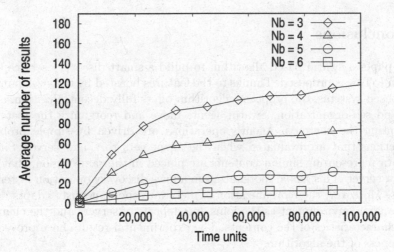

Fig. 5. Average number of results for different values of the number of bits of the metadata, N_b.

terminates its discovery operation when none neighbor has a similarity value better than the current server. Figure 6 shows the effectiveness of the algorithm to execute the range queries. The value of N_d was fixed to 4 and the number of the star bit was varied.

A range query does not discover all possible target metadata that would be discovered with the corresponding number of simple queries, but, in one shot, discover much many results than a simple query.

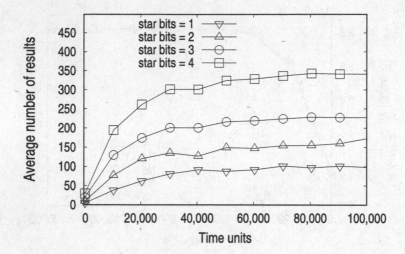

Fig. 6. Average number of results of range queries with $N_d = 4$ and different numbers star bits

5   Conclusions

In this paper a swarm based algorithm to build a smart discovery service CDN based in IoT, was proposed. Thanks to the features boasted by the swarm intelligence based systems, the proposed algorithm offers fully decentralization, adaptivity and self-organization. Swarm agents move and reorganize the metadata representing the contents. Agent's operations are driven by simple probability functions that are evaluated when the agent gets to a new server. Similar metadata representing similar contents are placed in the same region, that is in neighbor server. This global reorganization allows discovery operation faster and efficient. Moreover, the reorganization of metadata spontaneously adapts to the ever changing environment as the joins and departs of servers and the changing of the characteristics of the contents. The experimental results have proved the effectiveness of the algorithm.

References

1. Bonabeau, E., Dorigo, M., Theraulaz, G.: Swarm Intelligence: From Natural to Artificial Systems, vol. 4. Oxford University Press, New York (1999)
2. Bronzino, F., Gaeta, R., Grangetto, M., Pau, G.: An adaptive hybrid CDN/P2P solution for content delivery networks. In: Visual Communications and Image Processing (VCIP), pp. 1–6. IEEE, November 2012
3. Cai, M., Frank, M., Chen, J., Szekely, P.: MAAN: a multi-attribute addressable network for grid information services. J. Grid Comput. **2**(1), 3–14 (2004)
4. Cho, S., Cho, J., Shin, S.J.: Playback latency reduction for internet live video services in CDN-P2P hybrid architecture. In: 2010 IEEE International Conference on Communications (ICC), pp. 1–5, May 2010

5. Crespo, A., Garcia-Molina, H.: Routing indices for peer-to-peer systems. In: Proceedings of the 22nd International Conference on Distributed Computing Systems (ICDCS 2002), pp. 23–33 (2002)

6. Dorigo, M., Bonabeau, E., Theraulaz, G.: Ant algorithms and stigmergy. Future Gener. Comput. Syst. **16**(8), 851–871 (2000)

7. Forestiero, A., Mastroianni, C., Papuzzo, G., Spezzano, G.: A proximity-based self-organizing framework for service composition and discovery. In: 2010 10th IEEE/ACM International Conference on Cluster, Cloud and Grid Computing (CCGrid), pp. 428–437. IEEE (2010)

8. Forestiero, A., Mastroianni, C., Spezzano, G.: Building a peer-to-peer information system in grids via self-organizing agents. J. Grid Comput. **6**(2), 125–140 (2008)

9. Forestiero, A., Mastroianni, C., Spezzano, G.: Reorganization and discovery of grid information with epidemic tuning. Future Gener. Comput. Syst. **24**(8), 788–797 (2008)

10. Fortino, G., Mastroianni, C.: Next generation content networks. J. Netw. Comput. Appl. **32**(5), 941–942 (2009)

11. Huang, C., Wang, A., Li, J., Ross, K.W.: Understanding hybrid CDN-P2P: why limelight needs its own red swoosh. In: Proceedings of the 18th International Workshop on Network and Operating Systems Support for Digital Audio and Video, pp. 75–80. ACM (2008)

12. Jiang, W., Ioannidis, S., Massoulie, L., Picconi, F.: Orchestrating massively distributed CDNs. In: Proceedings of the 8th International Conference on Emerging Networking Experiments and Technologies (CoNEXT 2012), pp. 133–144. ACM, New York (2012)

13. Kang, S., Yin, H.: A hybrid CDN-P2P system for video-on-demand. In: Second International Conference on Future Networks (ICFN 2010), pp. 309–313, January 2010

14. Kim, T.N., Jeon, S., Kim, Y.: A CDN-P2P hybrid architecture with content/location awareness for live streaming service networks. In: 2011 IEEE 15th International Symposium on Consumer Electronics (ISCE), pp. 438–441, June 2011

15. Li, J., Shvartzshnaider, Y., Francisco, J.A., Martin, R.P., Nagaraja, K., Raychaudhuri, D.: Delivering internet-of-things services in mobilityfirst future internet architecture. In: 2012 3rd International Conference on the Internet of Things (IOT), pp. 31–38. IEEE (2012)

16. Liu, X., Dobrian, F., Milner, H., Jiang, J., Sekar, V., Stoica, I., Zhang, H.: A case for a coordinated internet video control plane. In: Proceedings of the ACM SIGCOMM 2012 Conference on Applications, Technologies, Architectures, and Protocols for Computer Communication (SIGCOMM 2012), pp. 359–370. ACM, New York (2012)

17. Lu, Z., Wang, Y., Yang, Y.R.: An analysis and comparison of CDN-P2P-hybrid content delivery system and model. J. Commun. **7**(3), 232–245 (2012)

18. Lumer, E.D., Faieta, B.: Diversity and adaptation in populations of clustering ants. In: Proceedings of the Third International Conference on Simulation of Adaptive Behavior: From Animals to Animats 3: From Animals to Animats 3 (SAB 1994), pp. 501–508. MIT Press (1994)

19. Nam, Y., Park, J.H., Chung, J.M.: Performance analysis of cooperative content delivery in wireless IoT networks. In: The 18th IEEE International Symposium on Consumer Electronics (ISCE 2014), pp. 1–2. IEEE (2014)

20. Oppenheimer, D., Albrecht, J., Patterson, D., Vahdat, A.: Design and implementation tradeoffs for wide-area resource discovery. In: Proceedings of the 14th IEEE International Symposium on High Performance Distributed Computing (HPDC 2005). Research Triangle Park, NC, USA, July 2005

21. Platzer, C., Dustdar, S.: A vector space search engine for web services. In: Proceedings of the Third European Conference on Web Services (ECOWS 2005), p. 62. IEEE Computer Society, Washington, DC (2005)

22. Rosário, D., Zhao, Z., Santos, A., Braun, T., Cerqueira, E.: A beaconless opportunistic routing based on a cross-layer approach for efficient video dissemination in mobile multimedia iot applications. Comput. Commun. **45**, 21–31 (2014)

23. Seyyedi, S., Akbari, B.: Hybrid CDN-P2P architectures for live video streaming: comparative study of connected and unconnected meshes. In: 2011 International Symposium on Computer Networks and Distributed Systems (CNDS), pp. 175–180, February 2011

24. Sivasubramanian, S., Pierre, G., Van Steen, M., Alonso, G.: Analysis of caching and replication strategies for web applications. IEEE Internet Comput. **11**(1), 60–66 (2007)

25. Van Dyke Parunak, H., Brueckner, S.A., Matthews, R., Sauter, J.: Pheromone learning for self-organizing agents. IEEE Trans. Syst. Man Cybern. Part A Syst. Hum. **35**(3), 316–326 (2005)

26. Yin, H., Liu, X., Min, G., Lin, C.: Content delivery networks: a bridge between emerging applications and future IP networks. IEEE Netw. **24**(4), 52–56 (2010)

GPU-Accelerated Evolutionary Induction
of Regression Trees

Krzysztof Jurczuk$^{(\boxtimes)}$, Marcin Czajkowski, and Marek Kretowski

Faculty of Computer Science, Bialystok University of Technology,
Wiejska 45a, 15-351 Bialystok, Poland
{k.jurczuk,m.czajkowski,m.kretowski}@pb.edu.pl

Abstract. In the paper, we investigate the speeding up of the evolutionary induction of decision trees, which is an emerging alternative to greedy top-down solutions. In particular, we design and implement graphics processing units (GPU)-based parallelization to generate
regression trees (decision trees employed to solve regression problems)
on large-scale data. The most time consuming part of the algorithm,
which is parallelized, is the evaluation of individuals in the population.
Other parts of the algorithms (like selection, genetic operators) are performed sequentially on a CPU. A data-parallel approach is applied to
split the dataset over the GPU cores. After each assigned chunk of
data is processed, the results calculated on all GPU cores are merged
and sent to the CPU. We use a Compute Unified Device Architecture
(CUDA) programming model, which supports general purpose computation on a GPU (GPGPU). Experimental validation of the proposed
approach is performed on artificial and real-life datasets. A computational performance comparison with the traditional CPU version shows
that GPU-accelerated evolutionary induction of regression trees is significantly (even up to 1000 times) faster and allows for processing of much
larger datasets.

Keywords: Evolutionary Algorithms · Decision trees
Parallel computing · Graphics processing unit (GPU) · Regression trees
Large-scale data

1 Introduction

Evolutionary Algorithms (EAs) [21] are naturally prone to parallelism. The artificial evolution process can be parallelized using various strategies [6] and different implementation platforms [13]. Recently, GPGPU has been widely used in
EAs parallelization due to its high computational power at a relatively low cost
[2]. It allows us to reduce the CPU load on the most time-consuming operations.
The paper covers the parallelization of the evolutionary induction of decision
trees (DT)s [18], which represents one of the major and frequently applied techniques for discriminant analysis prediction in data mining [12]. Traditionally,

© Springer International Publishing AG 2017
C. Martín-Vide et al. (Eds.): TPNC 2017, LNCS 10687, pp. 87–99, 2017.
https://doi.org/10.1007/978-3-319-71069-3_7

DTs are induced with greedy top-down strategy, however, in the recent past an evolutionary approach for the tree induction has attracted a great deal of interest. The evolutionary induced DTs [3] are much simpler than the ones generated by a greedy strategy [24] with at least comparable prediction performance. The main downside of the evolutionary approach is the relatively higher computational costs due to EA itself. Thus, evolutionary induction of DTs using large-scale data become very time-demanding.

In this paper, we focus on speeding up the evolutionary induction of regression trees that are considered as a variant of DTs, designed to approximate real-valued functions instead of being used for classification tasks [5]. The proposed GPU parallelization handles the most computing intensive jobs like fitness calculation, leaving the evolutionary flow control and communication to the CPU. It is applied to a framework called Global Decision Tree (GDT) that can be used for evolutionary induction of classification [19] and regression [9] trees. The manuscript can be seen as a continuation of previous study on GPU-based approach to evolutionary induced classification trees [16]. It extends the research to regression trees which demand a more advanced parallelization schema (e.g. for predictions calculation in the leaves, dipole mechanism) to evaluate and evolve individuals.

The paper is organized as follows. The next section provides a brief background. Section 3 describes our approach for GPU-accelerated evolutionary induction of regression trees. The experimental evaluation is performed in Sect. 4 on artificial and real-life datasets. In the last section, the paper is concluded and possible future works are outlined.

2 Background

In this section, we present some background information on evolutionary induced regression trees, GPGPU computing model and recent related works.

2.1 Evolutionary Induced Regression Trees

There are different variants of DTs in the literature [10]. They can be grouped according to the type of problem they are applied to and the way they are induced. In classification trees, a class label is assigned to each leaf. Regression trees may be considered as a variant of decision trees designed to approximate real-valued functions instead of being used for classification tasks. In a basic variant of a regression tree, each leaf contains a constant value, usually equal to an average value of the target attribute of all training instances that reach that particular leaf. To predict the value of the target attribute, the new tested instance is followed down the tree from a root node to a leaf using its attribute values to make routing decisions at each internal node. Next, the predicted value for the new instance is evaluated based on prediction associated with the leaf. Although regression trees are not as popular as classification ones, they are highly competitive with different machine learning algorithms [23].

Traditionally, DTs are induced with a greedy procedure known as recursive partitioning [24]. In this top-down approach the induction algorithm starts from a root node where the locally optimal split of the data is found according to the given optimality measure. Next, the training instances are redirected to newly created nodes, and this process is repeated for each node until a stopping condition is met. Additionally, post-pruning is usually applied after the induction to avoid the problem of over-fitting the training data.

An alternative concept for the decision tree induction focuses on a global approach which limits the negative effects of locally optimal decisions. It tries to simultaneously search for the tree structure and the tests in the internal nodes. This process is obviously much more computationally complex but can reveal hidden regularities that are often undetectable by greedy methods. Global induction is mainly represented by systems based on an evolutionary approach [3]. In the literature, there are relatively fewer evolutionary approaches for the regression trees than for the classification ones. Popular representatives of EA-based regression trees are the TARGET solution [11] that evolves a CART-like regression tree with basic genetic operators and a strongly typed genetic programming approach called STGP [15].

2.2   GPGPU

A general-purpose computation on GPUs (GPGPU) stands for the use of graphics hardware for generic problems. One of the most popular frameworks to facilitate GPGPU is a Compute Unified Device Architecture (CUDA) [27] created by the NVIDIA Corporation. In the CUDA programming model, a GPU is considered as a co-processor that can execute thousands of threads in parallel to handle the tasks traditionally performed by the CPU. This CPU load reduction using GPGPU is recently widely applied in many computational intelligence methods [26]. Application of GPUs in evolutionary data mining usually focuses on boosting the performance of the evolutionary process which is relatively slow due to high computational complexity, especially for the large scale data [2].

When the CPU delegates a job to the GPU, it calls a kernel that is a function run on the device. Then, a grid of (threads) blocks is created and each thread executes the same kernel code in parallel. The GPU computing engine is an array of streaming multiprocessors (SMs). Each SM consists of a collection of simple streaming processors (called CUDA cores). Each block of threads is mapped to one of the SMs, and the threads inside the block are mapped to CUDA cores.

There are two decomposition techniques that are most commonly used to parallelize EAs [1]: a data approach and a control approach. The first decomposition strategy, which is also applied in this paper, focuses on splitting the dataset and distributing its chunks across the processors of the parallel system. The second approach focuses on population decomposition as individuals from the population are evaluated at the same time on different cores [14]. The main drawback of this approach is relatively weak scalability for large-scale data.

2.3   Related Works

Speeding up the DT induction has so far been discussed mainly in terms of classification problems. In the literature, we may find some attempts at parallelization the tree building process, however, most of the implementations focus on either a greedy approach [20] or random forests [25]. Despite the fact that there is a strong need for parallelizing the evolutionary induced DT [3], the topic has not yet been adequately explored. One of the reasons is that the straightforward application of GPGPU to EA may be insufficient. In order to achieve high speedup and exploit the full potential of such parallelization, there is a need to incorporate knowledge about DT specifically and its evolutionary induction.

In one of the few papers that cover parallelization of evolutionary induced DT, a hybrid MPI+OpenMP approach is investigated for both classification [7] and regression [8] trees. The algorithms use the master-slave paradigm, and the most time-consuming operations, such as fitness evaluation and genetic operators, are executed in parallel on slaves nodes. The authors apply the control parallelization approach in which the population is evenly distributed to the available nodes and cores. The experimental validation shows that the possible speedup of such a hybrid parallelization is up to 15 times for 64 CPU cores.

To the best of our knowledge, in the literature there is one study that covers GPGPU parallelization of evolutionary induced DTs [16]. Experimental validation on artificial and real-life datasets showed that it was capable of inducing trees two orders of magnitude faster in comparison to the traditional CPU version. However, it concerned only classification trees.

3   GPU-Accelerated Induction of Regression Trees

In this section, we briefly describe the original evolutionary tree induction and next, we propose an efficient acceleration of it using GPGPU.

3.1   Global Decision Tree Induction Framework

The general structure of the GDT system follows a typical EA framework [21] with an unstructured population and a generational selection. GDT allows evolving different kinds of tree representations [10], however; in our description we focus on univariate trees in which each split in the internal node is based on a single attribute. Individuals are represented in their actual form as regression trees and initialized using a simple top-down greedy algorithm on a random subsample of the training data. The tests in the internal nodes are found on random subsets of attributes.

Tree-based representation requires developing specialized genetic operators corresponding to classical mutation and crossover. The GDT framework [9] offers several specialized variants that can modify simultaneously the tree structure and tests in internal nodes. The mutation operator makes random changes in nodes of the selected individuals by e.g. replacing the test, shifting its threshold, pruning the non-terminal nodes or expanding the leaves. To construct a new test in the internal node GDT uses a locally optimized strategy called 'long dipole' [9]. At first, an instance that will constitute the dipole is randomly selected from the set of instances from a current node. The rest of the objects are sorted in decreasing order according to the difference between the dependent variable values and the selected instance. Next, the second instance that constitutes the dipole with possibly a much different dependent variable value is searched for using a mechanism similar to the ranking linear selection [21]. Finally, the test that splits the dipole is constructed based on a randomly selected attribute. The threshold value is randomly selected from a range defined by the pairs that constitute the dipole.

The crossover operator attempts to combine elements of two existing individuals (parents) to create a new solution. Randomly selected nodes may exchange the tests, branches or even the subtrees in asymmetrical manner [9]. Both operators are applied with a given probability to a tree (default value is 0.8 for mutation and 0.2 for crossover). Selecting the point of mutation or crossover depends on the location (level) of the node in the tree and its average prediction error per instance. This way the weak nodes (with high error value) and the ones from the lower parts of the tree are selected with higher probability. Successful application of any operator results in the necessity for relocation of the learning instances between tree parts rooted in the modified nodes. In addition, in every node, information about training instances currently associated with the node is stored. This makes it faster to perform local structure and test modifications during applications of genetic operators. However, it increases the memory consumption.

Fitness function is one of the most important and sensitive elements in the design of EAs. It drives the evolutionary search process by measuring how good a single individual is in terms of meeting the problem objective. GDT framework offers different multi-objective strategies like weight formula, lexicographic analysis or Pareto dominance. Here, we use the first strategy and apply the following expression for the fitness function:

$$Fitness(T) = [1 - 1/(1 + RMSE(T))] + \alpha(S(T) - 1.0), \qquad (1)$$

where S is the tree size expressed as a number of nodes, $RMSE$s is root-mean-square error, α is the relative importance of the complexity term and a user supplied parameter (default value is 0.0005).

The selection mechanism is based on a ranking linear selection [21] with the elitist strategy, which copies the best individual founded so far to the next population. Evolution terminates when the fitness of the best individual in the population does not improve during a fixed number of generations (default: 1000) or maximum number of generations is reached (default: 5000).

3.2 GPU-Based Approach

The proposed algorithm is based on a data decomposition strategy. In this approach, each GPU thread operates on a small fraction of the dataset. The general flowchart of our GPU-based approach is illustrated in Fig. 1. It can be seen that only the most time consuming operation of EA, the evaluation of the individuals, is performed in parallel on GPU. The parallelization does not affect the behavior of the original EA as the evolutionary induction flow is driven by the CPU in a sequential manner.

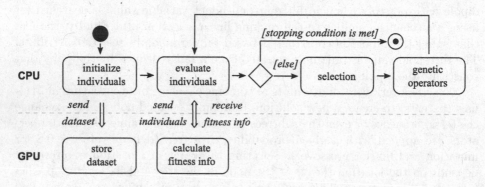

Fig. 1. Flowchart of a GPU-accelerated algorithm.

The first modification of the GDT framework concerns the initialization phase that begins by sending and saving the whole dataset from CPU to the global GPU memory. This way the GPU threads have constant access to the data and the heaviest data transfer is performed only once. The following operations: initialization of the population as well as selection of the individuals remain unchanged compared to original GDT system. The reason why these initial steps are not parallelized is that the initial population is created only once on small fractions of the dataset. In the evolutionary loop, CPU is also involved in relatively fast operations like genetic operators and selection. After successfully application of crossover or mutation, there is a need to evaluate the individuals. For calculating $RMSE$ and fitness, all objects in the training dataset need to be passed through the tree starting from the root node to an appropriate leaf. As this is a time-consuming operation and can be performed in parallel, it is delegated to the GPU which performs all necessary objects relocations and fitness calculation.

The cooperation between CPU and GPU is organized in four kernel calls that can be grouped into two sets: $Kernel1_{pre/post}$ and $Kernel2_{pre/post}$ (Fig. 2). They cover the decomposition phase (*pre*) and gathering phase (*post*) which is illustrated in Fig. 2. The role of the first function named $Kernel1_{pre}$ is to propagate objects from the root of the tree to the leaves. Each GPU block makes a copy of the evaluated individual that is later loaded into the shared memory that is visible in all threads within the block. The dataset is spread into smaller parts, first between different GPU blocks and then further between the threads. This way the threads can process the same individual but perform calculations on different chunks of the data. In each tree leaf the sum of predictions for the

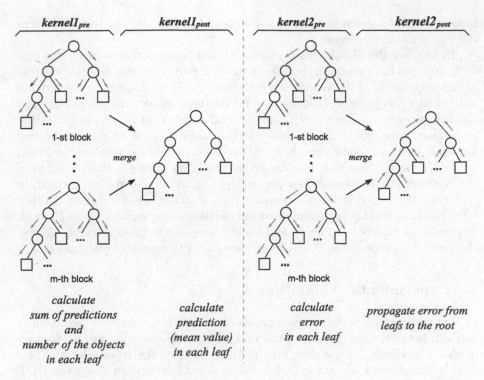

Fig. 2. Four kernel functions responsible finally for fitness info calculation for each individual.

training instances that reach that particular leaf as well as the number of the objects are stored. Next, the gathering function $Kernel1_{post}$ merges information from multiple copies of the individual allocated in each GPU block (see Fig. 2). For each individual, information that was calculated by the threads and stored in the leaves is combined.

The role of the $Kernel2$ functions is to enable the fitness calculation of the individual. In order to do that, the tree error must be determined using the information calculated by the $Kernel1$ functions and stored in the leaves. $Kernel2_{pre}$ function again splits the dataset into small parts and next in each GPU block its threads propagate and assign objects to the tree leaves. This operation is necessary to calculate the squared error of each tree leaf in $Kernel2_{pre}$ function and finally overall sum of squared residuals in the $Kernel2_{post}$ call. Like in $Kernel1_{pre}$ function, each GPU block stores a copy of the individual. The threads within the blocks calculate the prediction (mean value) for every leaf of every individual in the population from the information gathered in $Kernel1$ function. Next, each thread sums the squared differences between assigned objects predictions and the leaf prediction. The $Kernel2_{post}$ function gathers and merges the information of the squared error for each leaf from GPU blocks, determines sum of squared residuals and propagates the tree error from the leaves to the root node.

To improve the algorithm's performance, during the evolutionary induction CPU does not have access to the objects that fall into particular nodes of the tree as the propagation of the instances is performed on GPU. However, some variants of the mutation operator, that searches for the 'long dipole', require at least two objects to construct a new test in the internal node. That is why, in our GPU-accelerated approach each tree node contains additional information about two instances that may constitute 'long dipole'. First instance is randomly selected in the $Kernel1_{pre}$ function and the second one is set during gathering phase in the $Kernel2_{post}$ function. When the multiple copies of the tree are merged, in each node the second instance is searched from available set of instances in other GPU blocks according to the differences in the dependent variable value. As both instances are selected randomly and should have much different target values, the general concept of the 'long dipole' used in CPU version is maintained.

4 Experimental Validation

In this section, the performance analysis of the GPU-accelerated algorithm is verified, both on large-scale artificial and real-life datasets. As we are focused in this paper only on speeding up the GDT system, the results for the prediction performance are not included. For detailed information about the GDT prediction performance please see our previous papers [9,10].

4.1 Setup

In all experiments a default set of parameters from the sequential version of the GDT system is used and the results correspond to averages of 10 runs. We have tested two artificially generated datasets called *armchair* and *chess* (1, 5, 10 and 20 millions of instances, 2 real-valued attributes) [7,8] and two large real-life publicly available datasets: *Suzy* (5 millions of instances, 17 real-valued attributes) and *Year* (515 345 instances, 90 real-valued attributes) available in the UCI Machine Learning Repository [4]. Due to the lack of publicly available large-scale regression datasets, *Suzy* which originally concerned classification was transformed in such a way that in performed experiments the value of the last attribute is predicted instead of the class label. The only purpose of this operation was to investigate the algorithm's speedup and not the prediction performance.

All the experiments were performed on a regular PC equipped with a processor Intel Xeon E5-2620 v4 (20 MB Cache, 2.10 GHz), 64 GB RAM, and a single graphics card. We used a 64-bit Ubuntu Linux 16.04.02 LTS as an operating system. The sequential algorithm was implemented in C++ and compiled with the use of gcc version 5.4.0. The GPU-based parallelization was implemented in CUDA-C and compiled by nvcc CUDA 8.0 [22] (single-precision arithmetic was applied). We tested three NVIDIA GeForce GTX graphics cards:

- 780 (2304 CUDA cores, clock rate 863 MHz, 3 GB of memory with 288.4 GB/s bandwidth),
- Titan Black (2880 CUDA cores, clock rate 889 MHz, 6 GB of memory with 336.0 GB/s bandwidth),
- Titan X (3072 CUDA cores, clock rate 1000 MHz, 12 GB of memory with 336.5 GB/s bandwidth).

4.2 Results

Table 1 shows the obtained speedup of the proposed GPU-accelerated algorithm in comparison to its sequential version. Speedup for three GPUs and different datasets are included. It is clearly visible that the proposed GPU-acceleration provides a significant decrease in computation time. NVIDIA GTX Titan X GPU is able to speed up the evolutionary induction even more than ×1000, while other GPUs allow us to decrease the computation time at least ×100.

The scale of the improvement is even more visible when comparing the execution time between the sequential and parallel version of the GDT system (Table 2). For large data, the tree induction time for the proposed solution can be counted in minutes, while the original sequential algorithm often needs at least a few days. Moreover, the achieved speedup is much higher than the one obtained by a computer cluster of 16 nodes each equipped with 2 quad-core CPUs (Xeon 2.66 GHz) (128 CPU cores in total) and 16 GB RAM [8].

Table 1. Mean speedup for different datasets and various GPUs.

Dataset	GTX 780	GTX Titan Black	GTX Titan X
Armchair1M	×470	×496	×1189
Armchair5M	×572	×535	×1328
Armchair10M	×529	×546	×1372
Armchair20M	×505	×458	×1349
Chess1M	×140	×121	×232
Chess5M	×176	×192	×300
Chess10M	×181	×188	×249
Chess20M	×163	×129	×259
Year	×421	×512	×885
Suzy	×344	×324	×760

The results suggest that with the proposed approach even a regular PC with a medium-class graphics card is enough to significantly accelerate the GDT tree induction time. As it is expected, better graphics cards manage to achieve much better accelerations. However, the NVIDIA GTX 780 GPU is much cheaper (about 10 times) than NVIDIA GTX Titan X GPU and it provides only 2 or 3 times lower speedup.

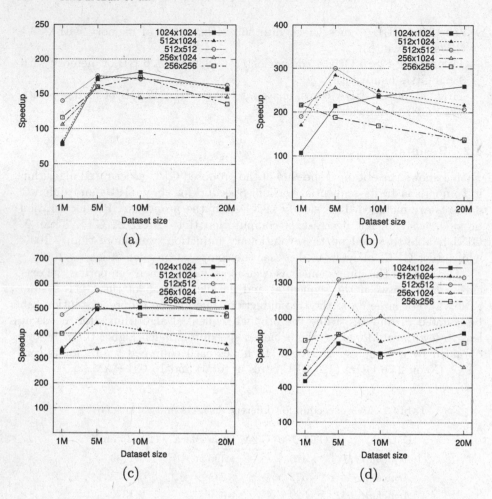

Fig. 3. The mean speedup for a few blocks × threads configurations and the different size of the dataset (1, 5, 10, and 20 million instances), successively for: (a) Geforce GTX 780, *Chess*, (b) Geforce GTX Titan X, *Chess*, (c) Geforce GTX 780, *Armchair*, (d) Geforce GTX Titan X, *Armchair*.

There is also a difference in speedup between datasets and/or their size. The highest acceleration was when using the *Armchair* dataset. This dataset is the simplest one and the induced trees are the smallest. This can suggest that the size of the generated regression trees (problem difficulty) influences time performance due to CUDA thread/branch divergence [27]. More investigation is needed here, e.g. detailed time profiling of both CPU and GPU.

We also experimentally verified whether different sizes of the data processed in each block/thread influences the algorithm time. For this purpose, we tested various blocks × threads configurations using two datasets (*Chess* and *Armchair*) and the slowest/quickest GPU (GTX 780 and GTX Titan X). Figure 3

Table 2. Mean execution time of the sequential algorithm as well as its GPU-accelerated version on the fastest GPU (in seconds and days/hours/minutes).

Dataset	Sequential	GPU-accelerated
Armchair1M	74 783 s $\approx$ 21 h	63 s $\approx$ 1 min
Armchair5M	404 388 s $\approx$ 4.5 days	304.5 s $\approx$ 5 min
Armchair10M	781 668 s $\approx$ 9 days	570 s $\approx$ 9.5 min
Armchair20M	1 492 440 s $\approx$ 17 days	1106 s $\approx$ 18.5 min
Chess1M	102 599 s $\approx$ 1 days 4 h	442 s $\approx$ 7 min
Chess5M	550 915 s $\approx$ 6 days 9 h	1 834 s $\approx$ 30.5 min
Chess10M	1 050 515 s $\approx$ 12 days	4 219 s $\approx$ 1 h 10.5 min
Chess20M	2 076 507 s $\approx$ 24 days	8 020 s $\approx$ 2 h 13.5 min
Year	90 360 s $\approx$ 25 h	102 s $\approx$ 1.5 min
Suzy	710 000 s $\approx$ 8 days 5 h	934 s $\approx$ 15 min

shows that for all larger datasets (starting with 10M), the configuration with more blocks/threads fits the best, whereas for smaller datasets configurations with less blocks/threads gives noticeably better results. There are at least two reasons that may explain the described algorithm behavior. Too small data portions per thread could cause more overhead as there are more threads to create, manage, and so on. On the other hand, the problem with load balancing can exist when the chunks of data are too big.

5   Conclusion

This paper focuses on GPU-accelerated evolutionary induction of regression trees. Proposed implementation takes an advantage of the specificity of evolutionary DT induction to exploit the full potential of GPGPU approach. Presented results show that our solution is fast, scalable and can easily explore large-scale data.

We see many promising directions for future research. In particular, we are currently working on extending our approach on regression trees with linear models in the leaves (model trees) and multi-GPU platforms. There are also many interesting ideas for optimization the proposed algorithm like processing only the modified by the genetic operators part of the tree instead of propagation all dataset objects. We also plan to verify the influence of various GPU specific memory improvements [17] in order to speed up the algorithm further.

Acknowledgments. This work was supported by the grants S/WI/2/13 (first and third author) and W/WI/1/2017 (second author) from Bialystok University of Technology founded by Ministry of Science and Higher Education.

References

1. Alba, E., Tomassini, M.: Parallelism and evolutionary algorithms. IEEE Trans. Evol. Comput. **6**(5), 443–462 (2002)
2. Bacardit, J., Llor, X.: Large-scale data mining using genetics-based machine learning. WIRE Data Min. Knowl. Discov. **3**(1), 37–61 (2013)
3. Barros, R.C., Basgalupp, M.P., Carvalho, A.C., Freitas, A.A.: A survey of evolutionary algorithms for decision-tree induction. IEEE Trans. SMC Part C **42**(3), 291–312 (2012)
4. Blake, C., Keogh, E., Merz, C.: UCI repository of machine learning databases (1998). http://www.ics.uci.edu/~mlearn/MLRepository.html
5. Breiman, L., Friedman, J.H., Olshen, R.A., Stone, C.J.: Classification and Regression Trees. Wadsworth and Brooks, Monterey (1984)
6. Chitty, D.: Fast parallel genetic programming: multi-core CPU versus many-core GPU. Soft Comput. **16**(10), 1795–1814 (2012)
7. Czajkowski, M., Jurczuk, K., Kretowski, M.: A parallel approach for evolutionary induced decision trees. MPI+OpenMP implementation. In: Rutkowski, L., Korytkowski, M., Scherer, R., Tadeusiewicz, R., Zadeh, L.A., Zurada, J.M. (eds.) ICAISC 2015. LNCS (LNAI), vol. 9119, pp. 340–349. Springer, Cham (2015). https://doi.org/10.1007/978-3-319-19324-3_31
8. Czajkowski, M., Jurczuk, K., Kretowski, M.: Hybrid parallelization of evolutionary model tree induction. In: Rutkowski, L., Korytkowski, M., Scherer, R., Tadeusiewicz, R., Zadeh, L.A., Zurada, J.M. (eds.) ICAISC 2016. LNCS (LNAI), vol. 9692, pp. 370–379. Springer, Cham (2016). https://doi.org/10.1007/978-3-319-39378-0_32
9. Czajkowski, M., Kretowski, M.: Evolutionary induction of global model trees with specialized operators and memetic extensions. Inf. Sci. **288**, 153–173 (2014)
10. Czajkowski, M., Kretowski, M.: The role of decision tree representation in regression problems an evolutionary perspective. Appl. Soft Comput. **48**, 458–475 (2016)
11. Fan, G., Gray, J.B.: Regression tree analysis using TARGET. J. Comput. Graph. Stat. **14**(1), 206–218 (2005)
12. Fayyad, U.M., Piatetsky-Shapiro, G., Smyth, P., Uthurusamy, R.: Advances in Knowledge Discovery and Data Mining. AAAI Press, Menlo Park (1996)
13. Gong, Y.J., Chen, W.N., Zhan, Z.H., Zhang, J., Li, Y., Zhang, Q., Li, J.J.: Distributed evolutionary algorithms and their models: a survey of the state-of-the-art. Appl. Soft Comput. **34**, 286–300 (2015)
14. Grama, A., Karypis, G., Kumar, V., Gupta, A.: Introduction to Parallel Computing. Addison-Wesley, Boston (2003)
15. Hazan, A., Ramirez, R., Maestre, E., Perez, A., Pertusa, A.: Modelling expressive performance: a regression tree approach based on strongly typed genetic programming. In: Rothlauf, F., et al. (eds.) EvoWorkshops 2006. LNCS, vol. 3907, pp. 676–687. Springer, Heidelberg (2006). https://doi.org/10.1007/11732242_64
16. Jurczuk, K., Czajkowski, M., Kretowski, M.: Evolutionary induction of a decision tree for large-scale data: a GPU-based approach. Soft Comput. (2017, in press)
17. Jurczuk, K., Kretowski, M., BezyWendling, J.: GPU-based computational modeling of magnetic resonance imaging of vascular structures. Int. J. High Perform. Comput. Appl. (2017, in press)
18. Kotsiantis, S.B.: Decision trees: a recent overview. Artif. Intell. Rev. **39**(4), 261–283 (2013)

19. Kretowski, M., Grześ, M.: Global learning of decision trees by an evolutionary algorithm. In: Saeed, K., Pejaś, J. (eds.) Information Processing and Security Systems, pp. 401–410. Springer, Boston (2005). https://doi.org/10.1007/0-387-26325-X_36
20. Lo, W., Chang, Y., Sheu, R., Chiu, C., Yuan, S.: CUDT: a CUDA based decision tree algorithm. Sci. World J. 1–12 (2014)
21. Michalewicz, Z.: Genetic Algorithms + Data Structures = Evolution Programs, 3rd edn. Springer, London (1996). https://doi.org/10.1007/978-3-662-03315-9
22. NVIDIA: CUDA C programming guide. Technical report (2017). https://docs.nvidia.com/cuda/cuda-c-programming-guide/
23. Ortuno, F.M., Valenzuela, O., Prieto, B., Saez-Lara, M.J., Torres, C., Pomares, H., Rojas, I.: Comparing different machine learning and mathematical regression models to evaluate multiple sequence alignments. Neurocomputing **164**, 123–136 (2015)
24. Rokach, L., Maimon, O.: Top-down induction of decision trees classifiers - a survey. IEEE Trans. Syst. Man Cybern. Part C (Appl. Rev.) **35**(4), 476–487 (2005)
25. Strnad, D., Nerat, A.: Parallel construction of classification trees on a GPU. Concurr. Comput. Pract. Exp. **28**(5), 1417–1436 (2016)
26. Tsutsui, S., Collet, P.: Massively Parallel Evolutionary Computation on GPGPUs. Springer, Heidelberg (2013). https://doi.org/10.1007/978-3-642-37959-8
27. Wilt, N.: CUDA Handbook: A Comprehensive Guide to GPU Programming. Addison-Wesley, Boston (2013)

Bezier Curve Parameterization Methods for Solving Optimal Control Problems of SIR Model

Tibor Kmet$^{(\boxtimes)}$ and Maria Kmetova

Department of Mathematics and Informatics, J. Selye University,
Bratislavska cesta 3322, 945 01 Komarno, Slovakia
{kmett,kmetovam}@ujs.sk
http://www.ujs.sk

Abstract. In this paper the optimal control strategies with two control variable of an SIR (susceptible-infected-recovered) epidemic model are introduced. The effect of dispersion of the population in a bounded habitat has been taken into consideration. The aim of this work is to minimize the infective and susceptible individuals and to maximize the total number of recovered individuals by using the possible control variables. To solve optimal control problem we use *direct* and *indirect* methods, Bernstein-Bezier parametrisation of control variable and invasive weed optimization of objective function, and adaptive critic design with echo state networks, respectively. Our results indicate that these two methods are able to solve optimal control problems.

Keywords: Bernstein-Bezier parametrisation
Invasive weed optimization · Adaptive critic design
Echo state networks · SIR model · Optimal control problem

1 Introduction

There are two general approaches to solve optimal control problems given mathematically as follows:

$$min \ F(u) = \psi(x(t_f)) + \int_{t_0}^{t_f} f_0(t, x(t), u(t)) \tag{1}$$

subject to

$$\dot{x}(t) = f(t, x(t), u(t)) \tag{2}$$

with initial condition $x(t_0) = x_0$, where $x \in R^m$, $u \in R^d$ and $f = (f_1, \ldots, f_m)$. These are often labeled as *indirect* and *direct* methods. In indirect methods there are some numerical methods to solve the challenges of obtaining an optimal control $\hat{u}$ and optimal trajectory $\hat{x}(t)$ [9,14]. The first indirect methods is

© Springer International Publishing AG 2017
C. Martín-Vide et al. (Eds.): TPNC 2017, LNCS 10687, pp. 100–110, 2017.
https://doi.org/10.1007/978-3-319-71069-3_8

based on solving the optimal systems, state $x(t)$ and co-state equations $\lambda(t)$, which consist of $2m$ differential equations and boundary conditions in time also. The second indirect method starting with an initial guess for the co-state equation, then the state equation and the control equation are solved by a forward method in time. These state and control values are used to solve the co-state equations by backward methods in time. In 1977, Werbos [15] introduced an approach for approximate dynamic programming which later became known under the name of adaptive critic design (ACD). A typical design of ACD consists of three modules: action, model (plant), and critic. The action consists of a parametrised control law. The critic approximates the value-related function and captures the effect that the control law has on the future cost. At any given time the critic provides a guidance on how to improve the control law. In return, the action can be used to update the critic. An algorithm that successively iterates between these two operations converges to the optimal solution over time. The plant dynamics are discrete, time-invariant, and deterministic, and they can be modelled by a difference equation. The action and critic networks are chosen as neural networks, for example feed forwards or echo state networks (ESNs). For detailed explanation see [10, 11, 13]. In the direct methods, optimal control is seen as a standard optimization problems: perform a search for the control function $u(t)$ that optimize the objective functional $F(u)$. However, optimization routines do not operate on infinite dimensional space, we used straightforward discretization of continues space [4]. To approximate optimal control $u(t)$ we use Bezier curve which can parameterize smooth, non-oscillatory function with minimum epistasis with minimum number of parameters. Given a large enough number of properly selected control points, any smooth function can be approximated by Bezier curve to arbitrary accuracy [3]. Here, Bezier Control Parameterization (BCP) is used to determine optimal control function. In this paper, using SIR model we compare *direct* method including Invasive Weed Optimization (IWO) and Bezier curve approximation with *indirect* method based on Pontryagin's maximum principle or on necessary conditions for the optimal control problem, ACD and ESNs. Rest of the paper is organized in the following way. Section 2 describes Berstein-Bezier parameterization. Section 3 elaborates the IWO algorithm. In Sect. 4, we present a mathematical model describing the population dynamics of infectious disease and optimal control problem of vaccine coverage threshold needed for disease control and eradication. Section 5 includes some numerical results of optimal control problem solving by BCP-IWO and ACD-ESNs methods. Finally, Sect. 6 concludes the paper.

2   Bernstein-Bezier Parameterisation

The first approach to Bezier curves was introduced by Paul de Casteljau in early 1960s at car company Citroen to modelling car shapes. He could not publish his results until 1986. De Casteljau algorithm is based on the repeated linear interpolation between pairs of control points. Linear interpolation between two distinct points A, B is the set of points $X(z) = (1-z)A + zB$ which, for $z \in [0,1]$

is a line segment AB interpreted as the affine image of the unit interval. We can also interpret the line segment AB as the affine image of any interval $[t_0, t_f]$. The interval $[t_0, t_f]$ may itself be obtained by an affine map from the interval $[0, 1]$ and vice versa. The mentioned map (with $z \in [0, 1]$ and $t \in [t_0, t_f]$) is given by $z = (t - t_0)/(t_f - t_0)$. The interpolated point X on AB is now given by both $X(z) = (1 - z)A + zB$ and $X(t) = (t_f - t)A/(t_f - t_0) + (t - t_0)B/(t_f - t_0)$.

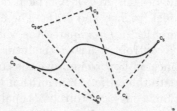

Fig. 1. General form of Bezier curve with control points $C_0, \ldots, C_5$.

For creating a Bezier curve of degree n, let us given $n + 1$ control points $C_i \in R^d$, $i = 0, 1, \ldots, n$ and a parameter $z \in [0, 1]$. Set $C_i^r(z) = (1 - z)C_i^{r-1}(z) + zC_{i+1}^{r-1}(z)$, $r = 1, \ldots, n$, $i = 0, \ldots, n - r$ and $C_i^0(z) = C_i$. Then $C_0^n(z) \in R^d$ is the point with parameter value z on the Bezier curve C^n, hence $C^n(z) = C_0^n(z)$. The general layout of Bezier curve is illustrated in Fig. 1. Now we give the example of the cubic case. Control points are C_i, $i = 0, 1, 2, 3$. According to de Casteljau algorithm we create Bezier Curve, see Fig. 2.

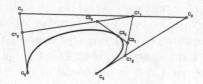

Fig. 2. Cubic Bezier curve construction via de Casteljau algorithm.

We got a point on the curve as affine combination of the origin control points. (Figure 2 shows the process and the result of linear interpolation for $z = 0.6$.) One can realize that the coefficients of the affine combination are Berstein polynomials. Bezier curves of degree n can be expressed also in terms of Berstein polynomials of degree n : $C^n(z) = \sum_{i=0}^{n} C_i B_i^n(z)$, where $B_i^n(z) = \binom{n}{i} z^i (1 - z)^{n-i}$ are Bernstein polynomials defined explicitly. $C^n(z) = \sum_{i=0}^{n} C_i B_i^n(z)$, One of the important properties of Bernstein polynomials is the following recursion: $B_i^n(z) = (1 - z)B_i^{n-1}(z) + zB_{i-1}^{n-1}(z)$. The property that Bernstein polynomials of degree n forms a partition of unity $\sum_{i=0}^{n} B_i^n(z) = 1$ is necessary for using them as coefficients of affine combination of control points of a Bezier curve. The following property is also important: $\sum_{i=0}^{n} \frac{i}{n} B_i^n(z) = z$. Bezier curves are invariant under affine parameter transformation. Previous definition of Bezier curve was given over the interval $[0, 1]$. This is done because it is convenient, not because it is necessary [3]. The curve can be defined over the arbitrary interval $t_0 \leq t \leq t_f$ of the real line. After the introduction of local coordinates $z = (t - t_0)/(t_f - t_0)$, the algorithm proceeds as usual. This property is inherited from the linear interpolation process. The corresponding generalized de Casteljau algorithm is of the form $C_i^r(t) = (t_f - t)/(t - t_0)C_i^{r-1}(t) + (t - t_0)/(t_f - t_0)C_{i+1}^{r-1}(t)$. Thus algebraic expression for Bezier curve C^n over the interval $[t_0, t_f]$ is the following $C^n(t) = \sum_{i=0}^{n} C_i B_i^n((t - t_0)/(t_f - t_0))$. In our model, we use Bezier curve in (t, u) space to estimate optimal control $u(t)$. Given a fixed set of t components of the control points $t_i = t_0 + hi$, $i = 0, \ldots, n$, where $h = \frac{t_f - t_0}{n}$ and the parameters u_i, $i = 0, \ldots, n$, the Bezier curve for $u(t)$ is

$$\begin{pmatrix} t \\ u(t) \end{pmatrix} = \sum_{i=0}^{n} \binom{n}{i} z^i (1 - z)^{n-i} \begin{pmatrix} t_i \\ u_i \end{pmatrix} \tag{3}$$

with control points $C_i = \binom{t_i}{u_i}$ and binomial coefficients $\binom{n}{i}$, $i = 0, \ldots, n$. A fixed regular mesh is used on the t-axis to make the curve single valued and to reduce the dimension of the optimization vectors to $n + 1$. The BCP with control points $C_i = \binom{t_i}{u_i}$, $i = 0, \ldots, n$ completely encodes the control function $u(t)$ as the n-th order parametric Bezier curve.

3   Invasive Weed Optimization Algorithm

Usually the parameters governing the optimization problem are presented as a vector $u = (u_1, \ldots, u_d)$ To measure the quality of each solution, an objective function or fitness function is used for single objective optimization. The task of optimization is to search for the parameter vector u^* to minimize the objective function $F(u)$. Invasive Weed Optimization (IWO) is a stochastic optimization algorithm inspired from colonizing weeds which was first introduced by Mehrabian and Locus in [1]. Since its invention, IWO has been used in many applications like the design and optimization of antenna array, solving optimal control problems [4], training neural networks [5]. In the basic IWO, weeds represent the feasible solutions of problems and population is the set of all weeds. A finite number of weeds is being dispread over the search area. Every weed produces new weeds depending on its fitness. The generated weeds are randomly distributed over the search space by normally distributed random numbers with a mean equal to zero. This process continues until maximum number of weeds is reached. Only the weeds with better fitness can survive and produce seed, others are being eliminated. The process continues until maximum iterations are reached or hopefully the weed with best fitness is closest to optimal solution. The process is addressed in detail as follows:

- Step 1: *Initialize a population*
  Set the maximum and the least value of a weed s_{max}, s_{min}, respectively. A population of initial solutions is being dispread over the d dimensional search space with random positions.

- Step 2: *Reproduction*
  The higher the weed's fitness is, the more seeds it produces. The formula of weeds producing seeds is $w_n = \frac{f - f_{min}}{f_{max} - f_{min}}(s_{max} - s_{min} + s_{min}$, where f is the current weed's fitness. f_{max} and f_{min} respectively represent the maximum and the least fitness of the current population.
- Step 3: *Spatial dispersal*
  This step ensures that the produced seeds will be generated around the parent weed, leading to a local search around each plant. The generated seeds are randomly spread out around the parent weeds according to a normal distribution with *mean* equal to zero and variance σ^2. The standard deviation of the seed dispersion σ decreases as a function of the number of iterations it. The equation for determining the standard deviation for each generation is presented in equation $\sigma_{it} = \frac{(It_{max} - it)^n}{(It_{max})^m}(\sigma_{init} - \sigma_{final}) + \sigma_{final}$, where It_{max} is the maximum number of iterations. σ_{it} is the standard deviation at the current iteration and m is the nonlinear modulation index.
- Step 4: *Competitive exclusion*
  After a number of iterations, the population reaches its maximum and an elimination mechanism is adopted: the seeds and their parents are ranked together and only those with better fitness can survive and become reproductive. Others are being eliminated.

Algorithm 1. Pseudo-code for the IWO algorithm [15].

Input: Generate random population W of M solution (weeds) over the $d-$ dimensional search space; Set maximum size of population M_{max}, maximum number of iteration It_{max}, s_{min} and s_{max}

Output: Weed with best fitness (optimal solution)

1 **for** $i \leftarrow 0$ **to** It_{max} **do**
2   Calculate the fitness of each weed based on the problem objective function
3   Compute the best and worst fitness in the population
4   Compute the standard deviation std depending on iteration
5   **for** *each weed w in the population W* **do**
6   Compute the number of seed for w depending on its fitness
7   Select the seeds from the feasible solutions around the parent weed w in a neighborhood with normal distribution having *mean* = 0 and *standard deviation* = σ_{it}
8   Add seeds produced to the population W
9   **if** $|W| > M_{max}$ **then**
10   Sort the population W according to their fitness
11   Truncate population W with worse fitness till $N = M_{max}$.

12 **return** *Weed with best fitness (optimal solution)*

---

4   SIR Model

Mathematical models describing the population dynamics of infectious disease have played an important role in better understanding epidemiological patterns and disease control. One of the most popular models of the infectious diseases is the classical SIR model [2, 16, 17]. In this model, the whole population is divided into three compartments which describe separated groups of individuals: susceptible which are able to contract the disease (denoted by S, x_1), infective which are capable of transmitting the disease (marked by I, x_2) and recovered which are permanently immune (denoted by R, x_3). The letters represent the number of individuals in each compartment at a particular time t and space p, and the whole population size N, x_4 is the sum of above fractional groups, i.e. $S + I + R = N$. For the optimal control problem we consider the control variable $u(t) = (u_1(t), u_2(t)) \in U$ relative to the state variables $x_1, \ldots, x_4$, where $U = \{(u_1, u_2),\ u_i(t)\ is\ measurable,\ 0 \le u_i(t) \le b_i\}$, says an admissible control set. The effect of dispersion of the population in a bounded habitat has been taken into consideration, and in this situation the governing equations for the population densities become a system of differential equations. The aim of this work is to minimize the infective and susceptible individuals and to maximize the total number of recovered individuals by using the possible minimal control variables $u_1(t)$ and $u_2(t)$. Susceptible individuals induce an optimal control vaccine $u_1(t)$ before the infection and an optimal control treatment $u_2(t)$ should be provided to infected individuals. The time evolutions of the populations compartments in the SIR model is described by four nonlinear differential equations:

$$\dot{x}_1(t) = \left(b - \mu \frac{r x_4(t)}{K_c} \right) x_4(t) - \frac{\beta x_1(t) x_2(t)}{x_4(t)} +$$

$$+ \omega u_2(t) \frac{x_2(t)}{x_4(t)} - \left(c + (1 - \mu) \frac{r x_4(t)}{K_c} \right) x_1(t) - u_1(t) x_1(t)$$

$$\dot{x}_2(t) = \frac{\beta x_1(t) x_2(t)}{x_4(t)} - u_2(t) \frac{x_2(t)}{x_4(t)} - \left(c + (1 - \mu) \frac{r x_4(t)}{K_c} \right) x_2(t) - \alpha x_2(t)$$

$$\dot{x}_3(t) = \alpha x_2(t) + (1 - \omega) u_2(t) \frac{x_2(t)}{x_4(t)} + u_1(t) x_1(t)$$

$$\dot{x}_4(t) = r x_4(t) \left(1 - \frac{x_4(t)}{K_c} \right) \tag{4}$$

with initial conditions

$$x_i(0) = x0_i,\ i = 1, \ldots, 4. \tag{5}$$

Here t denotes the time, $b > 0$, $c > 0$, $\alpha > 0$ and $\beta > 0$ are the birth, death, recovery and contact rate, respectively. $r = b - c$ is the intrinsic growth rate, μ is the convex combination constant, K_c is the carrying capacity of the population, and $u = (u_1, u_2)$ is the vaccination coverage of susceptible and infected individuals. Let us consider the whole population size x_4 given by the following equation:

$$\dot{x}_4(t) = r x_4(t) \left(1 - \frac{x_4(t)}{K_c} \right). \tag{6}$$

Equation (6) has two equilibrium $\bar{N}_1 = 0$, $\bar{N}_2 = K_c$, where N_1 is unstable and N_2 is asymptotically stable.

4.1 Optimal Control Problem

We set an optimal control problem in the SIR model to control the spread of diseases. The main goal of this problem is to investigate the optimal vaccine coverage threshold needed for disease control and eradication [8]. From these facts, our optimal control problem is given by the following. Find a control $u(t)$ to minimise the objective functional

$$\mathcal{J}(u) = \int_{t_0}^{t_f} a_1 x_1(t) + a_2 x_2(t) + \frac{1}{2} u_1(t)^2 + \frac{1}{2} u_2(t)^2 dt, \tag{7}$$

subject to the state system (4), where a_1, a_2 are small positive constants to keep a balance in the size of S and I, respectively. The theory of necessary conditions for the optimal control problem of form (7) is well developed, see e.g. [6,12]. The augmented Hamiltonian function for problem (7) is given by

$$\mathcal{H}(x, u, \lambda) = a_1 x_1(t) + a_2 x_2(t) + \frac{1}{2} u_1(t)^2 + \frac{1}{2} u_1(t)^2 + \sum_{j=1}^{4} \lambda_j F_j(x, u) =$$

$$\frac{1}{2} u_2(t)^2 + u_2(t) \frac{x_2(t)}{x_4(t)} \left(\omega \lambda_1(t) - \lambda_2(t) + (1 - \omega) \lambda_3(t) \right) +$$

$$\frac{1}{2} u_1(t)^2 + u_1(t) x_1(t) (\lambda_3(t) - \lambda_1(t)) + G(p, t), \tag{8}$$

where $\lambda \in R^4$ is the adjoint variable. Let $(\hat{x}, \hat{u})$ be an optimal solution for (7). Then the necessary optimality condition for (7) implies [6] that there exists a piecewise continuous and piecewise continuously differentiable co-state function $\lambda : Q \to R^4$ satisfying

$$\dot{\lambda} = -\frac{\partial \mathcal{H}}{\partial x} (\hat{x}, \hat{x}_\tau, \hat{u}, \lambda) \tag{9}$$

$$\lambda(t_f) = 0, \tag{10}$$

$$0 = \frac{\partial \mathcal{H}}{\partial u} (\hat{x}, \hat{u}, \lambda). \tag{11}$$

According to the optimality condition (11), we have

$$\frac{\partial \mathcal{H}(\hat{x}, \hat{u}, \lambda)}{\partial u_1} = \hat{u}_1(t) + x_1(t) (\lambda_3(t) - \lambda_1(t)) = 0$$

$$\frac{\partial \mathcal{H}(\hat{x}, \hat{u}, \lambda)}{\partial u_2} = \hat{u}_2(t) + \frac{\hat{x}_2(t)}{\hat{x}_4(t)} (\omega \lambda_1(t) - \lambda_2(t) + (1 - \omega) \lambda_3(t)) = 0.$$

Now, using the property of the control space $u_i \in \langle 0, u_{imax} \rangle$, we get

$$\hat{u}_1(t) = 0, \ if, \ (\lambda_3(t) - \lambda_1(t)) \leq 0,$$
$$\hat{u}_1(t) = x_1(t)(\lambda_3(t) - \lambda_1(t)), \tag{12}$$
$$if, \ 0 \leq x_1(t)(\lambda_3(t) - \lambda_1(t)) < u_{1max},$$
$$\hat{u}_1(t) = u_{1max}, \ if, \ x_1(t)(\lambda_3(t) - \lambda_1(t)) \geq u_{1max}$$

$$\hat{u}_2(t) = 0, \ if, \ \frac{x_2(t)}{x_4(t)}(-\omega\lambda_1(t) + \lambda_2(t) - (1-\omega)\lambda_3(t)) \leq 0,$$
$$\hat{u}_2(t) = \frac{x_2(t)}{x_4(t)}(-\omega\lambda_1(t) + \lambda_2(t) - (1-\omega)\lambda_3(t)), \tag{13}$$
$$if, \ 0 \leq \frac{x_2(t)}{x_4(t)}(-\omega\lambda_1(t) + \lambda_2(t) - (1-\omega)\lambda_3(t)) < u_{2max},$$
$$\hat{u}_2(t) = u_{imax}, \ if, \ \frac{x_2(t)}{x_4(t)}(-\omega\lambda_1(t) + \lambda_2(p,t) - (1-\omega)\lambda_3(t)) \geq u_{2max}.$$

To solve optimal control problem *indirectly* (7) we use ACD and ESNs, where state x and co-state variables λ are solved forward in time. In 1977, Werbos [15] introduced an approach for approximate dynamic programming, which later became known under the name of adaptive critic design. A typical design of ACD consists of three modules: action, model (plant), and critic. The action consists of a parametrised control law. The critic approximates the value-related function and captures the effect that the control law has on the future cost. At any given time the critic provides a guidance on how to improve the control law. In return, the action can be used to update the critic. An algorithm that successively iterates between these two operations converges to the optimal solution over time. The plant dynamics are discrete, time-invariant and deterministic, and they can be modelled by a difference equation. The action and critic networks are chosen as echo state networks [7]. For detail explanation see [11].

5   Numerical Simulation

The solution of optimal control problem (7) using Bezier curves approximation and adaptive critic neural network are displayed in Figs. 3, 4, 5 and 6. As follows from these figures optimal control $\hat{u}(t) = (\hat{u}_1(t), \hat{u}_2(t))$ and optimal trajectory $\hat{x}(t)$ are very closed. For Besier curve approximation and ESNs approximation the values of objective function are $J(u) = 1106$ and $J(u) = 593$, and $J(u) = 1114$ and $J(u) = 598$, for initial conditions $x(0) = (60, 30, 10, 100)$ and $x(0) = (8, 3, 1, 13)$, respectively. We have plotted susceptible, infected and recovered individuals by considering values of parameters [17] as $b = 0.07$, $c = 0.0123$, $\alpha = 0.0476$, $\beta = 0.21$, $\mu = 0.014$, $\omega = 0.35, K_c = 140$, $a_1 = 1$, $a_2 = 1$. The numerical results show that the number of susceptible and infected individuals decrease after the optimal control treatment and small number of individuals are infected from population $x_4(t)$, which converges to equilibrium K_c. The number of recovered individuals increase.

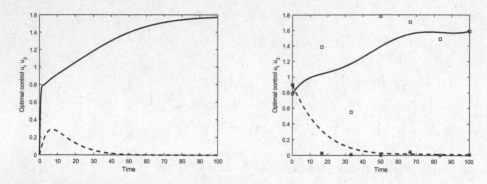

Fig. 3. Adaptive critic neural network and Bezier curve simulation of optimal controls $\hat{u}_1(t)$ (line) and $\hat{u}_2(t)$ (dosh line) and its control points with initial condition $x(0) = (2, 3, 8, 13)$.

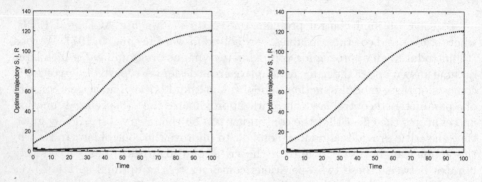

Fig. 4. The plot represents the population of susceptible (line), infected (dosh line) and recovered (dotted line) individuals with initial condition $x(0) = (2, 3, 8, 13)$ for adaptive critic neural network and Bezier curve simulation.

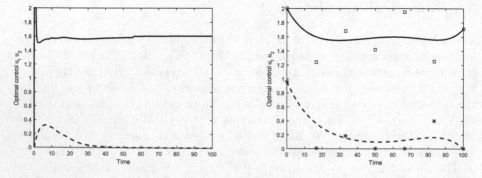

Fig. 5. Adaptive critic neural network and Bezier curve simulation of optimal controls $\hat{u}_1(t)$ (line) and $\hat{u}_2(t)$ (dosh line) and its control points with initial condition $x(0) = (60, 30, 10, 100)$.

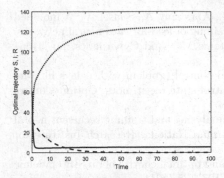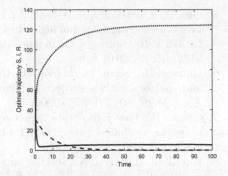

Fig. 6. The plot represents the population of susceptible (line), infected (dosh line) and recovered (dotted line) individuals with initial condition $x(0) = (60, 30, 10, 100)$ for adaptive critic neural network and Bezier curve simulation.

Our results are quite similar for two presented methods but the computation time for *direct* methods is very high.

6   Conclusion

In this paper, we have studied optimal control strategies to prevent the spread of infected individuals. Using MATLAB, we present a comparison between direct and indirect methods, respectively. Direct methods is based on Berstein-Bezier parametrisation of control variable $u(t)$ and invasive weed optimization. The second, indirect method is based on necessary conditions for the optimal control problem with adaptive critic design and echo state networks. It is easy to see that the optimal control is much more effective for reducing the number of susceptible and infected individuals. In order to illustrate the overall picture of the epidemic, the numbers of infected, susceptible and recovered individuals under the optimal control are shown in figures. We have shown that this approaches are applicable to a wide class of nonlinear systems.

References

1. Mehrabian, A.R.: A novel numerical optimization algorithm inspired from weed colonization. Ecol. Inform. **1**(4), 355–366 (2006)
2. Brauer, F., Castillo-Chavez, C.: Mathematical Models in Population Biology and Epidemiology. Springer, New York (2001). https://doi.org/10.1007/978-1-4614-1686-9
3. Farin, G.: Curves and Surfaces for Computer Aided Geometric Design — A Practical Guide. Academic Press Professional, San Diego (1993)
4. Ghosh, A., Das, S., Chowdhury, A., Giri, R.: An ecologically inspired direct search method for solving optimal control problems with Bezier parameterization. Eng. Appl. Artif. Intell. **24**, 1195–1203 (2011)

5. Giri, R., Chowdhury, A., Ghosh, A., Das, S., Abraham, A., Snasel, V.: A modified invasive weed optimization algorithm for training of feed-forward neural networks. In: IEEE International Conference on Systems Man and Cybernetics, pp. 3166–3173. IEEE (2010)

6. Gollman, L., Kern, D., Mauer, H.: Optimal control problem with delays in state and control variables subject to mixed control-state constraints. Optim. Control Appl. Meth. **30**, 341–365 (2006)

7. Jaeger, H.: The "Echo State" approach to analysing and training recurrent neural networks. Technical report GMD 148, German National Research Institute for Computer Science, Bonn (2001)

8. Kar, T.K., Batabyal, A.: Stability analysis and optimal control of an SIR epidemic model with vaccination. BioSyst. Sci. **104**, 127–135 (2011)

9. Kirk, D.E.: Optimal Control Theory: An Introduction. Dover Publications, New York (1989)

10. Kmet, T., Kmetova, M.: Neural networks simulation of distributed control problems with state and control constraints. In: Villa, A.E.P., Masulli, P., Pons Rivero, A.J. (eds.) ICANN 2016. LNCS, vol. 9886, pp. 468–477. Springer, Cham (2016). https://doi.org/10.1007/978-3-319-44778-0_55

11. Kmet, T., Kmetova, M.: Echo state networks simulation of sir distributed control. In: Rutkowski, L., Korytkowski, M., Scherer, R., Tadeusiewicz, R., Zadeh, L.A., Zurada, J.M. (eds.) ICAISC 2017. LNCS (LNAI), vol. 10245, pp. 86–96. Springer, Cham (2017). https://doi.org/10.1007/978-3-319-59063-9_8

12. Mittelmann, H.D.: Solving elliptic control problems with interior point and SQP methods: control and state constraints. J. Comput. Appl. Math. **120**, 175–195 (2000)

13. Padhi, R., Unnikrishnan, N., Wang, X., Balakrishnan, S.N.: Adaptive-critic based optimal control synthesis for distributed parameter systems. Automatica **37**, 1223–1234 (2001)

14. Pontryagin, L.S., Boltyanskii, V.G., Gamkrelidze, R., Mischenko, E.F.: Freshwater Ecosystems. Modelling and Simulation, Developments in Environmental Modelling. Nauka (in Russian), Moscow (1983)

15. Werbos, P.J.: Approximate dynamic programming for real-time control and neural modelling. In: White, D.A., Sofge, D.A. (eds.) Handbook of intelligent control: Neural Fuzzy, and Adaptive Approaches, pp. 493–525. Van Nostrand, New York (1992)

16. Yoshida, N., Hara, T.: Global stability of a delayed SIR epidemic model with density dependent birth and death rates. J. Comput. Appl. Math. **201**, 339–347 (2007)

17. Zaman, G., Kang, Y.H., Jung, I.H.: Optimal treatment of an SIR epidemic model with time delay. BioSystems **98**, 43–50 (2009)

Fuzzy Logic

Learning Interval-Valued Fuzzy Cognitive Maps with PSO Algorithm for Abnormal Stock Return Prediction

Petr Hajek[✉] and Ondrej Prochazka

Faculty of Economics and Administration, Institute of System Engineering
and Informatics, University of Pardubice, Studentska 84, 532 10 Pardubice,
Czech Republic
petr.hajek@upce.cz, st47576@student.upce.cz

Abstract. Stock return prediction is considered a challenging task in financial domain. The existence of inherent noise and volatility in daily stock price returns requires a highly complex prediction system. Generalizations of fuzzy systems have shown promising results for this task owing to their ability to handle strong uncertainty in dynamic financial markets. Moreover, financial variables are usually in difficult to interpret causal relationships. To overcome these problems, here we propose an interval-valued fuzzy cognitive map with PSO algorithm learning. This system is suitable for modelling complex non-linear problems through causal reasoning. As the inputs of the system, we combine causally connected financial indicators and linguistic variables extracted from management discussion in annual reports. Here we show that the proposed method is effective for predicting abnormal stock return. In addition, we demonstrate that this method outperforms fuzzy cognitive maps and adaptive neuro-fuzzy rule-based systems with PSO learning.

Keywords: Stock market · Interval-valued fuzzy cognitive map
PSO algorithm · Abnormal stock return

1 Introduction

Soft computing methods have recently attracted increasing attention in stock market prediction problems. This is mainly associated with the existence of inherent noise and volatility in stock market prices. On one hand, highly complex prediction systems are required to address this issue. On the other hand, these systems should not only be accurate but also easy to interpret. Developing transparent prediction models has become crucial especially after the recent financial crisis.

To capture the nonlinear behaviour of stock markets, intelligent systems such as neural networks [1], fuzzy systems [2] and evolutionary algorithms [3] have been extensively applied. Lately, hybrid systems have received increased interest because they integrate the advantages of multiple methods [4]. Thus, a high prediction accuracy can be achieved, without neglecting the interpretability of the system. Fundamental and technical financial indicators are usually used as the inputs of these systems. In addition, sentiment and other textual analyses have been rapidly developed to predict stock

© Springer International Publishing AG 2017
C. Martín-Vide et al. (Eds.): TPNC 2017, LNCS 10687, pp. 113–125, 2017.
https://doi.org/10.1007/978-3-319-71069-3_9

market movements [5, 6]. It has been shown that the combination of financial indicators and linguistic analysis of firm-related documents, such as news stories and corporate annual reports, may result in more accurate stock market predictions. This is mainly because these textual sources carry complementary information about the stock's current and future prospects, which is reflected by market participants in stock prices [7]. Thus, financial and linguistic indicators are causally related. On one hand, the linguistic indicators reflect the past financial performance. On the other hand, the linguistic indicators inform about future financial performance, affecting the expectations of market participants. Despite this empirical evidence, no one as far as we know has proposed a prediction system that incorporates these causal relationships. Here we attempt to fill this gap and propose an interval-valued fuzzy cognitive map (IVFCM) with particle swarm optimization (PSO) learning. Financial and linguistic indicators extracted from corporate annual reports are used as the inputs of this prediction system.

In traditional fuzzy cognitive maps (FCMs), causal relationships between variables are represented by directed edges labelled with fuzzy weights. Using interval-valued fuzzy sets (IVFSs) instead of fuzzy sets enables the incorporation of a higher level of uncertainty. Various learning algorithms have been proposed to automatically develop FCMs [8]. The set of variables is usually provided by an expert and the learning algorithm is then used to compute the weight matrix that best fits the data. Evolutionary approaches such as genetic algorithms (GAs) [9], particle swarm optimization (PSO) [10] and memetic algorithms (MAs) [11] have been particularly effective in learning FCMs. A comprehensive survey of nature-inspired metaheuristic algorithms was conducted in [12]. Interactive evolutionary computing has used partial expert estimations to handle incompleteness and natural uncertainty in expert evaluation [13]. Moreover, the learned FCM model was further improved by a multi-local and balanced local MA search algorithm in [14]. Chi and Liu [15] proposed a multi-objective evolutionary algorithm to address the issue of the high density of learned FCMs.

The problem of conventional FCMs in financial markets is that the precise values of a weight matrix must be determined under strong uncertainty in the dynamic environment of financial markets. This can be overcome by extending the concept of fuzzy sets in recently introduced FCM generalizations, such as IVFCMs [16], fuzzy grey cognitive maps (FGCMs) [17, 18], intuitionistic FCMs [19], interval-valued intuitionistic FCMs [20] and granular FCMs [21]. These systems all enable additional freedom in assigning the membership degrees to variables and causal relationships, but they have different motivation and inference mechanisms. Here we use FCMs based on IVFSs because in financial domain intervals are used to express the uncertainty related to the context or to the lack of model accuracy [16]. In the proposed prediction system, causal relationships in IVFCMs are estimated by using PSO. PSO was selected because it was effective in the dynamic optimization of FCMs in related time series forecasting problems [22]. We demonstrate that the proposed method is effective for one-day-ahead prediction of abnormal stock return. We also show that this method outperforms conventional FCMs [10], and the generalization of an adaptive neuro-fuzzy inference system (ANFIS) [23] with PSO learning.

The remainder of this paper is organized as follows. Section 2 briefly reviews previous literature on stock market prediction using fuzzy systems and their generalizations. In Sect. 3, we first provide the theoretical background on IVFCMs, and then we propose an IVFCM with PSO learning. Section 4 presents the data used for abnormal stock return prediction. In Sect. 5, we show the experimental results and compare the prediction accuracy with several neuro-fuzzy methods, such as conventional FCMs, adaptive neuro-fuzzy inference systems and intuitionistic neuro-fuzzy networks with PSO learning. Finally, we discuss the results and conclude this paper.

2 Related Literature on Stock Market Prediction

Here we briefly review hybrid soft computing systems that have been applied to stock market prediction. These systems usually incorporate the uncertainty processing and interpretability of fuzzy systems and integrate it with the learning capacity of neural networks or evolutionary algorithms.

ANFIS represents a typical neuro-fuzzy rule-based architecture applied for the task of stock market prediction. ANFIS was adopted by [24] to predict stock market return on the ISE National 100 Index. It was reported that the performance of stock price prediction can be significantly improved by using ANFIS. A similar architecture of Takagi-Sugeno fuzzy rule-based system was presented by [2], where a linear combination of the significant technical index was applied as a consequent to predict the stock price. A fuzzy rule-based expert system developed by [25] for portfolio managers performed superior relative to the benchmark stock market indexes. Short-term stock trends during turbulent stock market periods were predicted by using two ANFISs, one used as the controller and the other one as the stock market process [26].

To model additional uncertainty associated with stock market environment, interval type-2 fuzzy rule-based systems have been proposed. The empirical analyses showed that type-2 fuzzy systems outperform conventional type-1 fuzzy systems in predicting stock prices. Technical and fundamental indexes were used as the input variables of the proposed type-2 fuzzy rule based expert system in [27]. Type-2 fuzzy rules were generated automatically by a self-constructing clustering method and the obtained type-2 fuzzy rules were refined by a PSO learning algorithm for TAIEX and NASDAQ stock price prediction [28]. This approach outperformed conventional regression models, neural networks, fuzzy time series, and support vector regression. An integrated functional link interval type-2 fuzzy-neural system was presented by [29] for predicting stock market indexes. The model used a Takagi-Sugano type fuzzy rule base with type-2 fuzzy sets in the antecedent parts and the outputs from the functional link artificial neural network (FLANN) in the consequent parts. The parameters of all the prediction models were optimized by PSO. This approach performed better than FLANN, type-1 fuzzy logic system and local linear wavelet neural network irrespective of the time horizons spanning from 1 day to 1 month. An evolutionary interval-valued fuzzy rule-based classification system was developed by [30] for the prediction of real-world financial applications with imbalanced data. The proposed system outperformed C4.5 decision tree, type-1, and interval-valued fuzzy counterparts that use the synthetic minority oversampling technique.

3 IVFCMs with PSO Learning

3.1 FCMs

To effectively model nonlinear causal relationships, an FCM combines recurrent neural networks and fuzzy logic. It can be defined as a signed fuzzy weighted digraph with N nodes, where every node represents a concept. Fuzzy value c_i^k, usually within the range of [0, 1], is assigned to the i-th concept, where k denotes the index of iteration. The sign and strength of the causal relationship from concept j to concept i is expressed by using fuzzy weight w_{ji} in the range of [−1, 1]. Thus, the positive and negative relationships between the concepts can be represented. In other words, in the case of positive (negative) fuzzy weight w_{ji}, an increase in c_j^k will cause an increase (decrease) in c_i^{k+1}. When calculating the new value of the i-th concept, multiple edges connected to this concept usually have to be considered. Nonlinear activation function f (usually a sigmoid-type function) is then used to transform the linear values of the concepts. The new value of the i-th concept can be calculated as follows:

$$c_i^{k+1} = f\left(c_i^k + \sum_{\substack{j=1 \\ j \neq i}}^{N} c_j^k \times w_{ji} \right), \qquad (1)$$

where i and j denote the i-th and j-th concepts, respectively, k is the index of iteration and N is the number of concepts in the FCM. This recurrent neural network consists of N neurons organized in one layer and connected with each other, this is with $N \times (N-1)$ synapses.

3.2 Inference in IVFCMs

To reformulate reasoning in conventional FCMs, interval-valued fuzzy sets are used instead of fuzzy sets. In interval-valued fuzzy set A, the membership degree of an element $x \in X$ is defined by an interval as follows:

$$A = \{ \langle x, M_A(x) \rangle \mid x \in X \}, \qquad (2)$$

where the interval function $M_A: X \to D$ [0, 1] such that $x \to M_A(x) = \left[\mu_A^L(x), \mu_A^U(x) \right]$ denotes the lower and upper extremes, respectively, of the interval $M_A(x), 0 \leq \mu_A^L(x) \leq 1, 0 \leq \mu_A^U(x) \leq 1$. The degree of uncertainty of x can be expressed as:

$$\pi_A(x) = \mu_A^U(x) - \mu_A^L(x) \qquad (3)$$

and this represents the length of the interval $M_A(x) = \left[\mu_A^L(x), \mu_A^U(x) \right]$.

Generally, reasoning in IVFCMs can be expressed as [16]:

$$c_i^{k+1} = \{[\mu_A^L(c), \mu_A^U(c)]\}_i^{k+1} = f(\{[\mu_A^L(c), \mu_A^U(c)]\}_i^k \oplus$$
$$(\overset{N}{\underset{j=1}{\oplus}} (\{[\mu_A^L(c), \mu_A^U(c)]\}_j^k \otimes \{[\mu_A^L(w), \mu_A^U(w)]\}_{ji})))$$
$$j \neq i$$

$$(4)$$

Let A and B be interval-valued fuzzy sets. The addition, subtraction and multiplication operators for A and B used in this study are based on pseudo-t-representable t-norms, see [31] for more details. Specifically, the operators used in Eq. (4) can be defined as follows:

$$A \oplus B = \{\langle x, [\min(\mu_A^L(x) + \mu_B^U(x), \mu_A^U(x) + \mu_B^L(x)), \mu_A^U(x) + \mu_B^U(x)]\rangle | x \in X\}, \quad (5)$$

$$A - B = \{\langle x, [\mu_A^L(x) - \mu_B^U(x), \max(\mu_A^L(x) - \mu_B^L(x), \mu_A^U(x) - \mu_B^U(x))]\rangle | x \in X\}, \quad (6)$$

$$A \otimes B = \{\langle x, [\mu_A^L(x) \cdot \mu_B^L(x), \max(\mu_A^L(x) \cdot \mu_B^U(x), \mu_A^U(x) \cdot \mu_B^L(x))]\rangle | x \in X\}. \quad (7)$$

3.3 PSO Learning of IVFCMs

Here we use PSO algorithm [32] to learn the weight matrix $\mathbf{W} = \{w_{ji}\}$, $j \neq i$, of an IVFCM. The traditional variant of PSO was used to obtain results comparable to those produced by different neuro-fuzzy methods. PSO is a population based stochastic optimization algorithm that finds the global best solution by adjusting the trajectory (velocity and position) of individual particle towards its best location and towards the best particle of the entire population according to the following equations:

$$v_{i,j}(t+1) = \omega_i v_{i,j}(t) + c_1 r_{1,j}[p_{i,j}(t) - x_{i,j}(t)] + c_2 r_{2,j}[p_{g,j}(t) - x_{i,j}(t)], \quad (8)$$

$$x_{i,j}(t+1) = x_{i,j}(t) + v_{i,j}(t+1), \quad (9)$$

where ω_i is the inertia weight for the i-th particle, c_1 and c_2 are constants (cognitive and social parameter, respectively), $r_{1,j}$ and $r_{2,j}$ are uniformly distributed random numbers in the range [0, 1], $p_{i,j}(t)$ is the best position of the i-th particle remembered, and $p_{g,j}(t)$ is the best swarm position. The particle velocity at any instant is usually limited to v_{max}.

The weight matrix $\mathbf{W}$ comprises $N(N-1)$ variables, where N is the number of concepts in the IVFCM. Each particle encodes a set of $2N(N-1)$ variables because both lower and upper bounds $[\mu_A^L(w_{ji}), \mu_A^U(w_{ji}),]$ have to be learned. In other words, each particle represents a candidate IVFCM. Root mean squared error (RMSE), used as the fitness function, was calculated as the difference between the actual abnormal stock return of training data y_m, $k = 1, 2, ..., M$, and output $\bar{y}_k$ predicted by the IVFCM. Sigmoid function was used as activation function f. To avoid overfitting, the number of iterations in the IVFCM reasoning was fixed and set to 10 [9]. To obtain defuzzified output $\bar{y}_k$, we adopted the approach of [33] and calculated the average of the output interval-valued fuzzy set as $\bar{y}_k = \left(\bar{y}_K^L + \bar{y}_K^U\right)/2$. As a result, the fitness function can be expressed as:

$$RMSE = \sqrt{\frac{1}{M}\sum_{m=1}^{M}\left(\bar{y}_m - y_m\right)^2}. \tag{10}$$

The PSO learning of IVFCMs can be defined as follows:

Algorithm 1.
```
Inputs: training data vectors: {c(1), c(2), ... , c(M)}, number
of concepts: N, population size: P_size
Output: optimized weight matrix: W
For (i=1 to P_size){
    x_velocity←RandomVelocity()
    x_position←RandomPosition(P_size)
    p_i←x_position
    If (RMSE(p_i)≤RMSE(p_g))
        p_g←p_i
    }
}
While(stopping condition is not satisfied){
    For (x∈P)
    x_velocity←UpdateVelocity(x_velocity, p_i, p_g)
    x_position←UpdatePosition(x_position, x_velocity)
    If (RMSE(x_position)≤RMSE(p_i))
        p_i←x_position
        If (RMSE(p_i)≤RMSE(p_g))
            p_g←p_i
        }
    }
}
return p_g - particle with the best fitness value;
```

4   Data

In this study, we used data for 1380 U.S. firms listed on the New York Stock Exchange (NYSE) or Nasdaq. To reduce the contribution of bid/ask bounce in reaction to annual report filing (10-K filing), we followed [5] and used only the firms with a reported stock price of at least 3 USD before the filing date. To reduce the effect of risk factors for stocks, we also removed firms with market capitalisation less than 100 million USD. Publicly available EDGAR system was used as the source of corporate annual reports. All data were downloaded for the year 2013. In previous literature, the log of the market capitalisation (lnMC) was an important financial determinant of abnormal stock returns [34]. We therefore collected data for this fundamental financial indicator the Marketwatch database.

To perform textual analysis of the corporate annual reports, we first extracted the most important textual source of insider information from 10-K filings, this is management discussion and analysis section. This section provides a comprehensive overview of the firm's business and financial condition from the management point of view. Increasing interest in the analysis of firm-related narratives can be partly attributed to the requirements of the U.S. Securities and Exchange Commission for electronic filings. To maintain the interpretability of the prediction system, we used dictionary-based approach to calculate overall sentiment in the texts. More precisely, a finance-specific dictionary developed by [5] was used to measure the sentiment. Following previous studies [6], we used the raw term frequency of positive and negative word categories. The overall sentiment was defined as the count of positive words minus the count of negative words, divided by the sum of both positive and negative word counts.

This study also used the readability of the texts as another input. Specifically, Gunning fog index was applied as the most commonly applied readability measure. The Gunning fog index can be calculated as $0.4 \times$ (words per sentence + percent of complex words), where complex words are words with three syllables or more.

To analyse the semantic content of the texts, we first identified top 2000 terms (without stop-words) in terms of traditional term frequency inverse document frequency weighting scheme. Then, latent semantic analysis (LSA) combined with cosine similarity was performed [35]. The LSA was carried out using singular value decomposition to transform the original feature space to a low-dimensional semantic space. Documents with the same semantic concepts can then be detected. The number of concepts was 26. The weights of these concepts were then used to calculate cosine similarity to documents separately for two classes, one with positive and the other one with negative abnormal return (note that this was performed on training data only).

Following previous studies [5, 6], abnormal returns were calculated as accumulated returns in excess of the return on the Center for Research in Security Prices equal-weighted market portfolio. In agreement with these studies, we adopted a three-day event window (prediction horizon), from day $t - 1$ to $t + 1$, where t represents the 10-K filing day. Basic descriptive statistics of the data are presented in Table 1.

Table 1. Descriptive statistics of the data.

Category	Variable	Mean ± St. Dev.
Financial	lnMC	7.82 ± 1.70
Sentiment of annual report	Overall sentiment (Sent)	−0.34 ± 0.10
Readability of annual report	Gunning fog index (Fog)	10.53 ± 0.82
Cosine distance of concepts to stocks with positive abnormal return	LSA_{pos}	0.161 ± 0.109
Cosine distance of concepts to stocks with negative abnormal return	LSA_{neg}	0.168 ± 0.105
Predicted output	Abnormal stock return in $t + 1$	0.004 ± 0.072

5 Experimental Results

PSO algorithm was used to learn the weight matrix of the IVFCM. The setting of the PSO was as follows: population size $P_{size} = 40$, cognitive parameter $c_1 = 2$, social parameter $c_2 = 2$, inertia weight $\omega_i = 0.8$, maximum particle velocity $v_{max} = 0.4$, and maximum number of function evaluations $= 20000$ as termination criteria. To avoid overfitting, all experiments were performed by using 10-fold cross-validation (90% selected as the training set, the remaining 10% used as the testing set, repeated 10 times). Hereinafter, we report RMSE and MAPE (mean absolute percentage error) on testing data. All the values of the input variables in the IVFCM were transformed to a range of [0, 1] using center of gravity defuzzification method applied to regularly distributed lower and upper Gaussian membership functions with 0.1 and 0.15 spread, respectively. For example, Fig. 1 shows these functions for the overall sentiment variable. The initial value of abnormal stock return were collected from day $t - 3$ to $t - 1$.

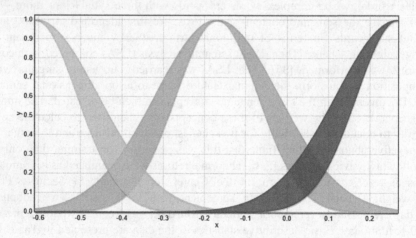

Fig. 1. Interval-valued membership functions for overall sentiment

Table 2 presents the average values of the interval-valued fuzzy weights in the trained IVFCMs. The large differences between the lower and upper bounds of the weights denote strong uncertainty in the causal relationships between LSA_{neg} and ASR (abnormal stock return) and lnMC and ASR, respectively. For the sake of inter-pretability [9], the weights in the interval [−0.1, 0.1] were not included in Table 2. In agreement with theoretical assumptions, lnMC had a strongly negative effect on ASR. Similarly, the effect of LSA_{pos} and LSA_{neg} on ASR was positive and negative, respectively. In contrast, the effect of readability (Fog) was rather weak. To demonstrate the increase in the uncertainty of the concept values, Fig. 2 shows the average values of the target concept ASR on the testing data. The increase corresponds to financial reality, as the degree of uncertainty is larger in the long run.

To compare the performance of the IVFCM-PSO, we employed conventional linear regression and three neuro-fuzzy methods with PSO learning: (1) FCM-PSO [10];

Table 2. Weight matrix of the IVFCM trained with PSO (average over 10 experiments).

	lnMC	Sent	Fog	LSA$_{pos}$	LSA$_{neg}$	ASR
lnMC				[−0.11, 0.06]	[−0.17, 0.13]	[−1.00, 0.06]
Sent	[−0.12, 0.01]		[−0.12, 0.04]		[−0.11, 0.09]	[−0.41, 0.04]
Fog				[−0.14, 0.08]		[−0.11, 0.04]
LSA$_{pos}$		[−0.15, 0.09]	[−0.02, 0.11]		[−0.26, 0.31]	[−0.06, 0.14]
LSA$_{neg}$	[−0.26, 0.11]	[−0.23, 0.08]	[−0.26, 0.12]	[−0.18, 0.15]		[−1.00, −0.26]
ASR	[−0.10, 0.11]	[−0.12, −0.04]			[−0.54, −0.05]	

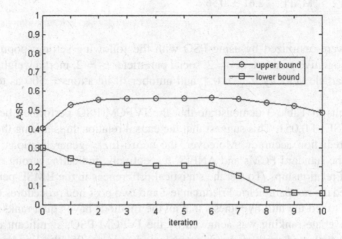

Fig. 2. Average lower and upper bounds of ASR in IVFCM iterations

(2) ANFIS-PSO [23]; and (3) intuitionistic neuro-fuzzy network (INFN-PSO) [23]. In the traditional FCM-PSO, each population comprises $N(N − 1)$ particles, thus having lower computational complexity compared with the IVFCM-PSO. In the experiments with the FCM-PSO, we used the same setting of the PSO parameters.

The ANFIS-PSO and INFN-PSO are rule-based neuro-fuzzy systems trained by using PSO. Here, we adopted the Pittsburgh approach to evolutionary-based fuzzy systems, where each particle encodes a set of M if-then rules. The PSO was used to tune the parameters of membership (and in the case of the INFN also non-membership) functions in the antecedent and parameters of the linear functions in the consequents of the if-then rules. Therefore, the dimension of each particle depends on both the length of if-then rules N and the number of if-then rules M, as each particle in the PSO comprises $M(4N + (N + 1))$ variables [23]. The learning of the ANFIS and INFN was performed in two steps. First, cluster centers (and thus also the number of membership/non-membership functions and number M of if-then rules) were found by using the subtractive clustering algorithm. To control complexity (granularity) and avoid the potential overfitting risk, we tested various numbers of membership/non-membership functions and if-then rules, $M = \{2, 3, 5, 7, 9\}$, for each training dataset. Thus, interpretability at the rule base and fuzzy partition levels was preserved. In the second step, the premise and consequent parameters of the ANFIS

Table 3. Results for the IVFCM-PSO vs. comparative methods (Mean ± St.Dev. over 10 experiments).

Method	Measure	Mean ± St. Dev.	Method	Measure	Mean ± St. Dev.
IVFCM-PSO	RMSE	0.051 ± 0.042	INFN-PSO	RMSE	0.055 ± 0.047
	MAPE	2.45 ± 0.45		MAPE	2.51 ± 0.42
FCM-PSO	RMSE	0.061 ± 0.045	Linear Regr.	RMSE	0.072 ± 0.054
	MAPE	2.52 ± 0.49		MAPE	2.79 ± 0.62
ANFIS-PSO	RMSE	0.059 ± 0.048			
	MAPE	2.61 ± 0.56			

and INFN were optimized by using PSO with the following setting: population size $P_{size} = 40$, cognitive parameter $c_1 = 2$, social parameter $c_2 = 2$, inertia weight $\omega_i = 0.8$, maximum particle velocity $v_{max} = 0.4$, and number of iterations = 500 as termination criteria.

The results in Table 3 demonstrate that the IVFCM-PSO performed best with an average RMSE of 0.051. This suggest that the causal relationships among the concepts improved prediction accuracy. Moreover, the neuro-fuzzy generalizations performed better than the standard FCMs and ANFIS, respectively, indicating strong uncertainty in the causal relationships. To test the statistical differences in the RMSE performance, we conducted the nonparametric Friedman test and two post-hoc procedures (Holm and Finner). We tested the null hypothesis that all the methods have equal ranks. Although the lowest average ranking was achieved by the IVFCM-PSO, significant differences between the evaluated methods were not detected at $p < 0.05$ (the Friedman p-value was 0.207). In the post-hoc procedures, the IVFCM-PSO was used as a control method. Significant differences at $p < 0.05$ were detected between the IVFCM-PSO and other methods by using the post-hoc procedures.

6   Conclusion

In this study, we demonstrate that the proposed novel IVFCM with PSO learning can be effectively used to the one-day-ahead prediction of abnormal stock returns. Similar to other economic and business domains, the interpretability of the relationships in terms of IVFSs is also appropriate for predicting abnormal stock returns. In addition, the degree of uncertainty increased over time, which is in agreement with financial expectations. We also demonstrate that the reasoning based on IVFSs can be for this task more effective than that based on traditional fuzzy sets or rule-based neuro-fuzzy inference systems.

Several important limitations need to be considered regarding the present study. Alternative evolutionary approaches can be used to learn FCMs. Specifically, the variants of GAs [36] and other optimization algorithms such as enhanced PSO, MA, differential evolution and artificial bee colony can be used to learn IVFCMs. Moreover, the current study only examined the learning of an IVFCM weight matrix. This may be noted as the main weakness of this study. Further experimental investigations are therefore needed to optimize the slope parameter of each sigmoid activation function. It would also be interesting to vary the IVFCM densities by using a multi-objective evolutionary algorithm. In fact, small weights can be excluded as no real-life map considers weak relationships. Finally, more complex prediction problems should be examined to investigate the scalability of IVFCMs with PSO learning.

Acknowledgments. This article was supported by the scientific research project of the Czech Sciences Foundation Grant No: 16-19590S.

References

1. Guresen, E., Kayakutlu, G., Daim, T.U.: Using artificial neural network models in stock market index prediction. Expert Syst. Appl. **38**(8), 10389–10397 (2011). https://doi.org/10.1016/j.eswa.2011.02.068
2. Chang, P.C., Liu, C.H.: A TSK type fuzzy rule based system for stock price prediction. Expert Syst. Appl. **34**(1), 135–144 (2008). https://doi.org/10.1016/j.eswa.2006.08.020
3. Majhi, R., Panda, G., Majhi, B., Sahoo, G.: Efficient prediction of stock market indices using adaptive bacterial foraging optimization (ABFO) and BFO based techniques. Expert Syst. Appl. **36**(6), 10097–10104 (2009). https://doi.org/10.1016/j.eswa.2009.01.012
4. Hadavandi, E., Shavandi, H., Ghanbari, A.: Integration of genetic fuzzy systems and artificial neural networks for stock price forecasting. Knowl. Based Syst. **23**(8), 800–808 (2010). https://doi.org/10.1016/j.knosys.2010.05.004
5. Loughran, T., Mcdonald, B.: When is a liability not a liability? Textual analysis, dictionaries, and 10-Ks. J. Fin. **66**, 35–65 (2011). https://doi.org/10.1111/j.1540-6261.2010.01625.x
6. Hajek, P.: Combining bag-of-words and sentiment features of annual reports to predict abnormal stock returns. Neural Comput. Appl. 1–16 (2017). https://doi.org/10.1007/s00521-017-3194-2
7. Hagenau, M., Liebmann, M., Neumann, D.: Automated news reading: stock price prediction based on financial news using context-capturing features. Decis. Support Syst. **55**, 685–697 (2013). https://doi.org/10.1016/j.dss.2013.02.006
8. Papageorgiou, E.I.: Learning algorithms for fuzzy cognitive maps – a review study. IEEE Trans. Syst. Man Cybern. **42**(2), 150–163 (2012). https://doi.org/10.1109/TSMCC.2011.2138694
9. Stach, W., Kurgan, L.A., Pedrycz, W., Reformat, M.: Genetic learning of fuzzy cognitive maps. Fuzzy Sets Syst. **153**(3), 371–401 (2005). https://doi.org/10.1016/j.fss.2005.01.009
10. Papageorgiou, E.I., Parsopoulos, K.E., Stylios, C.S., Groumpos, P.P., Vrahatis, M.N.: Fuzzy cognitive maps learning using particle swarm optimization. J. Intell. Inform. Syst. **25**(1), 95–121 (2005). https://doi.org/10.1007/s10844-005-0864-9
11. Acampora, G., Pedrycz, W., Vitiello, A.: A competent memetic algorithm for learning fuzzy cognitive maps. IEEE Trans. Fuzzy Syst. **23**(6), 2397–2411 (2015). https://doi.org/10.1109/TFUZZ.2015.2426311
12. Yang, X.S.: Nature-Inspired Metaheuristic Algorithms. Luniver Press, Frome (2010)
13. Mls, K., Cimler, R., Vascak, J., Puheim, M.: Interactive evolutionary optimization of fuzzy cognitive maps. Neurocomputing **232**, 58–68 (2017). https://doi.org/10.1016/j.neucom.2016.10.068
14. Salmeron, J.L., Ruiz-Celma, A., Mena, A.: Learning FCMs with multi-local and balanced memetic algorithms for forecasting industrial drying processes. Neurocomputing **232**, 52–57 (2017). https://doi.org/10.1016/j.neucom.2016.10.070

15. Chi, Y., Liu, J.: Learning of fuzzy cognitive maps with varying densities using a multiobjective evolutionary algorithm. IEEE Trans. Fuzzy Syst. **24**(1), 71–81 (2016). https://doi.org/10.1109/TFUZZ.2015.2426314

16. Hajek, P., Prochazka, O.: Interval-valued fuzzy cognitive maps for supporting business decisions. In: 2016 IEEE International Conference on Fuzzy Systems (FUZZ-IEEE), pp. 531–536. IEEE, Vancouver (2016). https://doi.org/10.1109/FUZZ-IEEE.2016.7737732

17. Salmeron, J.L.: Modelling grey uncertainty with fuzzy grey cognitive maps. Expert Syst. Appl. **37**(12), 7581–7588 (2010). https://doi.org/10.1016/j.eswa.2010.04.085

18. Papageorgiou, E., Iakovidis, D.K.: Intuitionistic fuzzy cognitive maps. IEEE Trans. Fuzzy Syst. **21**(2), 342–354 (2013). https://doi.org/10.1109/TFUZZ.2012.2214224

19. Froelich, W., Salmeron, J.L.: Evolutionary learning of fuzzy grey cognitive maps for the forecasting of multivariate, interval-valued time series. Int. J. Approx. Reason **55**(6), 1319–1335 (2014). https://doi.org/10.1016/j.ijar.2014.02.006

20. Hajek, P., Prochazka, O.: Interval-valued intuitionistic fuzzy cognitive maps for supplier selection. In: Czarnowski, I., Howlett, R.J., Jain, L.C. (eds.) IDT 2017. SIST, vol. 72, pp. 207–217. Springer, Cham (2018). https://doi.org/10.1007/978-3-319-59421-7_19

21. Pedrycz, W., Homenda, W.: From fuzzy cognitive maps to granular cognitive maps. IEEE Trans. Fuzzy Syst. **22**(4), 859–869 (2014). https://doi.org/10.1109/TFUZZ.2013.2277730

22. Salmeron, J.L., Froelich, W.: Dynamic optimization of fuzzy cognitive maps for time series forecasting. Knowl. Based Syst. **105**, 29–37 (2016). https://doi.org/10.1016/j.knosys.2016.04.023

23. Hajek, P., Olej, V.: Intuitionistic neuro-fuzzy network with evolutionary adaptation. Evol. Syst. **8**(1), 35–47 (2017). https://doi.org/10.1007/s12530-016-9157-5

24. Boyacioglu, M.A., Avci, D.: An adaptive network-based fuzzy inference system (ANFIS) for the prediction of stock market return: the case of the Istanbul stock exchange. Expert Syst. Appl. **37**(12), 7908–7912 (2010). https://doi.org/10.1016/j.eswa.2010.04.045

25. Yunusoglu, M.G., Selim, H.: A fuzzy rule based expert system for stock evaluation and portfolio construction: an application to Istanbul stock exchange. Expert Syst. Appl. **40**(3), 908–920 (2013). https://doi.org/10.1016/j.eswa.2012.05.047

26. Atsalakis, G.S., Protopapadakis, E.E., Valavanis, K.P.: Stock trend forecasting in turbulent market periods using neuro-fuzzy systems. Oper. Res. **16**(2), 245–269 (2016). https://doi.org/10.1007/s12351-015-0197-6

27. Zarandi, M.F., Rezaee, B., Turksen, I.B., Neshat, E.: A type-2 fuzzy rule-based expert system model for stock price analysis. Expert Syst. Appl. **36**(1), 139–154 (2009). https://doi.org/10.1016/j.eswa.2007.09.034

28. Liu, C.F., Yeh, C.Y., Lee, S.J.: Application of type-2 neuro-fuzzy modeling in stock price prediction. Appl. Soft Comput. **12**(4), 1348–1358 (2012). https://doi.org/10.1016/j.asoc.2011.11.028

29. Chakravarty, S., Dash, P.K.: A PSO based integrated functional link net and interval type-2 fuzzy logic system for predicting stock market indices. Appl. Soft Comput. **12**(2), 931–941 (2012). https://doi.org/10.1016/j.asoc.2011.09.013

30. Sanz, J.A., Bernardo, D., Herrera, F., Bustince, H., Hagras, H.: A compact evolutionary interval-valued fuzzy rule-based classification system for the modeling and prediction of real-world financial applications with imbalanced data. IEEE Trans. Fuzzy Syst. **23**(4), 973–990 (2015). https://doi.org/10.1109/TFUZZ.2014.2336263

31. Deschrijver, G.: Arithmetic operators in interval-valued fuzzy set theory. Inform. Sci. **177**(14), 2906–2924 (2007). https://doi.org/10.1016/j.ins.2007.02.003

32. Shi, Y., Eberhart, R.: A modified particle swarm optimizer. In: 1998 IEEE World Congress on Computational Intelligence, pp. 69–73. IEEE, Anchorage (1998). https://doi.org/10.1109/ICEC.1998.699146

33. Liang, Q., Mendel, J.M.: Interval type-2 fuzzy logic systems: theory and design. IEEE Trans. Fuzzy Syst. **8**(5), 535–550 (2000). https://doi.org/10.1109/91.873577
34. Price, S.M., Doran, J.S., Peterson, D.R., Bliss, B.A.: Earnings conference calls and stock returns: the incremental informativeness of textual tone. J. Bank Fin. **36**, 992–1011 (2012). https://doi.org/10.1016/j.jbankfin.2011.10.013
35. Egozi, O., Markovitch, S., Gabrilovich, E.: Concept-based information retrieval using explicit semantic analysis. ACM Trans. Inf. Syst. **29**, 1–34 (2011). https://doi.org/10.1145/1961209.1961211
36. Hajek, P., Prochazka, O.: Interval-valued fuzzy cognitive maps with genetic learning for predicting corporate financial distress. In: Frontiers in Artificial Intelligence and Applications (FAIA). IOS Press (2017)

Fuzzy Linguistic Labels in Multi-expert Decision Making

Alicja Mieszkowicz-Rolka(iD) and Leszek Rolka(✉)(iD)

Department of Avionics and Control, Rzeszów University of Technology,
Al. Powstańców Warszawy 8, 35-959 Rzeszów, Poland
{alicjamr,leszekr}@prz.edu.pl

Abstract. This paper presents an approach to modeling multi-expert decision systems. The proposed method is based on the idea of fuzzy linguistic label, which is suitable for analyzing real life decision-making process under uncertainty, where subjective criteria play an important role. A modified form of information system for modeling the action of a group of experts is introduced. The notions of dominating, boundary, and negative linguistic values are adopted. Furthermore, a novel definition of the fuzzy linguistic label, the measure of certainty of a linguistic label, and the compatibility function between elements of the universe and a linguistic label are given. Finally, a way of aggregating the experts' knowledge for selecting a set of objects that best fit the preference of a decision-maker is proposed. Independent vectors of preference degrees for both the attributes and their linguistic values are applied. A simple illustrating example is provided, which presents an analysis of a decision process performed by three experts.

Keywords: Information systems · Decision making · Fuzzy sets

1 Introduction

Multiple criteria decision making plays an important role in different areas of human activity. Many approaches have been proposed to obtain optimal solution, when several precisely defined criteria are taken into account. In a typical case, a single criterion is a function of several decision variables, which has to be minimized (cost criterion) or maximized (quality criterion). However, it is not always possible to formulate an objective quantitative measure of suitability in the form of an explicit mathematical function for various phenomena in real life. Evaluation and acceptance is often a matter of personal choice or feeling that can be expressed with vague linguistic terms only, such as "very attractive" or "comfortable". The fuzzy set theory [17] founded by Zadeh is a significant and successful attempt to deal with this kind of uncertainty. It has attracted interest of many researchers over recent decades. Many sophisticated extensions of the original fuzzy set concept were proposed, such as intuitionistic or hesitant fuzzy sets [1,16], which allow a refined representation of knowledge and help to achieve

© Springer International Publishing AG 2017
C. Martín-Vide et al. (Eds.): TPNC 2017, LNCS 10687, pp. 126–136, 2017.
https://doi.org/10.1007/978-3-319-71069-3_10

a more human-oriented nature of decision making. Moreover, several fuzzy-based variants of the well-known methods for multi-objective optimization, e.g., SAW, TOPSIS [3,4,6,8] were introduced.

The issue of subjective decision making becomes even more complicated, because we should, in general, consider the opinion of many human experts in order to find out a compromise or avoid taking extreme decisions. This involves the problem of discovering similarity, inconsistency, and contradiction between different decision models or information systems of particular experts. In this respect, the rough set theory [11] introduced by Pawlak seems to be a suitable tool which has been successfully combined with other methods in the form of a hybrid framework. It can also be applied to multi-criteria decision analysis, e.g., [7,15], in many works that were based on a dominance relation and preferences.

In this paper, we propose a solution of the multi-expert decision making problem, which could be classified as a fuzzy linguistic approach, e.g., [2,5,12–14]. The labeled fuzzy rough set approach, which we developed more recently [9,10], constitutes a simpler method of describing a decision model of a human expert with the help of attributes with fuzzy linguistic values. The crucial point of this method is the assumption that human experts try to build up and refine a set of fuzzy linguistic terms, which are then used for comparing and classifying all new objects or situations. Therefore, our goal is to identify an appropriate set of dominating fuzzy linguistic labels and to construct a system of consistent decision rules. Hence, we define new notions needed for extending the method to attain the ability of studying the properties of a complex of information systems obtained from a group of experts.

2   Multiple Information Systems with Fuzzy Attributes

Formal description and analysis of multi-expert decision making can be made more effectively, when we divide this process into two consecutive stages.

In the first stage, a group of experts E performs a task of evaluating particular objects from a finite universe U. The experts assign to every element x of the universe U, a value of membership degree in the linguistic values of all fuzzy attributes (criteria). Dominating linguistic values of attributes form a kind of linguistic labels, which represent the decision model of every expert.

In the second stage, a decision-maker selects a subset of certain linguistic labels obtained from the experts, and imposes a preference order on the fuzzy attributes (and their linguistic values) by applying suitable vectors of preference degrees. With the help of a ranking procedure, a set of objects is obtained that best fit the preference of the decision-maker, basing on the knowledge of experts.

By an appropriate selection of free parameters that are present in both stages of multi-expert decision making, one can meet requirements and restrictions in different real world applications.

For a given group E of experts, we define a fuzzy information system EISF of the experts group E, as a 5-tuple

$$\text{EISF} = \langle E, U, A, \mathbb{V}, f \rangle, \tag{1}$$

where:

E – is a finite set of experts,
U – is a nonempty set, called the universe,
A – is a finite set of fuzzy attributes,
$\mathbb{V}$ – is a set of fuzzy (linguistic) values of attributes, $\mathbb{V} = \bigcup_{a \in A} \mathbb{V}_a$,
    $\mathbb{V}_a$ is the set of linguistic values of an attribute $a \in A$,
f – is an information function, $f : E \times U \times \mathbb{V} \to [0, 1]$,
    $f(e, x, V) \in [0, 1]$, for all $e \in E$, $x \in U$, and $V \in \mathbb{V}$.

For every fuzzy attribute $a_i \in A$, where $i = 1, 2, \ldots, n$, we should specify a family of its linguistic values, denoted by $\mathbb{A}_i = \{A_{i1}, A_{i2}, \ldots, A_{in_i}\}$. The membership degree (in the interval $[0,1]$) of each element $x \in U$, in every linguistic value of all fuzzy attributes, will be assigned by the experts. However, this task should be performed by respecting the following requirements:

$$\exists A_{ik} \left(A_{ik} \in \mathbb{A}_i, \ \mu_{A_{ik}}(x) \geqslant 0.5 \right), \tag{2}$$

$$\text{power}\left(\mathbb{A}_i(x)\right) = \sum_{k=1}^{n_i} \mu_{A_{ik}}(x) = 1. \tag{3}$$

The requirements (2) and (3) can be perceived as a fuzzy counterpart of the properties of crisp decision systems, for which every element $x \in U$ must have a (unique) value of every attribute. In the case of fuzzy decision systems, more linguistic values are possible, and there must be a dominating linguistic value for any element $x \in U$.

Fuzzy generalization of the standard crisp rough set theory involves the issue of determining the degree of similarity between compared elements of a universe U. There are many different fuzzy connectives that can be used to this end. Moreover, there is no unique way to determine fuzzy rough approximations. This is why we introduced the labeled fuzzy rough set approach, assuming a simplified method of comparing the elements in a fuzzy information system. A human expert does not perform a comparison of objects with the help of a fuzzy similarity relation, but rather tries to assess how similar a new object is to a known prototype, which is a label that can be expressed using a tuple of linguistic values of fuzzy attributes. Therefore, the starting point of our method consists in identifying fuzzy labels used by the expert. It is necessary to find out those linguistic values of attributes, which are dominating in the decision process. In order to formally express domination of linguistic values, we use a level β which fulfills the following inequality

$$0.5 < \beta \leqslant 1. \tag{4}$$

One has to apply a suitable value of the parameter β to distinguish different kinds of linguistic values of fuzzy attributes for any element of the universe U. Given a fuzzy information system EISF, we define, for an expert $e \in E$, an element $x \in U$, and a fuzzy attribute $a \in A$, the set $\widehat{\mathbb{V}}_a(e,x) \subseteq \mathbb{V}_a$ of dominating linguistic values

$$\widehat{\mathbb{V}}_a(e,x) = \{V \in \mathbb{V}_a : f(e,x,V) \geqslant \beta\}, \tag{5}$$

the set $\overline{\overline{\mathbb{V}}}_a(e,x) \subseteq \mathbb{V}_a$ of boundary linguistic values

$$\overline{\overline{\mathbb{V}}}_a(e,x) = \{V \in \mathbb{V}_a : 0.5 \leqslant f(e,x,V) < \beta\}, \tag{6}$$

and the set $\check{\mathbb{V}}_a(e,x) \subseteq \mathbb{V}_a$ of negative linguistic values

$$\check{\mathbb{V}}_a(e,x) = \{V \in \mathbb{V}_a : 0 \leqslant f(e,x,V) < 0.5\}. \tag{7}$$

Due to the requirement (2), every element $x \in U$ can possess at most one dominating linguistic value, i.e., $\mathrm{card}\left(\widehat{\mathbb{V}}_a(e,x)\right) \leqslant 1$. By combining those positive linguistic values of attributes that are dominating for an element $x \in U$, a concise characteristic is obtained, which we call a linguistic label of the element x. For an expert $e \in E$ and a subset of fuzzy attributes $P \subseteq A$, we define the set of linguistic labels $\widehat{\mathbb{L}}^P(e,x)$ of an element $x \in U$, as the Cartesian product of the sets of dominating linguistic values $\widehat{\mathbb{V}}_p(e,x)$, for an attribute $p \in P$

$$\widehat{\mathbb{L}}^P(e,x) = \prod_{p \in P} \widehat{\mathbb{V}}_p(e,x). \tag{8}$$

For every $e \in E$, and every $x \in U$, it does hold: $\mathrm{card}\left(\widehat{\mathbb{L}}^P(e,x)\right) \leqslant 1$.

In the following, we will denote by:

- $L^P(e,x)$, the linguistic label (if it exists) for $e \in E$, and $x \in U$,
- $\mathbb{L}^P(e)$, the set of linguistic labels for $e \in E$, and for all $x \in U$,
- $\mathbb{L}^P$, the set of linguistic labels for all $e \in E$, and all $x \in U$.

Clearly, the cardinality of the set $\mathbb{L}^P(e)$ is depending on the parameter β, i.e., the number of linguistic labels belonging to the set $\mathbb{L}^P(e)$ can be restricted, when the value of β is increased.

By inspecting the decision table of a single expert $e \in E$, we determine which elements of the universe U do have a common linguistic label $L^P(e,x) \in \mathbb{L}^P(e)$. We denote by $X_{L^P}(e)$ the subset of elements of the universe U that correspond to a linguistic label $L^P \in \mathbb{L}^P(e)$, for selected fuzzy attributes $P \subseteq A$

$$X_{L^P}(e) = \{x \in U : L^P(e,x) = L^P\}. \tag{9}$$

$X_{L^P}(e)$ is called the set of characteristic elements of a linguistic label $L^P \in \mathbb{L}^P(e)$.

Any linguistic label $L^P(e, x) \in \mathbb{L}^P$ can be also represented in the form of an ordered tuple of dominating linguistic values, for all attributes $p \in P$

$$L^P(e, x) = \left(\hat{V}_{p_1}, \hat{V}_{p_2}, \ldots, \hat{V}_{p_{|P|}} \right). \tag{10}$$

For determining the resulting membership degree of $x \in U$ in the linguistic label $L^P(e, x) \in \mathbb{L}^P$, we should aggregate the membership degrees of dominating linguistic values for selected attributes. To this end, a T-norm operator, e.g., min can be used

$$\mu_{L^P(e,x)}(x) = \min \left(\mu_{\hat{V}_{p_1}}(x), \mu_{\hat{V}_{p_2}}(x), \ldots, \mu_{\hat{V}_{p_{|P|}}}(x) \right). \tag{11}$$

By calculating the membership degree for all elements of a universe U (containing N elements) in a linguistic label $L^P(e, x) \in \mathbb{L}^P$, we obtain a fuzzy similarity class denoted by $\tilde{L}^P(e, x)$

$$\tilde{L}^P(e, x) = \left\{ \mu_{L^P(e,x)}(x_1)/x_1, \mu_{L^P(e,x)}(x_2)/x_2, \ldots, \mu_{L^P(e,x)}(x_N)/x_N \right\}. \tag{12}$$

We need a measure of agreement between the experts, who may not always apply the same dominating linguistic values, when making their judgment about particular elements of the universe U. Hence, we define the certainty factor $\mathrm{cer}\left(x, L^P \right)$ of a label $L^P \in \mathbb{L}^P$, in evaluating an element $x \in U$, as follows

$$\mathrm{cer}\left(x, L^P \right) = \mathrm{card}\left(e: \ L^P(e, x) = L^P \right)/\mathrm{card}(E). \tag{13}$$

The certainty factor $\mathrm{cer}\left(x, L^P \right)$ will be equal to 1, only if all the experts regard x as characteristic element of the linguistic label L^P. When the linguistic label L^P is not used by any expert during evaluation of the element x, then the certainty factor $\mathrm{cer}\left(x, L^P \right)$ is equal to 0.

The linguistic labels which have a high value of certainty factor, constitute the most important part of the experts' knowledge. Therefore, they will be used at the second stage of decision-making for finding the most appropriate elements of the universe U. To this end, we construct a function which expresses the compatibility between an element $x \in U$ and a linguistic label. An independent threshold α, satisfying the inequality: $0.5 < \alpha \leqslant 1$, will be applied for selecting the most certain linguistic labels. Thus, we define the α-compatibility function $\mathrm{compat}_\alpha(x, L^P)$ between the element $x \in U$ and the linguistic label L^P, as follows

$$\mathrm{compat}_\alpha\left(x, L^P \right) = \mathrm{agr}_{e \in E}\left(\mu_{L^P(e,x)}(x): \ L^P(e, x) = L^P, \ \mathrm{cer}\left(x, L^P \right) \geqslant \alpha \right), \tag{14}$$

where $\mathrm{agr}_{e \in E}$ denotes an aggregation operator on the domain E.

It is open question how to choose a suitable aggregation operator. It depends on a particular application, whether one prefers to take into account the opinion of the most pessimistic expert ($\min_{e \in E}$), the most optimistic expert ($\max_{e \in E}$), or uses an averaging operator.

In the next stage, a decision-maker should specify his or her preferences concerning the linguistic values of particular attributes. For a given fuzzy attribute, we can interpret a preference degree of a linguistic value as membership in a special fuzzy set (on the domain of linguistic values), which could be called "the most preferred linguistic value".

Let us denote by pref (A_{ik}), the preference degree of the linguistic value A_{ik} of an attribute attribute $a_i \in A$, where $i = 1, 2, \ldots, n$, and $k = 1, 2, \ldots, n_i$. Furthermore, we denote by $L^P(x, a_i)$, the (dominating) linguistic value of the attribute $a_i \in A$, which appears in the tuple describing the linguistic label L^P for an element $x \in U$.

The decision-maker should also specify a vector $[w(a_1), w(a_2), \ldots, w(a_n)]$ of weights, representing preference for each fuzzy attribute, which satisfy the standard requirement imposed on weights: $\sum_{i=1}^{n} w(a_i) = 1$.

Finally, we should apply a suitable function for ranking all elements of the universe U. Certainly, there is no unique way of defining such a function. We calculate the rank of a given element $x \in U$ as follows

$$\text{rank}(x) = \text{compat}_\alpha \left(x, L^P\right) \times \text{cer} \left(x, L^P\right) \times \sum_{i=1}^{n} w(a_i) \times \text{pref} \left(L^P(x, a_i)\right). \quad (15)$$

In the formula (15), we make use of both the certainty factor of the linguistic label L^P connected with a particular $x \in U$ and the α-compatibility function between x and the linguistic label L^P.

3   Example

Let us consider a process of decision making performed by a group of three experts: $E = \{e_1, e_2, e_3\}$. They evaluate a universe of discourse consisting of six objects: $U = \{x_1, x_2, x_3, x_4, x_5, x_6\}$. The objects are described by three fuzzy attributes: $A = \{a_1, a_2, a_3\}$, and each attribute has three linguistic values. We will make use of all fuzzy attributes: $P = A$.

Table 1. Decision table of the expert e_1

	a_1			a_2			a_3		
	A_{11}	A_{12}	A_{13}	A_{21}	A_{22}	A_{23}	A_{31}	A_{32}	A_{33}
x_1	0.80	0.20	0.00	0.20	0.80	0.00	0.60	0.40	0.00
x_2	0.00	0.70	0.30	0.30	0.70	0.00	0.00	0.80	0.20
x_3	0.00	0.10	0.90	0.00	0.20	0.80	0.00	0.30	0.70
x_4	0.00	0.30	0.70	0.00	0.50	0.50	0.00	0.20	0.80
x_5	0.70	0.30	0.00	0.00	0.70	0.30	0.80	0.20	0.00
x_6	0.00	0.90	0.10	0.00	0.90	0.10	0.25	0.75	0.00

Every expert decides how to assign the membership in the linguistic values for all elements of the universe U (Tables 1, 2, and 3). Observe that the assignments of the experts satisfy the requirements (2) and (3).

In the first step, we seek out dominating linguistic values in the decision tables of all experts, and determine the linguistic labels for all elements $x \in U$. We assume a value of the level β equal to 0.55. The results are given in Tables 4, 5, and 6, which contain linguistic labels and their fuzzy similarity classes, according to the formulae (10), (11), and (12).

In the case of the expert e_1, we notice that the object x_4 is not a characteristic element of any linguistic label, because A_{22} and A_{23} are boundary linguistic values for that element. The linguistic labels (A_{11}, A_{22}, A_{31}), and (A_{12}, A_{22}, A_{32}) have two characteristic elements, whereas the linguistic label (A_{13}, A_{23}, A_{33}) has only one.

Table 2. Decision table of the expert e_2

	a_1			a_2			a_3		
	A_{11}	A_{12}	A_{13}	A_{21}	A_{22}	A_{23}	A_{31}	A_{32}	A_{33}
x_1	0.90	0.10	0.00	0.30	0.70	0.00	0.00	0.20	0.80
x_2	0.00	0.75	0.25	0.20	0.80	0.00	0.00	1.00	0.00
x_3	0.00	0.00	1.00	0.00	0.25	0.75	0.00	0.25	0.75
x_4	0.00	0.20	0.80	0.00	0.60	0.40	0.00	1.00	0.00
x_5	1.00	0.00	0.00	0.00	0.80	0.20	1.00	0.00	0.00
x_6	0.00	0.90	0.10	0.00	1.00	0.00	0.20	0.80	0.00

From the decision table of the expert e_2, we obtain five linguistic labels. By comparison with the expert e_1, we discover that x_1 is now a characteristic element of a different linguistic label: (A_{11}, A_{22}, A_{33}), and the element x_4 becomes a characteristic element of the linguistic label (A_{13}, A_{22}, A_{32}).

Table 3. Decision table of the expert e_3

	a_1			a_2			a_3		
	A_{11}	A_{12}	A_{13}	A_{21}	A_{22}	A_{23}	A_{31}	A_{32}	A_{33}
x_1	0.70	0.30	0.00	0.30	0.70	0.00	0.70	0.30	0.00
x_2	0.00	0.90	0.10	0.20	0.80	0.00	0.00	1.00	0.00
x_3	0.00	0.20	0.80	0.00	0.40	0.60	0.00	0.40	0.60
x_4	0.00	0.00	1.00	0.00	0.70	0.30	0.00	0.90	0.10
x_5	0.80	0.20	0.00	0.00	0.90	0.10	0.00	1.00	0.00
x_6	0.00	1.00	0.00	0.20	0.80	0.00	0.00	0.90	0.10

Table 4. Fuzzy similarity classes obtained for the expert e_1

	(A_{11}, A_{22}, A_{31})	(A_{12}, A_{22}, A_{32})	(A_{13}, A_{23}, A_{33})
x_1	**0.60**	0.20	0.00
x_2	0.00	**0.70**	0.00
x_3	0.00	0.10	**0.70**
x_4	0.00	0.20	0.50
x_5	**0.70**	0.20	0.00
x_6	0.00	**0.75**	0.00

Table 5. Fuzzy similarity classes obtained for the expert e_2

	(A_{11}, A_{22}, A_{31})	(A_{11}, A_{22}, A_{33})	(A_{12}, A_{22}, A_{32})	(A_{13}, A_{23}, A_{33})	(A_{13}, A_{22}, A_{32})
x_1	0.20	**0.70**	0.10	0.00	0.00
x_2	0.00	0.00	**0.75**	0.00	0.25
x_3	0.00	0.00	0.00	**0.75**	0.25
x_4	0.00	0.00	0.20	0.00	**0.60**
x_5	**0.80**	0.00	0.00	0.00	0.00
x_6	0.00	0.00	**0.80**	0.00	0.10

Table 6. Fuzzy similarity classes obtained for the expert e_3

	(A_{11}, A_{22}, A_{31})	(A_{11}, A_{22}, A_{32})	(A_{12}, A_{22}, A_{32})	(A_{13}, A_{23}, A_{33})	(A_{13}, A_{22}, A_{32})
x_1	**0.70**	0.30	0.30	0.00	0.00
x_2	0.00	0.00	**0.80**	0.00	0.10
x_3	0.00	0.00	0.20	**0.60**	0.40
x_4	0.00	0.00	0.00	0.10	**0.70**
x_5	0.00	**0.80**	0.20	0.00	0.00
x_6	0.00	0.00	**0.80**	0.00	0.00

Table 7. Characteristic elements of linguistic labels

	(A_{11}, A_{22}, A_{31})	(A_{12}, A_{22}, A_{32})	(A_{13}, A_{23}, A_{33})	(A_{13}, A_{22}, A_{32})	(A_{11}, A_{22}, A_{32})	(A_{11}, A_{22}, A_{33})
e_1	$\{x_1, x_5\}$	$\{x_2, x_6\}$	$\{x_3\}$	$\varnothing$	$\varnothing$	$\varnothing$
e_2	$\{x_5\}$	$\{x_2, x_6\}$	$\{x_3\}$	$\{x_4\}$	$\varnothing$	$\{x_1\}$
e_3	$\{x_1\}$	$\{x_2, x_6\}$	$\{x_3\}$	$\{x_4\}$	$\{x_5\}$	$\varnothing$

The expert e_3 assigns the element x_1 to the same linguistic label as the expert e_1, and x_4 to the linguistic label (A_{13}, A_{22}, A_{32}), as the expert e_2. We also get a new linguistic label (A_{11}, A_{22}, A_{32}) with the characteristic element x_5.

To facilitate a comparison of decision models of the experts, a summary of results is collected in Table 7. All the experts are in perfect agreement, when assigning objects to the linguistic labels (A_{12}, A_{22}, A_{32}), and (A_{13}, A_{23}, A_{33}).

The expert e_1 shares common characteristic elements with the other experts, for the linguistic label (A_{11}, A_{22}, A_{31}). However, we observe a strong disagreement with respect to the linguistic labels (A_{11}, A_{22}, A_{32}), and (A_{11}, A_{22}, A_{33}).

In the next step, the opinions of the experts are being aggregated for determining the compatibility between particular elements of the universe U and those linguistic labels, which have a degree of certainty factor above a threshold α. We set the value of α equal to 0.65. The operator min was chosen as the aggregation operator ($\text{agr}_{e \in E}$), in the α-compatibility function $\text{compat}_\alpha(x, L^P)$, according to the formula (14).

We observe that only the expert e_2 did not assign the element x_1 to the linguistic label $L_1 = (A_{11}, A_{22}, A_{31})$, so the certainty factor of that label, in evaluating the element x_1, is equal to 0.67. The value of the function $\text{compat}_{0.65}(x_1, L_1)$, between x_1 and L_1, is equal to 0.6. The results of analysis for all elements of the universe U are presented in Table 8.

Table 8. Compatibility between the elements $x \in U$ and selected linguistic labels

	L^P	cer x, L^P	compat_α x, L^P
x_1	$L_1 = (A_{11}, A_{22}, A_{31})$	0.67	0.60
x_2	$L_2 = (A_{12}, A_{22}, A_{32})$	1.00	0.70
x_3	$L_3 = (A_{13}, A_{23}, A_{33})$	1.00	0.70
x_4	$L_4 = (A_{13}, A_{22}, A_{32})$	0.67	0.60
x_5	$L_1 = (A_{11}, A_{22}, A_{31})$	0.67	0.70
x_6	$L_2 = (A_{12}, A_{22}, A_{32})$	1.00	0.75

As we can see, the linguistic labels (A_{11}, A_{22}, A_{32}), and (A_{11}, A_{22}, A_{33}) are missing, because a lower value of certainty factor, equal to 0.33, was obtained for them. Summarizing, four linguistic labels: L_1, L_2, L_3, and L_4, with a high level of certainty factor, can be used in further considerations.

The degrees of preference of a decision-maker, which express his or her preferences with respect to the linguistic values of particular attributes, are given in Table 9. In the case of the attribute a_1, we notice that the linguistic value A_{11} is the most preferred one, A_{12} is a significantly worse choice, whereas A_{13} is rather not acceptable.

Table 9. The degrees of preference of the linguistic values of attributes

a_1			a_2			a_3		
A_{11}	A_{12}	A_{13}	A_{21}	A_{22}	A_{23}	A_{31}	A_{32}	A_{33}
1.0	0.5	0.25	1.0	0.5	0.25	0.25	0.5	1.0

Let us assume that the vector of weights specified by the decision-maker for all used attributes is equal to [0.5 0.35 0.15]. We see that the attribute a_1 is the most important one, a_2 is slightly less important, and a_3 plays the smallest role in the decision process.

In the final step, we calculate the value of the ranking function for every element $x \in U$, with the help of the formula (15). Table 10 contains the results of ranking. The element x_6 turns out to be the most appropriate object, satisfying the preference of the decision-maker.

Table 10. Ranking of all elements $x \in U$

	rank(x)	Order of element
x_1	0.285	4
x_2	0.350	2
x_3	0.254	5
x_4	0.225	6
x_5	0.333	3
x_6	0.375	1

4   Conclusions

It is possible to describe and analyze the decision process of a group of experts basing on fuzzy linguistic labels, which have the form of tuples of dominating linguistic values of attributes. The proposed approach is straightforward and computationally not demanding. It can be implemented in real-world applications, where a set of subjective criteria is used for selecting objects according to preference of a decision-maker. In the future work, the presented approach will be further extended and combined with the most popular multi-criteria decision making methods.

References

1. Atanassov, K.T.: Intuitionistic fuzzy sets. Fuzzy Sets Syst. **20**(1), 87–96 (1986)
2. Cabrerizo, F., Pedrycz, W., Perez, I., Alonso, S., Herrera-Viedma, E.: Group decision making in linguistic contexts: an information granulation approach. Procedia Comput. Sci. **91**, 715–724 (2016). www.sciencedirect.com/science/article/pii/S1877050916312455
3. Chen, C.T.: Extensions of the TOPSIS for group decision making under fuzzy environment. Fuzzy Sets Syst. **114**, 1–9 (2000)
4. Chou, S.Y., Chang, Y.H., Shen, C.Y.: A fuzzy simple additive weighting system under group decision-making for facility location selection with objective/subjective attributes. Eur. J. Oper. Res. **189**, 132–145 (2008)

5. Chuu, S.J.: Interactive group decision-making using a fuzzy linguistic approach for evaluating the flexibility in a supply chain. Eur. J. Oper. Res. **213**(1), 279–289 (2011)
6. Deni, W., Sudana, O., Sasmita, A.: Analysis and implementation fuzzy multi-attribute decision making SAW method for selection of high achieving students in faculty level. Int. J. Comput. Sci. **10**(1), 674–680 (2013)
7. Greco, S., Matarazzo, B., Słowiński, R.: Rough sets theory for multicriteria decision analysis. Eur. J. Oper. Res. **129**, 1–47 (2001)
8. Kahraman, C., Onar, S.C., Oztaysi, B.: Fuzzy multicriteria decision-making: a literature review. Int. J. Comput. Intell. Syst. **8**(4), 637–666 (2015)
9. Mieszkowicz-Rolka, A., Rolka, L.: A novel approach to fuzzy rough set-based analysis of information systems. In: Wilimowska, Z., Borzemski, L., Grzech, A., Świątek, J. (eds.) Information Systems Architecture and Technology: Proceedings of 36th International Conference on Information Systems Architecture and Technology – ISAT 2015 – Part IV. AISC, vol. 432, pp. 173–183. Springer, Cham (2016). https://doi.org/10.1007/978-3-319-28567-2_15
10. Mieszkowicz-Rolka, A., Rolka, L.: Labeled fuzzy rough sets versus fuzzy flow graphs. In: Proceedings of the 8th International Joint Conference on Computational Intelligence, FCTA, vol. 1, pp. 115–120. SCITEPRESS Digital Library - Science and Technology Publications, Lda (2016). www.scitepress.org/DigitalLibrary
11. Pawlak, Z.: Rough Sets: Theoretical Aspects of Reasoning about Data. Kluwer Academic Publishers, Boston, Dordrecht, London (1991)
12. Rodríguez, R.M., Labella, Á., Martínez, L.: An overview on fuzzy modelling of complex linguistic preferences in decision making. Int. J. Comput. Intell. Syst. **9**(1), 81–94 (2016)
13. Rodríguez, R.M., Martínez, L.: An analysis of symbolic linguistic computing models in decision making. Int. J. Gen. Syst. **42**(1), 121–136 (2013)
14. Skorupski, J.: Interactive group decision-making using a fuzzy linguistic approach for evaluating the flexibility in a supply chain. Expert Syst. Appl. **41**, 7406–7414 (2014)
15. Sun, B., Ma, W.: Rough approximation of a preference relation by multi-decision dominance for a multi-agent conflict analysis problem. Inf. Sci. **315**, 39–53 (2015)
16. Yu, D., Zhang, W., Xu, Y.: Group decision making under hesitant fuzzy environment with application to personnel evaluation. Knowl. Based Syst. **52**, 1–10 (2013)
17. Zadeh, L.: Fuzzy sets. Inf. Control **8**, 338–353 (1965)

An Evolutionary Algorithm Based on Graph Theory Metrics for Fuzzy Cognitive Maps Learning

Katarzyna Poczeta[✉], Łukasz Kubuś, and Alexander Yastrebov

Kielce University of Technology, al. Tysiąclecia Państwa Polskiego 7,
25-314 Kielce, Poland
{k.piotrowska,l.kubus,a.jastriebow}@tu.kielce.pl

Abstract. Fuzzy cognitive map (FCM) is an effective tool for modeling dynamic decision support systems. It describes the analyzed phenomenon in the form of key concepts and causal connections between them. The main aspect of building of the FCM model is concepts selection. It is usually based on the expert knowledge. The aim of this paper is to introduce a new evolutionary algorithm for fuzzy cognitive maps learning. The proposed approach allows to select key concepts based on graph theory metrics and determine the connections between them. A simulation analysis was done with the use of synthetic and real-life data.

Keywords: Fuzzy cognitive maps · Evolutionary learning
Graph theory metrics

1 Introduction

Fuzzy cognitive map (FCM) is an effective tool for representing causal reasoning [7]. The advantage of fuzzy cognitive map is its graph-based representation. It allows to visualize the analyzed phenomenon in a clear and readable form of the collection of concepts (nodes) and causal connections (links) between them. The FCM model has the ability to describe the dynamics of the analyzed problems and can be used in a what-if analysis [1]. Fuzzy cognitive maps have been widely applied in modeling dynamic decision support systems, e.g. for decision making in radiation therapy [15], for time series prediction [5,14,19], for pattern recognition [16] or for forecasting of work of complex systems [24].

Fuzzy cognitive map can be initialized based on expert knowledge [15]. Experts determine the most significant concepts and weights of the connections between them. The second way to construct the FCM model are supervised [6] and evolutionary [2,22,23] learning algorithms that allow to determine the weights of the connections based on available data. Concepts are created for all data attributes. However, fuzzy cognitive maps with the large number of concepts are difficult to analyze and interpret. With the growth of the number of concepts, the number of connections between them that should be determined

© Springer International Publishing AG 2017
C. Martín-Vide et al. (Eds.): TPNC 2017, LNCS 10687, pp. 137–149, 2017.
https://doi.org/10.1007/978-3-319-71069-3_11

increases quadratically. So reduction of the number of concepts is very important issue that should be taken into consideration. Various approaches for reduction of fuzzy cognitive map have recently been proposed.

Concepts clustering techniques were used to merge related or similar concepts into the same cluster of nodes [13]. The resulting FCM models are easier to interpret and more readable. Homenda et al. [5] introduced a time series modeling framework based on simplifying complex FCM models using a priori nodes rejection criteria in order to achieve a reasonable balance between complexity and modeling accuracy. Selvin and Srinivasaraghavan applied the feature selection techniques to reduce the number of the input concepts of fuzzy cognitive map, however the influences of the connections between the concepts were not taken into consideration [20]. Salmeron and Froelich proposed the dynamic optimization of the FCM structure for univariate time series forecasting [19]. In [14] randomly selection of the most significant concepts and connections between them during learning process was proposed.

The aim of this paper is to introduce a new evolutionary algorithm for fuzzy cognitive maps learning that allows to select key concepts based on two metrics from the area of graph theory: the degree of the node and the total influence of the concept. The preliminary results of this approach were shown in [17]. This paper presents the improved version of the algorithm and more detailed analysis based on synthetic and real-life data. We carried out a comparison of the developed approach with the standard method for FCMs learning [22], the approach based on density evaluation [23], the approach based on system performance indicators [10] and the algorithm for random selection of FCM concepts [14]. Experiments confirm that the degree of the node and the total influence of the concept can be useful metrics to improve the learning process compared to the other techniques.

The paper is organized as follows. In Sect. 2, fuzzy cognitive maps with the selected metrics from the area of graph theory are described. Section 3 introduces the evolutionary algorithm based on graph theory metrics for fuzzy cognitive maps learning. Section 4 presents results of the experiments of the proposed approach. Finally, conclusions are covered in Sect. 5.

2   Fuzzy Cognitive Maps

Fuzzy cognitive map is a graph structure which nodes are variable concepts and edges are causal connections [7]. Model that contains n concepts is described by the n state vector X and a $n \times n$ connection matrix W. Each element $w_{j,i}$ of the matrix W determine the weight of the connection between concepts. A positive weight of the connection $w_{j,i}$ means node X_j causally increases node X_i. A negative weight of the connection $w_{j,i}$ means node X_j causally decreases node X_i. Figure 1 presents a sample FCM model to determine the risk of crisis in a country [1].

Fuzzy cognitive map is a useful tool for modeling behavior of the dynamic systems and can be used in a what-if analysis [1]. The state of the system is

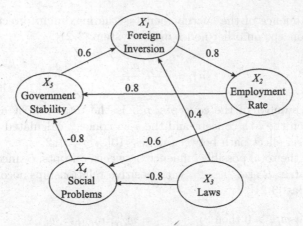

Fig. 1. Fuzzy cognitive map to determine the risk of crisis in a country

described by the vector X and contains values of the concepts at a t-th iteration. An initial state vector is required and next the values of the concepts are
calculated according to the selected dynamic model. Some of the concepts can
be determine as the output (decision) concepts and taken into account in the
analysis.

In this paper, the most commonly used dynamic model was applied [22,23]:

$$X_i(t+1) = F\left(\sum_{j=i}^{n} w_{j,i} \cdot X_j(t)\right) \tag{1}$$

where $X_i(t)$ is the value of the i-th concept at the t-th iteration, $i = 1, 2, ..., n$,
n is the number of concepts, $t = 0, 1, 2, ..., T$, T is the end time of simulation, $w_{j,i}$
is the weight of the connection between the j-th concept and the i-th concept,
taking on the values from the range $[-1, 1]$, $F(x)$ is a logistic transformation
function used to normalize values of the concepts to the range $[0, 1]$.

The advantage of fuzzy cognitive map in modeling complex systems is its
graph-based representation. Various metrics from the area of graph theory can
be used to analyze the structure and behavior of the modeled system [25]. In
this paper we analyzed two metrics: the degree of the node deg_i [4] and the total
influence of the concept inf_i [3,21].

The degree of the node (2) denotes its significance based on the number of
concepts it affects [4]:

$$deg_i = \frac{\sum_{j=1, j \neq i}^{n} \theta(w_{i,j})}{n-1},$$
$$\theta(w_{i,j}) = \begin{cases} 1, & w_{i,j} \neq 0 \\ 0, & w_{i,j} = 0 \end{cases} \tag{2}$$

where n is the number of concepts; $w_{j,i}$ is the weight of the connection between
the j-th and the i-th concept; $i, j = 1, 2, ..., n$.

The total influence of the concept denotes the maximum direct or indirect impact of the concept on other nodes in the system [3, 21]:

$$inf_i = \frac{\sum_j^n (p_{i,j})}{n} \tag{3}$$

where n is the number of the concepts, $p_{i,j}$ is the total (direct and indirect) influence between the i-th concept and the j-th concept calculated on the basis of the total causal effect path between nodes [10], $i, j = 1, 2, ..., n$.

To calculate the total possible influence between concepts, connection matrix W passes to matrix R size $2n \times 2n$ with positive relationships according to the following formulas [3, 21]:

$$\begin{aligned} &\text{if } w_{i,j} > 0 \text{ then } r_{2i-1,2j-1} = w_{i,j}, \, r_{2i,2j} = w_{i,j} \\ &\text{if } w_{i,j} < 0 \text{ then } r_{2i-1,2j} = -w_{i,j}, \, r_{2i,2j-1} = -w_{i,j} \end{aligned} \tag{4}$$

Next, operation of transitive closure of the matrix R is used [3, 21]:

$$R^* = R \vee R^2 \vee R^3 \vee ... \tag{5}$$

where $\vee$ means maximum operation, R^k is calculated according to the max-product composition:

$$R^k = R^{k-1} \circ R \tag{6}$$

Elements of the matrix R^* are transformed into elements of the matrix V [3, 21]:

$$\begin{aligned} v_{i,j} &= max(r_{2i-1,2j-1}, r_{2i,2j}) \\ v'_{i,j} &= -max(r_{2i-1,2j}, r_{2i-1,2j}) \end{aligned} \tag{7}$$

Based on the matrix V the total influence between concepts can be calculated according to the formula [3, 21]:

$$\begin{aligned} &\text{for } v_{i,j} \neq v'_{i,j} \\ p_{i,j} &= sign(v_{i,j} + v'_{i,j}) max(|v_{i,j}|, |v'_{i,j}|) \end{aligned} \tag{8}$$

3   Evolutionary Algorithm for FCMs Learning

Fuzzy cognitive map can be initialized based on expert knowledge or automatic constructed using learning algorithms and available data. The aim of the developed evolutionary algorithm for fuzzy cognitive maps learning is

- to reduce the number of concepts by selecting the most significant (key) nodes using metrics from the area of graph theory: the degree of the node and the total influence of the concept,
- to determine the weights of the connections between them,
- to approximate the input data.

The main steps of the developed algorithm for fuzzy cognitive maps learning are described below.

STEP 1. Initialize population.

First, the population of individuals is randomly initialized. Each individual is described by the vectors: W' and C. Vector W' describes values of the weights between concepts [22]:

$$W' = [w_{1,2}, ..., w_{1,n}, w_{2,1}, w_{2,3}, ..., w_{2,n}, ..., w_{n,n-1}]^T \tag{9}$$

where $w_{j,i} \in [-1, 1]$ is the weight of the connection between the j-th and the i-th concept, $i, j = 1, 2, ..., n$ and n is the number of concepts.

The second vector (10) describes the state of each concept:

$$C = [c_1, c_2, ..., c_{n,}]^T$$
$$c_i \in \{AS, IAS, AAS\} \tag{10}$$

where c_i is the state of the i-th concept and n is the number of concepts.

Each concept can be in one of the three states: active (AS), inactive (IAS) and always active (AAS). The proposed solution requires determination of the output (decision) concepts. Each output concept is always active. This mean, that obtained model always contains decision concepts. The concepts with states: AS and AAS make a collection of key concepts.

During the first step, the elements of the W' vector are initialized with the random values form the interval $[-1, 1]$. The state for each node is active for all individuals in the initial population. For this reason, the elements of the C vector are equal to AAS for the output concepts and AS for the other concepts.

STEP 2. Select key concepts.

Each individual in the population is decoded into the candidate FCM and next the selected graph theory metrics are calculated. The most significant concepts (key concepts) are selected in two ways: based on the degree of the node and based on the total influence of the concept.

1. Key concepts are selected based on the degree of the node (DEG).
   Values of the degree are calculated for each node (excluding output concepts) in the candidate FCM. Next, the state of each node is modified according to the following formula:

$$\text{if } deg_i \leq a \text{ then } c_i = \text{IAS}$$
$$\text{else } c_i = \text{AS} \tag{11}$$

where $i = 1, 2, ..., n$, n is the number of the concepts; a is a parameter determining an intensity of reduction of the number of concepts, it is selected experimentally, $a > 0$.
2. Key concepts are selected based on the total influence of each concept (INF).
   Values of the total influence are calculated for each concept (excluding output

concepts) in the candidate FCM. Next, the state of each node is modified according to the following formula:

$$\text{if } inf_i \le a \text{ then } c_i = \text{IAS} \\ \text{else } c_i = \text{AS} \qquad (12)$$

where $i = 1, 2, ..., n$, n is the number of the concepts; a is a parameter determining an intensity of reduction of the number of concepts, it is selected experimentally, $a > 0$.

In order to compare the proposed approach for concepts selection based on graph theory metrics, a random selection was implemented similar to [14] (RND). In this approach, the state of each concept can be changed with a certain probability described by the parameter a. The value of this parameter is in the range $(0, 1)$.

STEP 3. Evaluate population.

The fitness function evaluates the candidate FCM based on its ability to approximate the input data and is described as follows:

$$fitness(Error) = -Error \qquad (13)$$

where $Error$ is the objective function signifying the learning data error calculated for the output concepts:

$$Error = \sum_{t=1}^{T} \sum_{i=1}^{n_d} |Z_i(t) - X_i(t)| \qquad (14)$$

where $X_i(t)$ is the value of the i-th output concept at iteration t of the candidate FCM, $Z_i(t)$ is the value of the i-th output concept at iteration t in the input data, $t = 0, 1, 2, ..., T$, T is the input data length, $i = 1, ..., n_d$ and n_d is the number of the output concepts.

STEP 4. Check stop condition.

If the number of current generation is greater than $generation_{max}$ then the learning process is stopped.

STEP 5. Select new population.

The temporary population is created from a current base population using roulette-wheel selection with dynamic linear scaling of the fitness function. Additionally, elite strategy is applied [11].

STEP 6. Apply genetic operators.

To receive a new generation one of the most popular algorithms in fuzzy cognitive maps learning: Real-Coded Genetic Algorithm (RCGA) [11] and the developed Individually Directed Evolutionary Algorithm (IDEA) were used [9]. The genetic operators were applied only to the W' vector. For the RCGA method an uniform crossover and non-uniform mutation were used. For the IDEA algorithm a directed non-uniform mutation was applied.

STEP 7. Analyze population.

The values of weights from the interval $[-0.05, 0.05]$ are rounded down to 0 as suggested in [22]. Next the potential solutions are analyzed according to the previously developed approach [10]. Values of the total influence between concepts $p_{j,i}$ are calculated. If the value of $p_{j,i}$ is in the interval $[-0.1, 0.1]$, the corresponding weight value $w_{j,i}$ is rounded down to 0. Go to STEP 2.

STEP 8. Choose the best individual and calculate evaluation criteria.

To evaluate performance of the developed algorithm, we used two criteria that are commonly used in fuzzy cognitive maps learning:

1. Initial error allowing calculation of similarity between the input learning data and the data generated by the FCM model for the same initial state vector:

$$initial_{error} = \frac{1}{T \cdot n_d} \sum_{t=1}^{T} \sum_{i=1}^{n_d} |Z_i(t) - X_i(t)| \qquad (15)$$

where $X_i(t)$ is the value of the i-th decision concept at iteration t of the candidate FCM, $Z_i(t)$ is the value of the i-th decision concept at iteration t of the input model, $t = 0, 1, 2, ..., T$, T is the input data length, $i = 1, ..., n_d$, n_d is the number of decision concepts.

2. Behavior error evaluating generalization capabilities of the candidate FCM. It enables calculation of similarity between the input testing data and the data generated by the FCM model for the same initial state vectors:

$$behavior_{error} = \frac{1}{P \cdot T \cdot n_d} \sum_{p=1}^{P} \sum_{t=1}^{T} \sum_{i=1}^{n_d} |Z_i^p(t) - X_i^p(t)| \qquad (16)$$

where $X_i^p(t)$ is the value of the i-th decision concept at iteration t of the candidate FCM started from the p-th initial state vector, $Z_i^p(t)$ is the value of the i-th decision concept at iteration t of the input model started form the p-th initial state vector, $i = 1, ..., n_d$, n_d is the number of decision concepts, $p = 1, 2, ..., P$, P is the number of initial testing state vectors.

4 Experiments

The experiments were performed in order to analyze the performance of the proposed approach for fuzzy cognitive maps learning. Similarly as in [2,10,22,23] we used synthetic and real-life models to generate the input data, which are next used by the learning process to determine the weights of the connections. The evaluation was done based on the number of concepts n_c, $initial_{error}$ and $behavior_{error}$ calculated for the candidate FCMs. The learning process was done with the use of the RCGA and the IDEA algorithms. We carried out a comparison of the developed approach based on the degree of the node (DEG) and the total influence of the concept (INF) with other methods for learning FCMs: the standard approach (STD) [22], the approach based on density evaluation (DEN) [23], the approach based on system performance indicators (SPI) [10] and the algorithm for random selection of FCM concepts (RND) [14].

4.1   Data Sets

Synthetic data were obtained based on 3 randomly generated FCM models: with 5 concepts (1 output concept) and density 30% (S1), with 10 concepts (2 output concepts) and density of 30% (S2), with 20 concepts (3 output concepts) and density of 30% (S3).

Real-life data were obtained on the basis of three fuzzy cognitive maps reported in literature [8,12,18]. The first model is a decision support system in radiotherapy (R1) [12]. It contains 16 concepts: the factor-concepts, that represent the depth of tumor, the size of tumor, the shape of tumor, the type of the irradiation and the amount of patient thickness irradiated, the selector-concepts, representing size of radiation field, multiple field arrangements, beam directions, dose distribution from each field, stationery vs. rotation-isocentric beam therapy, field modification, patient immobilizing and use of 2D or 3D conformal technique, respectively and the three output-concepts: dose given to treatment volume, amount of irradiated volume of healthy tissues and amount of irradiated volume of sensitive organs. The next fuzzy cognitive map is a notional model for the evaluation of mining jurisdiction investment favorability (R2) [18]. It contains 12 concepts: national gov. stability, regional gob. stability, support for mining industry, workforce education, workforce skills/experience, infrastructure availability, permitting delays, gov. royalty rates, tax rates, environmental activism, union activism and output node investment favorability. The last map for modeling the behavior of soldiers (R3) consists of 10 concepts: cluster, proximity of enemy, receive fire, presence of authority, fire weapons, peer visibility, spread out, take cover, advance and fatigue [8]. Nodes: fire weapons, take cover and advance were chosen as the output concepts.

The input data for the learning process were generated starting from the one random initial state vector for every FCM model. The resulting fuzzy cognitive maps were tested on the basis of 10 testing state vectors ($P = 10$) and evaluated with the use of criteria (15), (16) and the number of concepts n.

4.2   Learning Parameters

The learning parameters were chosen experimentally based on the minimization of the average values of the initial and behavior error. The following parameters were used in simulations presented in the paper:

- the population size equal 100 and the maximum number of generations equal 100,
- RCGA: the number of elite individuals: 10, crossover probability: 0.75, mutation probability: 0.01,
- IDEA: mutation probability: $\frac{1}{n^2-n}$.

Additionally, we analyzed the parameter a that is responsible for the intensity of the concepts reduction. Results for the $a = 0.1$ (RND I, DEG I, INF I), $a = 0.2$ (RND II, DEG II, INF II) and $a = 0.3$ (RND III, DEG III, INF III) were presented.

Table 1. Average results with synthetic data

Approach	n_c Avg	$initial_{error}$ Avg ± Std	$behavior_{error}$ Avg ± Std	n_c Avg	$initial_{error}$ Avg ± Std	$behavior_{error}$ Avg ± Std
S1	IDEA			RCGA		
STD	5	0.0084 ± 0.0016	0.0107 ± 0.0038	5	0.0059 ± 0.0015	0.0079 ± 0.0026
DEN	5	**0.0051 ± 0.0014**	**0.0051 ± 0.0014**	5	0.0048 ± 0.0017	0.0046 ± 0.0031
SPI	5	0.0078 ± 0.0023	0.0086 ± 0.0033	5	0.0068 ± 0.0027	0.0085 ± 0.0054
RND I	4.4	0.0063 ± 0.0014	0.0079 ± 0.0020	4.5	**0.0041 ± 0.0007**	**0.0042 ± 0.0014**
DEG I	4.2	0.0061 ± 0.0017	0.0072 ± 0.0037	4.9	0.0046 ± 0.0016	0.0048 ± 0.0030
INF I	4.2	0.0052 ± 0.0018	0.0063 ± 0.0043	3.7	0.0054 ± 0.0021	0.0050 ± 0.0022
RND II	4.2	0.0063 ± 0.0010	0.0069 ± 0.0022	4.5	0.0043 ± 0.0008	0.0045 ± 0.0016
DEG II	4.4	0.0052 ± 0.0016	0.0053 ± 0.0029	4.8	0.0046 ± 0.0013	0.0044 ± 0.0013
INF II	3.5	0.0077 ± 0.0022	0.0081 ± 0.0035	3.3	0.0068 ± 0.0023	0.0072 ± 0.0038
RND III	4.1	0.0065 ± 0.0018	0.0071 ± 0.0023	4.6	**0.0041 ± 0.0007**	0.0051 ± 0.0019
DEG III	3.1	0.0066 ± 0.0028	0.0074 ± 0.0047	4	0.0052 ± 0.0012	0.0051 ± 0.0023
INF III	3.5	0.0085 ± 0.0029	0.0094 ± 0.0042	3.1	0.0072 ± 0.0024	0.0085 ± 0.0051
S2	IDEA			RCGA		
STD	10	0.0141 ± 0.0028	0.0157 ± 0.0035	10	0.0121 ± 0.0025	0.0164 ± 0.0043
DEN	10	0.0095 ± 0.0009	0.0096 ± 0.0010	10	0.0079 ± 0.0010	0.0083 ± 0.0015
SPI	10	0.0090 ± 0.0017	0.0099 ± 0.0024	10	0.0073 ± 0.0014	0.0073 ± 0.0016
RND I	7.7	0.0120 ± 0.0017	0.0153 ± 0.0029	7.2	0.0093 ± 0.0021	0.0109 ± 0.0032
DEG I	9.6	0.0097 ± 0.0014	0.0098 ± 0.0016	10	0.0074 ± 0.0021	0.0088 ± 0.0026
INF I	9.2	0.0111 ± 0.0018	0.0109 ± 0.0024	7.1	0.0085 ± 0.0010	0.0081 ± 0.0013
RND II	6.7	0.0131 ± 0.0019	0.0128 ± 0.0028	6.5	0.0086 ± 0.0018	0.0104 ± 0.0030
DEG II	8.1	0.0089 ± 0.0014	0.0093 ± 0.0023	9.3	0.0066 ± 0.0010	0.0072 ± 0.0019
INF II	8	0.0099 ± 0.0015	0.0097 ± 0.0020	5.9	0.0082 ± 0.0015	0.0081 ± 0.0017
RND III	7.1	0.0129 ± 0.0015	0.0149 ± 0.0031	6.6	0.0091 ± 0.0020	0.0103 ± 0.0022
DEG III	6	**0.0083 ± 0.0018**	**0.0085 ± 0.0022**	8.7	**0.0060 ± 0.0014**	**0.0062 ± 0.0013**
INF III	7.1	0.0101 ± 0.0014	0.0099 ± 0.0026	5.5	0.0076 ± 0.0013	0.0075 ± 0.0016
S3	IDEA			RCGA		
STD	20	0.0299 ± 0.0048	0.0342 ± 0.0065	20	0.0259 ± 0.0030	0.0312 ± 0.0039
DEN	20	0.0187 ± 0.0035	0.0216 ± 0.0029	20	0.0158 ± 0.0021	**0.0189 ± 0.0027**
SPI	20	0.0181 ± 0.0038	0.0211 ± 0.0033	20	0.0164 ± 0.0016	0.0208 ± 0.0024
RND I	14.1	0.0222 ± 0.0022	0.0264 ± 0.0042	11.7	0.0219 ± 0.0030	0.0255 ± 0.0048
DEG I	19.5	0.0176 ± 0.0024	0.0222 ± 0.0031	19.9	0.0157 ± 0.0023	0.0204 ± 0.0029
INF I	19.7	0.0195 ± 0.0019	0.0195 ± 0.0023	18.8	0.0151 ± 0.0023	0.0203 ± 0.0026
RND II	12	0.0225 ± 0.0031	0.0260 ± 0.0054	12.4	0.0253 ± 0.0025	0.0285 ± 0.0041
DEG II	15.5	0.0172 ± 0.0040	0.0197 ± 0.0035	19.1	**0.0145 ± 0.0017**	0.0192 ± 0.0028
INF II	19.4	0.0204 ± 0.0023	0.0214 ± 0.0043	19.4	0.0149 ± 0.0023	0.0205 ± 0.0033
RND III	13	0.0250 ± 0.0032	0.0280 ± 0.0057	11.8	0.0260 ± 0.0028	0.0301 ± 0.0039
DEG III	12.1	**0.0158 ± 0.0023**	**0.0191 ± 0.0025**	16.3	0.0152 ± 0.0021	0.0194 ± 0.0029
INF III	18.5	0.0180 ± 0.0034	0.0207 ± 0.0040	19.5	0.0156 ± 0.0025	0.0198 ± 0.0029

Table 2. Average results with real-life data

Approach	n_c Avg	$initial_{error}$ Avg ± Std	$behavior_{error}$ Avg ± Std	n_c Avg	$initial_{error}$ Avg ± Std	$behavior_{error}$ Avg ± Std
S1	IDEA			RCGA		
STD	16	0.0131 ± 0.0017	0.0138 ± 0.0019	16	0.0104 ± 0.0010	0.0131 ± 0.0020
DEN	16	0.0107 ± 0.0021	0.0096 ± 0.0016	16	**0.0083** ± 0.0011	0.0091 ± 0.0012
SPI	16	0.0106 ± 0.0020	0.0108 ± 0.0013	16	0.0088 ± 0.0016	0.0096 ± 0.0015
RND I	10.4	0.0113 ± 0.0018	0.0114 ± 0.0022	10.2	0.0117 ± 0.0020	0.0116 ± 0.0019
DEG I	15.9	0.0099 ± 0.0021	0.0099 ± 0.0015	16	0.0096 ± 0.0011	0.0098 ± 0.0015
INF I	15.9	0.0105 ± 0.0031	0.0104 ± 0.0022	15.7	0.0088 ± 0.0013	0.0097 ± 0.0012
RND II	11.2	0.0119 ± 0.0019	0.0117 ± 0.0021	10.6	0.0131 ± 0.0016	0.0136 ± 0.0012
DEG II	14.8	0.0168 ± 0.0231	0.0168 ± 0.0240	16	0.0085 ± 0.0016	0.0101 ± 0.0013
INF II	15.8	**0.0092** ± 0.0011	**0.0095** ± 0.0015	15	0.0090 ± 0.0013	0.0091 ± 0.0012
RND III	10.9	0.0143 ± 0.0016	0.0127 ± 0.0014	10	0.0136 ± 0.0018	0.0135 ± 0.0016
DEG III	13.7	0.0183 ± 0.0289	0.0196 ± 0.0291	14.8	0.0087 ± 0.0011	0.0092 ± 0.0009
INF III	15.7	0.0101 ± 0.0014	0.0099 ± 0.0018	15.1	0.0086 ± 0.0018	**0.0090** ± 0.0019
R2	IDEA			RCGA		
STD	12	0.0147 ± 0.0029	0.0133 ± 0.0038	12	0.0079 ± 0.0021	0.0118 ± 0.0044
DEN	12	0.0089 ± 0.0013	0.0095 ± 0.0038	12	0.0050 ± 0.0011	0.0069 ± 0.0028
SPI	12	0.0096 ± 0.0020	0.0100 ± 0.0041	12	0.0059 ± 0.0014	0.0079 ± 0.0015
RND I	7.5	0.0091 ± 0.0024	0.0104 ± 0.0031	7.6	0.0051 ± 0.0010	0.0075 ± 0.0010
DEG I	10.2	0.0089 ± 0.0009	0.0099 ± 0.0018	12	**0.0046** ± 0.0017	0.0069 ± 0.0012
INF I	11	0.0097 ± 0.0027	0.0096 ± 0.0030	8.3	0.0067 ± 0.0016	0.0077 ± 0.0021
RND II	7.5	0.0085 ± 0.0019	0.0117 ± 0.0032	7.7	0.0057 ± 0.0010	0.0083 ± 0.0023
DEG II	8.5	0.0091 ± 0.0018	0.0106 ± 0.0042	11.7	0.0057 ± 0.0014	0.0066 ± 0.0011
INF II	10.6	0.0084 ± 0.0018	**0.0089** ± 0.0025	7.3	0.0072 ± 0.0016	0.0083 ± 0.0010
RND III	7.2	**0.0075** ± 0.0025	0.0090 ± 0.0019	7.5	0.0055 ± 0.0012	0.0071 ± 0.0017
DEG III	6.6	0.0091 ± 0.0020	0.0093 ± 0.0015	11.1	0.0057 ± 0.0013	**0.0061** ± 0.0015
INF III	9	0.0086 ± 0.0013	0.0099 ± 0.0025	8.7	0.0076 ± 0.0017	0.0086 ± 0.0028
R3	IDEA			RCGA		
STD	10	0.0170 ± 0.0025	0.0214 ± 0.0025	10	0.0165 ± 0.0022	0.0212 ± 0.0027
DEN	10	0.0134 ± 0.0016	0.0178 ± 0.0017	10	**0.0124** ± 0.0015	0.0179 ± 0.0029
SPI	10	0.0153 ± 0.0018	0.0195 ± 0.0019	10	0.0127 ± 0.0007	**0.0177** ± 0.0017
RND I	7.3	0.0161 ± 0.0017	0.0208 ± 0.0020	7.4	0.0163 ± 0.0026	0.0219 ± 0.0019
DEG I	9.6	**0.0130** ± 0.0007	**0.0176** ± 0.0013	10	0.0126 ± 0.0009	0.0179 ± 0.0012
INF I	9	0.0147 ± 0.0016	0.0194 ± 0.0019	7.1	0.0128 ± 0.0008	0.0179 ± 0.0012
RND II	7.7	0.0168 ± 0.0019	0.0205 ± 0.0018	6.9	0.0156 ± 0.0014	0.0202 ± 0.0022
DEG II	8.5	0.0135 ± 0.0013	0.0189 ± 0.0010	9.4	0.0125 ± 0.0010	0.0181 ± 0.0008
INF II	8.3	0.0140 ± 0.0016	0.0189 ± 0.0019	6.5	0.0130 ± 0.0006	0.0179 ± 0.0010
RND III	7.2	0.0159 ± 0.0018	0.0212 ± 0.0030	6.6	0.0167 ± 0.0017	0.0221 ± 0.0030
DEG III	6.7	0.0140 ± 0.0010	0.0190 ± 0.0018	8.9	**0.0124** ± 0.0010	0.0183 ± 0.0017
INF III	8.3	0.0140 ± 0.0011	0.0190 ± 0.0022	5.4	0.0137 ± 0.0007	0.0185 ± 0.0010

4.3 Results

Table 1 presents the average results of the experiments with the synthetic data: the number of concepts for the resulted FCM models n_c, the initial and the behavior error. The columns with the number of concepts n_c and the initial error were averaged over the 10 experiments performed for every set of the learning parameters, whereas the behavior error was additionally averaged over the 10 simulations performed with different initial state vectors. The highlighted values in bold show the best average values of the initial and behavior error obtained for the analyzed FCM models. For the first map S1, the proposed approaches allowed to slightly reduce the number of nodes keeping similar level of the initial and behavior error. However, for larger FCM models S2 and S3, in most of the cases the methods of concepts selection based on the degree of the node (DEG) and the total influence of the concepts (INF) reduced the number of concepts n_c giving the lowest or very close to the lowest values of initial and behavior error.

Table 2 summarizes the average results of the experiments with the real-life data. In most of the cases, the standard approaches (STD, DEN, SPI) and the approach based on random selection of key concepts (RND) gave higher errors than the developed algorithms (DEG, INF). The appropriate determination of the parameter a allows to control the number of removed nodes and obtain some compromise between the number of concepts (n_c) and data errors ($initial_{error}$ and $behavior_{error}$).

5 Conclusion

This paper presents the evolutionary algorithm for fuzzy cognitive maps learning. Graph theory metrics: the degree of the node and the total influence of the concepts were used to select key concepts during learning process. The RCGA and IDEA were used to determine the weights of the connections between concepts. Experiments were performed on the basis of synthetic and real-life data. The obtained results confirm that the degree of the node and the total influence of the concept can be useful metrics to improve the learning process compared to the standard approach based on all available concepts or the approach based on random selection of the concepts. The developed approach allows to reduce the number of concepts of the FCM model and determine the weights of the connections between them keeping the lowest or very close to the lowest values of the initial error and the behavior error. We plan to continue analysis of the developed approach using historical data.

References

1. Aguilar, J.: Dynamic random fuzzy cognitive maps. Computación y Sistemas **7**(4), 260–270 (2004)
2. Ahmadi, S., Forouzideh, N., Alizadeh, S., Papageorgiou, E.I.: Learning fuzzy cognitive maps using imperialist competitive algorithm. Neural Comput. Appl. **26**(6), 1333–1354 (2015)
3. Borisov, V.V., Kruglov, V.V., Fedulov, A.C.: Fuzzy Models and Networks. Publishing House Telekom, Moscow (2004). (in Russian)
4. Christoforou, A., Andreou, A.S.: A framework for static and dynamic analysis of multi-layer fuzzy cognitive maps. Neurocomputing **232**, 133–145 (2017)
5. Homenda, W., Jastrzebska, A., Pedrycz, W.: Nodes selection criteria for fuzzy cognitive maps designed to model time series. In: Filev, D., et al. (eds.) Intelligent Systems'2014. AISC, vol. 323, pp. 859–870. Springer, Cham (2015). https://doi.org/10.1007/978-3-319-11310-4_75
6. Jastriebow, A., Poczęta, K.: Analysis of multi-step algorithms for cognitive maps learning. Bullet. Polish Acad. Sci. Tech. Sci. **62**(4), 735–741 (2014)
7. Kosko, B.: Fuzzy cognitive maps. Int. J. Man Mach. Stud. **24**(1), 65–75 (1986)
8. Kosko, B.: Fuzzy Engineering. Prentice-Hall, Englewood Cliffs (1997)
9. Kubuś, Ł.: Individually directional evolutionary algorithm for solving global optimization problems - comparative study. IJISA **7**(9), 12–19 (2015)
10. Kubuś, Ł., Poczęta, K., Yastrebov, A.: A new learning approach for fuzzy cognitive maps based on system performance indicators. In: 2016 IEEE International Conference on Fuzzy Systems, Vancouver, Canada, pp. 1398–1404 (2016)
11. Michalewicz, Z.: Genetic Algorithms + Data Structures = Evolution Programs. Springer, Heidelberg (1996). https://doi.org/10.1007/978-3-662-03315-9
12. Papageorgiou, E.: A novel approach on constructed dynamic fuzzy cognitive maps using fuzzified decision trees and knowledge-extraction techniques. In: Glykas, M. (ed.) Fuzzy Cognitive Maps: Advances in Theory. Methodologies, Tools and Applications, pp. 43–70. Springer, Heidelberg (2010). https://doi.org/10.1007/978-3-642-03220-2_3
13. Papageorgiou, E.I., Hatwágner, M.F., Buruzs, A., Kóczy, L.T.: A concept reduction approach for fuzzy cognitive map models in decision making and management. Neurocomputing **232**, 16–33 (2017)
14. Papageorgiou, E.I., Poczeta, K.: A two-stage model for time series prediction based on fuzzy cognitive maps and neural networks. Neurocomputing **232**, 113–121 (2017)
15. Papageorgiou, E.I., Stylios, C.D., Groumpos, P.P.: An integrated two-level hierarchical system for decision making in radiation therapy based on fuzzy cognitive maps. IEEE Trans. Biomed. Eng. **50**(12), 1326–1339 (2003)
16. Papakostas, G.A., Boutalis, Y.S., Koulouriotis, D.E., Mertzios, B.G.: Fuzzy cognitive maps for pattern recognition applications. Int. J. Pattern Recognit. Artif. Intell. **22**(8), 1461–1468 (2008)
17. Poczeta, K., Kubuś, Ł., Yastrebov, A.: concepts selection in fuzzy cognitive map using evolutionary learning algorithm based on graph theory metrics. In: FedCSIS 2017 (2017)
18. Rickard, J.T., Aisbett, J., Yager, R.R.: A new fuzzy cognitive map structure based on the weighted power mean. IEEE Trans. Fuzzy Syst. **23**(6), 2188–2201 (2015)
19. Salmeron, J.L., Froelich, W.: Dynamic optimization of fuzzy cognitive maps for time series forecasting. Knowl. Based Syst. **105**, 29–37 (2016)

20. Selvin, N.N., Srinivasaraghavan, A.: Dimensionality reduction of inputs for a fuzzy cognitive map for obesity problem. In: 2016 International Conference on Inventive Computation Technologies (ICICT) (2016)

21. Silov, V.B.: Strategic decision-making in a fuzzy environment. INPRO-RES, Moscow (1995). (in Russian)

22. Stach, W., Kurgan, L., Pedrycz, W., Reformat, M.: Genetic learning of fuzzy cognitive maps. Fuzzy Sets Syst. **153**(3), 371–401 (2005)

23. Stach, W., Pedrycz, W., Kurgan, L.A.: Learning of fuzzy cognitive maps using density estimate. IEEE Trans. Syst. Man Cybern. Part B **42**(3), 900–912 (2012)

24. Słoń, G.: Application of models of relational fuzzy cognitive maps for prediction of work of complex systems. In: Rutkowski, L., Korytkowski, M., Scherer, R., Tadeusiewicz, R., Zadeh, L.A., Zurada, J.M. (eds.) ICAISC 2014. LNCS (LNAI), vol. 8467, pp. 307–318. Springer, Cham (2014). https://doi.org/10.1007/978-3-319-07173-2_27

25. Wilson, R.J.: An Introduction to Graph Theory. Pearson Education, Delhi (1970)

Fuzzy Petri Nets with Linear Orders for Intervals

Zbigniew Suraj$^{(\boxtimes)}$ and Piotr Grochowalski

Chair of Computer Science, University of Rzeszów, Rzeszów, Poland
{zbigniew.suraj,piotrg}@ur.edu.pl

Abstract. Recently, an extended class of generalized fuzzy Petri nets (*GFP*-nets) called type-2 generalized fuzzy Petri nets (*T2GFP*-nets) were proposed. This class extends the existing *GFP*-nets by introducing a triple of operators (In, Out_1, Out_2) in a *T2GFP*-net in the form of interval triangular norms, which are supposed to function as substitute for the triangular norms in *GFP*-nets. In this paper we enrich the *T2GFP*-net model by adding to it instead of the usual partial order relation between interval numbers some of the most used examples of total orders that appear in the literature. This addition has significant influence on extending the use of *T2GFP*-nets in many different fields. In particular, the proposed approach can be used in intelligent control design, approximate reasoning, decision making or classification.

Keywords: Fuzzy Petri nets · Decision making · Classification
Approximate reasoning · Expert systems

1 Introduction

Petri nets are being widely accepted by the research community for modeling and simulation of a broad class of systems. As a computational paradigm for intelligent systems, they provide a graphical language to visualize, communicate and interpret engineering problems [3].

In 1988, Looney proposed in [6] so called fuzzy Petri nets. In his model logical propositions can be associated with Petri nets allowing for logical reasoning about the modeled system and its behavior. The application of fuzzy Petri nets includes the design and implementation of decision support systems. In particular, they can be used for knowledge representation and modeling of reasoning processes in such systems. In this class of Petri net models not only crisp but also imprecise, vague and uncertain information is admissible and taken into account. Several authors have proposed different classes of fuzzy Petri nets [2,5,11,14,15]. These models are based on different approaches combining Petri nets and fuzzy sets introduced by Zadeh in 1965 [17].

In 2013, the generalized fuzzy Petri nets (*GFP*-nets) were proposed [14]. However, an extended class of *GFP*-nets called generalized fuzzy Petri nets of type 2 (*T2GFP*-nets) is provided in the paper [15]. *T2GFP*-nets extend the existing generalized fuzzy Petri nets by introducing a triple of operators (In, Out_1, Out_2)

© Springer International Publishing AG 2017
C. Martín-Vide et al. (Eds.): TPNC 2017, LNCS 10687, pp. 150–161, 2017.
https://doi.org/10.1007/978-3-319-71069-3_12

in a *T2GFP*-net in the form of interval triangular norms, which are supposed to function as substitute for the t-norms and s-norms operators in *GFP*-nets. Therefore the *T2GFP*-net model gives a faithful extension of the *GFP*-net one as in the former class the user has the chance to define the input/output operators being interval triangular norms. Moreover, this extension has significant influence on presentation and analysis of the modeled system by the *T2GFP*-nets on generalized level abstraction. The choice of suitable operators for the modeled system in more generalized form is very important, especially in systems described by incomplete, imprecise and/or vague information using fuzzy sets. In classical situation a fuzzy set is defined in terms of a function from a universe to the unit interval [0,1]. That is, the membership of each element belonging to a fuzzy set is a single value between 0 and 1. In practical applications, there is also a need to represent the membership of an element by using a fuzzy set in [0,1], instead of a single value. The *T2GFP*-net model gives such possibility. Nevertheless, in general, some interval numbers can be incomparable by means of the usual partial order which was used in the definition of *T2GFP*-nets presented in the paper [15]. In order to avoid such situation, we enrich the *T2GFP*-net model by adding to it instead of the usual partial order relation between interval numbers some of the most used examples of total orders that appear in the literature [1]. This addition has significant influence on extending the use of *T2GFP*-nets in many different fields such as intelligent control design [10], decision making [5] or classification [13].

The structure of this paper is the following: we start with some preliminaries and, in Sect. 3, we present the main result of the paper, including an extension of the *T2GFP*-net model. Then, in Sect. 4, we present both a method for transforming production rules into a *T2GFP*-net as well as an algorithm for construction of a *T2GFP*-net on the base of a set of production rules. Next, an example coming from the domain of train traffic control illustrating our methodology we give in Sect. 5. We finish with some conclusions and the references.

2   Preliminaries

We start recalling some well-known concepts that will be useful for subsequent developments in the paper.

2.1   Interval Computation

An interval number $[a, a']$ with $a \leq a'$ is the set of real numbers defined by $[a, a'] = \{x : a \leq x \leq a'\}$. Degenerate intervals of the form $[a, a]$ are equivalent to real numbers. One can perform arithmetic operations with interval numbers through the arithmetic operations on their members.

Let $A = [a, a']$ and $B = [b, b']$ be two interval numbers, and let $+$, $-$, $\cdot$, $/$, and $=$ denote arithmetic operations (addition, subtraction, multiplication, division, respectively) and arithmetic equality relation on pairs of real numbers. The arithmetic operations with real numbers may be easily extended to pairs of interval numbers in the following way: $A + B = [a + b, a' + b']$, $A - B = [a - b', a' - b]$, $A \cdot B = [min(a \cdot b, a \cdot b', a' \cdot b, a' \cdot b'), max(a \cdot b, a \cdot b', a' \cdot b, a' \cdot b')]$, $A/B = [a, a'] \cdot [1/b', 1/b]$ for $0 \notin [b, b']$. We shall write $A = B \Leftrightarrow a = a'$ and $b = b'$. In the special case where both A and B are non-negative intervals, the multiplication can be simplified to $A \cdot B = [a \cdot b, a' \cdot b']$, $0 \leq a \leq a'$, $0 \leq b \leq b'$.

2.2 Ordering of Intervals

Let L be a non-empty set and $\preceq$ be a binary relation on L. The relation $\preceq$ is a partial order on the set L if the following three conditions are satisfied: (1) it is reflexive, i.e., for each $a \in L$, $a \preceq a$, (2) it is antisymmetric, i.e., for all $a, b \in L$, if $a \preceq b$ and $b \preceq a$, then $a = b$, (3) it is transitive, i.e., for all $a, b, c \in L$, if $a \preceq b$ and $b \preceq c$, then $a \preceq c$. We will write $a \prec b$ if a couple (a, b) is in a relation $\preceq$ but $a \neq b$. A set L with a partial order $\preceq$ is called a partially ordered set (poset) and denoted by $(L, \preceq)$. If in a poset $(L, \preceq)$ any two elements a, b are comparable, i.e., either $a \preceq b$ or $b \preceq a$, the partial order $\preceq$ is called a linear order (and then a pair $(L, \preceq)$ is called a totally ordered set).

Let us denote by $L([0, 1])$ the set of all closed subintervals of the unit interval, i.e., $L([0, 1]) = \{[a, b] : 0 \leq a \leq b \leq 1\}$. Now we recall four well known order relations on $L([0, 1])$: (i) $[a, a'] \preceq_{Upo} [b, b'] \Leftrightarrow a \leq b$ and $a' \leq b'$ (the usual partial order), (ii) $[a, a'] \preceq_{Lex1} [b, b'] \Leftrightarrow a < b$ or $a = b$ and $a' \leq b'$ (the first lexicographical order), (iii) $[a, a'] \preceq_{Lex2} [b, b'] \Leftrightarrow a' < b'$ or $a' = b'$ and $a \leq b$ (the second lexicographical order), (iv) $[a, a'] \preceq_{YX} [b, b'] \Leftrightarrow a + a' < b + b'$ or $a + a' = b + b'$ and $a' - a \leq b' - b$ (the order introduced by Xu and Yager in [16]). It is easy to see that the order (i) is partial, but the orders defined by (ii)–(iv) are linear. In the sequel we shall write $[a, a'] \prec_i [b, b'] \Leftrightarrow [a, a'] \preceq_i [b, b']$ and $[a, a'] \neq [b, b']$, where i denotes one of the orders presented above.

For further details, the reader is referred to [1].

2.3 Triangular Norms

A triangular norm (t-norm for short) is a binary operation t on the unit interval $[0,1]$, i.e., a function $t: [0, 1]^2 \rightarrow [0, 1]$, such that for all $a, b, c \in [0, 1]$ the following four conditions are satisfied: (1) it has 1 as the unit element, i.e., $t(a, 1) = a$; (2) it is monotone, i.e., if $a \leq b$ then $t(a, c) \leq t(b, c)$; (3) it is commutative, i.e., $t(a, b) = t(b, a)$; (4) it is associative, i.e., $t(t(a, b), c) = t(a, t(b, c))$.

More relevant examples of t-norms are $ZtN(a, b) = min(a, b)$ (minimum, Zadeh t-Norm), $GtN(a, b) = a \cdot b$ (algebraic product, Goguen t-Norm), and $LtN(a, b) = max(0, a + b - 1)$ (Lukasiewicz t-Norm). Since t-norms are just functions from the unit square into the unit interval, the comparison of t-norms is done in the usual way, i.e., pointwise. For the three basic t-norms and for each $(a, b) \in [0, 1]^2$ we have the following order $LtN(a, b) \leq GtN(a, b) \leq ZtN(a, b)$.

An s-norm is a binary operation s on the unit interval $[0, 1]$, i.e., a function $s: [0, 1]^2 \rightarrow [0, 1]$ such that for all $a, b, c \in [0, 1]$ the following four conditions are satisfied: (1) it has 0 as the unit element, i.e., $s(a, 0) = a$, (2) it is monotone, i.e., if $a \leq b$ then $s(a, c) \leq s(b, c)$, (3) it is commutative, i.e., $s(a, b) = s(b, a)$, and (4) it is associative, i.e., $s(s(a, b), c) = s(a, s(b, c))$.

However, the examples of s-norms corresponding respectively to the three basic t-norms presented above are $ZsN(a, b) = max(a, b)$ (maximum, Zadeh s-Norm), $GsN(a, b) = a + b - a \cdot b$ (probabilistic sum, Goguen s-Norm), and $LsN(a, b) = min(1, a + b)$ (bounded sum, Lukasiewicz s-Norm). As in the case of t-norms, we also have for the three basic s-norms and for each $(a, b) \in [0, 1]^2$ the following order: $ZsN(a, b) \leq GsN(a, b) \leq LsN(a, b)$.

For further details, the reader is referred to [4].

2.4   Interval Triangular Norms

The notion of t-norms on single values in [0,1] can be extended to subintervals of [0,1]. Moreover, basic properties of interval t-norms can be obtained from t-norms.

Let $A = [a, a']$ and $B = [b, b']$ be two interval real numbers such that $0 \leq a \leq a'$, $0 \leq b \leq b'$. Then for a given t-norm t, an extended t-norm T is defined by: $T(A, B) = \{t(x, y) : x \in A, y \in B\}$. Similarly, an extended s-norm S is defined by: $S(A, B) = \{s(x, y) : x \in A, y \in B\}$. Moreover, the following facts are true for any continuous t-norm or s-norm: (1) The interval t-norm T of a continuous t-norm t produces the interval $T(A, B) = [t(a, b), t(a', b')]$. (2) The interval s-norm S of a continuous s-norm s produces the interval $S(A, B) = [s(a, b), s(a', b')]$.

Interval t-norms corresponding to ZtN, GtN, and LtN can be computed by the following formulas: $iZtN(A, B) = [min(a, b), min(a', b')]$ (interval minimum, interval Zadeh t-Norm), $iGtN(A, B) = [a \cdot b, a' \cdot b']$ (interval algebraic product, interval Goguen t-Norm), $iLtN(A, B) = [max(0, a + b - 1), max(0, a' + b' - 1)]$ (interval Lukasiewicz t-Norm). The corresponding interval s-norms are: $iZsN(A, B) = [max(a, b), max(a', b')]$ (interval maximum, interval Zadeh s-Norm), $iGsN(A, B) = [a + b - a \cdot b, a' + b' - a' \cdot b']$ (interval probabilistic sum, interval Goguen s-Norm)), $iLsN(A, B) = [min(1, a + b), min(1, a' + b')]$ (interval bounded sum, interval Lukasiewicz s-Norm). With the order relation $\leq_{Upo}$, defined in the Subsect. 2.2, the counterpart of the order for the three basic t-norms presented above can be expressed as: $iLtN \preceq_{Upo} iGtN \preceq_{Upo} iZtN$. Similarly as for interval t-norms with the relation $\preceq_{Upo}$, the counterpart of the order for the three basic s-norms presented above can be expressed as: $iZsN \preceq_{Upo} iGsN \preceq_{Upo} iLsN$.

For further details, the reader is referred to [9].

3   Type-2 Generalized Fuzzy Petri Net

In this paper, we assume that the reader is familiar with the basic notions of Petri nets [3, 12].

Let $L([0, 1])$ be the set of all closed subintervals of the unit interval. A type-2 generalized fuzzy Petri net ($T2GFP$-net) [15] is a tuple $N = (P, T, S, I, O, \alpha, \beta, \gamma, Op, \delta, M_0)$ with (1) $P = \{p_1, p_2, \ldots, p_n\}$ is a finite set of places; (2) $T =$

$\{t_1, t_2, \ldots, t_m\}$ is a finite set of transitions; (3) $S = \{s_1, s_2, \ldots, s_n\}$ is a finite set of statements; (4) the sets P, T, S are pairwise disjoint; (5) $I: T \to 2^P$ is the input function; (6) $O: T \to 2^P$ is the output function; (7) $\alpha: P \to S$ is the statement binding function; (8) $\beta: T \to L([0, 1])$ is the truth degree function; (9) $\gamma: T \to L([0, 1])$ is the threshold function; (10) Op is a union of interval t-norms and interval s-norms called the set of operators; (11) $\delta: T \to Op \times Op \times Op$ is the operator binding function; (12) $M_0: P \to L([0, 1])$ is the initial marking, where 2^P denotes a family of all subsets of the set P.

As for the graphical representation, places are denoted by circles and transitions by rectangles. The function I describes the oriented arcs connecting places with transitions, and the function O describes the oriented arcs connecting transitions with places. If $I(t) = \{p\}$ then a place p is called an input place of a transition t, and if $O(t) = \{p'\}$, then a place p' is called an output place of t. The initial marking M_0 is an initial distribution of interval numbers in the places. It can be represented by a vector of dimension n of interval numbers from $L([0, 1])$. For $p \in P$, $M_0(p)$ can be interpreted as a truth value of the statement s bound with a given place p by means of the statement binding function α. Pictorially, the tokens are represented by means of suitable closed subintervals of $[0, 1]$ placed over the circles corresponding to appropriate places.

The interval numbers corresponding to values of $\beta(t)$ and $\gamma(t)$ functions are placed in a net picture under the transition t. The first interval number is interpreted as the truth degree of an implication corresponding to a given transition t. The role of the second one is to limit the possibility of transition firings, i.e., if the input operator In value for all values corresponding to input places of the transition t is less than a threshold value $\gamma(t)$ then this transition cannot be fired (activated). The operator binding function δ connects transitions with triples of operators (In, Out_1, Out_2). The first operator in the triple is called the input operator, and two remaining ones are the output operators. The input operator In concerns the way in which all input places are connected with a given transition t (more precisely, statements corresponding to those places). However, the output operators Out_1 and Out_2 concern the way in which the next marking is computed after firing the transition t. In the case of the input operator we assume that it can belong to one of two classes, i.e., interval t- or interval s-norms, whereas the second one belongs to the class of interval t-norms, and the third to the class of interval s-norms.

In the $T2GFP$-net model its elements from (8) to (12) are more general in comparing to the corresponding elements in the GFP-net [14]. Moreover, in this paper we enrich a description of the $T2GFP$-net behavior replacing the usual partial order relation between interval numbers by the most used examples of total orders that appear in the literature (see Subsect. 2.2. This issue is more precisely discussed further on. The $T2GFP$-net dynamics defines how new markings are computed from the current marking when transitions are fired.

Let N be a $T2GFP$-net and $(L([0, 1]), \preceq_i)$ be a i-poset, where i denotes one of the orders presented in Subsect. 2.2. A marking of N is a function $M: P \to L([0, 1])$. We assume that if $M(p) = [0, 0]$ then the token does not exist in the place p.

A transition $t \in T$ is i-enabled for marking M and $i = Upo, Lex1, Lex2, YX$, if the number interval produced by input operator In for all input places of the transition t by M is (strictly) greater than $[0,0]$ and greater than, or equal to the number interval being a value of threshold function γ corresponding to the transition t w.r.t. the order relation $\preceq_i$, i.e., $In(M(p_{i1}), M(p_{i2}), \ldots, M(p_{ik})) \succeq_i \gamma(t) \succ_i [0,0]$. Only enabled transitions can be fired. Firing the enabled transition t in practice consists of removing the tokens from its input places $I(t)$ and adding the tokens to all its output places $O(t)$ without any alteration of the tokens in other places.

Let $N = (P, T, S, I, O, \alpha, \beta, \gamma, Op, \delta, M_0)$ be a $T2GFP$-net and $(L([0,1]), \succeq_i)$ be an i-poset, where $i = Upo, Lex1, Lex2, YX$, $t \in T$, $I(t) = \{p_{i1}, p_{i2}, \ldots, p_{ik}\}$ be a set of input places for a transition t and $\beta(t) \in L((0,1])$. (0 does not belong to the unit interval.) Moreover, let In be an input operator and Out_1, Out_2 be output operators for the transition t. If M is a marking of N i-enabling transition t and M' is the marking derived from M by firing transition t, then for each $p \in P$: $M'(p) = [0,0]$ if $p \in I(t)$; $Out_2(Out_1(In(M(p_{i1}), M(p_{i2}), \ldots, M(p_{ik})), \beta(t)), M(p))$ if $p \in O(t)$; and $M(p)$ otherwise.

Example 1. Consider a type-2 generalized fuzzy Petri net in Fig. 1(a). For the net we have: the set of places $P = \{p_1, p_2, p_3\}$, the set of transitions $T = \{t_1\}$, the input function I and the output function O in the form: $I(t_1) = \{p_1, p_2\}$, $O(t_1) = \{p_3\}$, the set of statements $S = \{s_1, s_2, s_3\}$, the statement binding function α: $\alpha(p_1) = s_1$, $\alpha(p_2) = s_2$, $\alpha(p_3) = s_3$, the truth degree function β: $\beta(t_1) = [0.5, 0.8]$ and the threshold function γ: $\gamma(t_1) = [0.3, 0.4]$. Moreover, there are: the set of operators $Op = \{iZtN, iGtN, iZsN\}$, the operator binding function δ: $\delta(t_1) = (iZtN, iGtN, iZsN)$ and the initial marking M_0: $M_0(p_1) = [0.2, 0.5]$, $M_0(p_2) = [0.7, 0.8]$, $M_0(p_3) = [0,0]$). The transition t_1 is $Lex2$-enabled by the initial marking M_0, since $iZtN$ $(M_0(p_1), M_0(p_2)) = [min(0.2, 0.7), min(0.5, 0.8)] = [0.2, 0.5] \succeq_{Lex2} [0.3, 0.4] = \gamma(t_1)$. Firing transition t_1 by the marking M_0 with the order relation $Lex2$ transforms M_0 to the marking $M' = ([0,0], [0,0], [0.1, 0.4])$, because $iGtN(iZtN(M_0(p_1), M_0(p_2)), \beta(t_1)) = iGtN([0.2, 0.5], [0.5, 0.8]) = [0.2 \cdot 0.5, 0.5 \cdot 0.8] = [0.1, 0.4]$ and $iZsN$

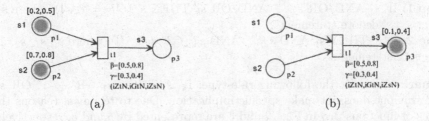

(a)   (b)

Fig. 1. A $T2GFP$-net with: (a) the initial marking, (b) the marking after firing t_1

$(M_0(p_3), iGtN(iZtN(M_0(p_1), M_0(p_2)), \beta(t_1)) = iZsN([0,0], [0.1, 0.4]) = [max(0, 0.1), max(0, 0.4)] = [0.1, 0.4]$ (see Fig. 1(b)). It is easy to see that t_1 by the marking M' is already disabled. In a similar way as above one can check that transition t_1 is YX-enabled by M_0 too. However, it is not i-enabled by the initial marking M_0 with $i = Upo, Lex1$.

For further details, the reader is referred to [15].

4   Transformation of Production Rules into *T2GFP*-net

A production rule is an important and fruitful approach to knowledge representation and a fuzzy Petri net is a very useful way to represent this production rule graphically [14]. In the paper, we consider three structural forms of production rules. The transformation of production rules into a *T2GFP*-net is realized depending on the form of a transformed rule.

Type 0: IF s THEN s' $(CF = [c, c'])$, where s, s' denote statements, $[a, a']$, $[b, b']$ are the interval numbers corresponding to their values, and CF is a certainty factor. The truth values of s, s', and CF belong to $L([0, 1])$.

A *T2GFP*-net structure of this rule is shown in Fig. 2.

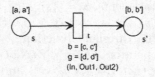

Fig. 2. A *T2GFP*-net representation of rule type 0

If the antecedence or the consequence of a production rule contains AND or OR (classical propositional connectives), it is called a *composite production rule*. Below, two types of composite production rules are presented together with their *T2GFP*-net representation (see Fig. 3).

Type 1: IF s_1 AND/OR s_2 ... AND/OR s_k THEN s' $(CF = [c, c'])$, where s_1, s_2, ..., s_k, s' denote statements.

Type 2: IF s' THEN s_1 AND s_2 ... AND s_n $(CF = [c, c'])$, where s', s_1, s_2, ..., s_n denote statements.

Remark: We omit the following rule-type: IF s' THEN s_1 OR s_2 ... OR s_n since this one does not make specific implication. Due to technical reasons the names of functions β, γ in Figs. 2 and 3 are represented by b and g, respectively.

Now we are ready to present an algorithm which constructs a Petri net on the base of a given set of production rules.

For further details, the reader is referred to [14].

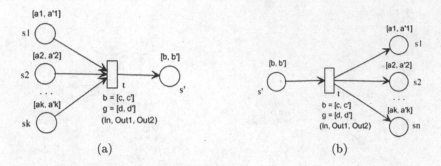

Fig. 3. A *T2GFP*-net representation of production rule: (a) type 1, (b) type 2

Algorithm 1. Construction of *T2GFP*-net using a set of production rules

---

Input : A finite set R of production rules
Output: A *T2GFP*-net N
$F \leftarrow \emptyset$; (* The empty set. *)
for each $r \in R$
if *r is a rule of type 0* **then**
    └ construct a subnet N_r as shown in Fig. 2;

if *r is a rule of type 1* **then**
    └ construct a subnet N_r as shown in Fig. 3(a);

if *r is a rule of type 2* **then**
    └ construct a subnet N_r as shown in Fig. 3(b);
$F \leftarrow F \cup \{N_r\}$;
integrate all subnets from a family F on joint places and create a result net N;
return N;

---

5 Example

In order to illustrate our methodology, let us discuss a simple example coming from the domain of train traffic control.

Consider the following situation: a train B waits at a certain station for a train A to arrive in order to allow some passengers to change train A to train B. Now, a conflict arises when the train A is late. In this situation, the following alternatives can be taken into account: (1) Train B waits for train A to arrive. In this case, train B will depart with delay. (2) Train B departs in time. In this case, passengers disembarking train A have to wait for a later train. (3) Train B departs in time, and an additional train is employed for the train A's passengers. In order to describe the traffic conflict, we propose to consider the following four production rules: (1) IF s_2 THEN s_6; (2) IF s_3 THEN s_6; (3) IF s_1 AND s_4 AND s_6 THEN s_7; (4) IF s_4 AND s_5 THEN s_8, where: $s_1 =$ 'Train B is the last train in this direction today', $s_2 =$ 'The delay of train A is huge', $s_3 =$ 'There is an urgent need for the track of train B', $s_4 =$ 'Many passengers would like to change for train B', $s_5 =$ 'The delay of train A is short', $s_6 =$ '(Let) train B

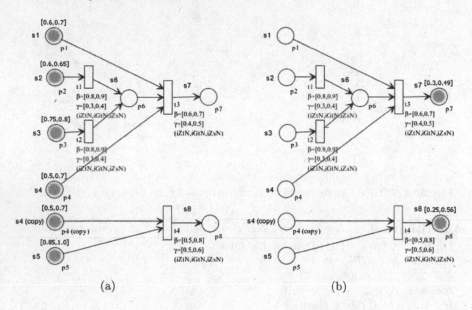

(a)   (b)

Fig. 4. *T2GFP*-net model of train traffic control: (a) the initial marking, (b) the marking after firing a sequence of transitions $t_1 t_2 t_3$, and the transition t_4

depart according to schedule', s_7 = 'Employ an additional train C (in the same direction as train B)', and s_8 = 'Let train B wait for train A'.

Using the Algorithm 1 presented in Sect. 4, we construct the *T2GFP*-net model corresponding to these rules, where the logical operator AND is interpreted as $iZtN$ (interval minimum). This net model is shown in Fig. 4. Note that the places $p_1, p_2, p_3, p_4, p_4(copy)$, p_5, p_6, p_7 and p_8 include the interval numbers [0.6,0.7], [0.6,0.65], [0.75,0.8], [0.5,0.7], [0.5,0.7], [0.85,1.0], [0,0], [0,0] and [0,0] corresponding to the statements $s_1, s_2, s_3, s_4, s_4(copy), s_5, s_6, s_7$ and s_8, respectively. Moreover, there are: the truth degree function β: $\beta(t_1)$ = $\beta(t_2)$ = [0.8, 0.9], $\beta(t_3)$ = [0.6, 0.7], $\beta(t_4)$ = [0.5, 0.8], the threshold function γ: $\gamma(t_1) = \gamma(t_2)$ = [0.3, 0.4], $\gamma(t_3)$ = [0.4, 0.5], $\gamma(t_4)$ = [0.5, 0.6], the set of operators $Op = \{iZtN, iGtN, iZsN\}$ and the operator binding function δ: $\delta(t_1) = \delta(t_2)$ = $\delta(t_3) = \delta(t_4) = (iZtN, iGtN, iZsN)$. Assessing the statements attached to the places from p_1 up to p_5, we observe that the transitions t_1, t_2 and t_4 are i-enabled by the initial marking M_0 (see Fig. 4(a)), where $i = Upo, Lex1, Lex2, YX$. Firing these transitions according to the firing rules for the *T2GFP*-net model allows computation of the support for the alternatives in question. In this way, the possible alternatives are ordered with regard to our preferences. This order forms the basis for further examinations and simulations and, ultimately, for the dispatching proposal. If one chooses a sequence of transitions $t_1 t_2 t_3$ then they obtain the final value, corresponding to the statement s_7, equal to the interval number [0.3,0.49]. The detailed computation in this case proceeds as follows. We can see that the transition t_1 is i-enabled by the initial marking M_0 since

$iZtN(M_0(p_2)) = iZtN([0.6, 0.65]) = [0.6, 0.65] \succeq_i [0.3, 0.4] = \gamma(t_1)$. Firing transition t_1 by the marking M_0 transforms M_0 to the marking $M_1 =.([0.6,\ 0.7],$ $[0, 0], [0.75, 0.8], [0.5, 0.7], [0.5, 0.7], [0.85, 1], [0.48, 0.585], [0, 0], [0, 0])$, because $iGtN(iZtN(M0(p_2)), \beta(t_1)) = iGtN([0.6, 0.65], [0.8, 0.9]) = [0.6 \cdot 0.8, 0.65 \cdot 0.9] = [0.48, 0.585]$. It is easy to see that the transition t_2 is still i-enabled by the marking M_1. Firing transition t_2 by the marking M_1 transforms M_1 to the marking $M_2 = ([0.6, 0.7], [0, 0], [0, 0], [0.5, 0.7],\ [0.5, 0.7], [0.85, 1],\ [0.6, 0.72], [0, 0], [0, 0])$, where the transition t_3 is now i-enabled. After firing this transition by the marking M_2 we obtain the marking $M_3 = ([0, 0], [0, 0], [0, 0], [0, 0], [0.5, 0.7], [0.85, 1], [0, 0], [0.3, 0.49], [0, 0])$, where the transitions t_1, t_2, t_3 are already disabled. In the other case (i.e., for the transition t_4 only), the final value, this time corresponding to the statement s_8, equals the interval number [0.25,0.56], where now all transitions are disabled. We omit the particular calculations for firing the transitions t_2, t_3 and t_4 because they run similarly as for the transition t_1 presented above.

If we interpret the logical operator AND as the interval Lukasiewicz t-norm and accept for the output operators Out_1 and Out_2 the interval algebraic product $iGtN$ and the interval Lukasiewicz s-norm, respectively, for all transitions, and if we choose a sequence of transitions $t_1 t_2 t_3$ then the final value is not possible to obtain, because after firing the transitions t_1, t_2 with $i = Upo, Lex1, Lex2, YX$ by the initial marking M_0 we achieve the result marking by which the transition t_3 is not able to fire by any order relation. In the other case, i.e., for the transition t_4, we obtain the final value for the statement s_8 equal to [0.175,0.56] only with the order relation $Lex2$ and YX. A similar situation occurs as before, if we accept the interval Goguen t-norm as the interpretation of the logical operator AND, and interval Goguen t-norm and interval Goguen s-norm for the output operators Out_1, Out_2, respectively. It is easy to observe that this time the transition t_4 is i-enabled with $i = Lex2$ or $i = YX$, by the initial marking M_0. After firing this transition by M_0, we obtain the final value for the statement s_8 equal to [0.2125,0.56]. The detailed computation in this case is also omitted.

At the end of this example we would still like to mention about one more interesting problem. In the first case we have obtained two final decisions corresponding to the statements s_7 and s_8 equal to the interval numbers [0.3,0.49], [0.25,0.56], respectively. In order to determine which is the best alternative, we need to order these values. But, if we consider the order generated by the order relation $Lex1$, our approach leads to the ordering $[0.3,0.49] \succeq_{Lex1} [0.25,0.56]$. This means that the interval number [0.3,0.49] is the best alternative. On the other hand, the order generated by the order relation $i = Lex2$ or YX provides the opposite ranking $[0.25,0.56] \succeq_i [0.3,0.49]$. In this case the best decision is [0.25,0.56]. Finally, if we choose the order generated by the usual partial order Upo we will see that these two intervals are not comparable, i.e., in this situation it is not possible to indicate the best decision result. This example shows clearly that different interpretations for the logical operator AND, different substitutions for the output operators, and different order relations for comparing of intervals may lead to quite different decision results. The fuzzy Petri net model proposed in the paper gives us such possibility. Therefore, we can say that it is more flexible than the ones known from the subject literature. Choosing a suitable interpretation for the logical operator AND we may apply the mathematical relationships between interval t-norms, and for the order relations presented in Subsects. 2.4 and 2.2, respectively. The rest in this case certainly depends on the experience of the model designer to a significant degree.

6   Concluding Remarks

In this paper, a modified type-2 generalized fuzzy Petri net model has been proposed. The model uses interval triangular norms instead of classical triangular ones. Moreover, we enhance this model by adding to it instead of the usual partial order relation between interval numbers [15] some of the most used examples of total orders that appear in the literature. The orders considered in the paper include the total orders such as the lexicographical orders or the order defined by Xu and Yager [16]. In general, it is possible to define many other total orders between interval numbers [1]. However, we have shown in the paper by means of the simple example that there exist problems in which, by choosing the appropriate order, we can force the conclusion. This is the novelty of this research work. In the approach based on the interval fuzzy sets, it is assumed that one is not able to specify the exact membership or truth value. An interval is adopt to indicate the range of the exact value. It makes the model as proposed in this paper more flexible and general. Moreover, this model is concerned with the reliability of the information provided, leading to more generalization in approximate reasoning process in decision support system. Using the intuitive real-life example suitability and usefulness of the proposed approach have been proved for the decision-making. The elaborated approach looks promising with regard to alike application problems that could be solved in a similar manner.

In this paper, we have only considered the extension of t-norms to interval t-norms in a numeric framework. It is useful to study fuzzy Petri nets in the context of the notion of t-norms and their interval extensions using more general mathematic structures (see e.g. [7,8]). Moreover, the comment presented above and related to ordering of interval numbers leads to the following question. Which is the most appropriate order for a given practical problem, in order to avoid spurious conclusions? In other words: How can these orders be related to the data in the different problems that can be considered? In future works, we intend to handle these issues, focusing in particular on the approach presented here.

Acknowledgments. This research was partially supported by the Center for Innovation and Transfer of Natural Sciences and Engineering Knowledge at the University of Rzeszów. The authors are grateful to the anonymous referees for their helpful comments.

References

1. Bustince, H., Fernandez, J., Kolesarova, A., Mesiar, R.: Generation of linear orders for intervals by means of aggregation functions. Fuzzy Sets Syst. **220**, 69–77 (2013)
2. Cardoso, J., Camargo, H.: Fuzziness in Petri Nets. Springer, Heidelberg (1999)
3. David, R., Alla, H.: Petri Nets and Grafcet: Tools for Modelling Discrete Event Systems. Prentice-Hall, Upper Saddle River (1992)
4. Klement, E., Mesiar, R., Pap, E.: Triangular Norms. Kluwer, Dordrecht (2000)
5. Li, X., Lara-Rosano, F.: Adaptive fuzzy petri nets for dynamic knowledge representation and inference. Expert Syst. Appl. **19**, 235–241 (2000)
6. Looney, C.: Fuzzy petri nets for rule-based decision-making. IEEE Trans. Syst. Man Cybern. **18**(1), 178–183 (1988)
7. Ma, Z., Wu, W.: Logical operators on complete lattices. Inf. Sci. **55**, 77–97 (1991)
8. Mayor, G., Torrens, J.: On a class of operators for expert systems. Int. J. Intell. Syst. **8**, 771–778 (1993)
9. Moore, R.: Methods and Applications of Interval Analysis. SIAM Studies in Applied Mathematics, vol. 2 (1979)
10. Pedrycz, W.: Fuzzy Control and Fuzzy Systems, 2nd edn. Wiley, New York (1993)
11. Pedrycz, W., Gomide, F.: A generalized fuzzy Petri net model. IEEE Trans. Fuzzy Syst. **2**(4), 295–301 (1994)
12. Peterson, J.: Petri Net Theory and the Modeling of Systems. Prentice-Hall Inc., Upper Saddle River (1981)
13. Sanz, J., Fernandez, A., Bustince, H., Herrera, F.: A genetic tuning to improve the performance of fuzzy rule-based classification systems with interval-valued fuzzy sets: degree of ignorance and lateral position. Int. J. Approx. Reas. **52**(6), 751–766 (2011)
14. Suraj, Z.: A new class of fuzzy petri nets for knowledge representation and reasoning. Fundam. Informat. **128**(1–2), 193–207 (2013)
15. Suraj, Z., Grochowalski, P.: Fuzzy Petri nets over interval triangular norms. In: Proceedings of the 2nd International Symposium Fuzzy and Rough Sets (ISFUROS 2017), 24–26 October 2017, Santa Maria Key, Villa Clara, Cuba (2017)
16. Xu, Z., Yager, R.: Some geometric aggregation operators based on intuitionistic fuzzy sets. Int. J. Gen. Syst. **35**, 417–413 (2006)
17. Zadeh, L.: Fuzzy sets. Inform. Control **8**, 338–353 (1965)

Molecular Computation

Networks of Polarized Splicing Processors

Henning Bordihn[1], Victor Mitrana[2,3(✉)], Andrei Păun[3], and Mihaela Păun[3]

[1] Department of Computer Science, University of Potsdam,
August-Bebel-Str. 89, 14482 Potsdam, Germany
henning@cs.uni-potsdam.de

[2] Faculty of Mathematics and Computer Science, University of Bucharest,
Str. Academiei 14, 010014 Bucharest, Romania
mitrana@fmi.unibuc.ro

[3] Bioinformatics Department, National Institute for R&D for Biological Sciences,
060031 Bucharest, Romania
apaun@incdsb.ro, mihaela.paun@incdsb.ro

Abstract. In this paper, we consider the computational power of a new variant of networks of splicing processors in which each processor as well as the data navigating throughout the network are now considered to be polarized. While the polarization of every processor is predefined (negative, neutral, positive), the polarization of data is dynamically computed by means of a valuation mapping. Consequently, the protocol of communication is naturally defined by means of this polarization. We show that networks of polarized splicing processors (NPSP) of size 2 are computationally complete, which immediately settles the question of designing computationally complete NPSPs of minimal size. We prove that NPSP of size 4 can accept all languages in **NP** in polynomial time. All these results can be obtained with NPSPs with valuations in the set $\{-1, 0, 1\}$ as well. We finally show that Turing machines can simulate a variant of NPSPs and discuss the time complexity of these simulations.

Keywords: Computing with DNA · Splicing · Splicing processor Polarization

1 Introduction

Networks of bio-inspired processors is one of the well known bio-inspired families of highly parallel and distributed computational models based on the string processing. Networks of bio-inspired processors resemble other models of computation with different origins: *evolutionary systems* inspired by the evolution of cell populations [2], *tissue-like P systems* in the membrane computing area [10], *networks of parallel language processors* as a formal languages generating device [3], *flow-based programming* as a well-known programming paradigm [11], *distributed computing using mobile programs* ([4] and the references therein), etc.

This work was supported by a grant of the Romanian National Authority for Scientific Research and Innovation, project number POC P-37-257. Victor Mitrana has also been supported by the Alexander von Humboldt Foundation.

© Springer International Publishing AG 2017
C. Martín-Vide et al. (Eds.): TPNC 2017, LNCS 10687, pp. 165–177, 2017.
https://doi.org/10.1007/978-3-319-71069-3_13

Informally speaking, a network of bio-inspired processors can be defined as a graph whose nodes host processors performing bio-inspired operations on the strings contained in the corresponding nodes. Every node has filters that block some strings from being sent out and/or receiving in. A network of bio-inspired processors alternates processing and communication steps, until a predefined halting condition is fulfilled. In each processing step, all processors change simultaneously the contents of their nodes according to their associated sets of rules. In the communication step, all the strings that pass the corresponding filters are interchanged between the connected nodes.

Two main types of processors have been considered so far: evolutionary processors and splicing processors. An evolutionary processor can perform very simple operations on strings. These operations, which might be viewed as formal operations of the gene mutations in DNA molecules, consist in: delete a symbol, insert a symbol, and substitute one symbol by another. A splicing processor can perform an operation inspired from one of the basic mechanisms by which the genetic material is merged, namely recombination of DNA sequences under the effect of enzymatic activities called *splicing*. This process has been formalized as a word rewriting operation as follows [5]: the restriction enzymes have been approximated by a finite set of rules defining the restriction sites and the DNA sequences, on which the enzymes act, have been approximated by a finite set of words. A computing model based on the splicing operation as defined above, called *network of splicing processors* (NSP), was introduced in [8] In this paper we change the protocol of communication which is now regulated by a sort of compatibility between nodes and data, called here polarity. The NSP model is similar in some extent to the test tube distributed systems based on splicing introduced in [1] and further explored in [16]. However, there are several differences between the models considered in [1,8] which are precisely pointed out in [8]. Along the same lines, in [8] one discusses the differences between NSP and the time-varying distributed H systems, a generative model introduced in [15] and further studied in [9,13,14]. A restricted version of NSPs (in which the splicing operations were performed if and only if exactly one of the two strings spliced was an auxiliary string) was introduced in [8], where it was shown that this computing model is computationally complete. Also, the complexity class **NP** was proved to correspond to the class of languages accepted by restricted NSPs in polynomial time and **PSPACE** to the class accepted by restricted NSPs with at most polynomial length of the stings used in the derivation.

In this paper, we consider the computational power of a new variant of networks of splicing processors in which the communication protocol is not anymore regulated by random-context conditions. Each processor as well as the data navigating throughout the network are now considered to be polarized, that is having a value in the set $\{-, 0, +\}$. While the polarization of every processor is predefined, the polarization of data is dynamically computed by means of a valuation mapping. The valuation mapping associates an integer value with each symbol and computes the value associated with the whole word as the algebraic sum of the values of its symbols, taking into consideration the number of occurrences of each symbol. Then the polarization of the word is nothing else then the sign of this value. Consequently, the protocol of communication is naturally defined by means of this polarization, namely each word will migrate to a node of the same polarity as it has. We show that networks of polarized splicing processors (NPSP) of size 2 are computationally complete by simulating a deterministic Turing machine. As a non-trivial NPSP must have at least two nodes, this result settles the question of designing computationally complete NPSPs of minimal size. We prove that NPSP of size 4 can decide all languages in **NP** in polynomial time by efficiently simulating a nondeterministic Turing machine. All these results can be easily obtained with NPSPs with valuations in the set $\{-1, 0, 1\}$, by encoding each symbol having a value out of the set $\{-1, 0, 1\}$ with a block of identical new symbols. As the proofs of all previous results use a restricted version of NPSP in which the splicing operations are performed if and only if exactly one of the two strings spliced is an auxiliary word, we finally show that Turing machines can simulate this variant of NPSPs. The time complexity of these simulations is also discussed.

2   Basic Definitions and Notations

We assume the reader's familiarity with the basic concepts in complexity classes and formal language theory. The reader may refer to [6,12] for definitions.

For any finite set A, $card(A)$ denotes the cardinality of A and for a word w, $|w|$ denotes the length of w. The smallest alphabet W such that $w \in W^*$ is denoted by $alph(w)$ and the empty word is denoted by λ.

A homomorphism from the monoid V^* into the additive monoid (group) of integers $\mathbf{Z}$ is called *valuation* of V^* in $\mathbf{Z}$. The absolute value of an integer k is denoted by $|k|$. Although the length of a word and the absolute value of an integer is denoted in the same way, this cannot cause any confusion as the arguments are understood from the context.

A nondeterministic Turing machine is a construct $M = (Q, V, U, \delta, q_0, B, F)$, where Q is a finite set of states, V is the input alphabet, U is the tape alphabet, $V \subset U$, q_0 is the initial state, $B \in U \setminus V$ is the "blank" symbol, $F \subseteq Q$ is the set of final states, and δ is the partial transition function, $\delta : (Q \setminus F) \times U \xrightarrow{\circ} 2^{Q \times (U \setminus \{B\}) \times \{R, L\}}$. The variant of a Turing machine we use in this paper can be described intuitively as follows: it has a semi-infinite tape (bounded to the left) divided into cells (each cell may store exactly one symbol from U). The machine has a central unit storing a state from a finite set of states, and a reading/writing tape head which scans the tape cells; the head cannot write blank symbols. The input is a word over V stored on the tape starting with the leftmost cell while all the other tape cells initially contain the symbol B. When M starts a computation, the tape head scans the leftmost cell and the central unit is in the state q_0. The machine performs moves that depend on the content of the cell currently scanned by the tape head and the current state stored in the central unit. A move consists of: change the state, write a symbol from U on the current cell and move the tape head one cell either to the left (provided that the cell scanned was not the leftmost one) or to the right. An input word is accepted iff after a finite number of moves the Turing machine enters a final state. A Turing machine is deterministic if for every state and symbol, the machine can make at most one move. The deterministic Turing machine halts if it reaches a state q and reads a symbol a such that $\delta(q, a)$ is not defined. Note that, in particular, no transition is defined for any final state. An instantaneous description (ID for short) of a Turing machine M as above is a word over $(U \setminus \{B\})^* Q (U \setminus \{B\})^*$. Given an ID $\alpha q \beta$, this means that the tape contents is $\alpha\beta$ followed by an infinite number of cells containing the blank symbol B, the current state is q, and the symbol currently scanned by the tape head is the first symbol of β provided that $\beta \neq \lambda$, or B, otherwise. Usually, we say that an ID $\alpha q \beta$ is final when $q \in F$, and we say that such an ID is blocking when $\delta(q, x)$ is not defined, where x is the first symbol of β (if $\beta \neq \lambda$) or $x = B$ (if $\beta = \lambda$). An input word $w \in V^*$ is accepted by M iff there exists a computation of M on w that halts in a final state. The language accepted by M is the language of all accepted words by M.

For a deterministic Turing machine M that halts on every input, we say that the language of all accepted words by M is decided by M.

We now pass to the definition of the splicing operation following [5]. A *splicing rule* over a finite alphabet V is a quadruple of words of the form $[(u_1, u_2); (v_1, v_2)]$ such that $u_1, u_2, v_1,$ and v_2 are in V^*. For a splicing rule $r = [(u_1, u_2); (v_1, v_2)]$ and for $x, y, w, z \in V^*$, we say that r produces z from x and y (denoted by $(x, y) \vdash_r z$) if there exist some $x_1, x_2, y_1, y_2 \in V^*$ such that $x = x_1 u_1 u_2 x_2$, $y = y_1 v_1 v_2 y_2$, and $z = x_1 u_1 v_2 y_2$.

For a language L over V and a set of splicing rules R we define

$$\sigma_R(L) = \{z \in V^* \mid \exists u, v \in L, \exists r \in R \text{ such that } (u, v) \vdash_r z\}.$$

A *polarized splicing processor* over V is a triple (S, A, π) where

- S a finite set of splicing rules over V,
- A a finite set of auxiliary words over V,
- $\pi \in \{-, +, 0\}$ is the polarization of the node (negatively or positively charged, or neutral, respectively).

A *network of polarized splicing processors* (NPSP for short) is a construct

$$\Gamma = (V, U, \langle, \rangle, G, \mathcal{N}, \varphi, \underline{In}, \underline{Halt}),$$

where

- U is the network alphabet and $V \subseteq U$ is the input alphabet.
- $\langle, \rangle \in U \setminus V$ are two special symbols.
- $G = (X_G, E_G)$ is an undirected graph with nodes X_G and edges E_G.
- $\mathcal{N}$ is a mapping which associates with each node $x \in X_G$ the splicing processor over U, $\mathcal{N}(x) = (S_x, A_x, \pi_x)$.
- φ is a valuation of U^* in $\mathbf{Z}$.
- $\underline{In}$ and $\underline{Halt}$ are the *input* and the *halting* nodes, respectively.

The graph G is called the *underlying graph* of the network. We say that $card(X_G)$ is the size of Γ.

A *configuration* of an NPSP Γ is a mapping $C : X_G \to 2^{U^*}$ which associates a set of words to every node of the graph. A configuration can be seen as the sets of words which are present in any node at a given moment. For a word $w \in V^*$ the initial configuration of Γ on w is defined by $C_0^{(w)}(x_{\underline{In}}) = \{\langle w \rangle\}$ and $C_0^{(w)}(x) = \emptyset$ for all other $x \in X_G$. By convention, the auxiliary words do not appear in any configuration.

There are two ways to change a configuration, by a splicing step or by a communication step. When changing by a splicing step, each component $C(x)$ of the configuration C is changed according to the set of splicing rules S_x, whereby the words in the set A_x are available for splicing. Formally, configuration C' is obtained in one splicing step from the configuration C, written as $C \Rightarrow C'$, iff for all $x \in X_G$

$$C'(x) = \sigma_{S_x}(C(x) \cup A_x).$$

When changing by a communication step, each node processor $x \in X_G$ sends out copies of all its words, keeping a local copy of the words having the same polarity to that of x only, to all the node processors connected to x and receives a copy of each word sent by any node processor connected with x providing that it has the same polarity as that of x. Note that, for simplicity reasons, we prefer to consider that a word migrates to a node with the same polarity and not an opposed one. Formally, we say that the configuration C' is obtained in *one communication step* from configuration C, written as $C \vdash C'$, iff

$$C'(x) = (C(x) \setminus \{w \in C(x) \mid sign(\varphi(w)) \neq \pi_x\}) \cup$$
$$\bigcup_{\{x,y\} \in E_G} (\{w \in C(y) \mid sign(\varphi(w)) = \pi_x\}),$$

for all $x \in X_G$. Here $sign(m)$ is the sign function which returns $+, 0, -$, provided that m is a positive integer, is 0, or is a negative integer, respectively. Note that all words with a different polarity than that of x are expelled from x. Further, each expelled word from a node x that cannot enter any node connected to x (no such node has the same polarity as the word has) is lost.

Let Γ be an NPSP, the computation of Γ on the input word $w \in V^*$ is a sequence of configurations $C_0^{(w)}, C_1^{(w)}, C_2^{(w)}, \ldots$, where $C_0^{(w)}$ is the initial config-uration of Γ on w, $C_{2i}^{(w)} \Longrightarrow C_{2i+1}^{(w)}$ and $C_{2i+1}^{(w)} \vdash C_{2i+2}^{(w)}$, for all $i \geq 0$. Note that the configurations are changed by alternative steps. By the previous definitions, each configuration $C_i^{(w)}$ is uniquely determined by the configuration $C_{i-1}^{(w)}$.

A computation as above *halts* as soon as there exists a configuration in which the set of words from the halting node $\underline{Halt}$ is non-empty, or no further step is possible anymore. Given an NPSP Γ and an input word w, we say that Γ accepts w if the computation of Γ on w halts and the node $\underline{Halt}$ is non-empty. The language accepted by an NPSP Γ consists of all words accepted by Γ and is denoted by $L(\Gamma)$. A language is decided by an NPSP Γ if it is accepted by Γ and moreover the computation of Γ on every input halts.

We now define the time computational complexity of an NPSP Γ with the input alphabet V that halts on every input. The *time complexity* of the finite computation $C_0^{(x)}, C_1^{(x)}, C_2^{(x)}, \ldots C_m^{(x)}$ of Γ on $x \in V^*$ is denoted by $Time_\Gamma(x)$ and equals m, that is the number of steps required for the network to halt on x. The time complexity of Γ is the partial function from N to N,

$$Time_\Gamma(n) = \max\{Time_\Gamma(x) \mid x \in V^*, |x| = n\}.$$

An NPSP Γ is said to be working in $\mathcal{O}(f(n))$ time if $Time_\Gamma(n) \leq cf(n)$ for some $c \geq 0$ and $n \geq n_0$.

3   NPSPs Simulating Turing Machines

In this section, we provide simulations of Turing machines by NPSPs. First we simulate deterministic Turing machines as follows.

Theorem 1.

1. *All recursively enumerable (recursive) languages are accepted (decided) by NPSPs of size 2.*
2. *Every language decided by a deterministic Turing Machine in $\mathcal{O}(f(n))$ time, for some function $f(n)$, is decided by an NPSP of size 2 in $\mathcal{O}(f(n))$ time.*

Proof. 1. The construction is essentially the same as that in the proof of Theorem 1 from [7] so that, due to space limitations we prefer to skip it. In that proof it suffices to consider that the valuation of each symbol in U_Γ is 0, except the final state q_f whose valuation is 1. Moreover, the input node has a neutral polarization, while the halting node has a positive polarization. We also note that, the given Turing machine halts in a non-final state, if and only if the computation of the network halts because no further step is possible anymore, and the halting node is empty.
2. As one can see in the aforementioned construction, each move of the Turing machine is simulated by a constant number of computational steps in the network.   □

Note that the NPSPs constructed above have a valuation mapping with values in $\{-1, 0, 1\}$, actually in $\{0, 1\}$, only. Furthermore, we have:

Corollary 1. *The class of polynomially recognizable languages is included in the class of languages decided by NPSPs of size 2 in polynomial time.*

We present now a more involved construction of an NPSP with 4 nodes that can simulate in parallel the computations of non-deterministic Turing machines.

Theorem 2. *Every language accepted by a nondeterministic Turing machine is accepted by an NPSP of size 4. Moreover, if the Turing machine works in $\mathcal{O}(f(n))$, for some function $f(n)$, then the time complexity of the simulating network is in $\mathcal{O}(f(n))$.*

Proof. Let $M = (Q, V, U, q_0, \{q_f\}, \delta, B)$ be a nondeterministic Turing machine accepting L, with Q the set of states, V and U respectively the input and tape alphabet, q_0 the initial state, B the blank symbol and $\delta : Q \times U \to Q \times U \times \{L, R\}$ the transition function. We assume without loss of generality that M has a single accepting state q_f. Moreover, we may assume that M has no deadlock state different than q_f, that is a state in which M may halt its computation. Given that M accepts L, we construct an NPSP $\Gamma = (V, U\langle, \rangle, G, \mathcal{N}, \varphi, \underline{In}, \underline{Halt})$ accepting L as follows.

We make the following assumptions:

- $V = \{1, 2, \ldots, p\}$.
- $U = \{p + 1, p + 2, \ldots, n + 1\}$, $n \geq p$, and $B = n + 1$.
- The transitions to the right are labeled with labels from 1 to k, while the transitions to the left, if any, are labeled with labels from $k + 1$ to m.

We shall not give the whole construction from the beginning. We prefer to construct the network step by step with explanations about every step. The underlying network is a star graph with nodes: $\underline{In}$, $\underline{Plus}$, $\underline{Minus}$, and $\underline{Halt}$, hence a claw graph with $\underline{In}$ of degree 3.

We first show how the input word $\langle w \rangle$ in $\underline{In}$ is transformed into $\langle q_0 w \# \rangle$, which eventually enters $\underline{In}$. To this aim, for each of the nodes $\underline{In}$, $\underline{Plus}$, and $\underline{Minus}$ we set:

$$\underline{In} \begin{cases} \{[(\langle, a); (\$q_0, \mathbb{c})] \mid 1 \leq a \leq n\} \cup \{[(\$, q_0); (\langle, \dagger)]\} \subseteq S_{\underline{In}}, \\ \{\$q_0\mathbb{c}, \langle\dagger\} \subseteq A_{\underline{In}}, \\ \pi_{\underline{In}} = 0. \end{cases}$$

$$\underline{Plus} \begin{cases} \{[(a, \rangle); (\yen, \#\pounds)] \mid 1 \leq a \leq n\} \subseteq S_{\underline{Plus}}, \\ \{\yen\#\pounds\} \subseteq A_{\underline{Plus}}, \\ \pi_{\underline{Plus}} = +. \end{cases}$$

$$\underline{Minus} \begin{cases} \{[(\#, \pounds); (\ddagger, \rangle)]\} \subseteq S_{\underline{Minus}}, \\ \{\ddagger\rangle\} \subseteq A_{\underline{Minus}}, \\ \pi_{\underline{Minus}} = -. \end{cases}$$

We define $\varphi(x) = 0$ for any $1 \leq x \leq n$ and $x \in Q \cup \{\#\}$. Furthermore, $\varphi(\$) = 1, \quad \varphi(\mathbb{c}) = -1, \quad \varphi(\yen) = 2,$ $\varphi(\pounds) = -1, \quad \varphi(\dagger) = 0, \quad \varphi(\ddagger) = -1.$

We now explain how an input word $\langle w \rangle$ in $\underline{In}$ is transformed into $\langle q_0 w \# \rangle$, which eventually enters $\underline{In}$. In $\underline{In}$ the splicing rule $[(\langle, a); (\$q_0, \mathbb{c})]$, where a is the first symbol of w, is applied to the pair of words $(\langle w \rangle, \$q_0\mathbb{c})$. Two words are obtained: $\$q_0 w \rangle$ and $\langle \mathbb{c}$. The first one has a positive polarization, hence it migrates to $\underline{Plus}$, while the second one will enter $\underline{Minus}$, where it remains trapped and cannot be used in any further computational step.. The word $\$q_0 w \rangle$ enters together with $\yen\#\pounds$ into a splicing step under the rule $[(b, \rangle); (\yen, \#\pounds)]$, where b is the last symbol of w. Two words result from this slicing step: $\$q_0 w \# \pounds$ and $\yen\rangle$. As the first word has a neutral polarization, it enters $\underline{In}$, while the second one remains in $\underline{Plus}$ forever and will not intervene in any further computation.

We continue with the word $\$q_0w\#\pounds$ that entered $\underline{In}$. Here the rule $[(\$, q_0); (\langle, \dagger)]$ is applied to the pair of words $(\$q_0w\#\pounds, \langle\dagger)$ yielding $\langle q_0w\#\pounds$ and $\$\dagger$. The first word goes to $\underline{Minus}$ while the second one goes to $\underline{Plus}$, where it will remain forever. The word $\langle q_0w\#\pounds$ is transformed into $\langle q_0w\#\rangle$ in $\underline{Minus}$ and goes back to $\underline{In}$. Note that all the other words obtained during the splicing steps discussed here remain trapped in some nodes and are inert for further computations.

Inductively, assuming that a word of the form $\langle qx\#y\rangle$ is in $\underline{In}$, such that yqx is an ID of M, we show how the network simulates a move of M to the right in the state q, provided that such a transition is defined. Let $1 \leq a \leq n$ be the first symbol of x and $(s, b, R) \in \delta(q, a)$ be a transition to the right labeled by the number $1 \leq i \leq k$. The simulation of such a transition is pretty much similar to the previous case. To this aim, for each transition $(s, b, R) \in \delta(q, a)$, labeled by i, with $1 \leq a \leq n$, and each of the nodes $\underline{In}$, $\underline{Plus}$, and $\underline{Minus}$ we set:

$$\underline{In} \begin{cases} \{[(\langle qa, c); (\$_i, \mathfrak{c}_i)] \mid c \in \{1, 2, \ldots, n\} \cup \{\#\}\} \cup \\ \quad \{[(\$_i, c); (\langle s, \Diamond)] \mid c \in \{1, 2, \ldots, n\} \cup \{\#\}\} \subseteq S_{\underline{In}}, \\ \{\$_i\mathfrak{c}_i, \langle s\Diamond\} \subseteq A_{\underline{In}}. \end{cases}$$

$$\underline{Plus} \begin{cases} \{[(c, \rangle); (\clubsuit, \widetilde{b}_i)] \mid c \in \{1, 2, \ldots, n\} \cup \{\#\}\} \subseteq S_{\underline{Plus}}, \\ \{\clubsuit\widetilde{b}_i\} \subseteq A_{\underline{Plus}}. \end{cases}$$

$$\underline{Minus} \begin{cases} \{[(c, \widetilde{b}_i); (\pounds, b)] \mid c \in \{1, 2, \ldots, n\} \cup \{\#\}\} \subseteq S_{\underline{Minus}}, \\ \{\pounds b\rangle\} \subseteq A_{\underline{Minus}}. \end{cases}$$

We further extend φ in the following way: $\varphi(\$_i) = i + 2$, $\varphi(\mathfrak{c}_i) = -(i + 2)$, $\varphi(\widetilde{b}_i) = -(i + 2)$, $\varphi(\Diamond) = 0$, and $\varphi(\clubsuit) = 2m + 3$.

We now explain how a move of M to the right using the transition $(s, b, R) \in \delta(q, a)$ is simulated by the network. Assume that $\langle qax'\#y\rangle$ is in $\underline{In}$; the rule $[(\langle qa, c); (\$_i, \mathfrak{c}_i)]$ can be applied to the pair formed by $\langle qax'\#y\rangle$ and $\$_i\mathfrak{c}_i$ yielding the pair of words $(\$_ix'\#y\rangle, \langle qa\mathfrak{c}_i)$. The first word enters $\underline{Plus}$ while the second one enters $\underline{Minus}$. As in the previous case, the word $\langle qa\mathfrak{c}_i$ that arrives in $\underline{Minus}$ remains there forever being inactive for the rest of the computation. Let us follow what is the itinerary of the word $\$_ix'\#y\rangle$ that arrives in $\underline{Plus}$. Here its rightmost symbol $\rangle$ is replaced by a symbol $\widetilde{d}_j$ in a splicing step. It is worth mentioning that if $j = i$, then $d = b$ must hold. Furthermore, if $j \neq i$, the polarization of the word will be either positive or negative. If the polarization is negative, the word goes out from $\underline{Plus}$, but cannot enter any node such that it is lost. If the polarization is positive, the word remains in $\underline{Plus}$ forever and becomes inactive for the rest of the computation. Therefore $i = j$ must hold. Now the word has a neutral polarization such that it enters $\underline{In}$, where its first symbol $\$_i$ is substituted by s via a splicing rule. The new word enters $\underline{Minus}$, where by the splicing rule $[(c, \widetilde{b}_i); (\pounds, b)]$, for some $c \in \{1, 2, \ldots, n\} \cup \{\#\}$, $\widetilde{b}_i$ is replaced by $b\rangle$, yielding the word $\langle sx'\#yb\rangle$. This word enters $\underline{In}$ and the simulation is completed.

We analyze now the case when $a = n+1$. If the transition $(s, b, R) \in \delta(q, n+1)$ is labeled by some r, then it suffices to add the following sets of splicing rules and auxiliary words to the nodes of Γ:

- The set $\{[(\langle q, \# \rangle; (\$_r, \mathfrak{c}_r)], [(\$_r, \#); (\langle s, \Diamond \rangle)]\}$ to S_{In}, and $\{\$_r \#_r, \langle s \Diamond \}$ to A_{In}.
- The set $\{[(c, \rangle); (\clubsuit, \widetilde{b}_r)] \mid c \in \{1, 2, \ldots, n\} \cup \{\#\}\}$ to S_{Plus}, and $\clubsuit \widetilde{b}_r$ to A_{Plus}.
- The set $\{[(c, \widetilde{b}_r); (\pounds, b)] \mid c \in \{1, 2, \ldots, n\} \cup \{\#\}\}$ to S_{Minus}, and $\pounds b$ to A_{Minus}.

Furthermore, $\varphi(\$_r) = r + 2$, $\varphi(\mathfrak{c}_r) = -(r + 2)$, $\varphi(\widetilde{b}_r) = -(r + 2)$.

Now, we show how the network simulates a move of M to the left. To this aim, for each transition $(s, b, L) \in \delta(q, a)$, labeled by $k + 1 \leq j \leq m$, with $1 \leq a \leq n$, and each of the nodes $\underline{In}$, $\underline{Plus}$, and $\underline{Minus}$ we set:

$$\underline{In} \begin{cases} \{[(\langle qa, c\rangle; (\$_{j,d}, \mathfrak{c}_{j,d})] \mid c \in \{1, 2, \ldots, n\} \cup \{\#\}, 1 \leq d \leq n\} \cup \\ \quad \{[(\$_{j,d}, c); (\langle sdb, \heartsuit)] \mid c \in \{1, 2, \ldots, n\} \cup \{\#\}, 1 \leq d < n\} \subseteq S_{In}, \\ \{\$_{j,d}\mathfrak{c}_{j,d} \mid 1 \leq d \leq n\} \cup \{\langle sdb\heartsuit \mid 1 \leq d \leq n\} \subseteq A_{In}. \end{cases}$$

$$\underline{Plus} \begin{cases} \{[(c, d)); (\spadesuit, \widehat{d}_j)] \mid c \in \{1, 2, \ldots, n\} \cup \{\#\}, 1 \leq d \leq n\} \subseteq S_{Plus}, \\ \{\spadesuit \widehat{d}_j \mid 1 \leq d \leq n\} \subseteq A_{Plus}. \end{cases}$$

$$\underline{Minus} \begin{cases} \{[(c, \widehat{d}_j); (\pounds, \rangle)] \mid c \in \{1, 2, \ldots, n\} \cup \{\#\}, 1 \leq d \leq n\} \subseteq S_{Minus}, \\ \{\pounds\rangle\} \subseteq A_{Minus}. \end{cases}$$

We further extend φ in the following way: $\varphi(\$_{j,d}) = 2^{m+j+2}3^{m+d+2}$, $\varphi(\mathfrak{c}_{j,d}) = -2^{m+j+2}3^{m+d+2}$, $\varphi(\widehat{d}_j) = -2^{m+j+2}3^{m+d+2}$, for all $1 \leq d \leq n$. Moreover, $\varphi(\heartsuit) = 0$ and $\varphi(\spadesuit) = 7^{2m+3}$.

We now explain how a move of M to the left using the transition $(s, b, L) \in \delta(q, a)$, with $a \neq n+1$, is simulated by the network. Assume that $\langle qax\#yd \rangle$ is in $\underline{In}$, for some $1 \leq d \leq n$; the rule $[(\langle qa, c\rangle; (\$_{j,t}, \mathfrak{c}_{j,t})]$, for some $1 \leq t \leq n$, can be applied to the pair formed by $\langle qax\#yd \rangle$ and $\$_{j,t}\mathfrak{c}_{j,t}$ yielding the pair of words $(\$_{j,t}x\#yd \rangle, \langle qa\mathfrak{c}_{j,t})$. A short discussion is in order here. With a symbol $\$_{j,d}$, we guess the last symbol of the current word $\langle qax\#yd \rangle$. Our guess is checked with the values associated with the symbols $\$_{j,d}$ and $\widehat{d}_j$, which uniquely identify the pair (j, d). The first word enters $\underline{Plus}$ while the second one enters $\underline{Plus}$, where it becomes inactive. Let us follow which is the itinerary of the word $\$_{j,d}x\#yd \rangle$ that arrives in $\underline{Plus}$. Here its suffix $d\rangle$ is replaced by the symbol $\widehat{t}_r$ in a splicing step. It is worth mentioning that if $d \neq t$, the polarization of the word will be either positive or negative. If the polarization is negative, the word goes out from $\underline{Plus}$, but cannot enter any node such that it is lost. If the polarization is positive, the word remains in $\underline{Plus}$, but it cannot participate in any further slicing step. Therefore $t = d$ must hold; furthermore, as in the previous case $r = j$ must also hold. Now the word has a neutral polarization such that it enters $\underline{In}$, where its first symbol $\$_{j,d}$ is replaced by $\langle sdb$. The new word enters $\underline{Minus}$, where by the splicing rule $[(c, \widehat{d}_j); (\pounds, \rangle)]$, for some $c \in \{1, 2, \ldots, n\} \cup \{\#\}$, $\widehat{d}_j$ is replaced by $\rangle$, yielding the word $\langle sdbx\#y \rangle$. This word enters $\underline{In}$ and the simulation is completed.

We analyze now the case when $a = n+1$. If the transition $(s, b, L) \in \delta(q, n+1)$ is labeled by some u, then it suffices to add the following sets of splicing rules and auxiliary words to the nodes of Γ:

- The set $\{[(\langle q, \# \rangle); (\$_{u,d}, \mathfrak{c}_{u,d})] \mid 1 \leq d \leq n\} \cup \{[(\$_{u,d}, \#); (\langle sdb, \heartsuit \rangle)] \mid 1 \leq d \leq n\}$ to S_{In}, and $\{\$_{u,d} \mathfrak{c}_{u,d} \mid 1 \leq d \leq n\} \cup \{\langle sdb \heartsuit \mid 1 \leq d \leq n\}$ to A_{In}.

- The set $\{[(c,d)); (\spadesuit, \widehat{d_u})] \mid c \in \{1, 2, \ldots, n\} \cup \{\#\}, 1 \leq d \leq n\}$ to S_{Plus}, and $\{\spadesuit \widehat{d_j} \mid 1 \leq d \leq n\}$ to A_{Plus}.

- The set $\{[(c, \widehat{d_u}); (\pounds, \rangle)] \mid c \in \{1, 2, \ldots, n\} \cup \{\#\}, 1 \leq d \leq n\}$ to S_{Minus}. Furthermore, $\varphi(\$_{u,d}) = 2^{m+u+2} 3^{m+d+2}$, $\varphi(\mathfrak{c}_{u,d}) = -2^{m+u+2} 3^{m+d+2}$, $\varphi(\widehat{d_u}) = -2^{m+u+2} 3^{m+d+2}$, for all $1 \leq d \leq n$.

We finish the construction by considering the case when the current state is q_f. If the current word is of the form $\langle q_f x \rangle$, for some x, it will be spliced in $\underline{In}$ by the splicing rule $[(\langle, q_f); (\$_0, \mathfrak{c}_0)]$, which is added to S_{In} together with the word $\$_0 \mathfrak{c}_0$ to A_{In}. We set $\varphi(\$_0) = \varphi(\mathfrak{c}_0) = 0$, hence both words produced by the splicing rule above will enter $\underline{Halt}$ and the computational process if stopped. It follows that the input word is accepted but it is accepted by the Turing machine as well.   □

As we have seen in the proof of Theorem 1, a valuation mapping with values in $\{-1, 0, 1\}$ was sufficient. A natural question is whether the construction in the previous proof can be modified such that the valuation mapping of any symbol is just one of the three values. The answer is positive and the modification is simple because it suffices to replace each occurrence of a symbol x in the splicing rules and auxiliary words, such that $\varphi(x) = k$, $k \notin \{-1, 0, 1\}$, by a word which is defined as follows:

(i) $a_x^{k-1} \triangle$, if $\varphi(x) > 0$, where a_x are new symbols and $\varphi(a_x) = \varphi(\triangle) = 1$,

(ii) $a_x^{-k-1} \nabla$, if $\varphi(x) < 0$, where a_x are new symbols and $\varphi(a_x) = \varphi(\nabla) = -1$.

Therefore, we can state:

Theorem 3. *Every language accepted (decided) by a nondeterministic Turing machine is accepted (decided) by an NPSP of size 4 having a valuation in the set $\{-1, 0, 1\}$. Moreover, if the Turing machine works in $\mathcal{O}(f(n))$, for some function $f(n)$, then the time complexity of the simulating network is in $\mathcal{O}(f(n))$.*

4   Turing Machines Simulating NPSPs

Clearly, every NPSP can be simulated by a Turing machine. However, the simulation might be very inefficient. As one can easily see, in all constructions presented so far, one of the two words in each splicing step was always an auxiliary word. If we consider these NPSPs such that one of the two words in each splicing step is an auxiliary word, we can construct a Turing machine able to simulate such a network in an efficient way.

Theorem 4. *Every language accepted by an NPSP Γ such that one of the two words in each splicing step is an auxiliary word is accepted by a Turing machine M. If $Time_\Gamma(n) \in \mathcal{O}(f(n))$, then M accepts any input word of length n in $\mathcal{O}((f(n) + n)(f(n) + n + K))$, where K is the maximal absolute value of the valuations of symbols in the working alphabet of Γ.*

Proof. Let L be a language accepted by an NPSP Γ; we construct a nondeterministic Turing machine that accepts L. Such a machine M may be constructed as follows. For each node of Γ, a set of states of M is constructed, which is partitioned into several subsets mutually disjoint. For each splicing rule of the node, there is a subset of states used in the process when M simulates the application of the rule to the word on the tape of M and an auxiliary word, which is identified by some subset of disjoint states associated with the node. F Furthermore, a subset of states is used for the process of computing the polarity of the words in that node.

M chooses nondeterministically a copy of the input word from those existing in the initial node of Γ. This word is actually on the tape of M in its initial ID. First the Turing machine places this word between the two symbols $<, >$ and then follows its itinerary through the underlying network of Γ. Let us suppose that the contents of the tape of M in the current ID is α; M works according to the following strategy:

(i) When M enters a state from the subset of states associated with a rule of the node $N: [(x, y); (z, t)]$, it searches in α for the occurrences of the word xy. If any such occurrence is found, and there exists an auxiliary word in the node N that contains an occurrence of zt as a subword (this could be checked by storing the state associated with the above splicing rule, and using the states associated with the auxiliary words of the node), the splicing rule is applied nondeterministically for any pair of such occurrences. One of the two newly obtained words, chosen nondeterministically, becomes the word whose evolution in the network is followed from now on, and M enters a state associated with the process of computing the polarity of the current word. If α does not contain any occurrence of xy, or no auxiliary word in the currently simulated node contains zt, then M blocks the computation.

(ii) The process of computing the polarity of the current word is accomplished in a nondeterministic way as follows:

- Mark all the occurrences of the symbols that have a neutral valuation.
- Mark an unmarked symbol and write its valuation in unary on an auxiliary tape using the symbol a, if its valuation is a positive integer or b, if its valuation is a negative integer.
- If the auxiliary tape contains only a's and 0's, then mark an unmarked symbol of a negative valuation and modify accordingly the contents of the auxiliary tape. For instance, if the number of a's on the tape is k and the marked symbol has valuation $-p$, then change p occurrences of a into 0, provided that $k \geq p$, or change all occurrences of a into 0 and write $p - k$ b's on the tape, otherwise. If there is no unmarked symbol of a negative

value, then halt the process and set the valuation of the current word as positive. The situation when the auxiliary tape contains only b's and 0's is treated analogously. If all symbols of the current word are marked, the polarity of the word is on the tape. Then M enters a state from the subset of states associated with a node with the same polarity as that of the current word, connected to the current node.

(iii) As soon as M enters a state associated with the output node of Γ, it accepts its input string. It is rather plain that M accepts L.

The following complexity related observations can be made. Assume that Γ needs at most $f(n)$ steps to accept any word of length n. In any splicing step the length of the current word increases at most by a constant which is given by the maximal length of an auxiliary word. Therefore, the maximal length of the current word is of order $\mathcal{O}(f(n) + n)$. In the simulation of each of the $f(n)$ steps of the computation of Γ, M needs to perform subword matchings in the word on its tape and to replace a part of the word on its tape with another word; in both phases the number of steps needed to perform these operations is $\mathcal{O}(f(n) + n)$. Therefore, the overall time for simulating splicing steps is of order $\mathcal{O}(f(n) + n)^2$. On the other hand, the process of computing the polarity of a word of length m is $\mathcal{O}(Km)$, where $K = \max\{|\varphi(a)| \mid a \in V\}$. Therefore, the overall time complexity of the Turing machine is $\mathcal{O}((f(n) + n)(f(n) + n + K))$.□

We finish with a few problems that remained unsolved here. The first one concerns the possibility to simulate a nondeterministic Turing machine with an NPSP of size 3. In the case that this is possible, is the simulation time efficient? Another problem refers to the possibility of simulating efficiently a non restricted NPSP with a Turing machine. It is clear that a Turing machine can simulate an arbitrary NPSP; however, it appears that such a machine should store all words obtained during the computation of the network on its tape. This means that the machine requires both space and time resources which are huge, making the simulation extremely inefficient.

References

1. Csuhaj-Varjú, E., Kari, L., Păun, G.: Test tube distributed systems based on splicing. Comput. AI **15**, 211–232 (1996)
2. Csuhaj-Varjú, E., Mitrana, V.: Evolutionary systems: A language generating device inspired by evolving communities of cells. Acta Informatica **36**(11), 913–926 (2000)
3. Csuhaj-Varjú, E., Salomaa, A.: Networks of parallel language processors. In: Păun, G., Salomaa, A. (eds.) New Trends in Formal Languages. LNCS, vol. 1218, pp. 299–318. Springer, Heidelberg (1997). https://doi.org/10.1007/3-540-62844-4_22
4. Gray, R., Kotz, D., Nog, S., Rus, D., Cybenko, G.: Mobile agents: the next generation in distributed computing. In: Proceedings of the 2nd AIZU International Symposium on Parallel Algorithms/Architecture Synthesis, PAS 1997, pp. 8–24. IEEE Computer Society (1997)
5. Head, T.: Formal language theory and dna: An analysis of the generative capacity of specific recombinant behaviors. Bull. Math. Biol. **49**, 737–759 (1987)

6. Hopcroft, J.E., Ullman, J.D.: Introduction to Automata Theory. Addison Wesley, Languages and Computation (1979)

7. Loos, R., Manea, F., Mitrana, V.: On small, reduced, and fast universal accepting networks of splicing processors. Theoret. Comput. Sci. **410**, 406–416 (2009)

8. Manea, F., Martín-Vide, C., Mitrana, V.: Accepting networks of splicing processors: Complexity results. Theoret. Comput. Sci. **371**, 72–82 (2007)

9. Margenstern, M., Rogozhin, Y.: Time-varying distributed h systems of degree 1 generate all recursively enumerable languages. In: Words, Semigroups, and Transductions, pp. 329–340. World Scientific (2001)

10. Martín-Vide, C., Pazos, J., Păun, G., Rodríguez-Patón, A.: A new class of symbolic abstract neural nets: tissue P systems. In: Ibarra, O.H., Zhang, L. (eds.) COCOON 2002. LNCS, vol. 2387, pp. 290–299. Springer, Heidelberg (2002). https://doi.org/10.1007/3-540-45655-4_32

11. Morrison, J.P.: Flow-Based Programming: A New Approach to Application Development. J.P. Enterprises Ltd. (2010)

12. Papadimitriou, C.H.: Computational Complexity. Addison-Wesley, Reading (1994)

13. Păun, A.: On time-varying H systems. Bull. EATCS **67**, 157–164 (1999)

14. Păun, G.: Regular extended H systems are computationally universal. J. Automata Lang. Comb. **1**, 27–36 (1996)

15. Păun, G.: DNA computing: distributed splicing systems. In: Mycielski, J., Rozenberg, G., Salomaa, A. (eds.) Structures in Logic and Computer Science. LNCS, vol. 1261, pp. 353–370. Springer, Heidelberg (1997). https://doi.org/10.1007/3-540-63246-8_22

16. Păun, G.: Distributed architectures in DNA computing based on splicing: limiting the size of components. In: Unconventional Models of Computation, pp. 323–335. Springer (1998)

Robust Combinatorial Circuits in Chemical Reaction Networks

Samuel J. Ellis[1], Titus H. Klinge[2(✉)], and James I. Lathrop[1]

[1] Department of Computer Science, Iowa State University, Ames, IA 50012, USA
{sjellis,jil}@iastate.edu
[2] Department of Computer Science, Grinnell College, Grinnell, IA 50112, USA
klingeti@grinnell.edu

Abstract. We introduce a general method for compiling any combinatorial circuit into an input/output chemical reaction network (I/O CRN). An I/O CRN receives a robust input signal over time, processes it catalytically to produce an output signal, and operates under deterministic mass action semantics (mass action kinetics). Our construction is reusable in the sense that it continues to operate correctly under changing input signals, and we prove that the construction is robust with respect to perturbations in (1) input signals; (2) initial concentrations; (3) rate constants; and (4) output measurements.

Keywords: Nanocomputing · Molecular programming
Combinatorial circuits · Robustness · Chemical reaction networks

1 Introduction

Logic circuits are foundational to the computing industry, and over the years Moore's law has forced circuit components to the nanoscale. Furthermore, circuits are being used increasingly often in biological applications and becoming an important field of study for nano-robotics [2,6,7]. DNA has been proposed as a universal medium for building bio-compatable logic circuits and has been thoroughly explored in [3,20,21].

Chemical reaction networks (CRNs) model the behavior of molecular systems and have been used for over a half-century [1]. In the last decade, CRNs have become a prominent programming language for developing algorithms for nanoscale applications for two reasons. First, they are capable of computing any algorithm [18], and second, they can be systematically compiled into DNA molecules that simulate their behavior [4,5,19]. CRNs are also a model of *analog* computation which makes them a natural choice for implementing Boolean circuits, since concentrations of molecules can be used as signals which are analogous to electrical signals in traditional silicon circuits.

Many molecular circuit motifs have been proposed over the years [10,16,17]. Recently Ge, Zhong, Wen, You, and Zhang introduced five approaches for constructing combinatorial logic gates with CRNs using Karnaugh maps and compared their stability and robustness using simulations [9]. Since many applications

This work is supported by National Science Foundation grants 1247051 and 1545028.

C. Martín-Vide et al. (Eds.): TPNC 2017, LNCS 10687, pp. 178–189, 2017.
https://doi.org/10.1007/978-3-319-71069-3_14

of molecular programming are safety-critical, ensuring the correctness and robustness of molecular systems is crucial [8, 11–13, 15].

In this paper, we propose a general scheme for robustly implementing combinatorial circuits with chemical reaction networks. Our circuit construction compliments the current literature in the following four ways. (1) They are reusable and dynamically adjust to changes in the input within a programmable propagation delay. (2) Inputs signals are used non-destructively as catalysts. (3) We formally prove robustness of the CRN construction with respect to perturbations (noise) in the input signals, initial concentrations, rate constants, and output measurements. (4) We prove that *all* combinatorial circuits can be robustly implemented in this way.

Since input signals may be used by other gates or circuits, it is critical that our construction read input signals without modifying or destroying them. CRNs that receive input signals over time in this manner are referred to as *input/output chemical reaction networks* in [14]. Also defined in [14] is a definition of robustness in which the input signal, initial concentrations, and output signal may be perturbed. (Such perturbations correspond to noisy systems.) This definition of robustness also takes into account perturbations in the rate constants, which could be the result of variations in temperature or salinity of the solution. In this paper, we prove that our construction is not only robust to perturbations in the input signal, initial concentrations, and output signal, but also to malicious perturbations of the rate constants, i.e., in the presence of an adversary manipulating the rate constants within a bounded error.

The rest of this paper is organized as follows. Section 2 reviews the I/O CRN model and the notion of robustly satisfying requirements; Sect. 3 provides an I/O CRN construction of a NAND gate and formally proves that it is robust; and Sect. 4 contains our main theorem that all combinatorial circuits can be robustly implemented by I/O CRNs.

2   Preliminaries

We now review the definitions of an input/output chemical reaction network and what it means to robustly satisfy a set of requirements. These were first introduced in 2016 by [14] and are closely related to well-known definitions in control theory.

2.1   Input/Output Chemical Reaction Networks

We fix a countably infinite set $S = \{X_0, X_1, X_2 \ldots\}$ of *species*, and we refer to them with capital Roman characters such as X, Y, and Z. A *reaction* over a finite set $S \subseteq \mathbf{S}$ of species is a triple $\rho = (\mathbf{r}, \mathbf{p}, k) \in \mathbb{N}^{|S|} \times \mathbb{N}^{|S|} \times (0, \infty)$ such that $\mathbf{r} \neq \mathbf{p}$. The elements of a reaction $\rho = (\mathbf{r}, \mathbf{p}, k)$ are called the *reactant vector*, *product vector* and *rate constant*, respectively, and the *net effect* of a reaction $\rho = (\mathbf{r}, \mathbf{p}, k)$ is the vector $\Delta\rho = \mathbf{p} - \mathbf{r}$. Given a reaction $\rho = (\mathbf{r}, \mathbf{p}, k)$, we use the notation $\mathbf{r}(\rho) = \mathbf{r}$, $\mathbf{p}(\rho) = \mathbf{p}$, and $k(\rho) = k$ for the individual components of ρ.

The formal definition of a reaction mirrors our intuitive understanding from chemistry. The reaction $A + B \xrightarrow{k} 2B + C$ over the set $S = \{A, B, C\}$ can be written $\rho = (\mathbf{r}, \mathbf{p}, k)$ where $\mathbf{r} = (1, 1, 0)$ and $\mathbf{p} = (0, 2, 1)$. Its net effect is $\Delta\rho = (-1, 1, 1)$, meaning it consumes one A and produces one B and C. For convenience, we treat the vectors $\mathbf{r}$, $\mathbf{p}$, and $\Delta\rho$ as functions from the set S into the natural numbers. We call a species $Y \in S$ a *reactant* of $\rho = (\mathbf{r}, \mathbf{p}, k)$ if $\mathbf{r}(Y) > 0$, a *product* of ρ if $\mathbf{p}(Y) > 0$, and a *catalyst* of ρ if $\mathbf{r}(Y) > 0$ and $\Delta\rho(Y) = 0$.

An *input/output chemical reaction network* (*I/O CRN*) is a tuple $N = (U, R, S)$ where $U, S \subseteq \mathbf{S}$ are finite sets of species satisfying $U \cap S = \emptyset$ and R is a finite set of reactions over $U \cup S$ where $\Delta\rho(X) = 0$ for each $\rho \in R$ and $X \in U$. We call the elements of S *state species* and the elements of U *input species*.

Under *deterministic mass action semantics* (also called *mass action kinetics*), a *state* of an I/O CRN $N = (U, R, S)$ is a vector $\boldsymbol{x} \in [0, \infty)^{|S|}$ that assigns to each $Y \in S$ a real-valued *concentration* denoted $\boldsymbol{x}(Y)$. Similarly, an *input state* is a vector $\boldsymbol{u} \in [0, \infty)^{|U|}$, and a *global state* is a vector $(\boldsymbol{x}, \boldsymbol{u}) \in [0, \infty)^{|S \cup U|}$.

For a finite set $W \subseteq \mathbf{S}$, we define the *W-signal space* to be the set $C[W] = C([0, \infty), [0, \infty)^{|W|})$ where $C(\mathcal{X}, \mathcal{Y})$ is the set of all continuous functions from $\mathcal{X}$ to $\mathcal{Y}$. A *context* of an I/O CRN $N = (U, R, S)$ is a tuple $\boldsymbol{c} = (\boldsymbol{u}, V, h)$ where $\boldsymbol{u} \in C[U]$, $V \subseteq S$, and $h : [0, \infty)^{|S \cup U|} \to [0, \infty)^{|V|}$. We call the components of the context $\boldsymbol{c} = (\boldsymbol{u}, V, h)$ the *input function*, the *output species*, and the *measurement function*, respectively. The set of all contexts of an I/O CRN N is denoted $\mathcal{C}_N$.

Given a global state $(\boldsymbol{x}, \boldsymbol{u}) \in [0, \infty)^{|S \cup U|}$ and a reaction $\rho \in R$, the *rate* of ρ in $(\boldsymbol{x}, \boldsymbol{u})$ is the real-value

$$\text{rate}_{\boldsymbol{x}, \boldsymbol{u}}(\rho) = k(\rho) \prod_{Y \in S \cup U} (\boldsymbol{x}, \boldsymbol{u})(Y)^{\mathbf{r}(\rho)(Y)}. \tag{1}$$

For each species $Y \in S$, the *deterministic mass action function* for Y is

$$F_Y(\boldsymbol{x}, \boldsymbol{u}) = \sum_{\rho \in R} \Delta\rho(Y) \cdot \text{rate}_{\boldsymbol{x}, \boldsymbol{u}}(\rho). \tag{2}$$

In the context $\boldsymbol{c} = (\boldsymbol{u}, V, h)$, the concentration of each species $Y \in S$ of an I/O CRN evolves according to ordinary differential equation (ODE)

$$y'(t) = F_Y(\boldsymbol{x}(t), \boldsymbol{u}(t)), \tag{3}$$

for all $t \in [0, \infty)$. (Our occasional use of $\boldsymbol{x}$ and $\boldsymbol{u}$ as single states as well as states parameterized by time is intentional and helps reduce obfuscation.) If we define the vector-valued function $F(\boldsymbol{x}, \boldsymbol{u})(Y) = F_Y(\boldsymbol{x}, \boldsymbol{u})$ for each $Y \in S$, then we can rewrite the ODEs of (3) in the vector form

$$\boldsymbol{x}'(t) = F(\boldsymbol{x}(t), \boldsymbol{u}(t)), \tag{4}$$

for all $t \in [0, \infty)$.

According to the standard theory of ODEs, the system (4) along with an initial state $\boldsymbol{x}_0 \in [0, \infty)^{|S|}$ has a unique solution $\boldsymbol{x}(t)$ satisfying $\boldsymbol{x}(0) = \boldsymbol{x}_0$. Finally, we define the *output signal* of an I/O CRN $N = (U, R, S)$ with initial state $\boldsymbol{x}_0 \in [0, \infty)^{|S|}$ in context $\boldsymbol{c} = (\boldsymbol{u}, V, h)$ as

$$N_{\boldsymbol{x}_0, \boldsymbol{c}}(t) = h(\boldsymbol{x}(t)), \tag{5}$$

for all $t \in [0, \infty)$ where $\boldsymbol{x}(t)$ is the unique solution to (4) with initial state $\boldsymbol{x}_0$. The output signal $N_{\boldsymbol{x}_0, \boldsymbol{c}}$ exactly defines the behavior of the I/O CRN.

2.2   Time-Dependent I/O CRNs

In order to define robustness with respect to rate constants, we define a variation of the I/O CRN model that replaces the rate constants of reactions with non-negative functions of time. For the purposes of this definition, we define a *time-dependent reaction* over the set S to be tuple $\rho = (\mathbf{r}, \mathbf{p}, \hat{k})$ where $\mathbf{r}, \mathbf{p} \in \mathbb{N}^{|S \cup U|}$ and $\hat{k} : [0, \infty) \to (0, \infty)$. A *time-dependent input/output chemical reaction network* (*I/O tdCRN*) is a tuple $N = (U, \widehat{R}, S)$ where $U, S \in \boldsymbol{S}$ are finite sets of species such that $S \cap U = \emptyset$ and $\widehat{R}$ is a finite set of time-dependent reactions that only use species in U as catalysts.

The deterministic mass action semantics of an I/O tdCRN are the same as that of an I/O CRN except that the rate function of (1) changes to

$$\text{rate}_{\boldsymbol{x}(t), \boldsymbol{u}(t)}(\rho) = \hat{k}(\rho)(t) \prod_{Y \in S \cup U} (\boldsymbol{x}, \boldsymbol{u})(t)(Y)^{\mathbf{r}(\rho)(Y)}, \tag{6}$$

for all time $t \in [0, \infty)$ in order to incorporate the time-dependent reactions. The Eqs. (2)–(5) also change in the obvious way.

For an I/O CRN $N = (U, R, S)$ and constant $\delta > 0$, we say that an I/O tdCRN $\widehat{N} = (U, \widehat{R}, S)$ is δ-*close* to N if each $\hat{\rho} \in \widehat{R}$ is the time-dependent equivalent of $\rho \in R$ and satisfies $|k(\rho) - \hat{k}(\hat{\rho})(t)| \leq \delta$ for all $t \in [0, \infty)$.

2.3   Robustness

A *requirement* of an I/O CRN $N = (U, R, S)$ is an ordered-pair $\Phi = (\alpha, \phi)$ consisting of two Boolean predicates $\alpha : \mathcal{C}_N \to \{\mathbf{true}, \mathbf{false}\}$ and $\phi : C[U] \times C[V] \to \{\mathbf{true}, \mathbf{false}\}$ called the *context assumption* and the *I/O requirement*, respectively. We say that an I/O CRN $N = (U, R, S)$ *satisfies* the requirement $\Phi = (\alpha, \phi)$, and we write $N \models \Phi$, if there exists an initial state $\boldsymbol{x}_0 \in [0, \infty)^{|S|}$ such that for all $\boldsymbol{c} \in \mathcal{C}_N$

$$\alpha(\boldsymbol{c}) \implies \phi(\boldsymbol{u}, N_{\boldsymbol{x}_0, \boldsymbol{c}}).$$

In order to capture the notion of approximately satisfying a requirement, we use the *supremum norm* defined by $\|f\| = \sup_{t \in [0, \infty)} |\boldsymbol{w}(t)|$ for all $\boldsymbol{w} \in C[W]$ where $|\boldsymbol{w}(t)| = \sqrt{\sum_{Y \in W} \boldsymbol{w}(t)(Y)^2}$ is the Euclidean distance function in $\mathbb{R}^{|W|}$. For two functions $\boldsymbol{w}, \widehat{\boldsymbol{w}} \in C[W]$, it is well known that $\|\boldsymbol{w} - \widehat{\boldsymbol{w}}\|$ is a well behaved distance function. Therefore for $w \in C[W]$ and $\epsilon > 0$, we define the *closed ball of radius ϵ around w* to be the set $B_\epsilon(w) = \{\hat{w} \mid \|w - \hat{w}\| \leq \epsilon\}$. If $\hat{w} \in B_\epsilon(w)$, then we say that $\hat{w}$ is ϵ-*close* to w.

We say that an I/O CRN $N = (U, R, S)$ ϵ-*satisfies* a requirement $\Phi = (\alpha, \phi)$, and we write $N \models_\epsilon \Phi$, if there exists an initial state $x_0 \in [0, \infty)^{|S|}$ such that

$$\alpha(u, V, h) \implies \exists v \in B_\epsilon(N_{x_0, c}) \, [\phi(u, v)].$$

Given a context $c = (u, V, h)$ and real numbers $\delta_1, \delta_2 > 0$, we say that $\hat{c} = (\hat{u}, V, \hat{h})$ is (δ_1, δ_2)-*close* to c if $\|u - \hat{u}\| \leq \delta_1$ and $\|h - \hat{h}\| \leq \delta_2$. Given states $x, \hat{x} \in [0, \infty)^{|S|}$ and $\delta > 0$, we say that $\hat{x}$ is δ-*close* to x if $|x - \hat{x}| \leq \delta$.

Finally we state what it means for an I/O CRN to robustly satisfy a requirement. Given $N = (U, R, S)$, $\Phi = (\alpha, \phi)$, $\epsilon > 0$, and $\delta = (\delta_1, \delta_2, \delta_3, \delta_4)$ such that $\delta_1, \delta_2, \delta_3, \delta_4 > 0$, we say that N δ-*robustly* ϵ-*satisfies* Φ, and we write $N \models_\epsilon^\delta \Phi$, if there exists an initial state $x_0 \in [0, \infty)^{|S|}$ such that for all contexts $c = (u, V, h)$ satisfying $\alpha(c)$, for each context $\hat{c} = (\hat{u}, V, \hat{h})$ (δ_1, δ_2)-close to c, for each state $\hat{x}_0 \in [0, \infty)^{|S|}$ δ_3-close to x_0, and for each I/O tdCRN $\hat{N}$ δ_4-close to N, there exists a concentration signal $v \in C[V]$ that is ϵ-close to the output signal $\hat{N}_{\hat{x}_0, \hat{c}}$ that satisfies $\phi(u, v)$.

3   A Robust NAND Gate

In this section, we prove that a single NAND gate can be robustly implemented by an I/O CRN. First, we formally specify the requirement for an I/O CRN that implements a NAND gate. We then present an I/O CRN construction and prove that it robustly satisfies its requirement.

An implicit parameter of the NAND gate requirement is the set of input species. Therefore we begin by defining the set

$$U = \{X_1, X_2, \overline{X}_1, \overline{X}_2\}. \tag{7}$$

The species X_1 and X_2 represent the two inputs of the NAND gate, and the species $\overline{X}_1$ and $\overline{X}_2$ are their *duals*. Intuitively, a dual species represents the Boolean complement of its counterpart. For example, whenever a species Z has high concentration, $\overline{Z}$ must have low concentration and vice versa.

Given a positive real number τ, often called the *propagation delay*, we define the NAND gate requirement $\Phi(\tau) = (\alpha, \phi)$. The context assumption α of $\Phi(\tau)$ is defined by

$$\alpha(u, V, h) \equiv \left[V = \{Y, \overline{Y}\} \text{ and } h = h_0 \right], \tag{8}$$

where h_0 is the *zero-error measurement function* defined by $h_0(x)(Y) = x(Y)$ for all $x \in [0, \infty)^{|S \cup U|}$ and $Y \in V$. Thus α has no constraints on the input signal $u \in C[U]$ and requires that the output species be $\{Y, \overline{Y}\}$, and the measurement function is initially error-free. (Errors are introduced into the measurement function when we prove that $\Phi(\tau)$ can be *robustly* satisfied.)

Before we specify the I/O requirement ϕ of $\Phi(\tau)$, we first define some useful notation. Recall that ϕ is a predicate that takes two parameters, an input signal $u \in C[U]$ and an output signal $v \in C[V]$. For convenience, we use these parameters in two definitions that help us define ϕ.

First, we define the set of all closed intervals of length at least τ as

$$I(\tau) = \{I = [t_1, t_2] \subseteq [0, \infty) \mid t_2 - t_1 \geq \tau\}.$$

For an interval $I = [t_1, t_2] \subseteq [0, \infty)$, we define the τ-left-truncation of I to be the interval $I_\tau = [t_1 + \tau, t_2]$.

For two bits $a, b \in \{0, 1\}$, we define the predicate

$$\phi_{ab}(I) \equiv (\forall t \in I)\big[u(X_1)(t) = a = 1 - u(\overline{X}_1)(t) \text{ and} \tag{9}$$
$$u(X_2)(t) = b = 1 - u(\overline{X}_2)(t)\,\big],$$

for all intervals $I \in I(\tau)$. Therefore the predicate $\phi_{01}(I)$ simply means that the input species X_1 and X_2 encode the values 0 and 1 in the interval I, respectively. Furthermore, their duals encode values of 1 and 0 in I.

Similarly, for a bit $a \in \{0, 1\}$ we define the Boolean predicate

$$\psi_a(I) \equiv (\forall t \in I)\big[v(Y)(t) = a = 1 - v(\overline{Y})(t)\,\big], \tag{10}$$

for all $I \in I(\tau)$. Thus the predicate $\psi_1(I)$ simply means that the output species Y and $\overline{Y}$ encode the numbers 1 and 0 in the interval I, respectively.

We now have the terminology to define the I/O requirement ϕ of $\Phi(\tau)$ as

$$\phi(u, v) \equiv \big(\forall I \in I(\tau)\big)\big[\,[\phi_{11}(I) \implies \psi_0(I_\tau)] \text{ and} \tag{11}$$
$$[(\phi_{00}(I) \vee \phi_{01}(I) \vee \phi_{10}(I)) \implies \psi_1(I_\tau)]\,\big]$$

for all $u \in C[U]$ and $v \in C[V]$. Intuitively, this means that if X_1 and X_2 encode the values of 1 and 1, respectively, then the output species Y must converge to 0 in at most τ time. In addition, Y remains there as long as the inputs are held constant. Similarly, if either of the inputs is 0, then the output must converge to 1 in at most τ time and remain there while the inputs are held constant.

We now specify our I/O CRN that robustly simulates a NAND gate.

Construction 1. Given parameters $\boldsymbol{\delta} = (\delta_1, \delta_2, \delta_3, \delta_4)$, and τ, define the CRN

$$N(\boldsymbol{\delta}, \tau) = (U, R, S),$$

where $U = \{X_1, X_2, \overline{X}_1, \overline{X}_2\}$, $S = \{Y, \overline{Y}\}$, and R consists of the reactions

$$X_1 + X_2 + Y \xrightarrow{k} X_1 + X_2 + \overline{Y} \tag{12}$$

$$\overline{X}_1 + \overline{Y} \xrightarrow{k} \overline{X}_1 + Y \tag{13}$$

$$\overline{X}_2 + \overline{Y} \xrightarrow{k} \overline{X}_2 + Y \tag{14}$$

$$2Y + \overline{Y} \xrightarrow{3k} 3Y \tag{15}$$

$$2\overline{Y} + Y \xrightarrow{3k} 3\overline{Y}, \tag{16}$$

and where k is the constant

$$k = 100\delta_4 + \frac{13}{\tau} \tag{17}$$

In the above construction, reaction (12) biases the output toward $\overline{Y}$ when the inputs X_1 and X_2 are both present, reactions (13) and (14) bias the output toward Y in the presence of $\overline{X}_1$ or $\overline{X}_2$ (i.e. when X_1 or X_2 is low), and reactions (15) and(16) give extra bias to the output species with majority concentration. The latter two reactions are essential for the I/O CRN to produce an output signal that is at least as clean as its input.

Theorem 2. *If $\boldsymbol{\delta} = (\delta_1, \delta_2, \delta_3, \delta_4) \in (0, \infty)^4$ and $\tau > 0$ are constants satisfying*

$$\delta_2 + \delta_3 < \delta_1 < \frac{1}{25} \tag{18}$$

$$\delta_2 + \delta_3 < \frac{1}{100} \tag{19}$$

and $N = N(\boldsymbol{\delta}, \tau)$ is constructed according to Construction 1, then $N \models_{\delta_1}^{\boldsymbol{\delta}} \Phi(\tau)$.

The remainder of this section is devoted to proving this theorem. Since the proof requires examining an arbitrary perturbation of a variety of parameters, we begin the proof by fixing these arbitrary perturbations.

Assume the hypothesis of Theorem 2 with $N = (U, R, S) = N(\boldsymbol{\delta}, \tau)$. We fix initial state $\boldsymbol{x}_0 \in [0, \infty)^S$ defined by

$$\boldsymbol{x}_0(Y) = 1 \quad \text{and} \quad \boldsymbol{x}_0(\overline{Y}) = 0.$$

(Note that any choice satisfying $\boldsymbol{x}_0(Y) + \boldsymbol{x}_0(\overline{Y}) = 1$ suffices for our argument.) Let $\boldsymbol{c} = (\boldsymbol{u}, V, h)$ be a context that satisfies the context assumption $\alpha(\boldsymbol{c})$. Let $\hat{\boldsymbol{c}} = (\hat{\boldsymbol{u}}, V, \hat{h})$ be (δ_1, δ_2)-close to $\boldsymbol{c}$, let $\hat{\boldsymbol{x}}_0$ be δ_3-close to $\boldsymbol{x}_0$, and let $\widehat{N}$ be δ_4-close to N. It now suffices to show that the output function $\widehat{N}_{\hat{\boldsymbol{c}}, \hat{\boldsymbol{x}}_0}$ is δ_1-close to a signal $\boldsymbol{v} \in C[V]$ satisfying the I/O requirement $\phi(\boldsymbol{u}, \boldsymbol{v})$. Thus we fix $\hat{\boldsymbol{x}} \in C[S]$ as the unique solution generated by $\widehat{N}$ in context $\hat{\boldsymbol{c}}$ on the initial state $\hat{\boldsymbol{x}}_0$.

Since the I/O requirement $\phi(\boldsymbol{u}, \boldsymbol{v})$ is naturally broken down into two parts, Lemmas 3 and 4 suffice to prove the theorem.

Lemma 3. *If $I \in \boldsymbol{I}(\tau)$ is an interval such that $\phi_{11}(I)$ holds, then $\psi_0(I_\tau)$ holds.*

Proof. Assume the hypothesis. To show that $\psi_0(I_\tau)$ holds, we need to show that for all $t \in I_\tau$, $1 - \delta_2 < \hat{\boldsymbol{x}}(t)(\overline{Y}) < 1 + \delta_2$ and $\hat{\boldsymbol{x}}(t)(Y) < \delta_2$. For convenience, we will write $y(t)$ and $\overline{y}(t)$ to denote $\hat{\boldsymbol{x}}(t)(Y)$ and $\hat{\boldsymbol{x}}(t)(\overline{Y})$, respectively.

Using the reactions from Construction 1 along with the definition of the deterministic mass action system for a time-varying I/O CRN, we observe that $y(t)$ and $\overline{y}(t)$ conform to the ODEs

$$\frac{dy}{dt} = 3\hat{k}_1 y^2 \overline{y} - 3\hat{k}_2 y \overline{y}^2 - \hat{k}_3 x_1 x_2 y + \hat{k}_4 \overline{x}_1 \overline{y} + \hat{k}_5 \overline{x}_2 \overline{y}, \tag{20}$$

$$\frac{d\overline{y}}{dt} = -\frac{dy}{dt}, \tag{21}$$

where $\hat{k}_1$, $\hat{k}_2$, $\hat{k}_3$, $\hat{k}_4$, and $\hat{k}_5$ are all time-varying δ_4-perturbations of the rate constant k and $x_1(t)$, $x_2(t)$, $\overline{x}_1(t)$, and $\overline{x}_2(t)$ are the four components of the δ_1-perturbed input signal $\hat{u}(t)$.

Equation (21) immediately implies that

$$p = y(t) + \overline{y}(t), \tag{22}$$

where $p = \hat{x}_0(Y) + \hat{x}_0(\overline{Y})$. It is also useful to note that $|p - 1| < \delta_3$ since $\hat{x}_0$ is a δ_3-perturbation of x_0 which satisfies $x_0(Y) + x_0(\overline{Y}) = 1$.

Recall that our goal is to show for all $t \in I_\tau$ that $y(t)$ and $\overline{y}(t)$ are δ_1-close to 0 and 1, respectively. It now suffices to show that $\overline{y}(t) > p - \gamma$ where $\gamma = \delta_1 - \delta_2 - \delta_3$. We will show this by examining the ODE (21) of $\overline{Y}$.

Since all of the perturbed rate constants are within δ_4 of the constant k, we know that

$$\frac{d\overline{y}}{dt} \geq 3(k - \delta_4)\overline{y}^2 y - 3(k + \delta_4)\overline{y}y^2 + (k - \delta_4)\hat{k}_3 x_1 x_2 y$$
$$- (k + \delta_4)\hat{k}_4 \overline{x}_1 \overline{y} - (k + \delta_4)\overline{x}_2 \overline{y}.$$

Thus if we let $d = \frac{\delta_4}{k}$, we can write

$$\frac{d\overline{y}}{dt} \geq k \left[3(1 - d)\overline{y}^2 y - 3(1 + d)\overline{y}y^2 + (1 - d)x_1 x_2 y - (1 + d)(\overline{x}_1 + \overline{x}_2)\overline{y} \right]. \tag{23}$$

It is also not difficult to show that the expression $3(1 - d)\overline{y}^2 y - 3(1 + d)\overline{y}y^2$ can be minimized by setting $\overline{y} = \frac{p}{6}\left(d + 3 - \sqrt{d^2 + 3}\right)$. By substituting this back into the expression, we obtain the bound

$$3(1 - d)\overline{y}^2 y - 3(1 + d)\overline{y}y^2 \geq -\frac{p^3}{18}\left(3\sqrt{d^2 + 3} + d\left(d\left(\sqrt{d^2 + 3} - d\right) + 9\right)\right)$$
$$\geq -\frac{p^3}{18}\left((3 + d)^{3/2} + 9d\right).$$

Substituting this into (23), we obtain

$$\frac{d\overline{y}}{dt} \geq k \left[-\frac{p^3}{18}\left((3 + d)^{3/2} + 9d\right) + (1 - d)x_1 x_2 y - (1 + d)(\overline{x}_1 + \overline{x}_2)\overline{y} \right].$$

Since $\phi_{11}(I)$ holds, we know that within the interval I that x_1, x_2, $\overline{x}_1$, and $\overline{x}_2$ are encoding 1, 1, 0, and 0, respectively. However, these are only δ_1-approximating these because of the input perturbations. Thus for all $t \in I$ we have

$$\frac{d\overline{y}}{dt} \geq k \left[-a + b(p - \overline{y}) - c\overline{y} \right],$$

where $a = \frac{p^3}{18}\left((3 + d)^{3/2} + 9d\right)$, $b = (1 - d)(1 - \delta_1)^2$, and $c = 2\delta_1(1 + d)$. This equation can easily be solved by separation of variables and integrating which yields the bound

$$\overline{y}\left(t_0 + \frac{\tau}{2}\right) \geq \frac{bp - a}{b + c}\left(1 - e^{-k(b+c)\frac{\tau}{2}}\right),$$

for all $t \in I$ where t_0 is the time at the beginning of the interval I.

Using the facts that $\delta_1 \leq \frac{1}{25}$, $d < \frac{1}{100}$, $\delta_3 \leq \frac{1}{100}$, $|p - 1| \leq \delta_3$ and $k \geq \frac{13}{\tau}$, it is not difficult to verify via substitution that

$$\overline{y}\left(t_0 + \frac{\tau}{2}\right) \geq \frac{3}{5}. \tag{24}$$

To bound the behavior of $\overline{Y}$ after time $t_0 + \frac{\tau}{2}$, we take another look at (23) and see that

$$\frac{d\overline{y}}{dt} \geq k\left[3(1 - d)\overline{y}^2 y - 3(1 + d)\overline{y}y^2 - 2\delta_1(1 + d)\overline{y}\right]$$
$$\geq a\overline{y}^2(p - \overline{y}) - b\overline{y}(p - \overline{y})^2 - c\overline{y},$$

where $a = 3k(1 - d)$, $b = 3k(1 + d)$, and $c = 2k\delta_1(1 + d)$.

This ODE is sometimes referred to as a signal restoration algorithm. According to two theorems proved in [12], if the inequalities

$$c < \frac{p^2 a^2}{4(a + b)} \tag{25}$$

$$\overline{y}\left(t_0 + \frac{\tau}{2}\right) > E_1, \tag{26}$$

hold where $E_1 = p\left(\frac{b}{a+b}\right) + A$ and where $A = \frac{p}{2}\left(\frac{a}{a+b}\right)\left(1 - \sqrt{1 - c^*}\right)$ and $c^* = \frac{4c(a+b)}{p^2 a^2}$, then $\overline{Y}$ exponentially quickly converges to the concentration $E_2 = p - A$. Using the facts that $d < \frac{1}{100}$, $\delta_1 < \frac{1}{25}$, $\delta_3 < \frac{1}{100}$ and $\overline{y}\left(t_0 + \frac{\tau}{2}\right) > \frac{3}{5}$, it is easy to verify that both of the above inequalities hold.

Corollary 4.5 of [12] shows that under these conditions $\overline{Y}$ will converge to the quantity $p - \gamma$ in at most time

$$T = \frac{a + b}{abp^2(1 - c^*)} \log u,$$

where $u = \frac{(p - \gamma - E_1)(E_2 - \frac{3}{5})}{(\frac{3}{5} - E_1)(E_2 - p + \gamma)}$. Using the bounds of d, δ_1, and δ_3 and the fact that $k \geq \frac{13}{\tau}$, it is easy to verify that $T \leq \frac{\tau}{2}$. Consequently, for all time $t \in I_\tau$, $\overline{y}(t) \geq p - \gamma$ and therefore $y(t) < \gamma$.

Finally, since $p > 1 - \delta_3$, $\gamma = \delta_1 - \delta_2 - \delta_3$ and the measurement function can only introduce δ_2 amount of error, $\widehat{N}_{\hat{x}_0, \hat{c}}(t)(\overline{Y}) > 1 - \delta_1$ and $\widehat{N}_{\hat{x}_0, \hat{c}}(t)(Y) < \delta_1$. Therefore $\widehat{N}_{\hat{x}_0, \hat{c}}$ is δ_1-close to encoding an output of $Y = 0$ and $\overline{Y} = 1$ in the interval I_τ. $\qquad\square$

Lemma 4. *If $I \in \mathbf{I}(\tau)$ is an interval such that $\phi_{00}(I)$, $\phi_{01}(I)$, or $\phi_{10}(I)$ holds, then $\psi_1(I)$ holds.*

Proof. This lemma follows by symmetry of Lemma 3. This is even more pronounced by comparing the bias introduced by the reactions (12)–(14). In the case of this lemma, the bias in favor of Y is $(\overline{x}_1 + \overline{x}_2) \geq 1 - \delta_1$ and the bias in favor of $\overline{Y}$ is $x_1 x_2 \leq (1 - \delta_1)\delta_1$. This is far more favorable when the corresponding bias in Lemma 3 was $(1 - \delta_1)^2$ and δ_1, respectively. $\qquad\square$

4   Robust Combinatorial Circuits

In this section, we state and prove our main theorem, namely, that every combinatorial circuit can be robustly simulated by an I/O CRN. The proof is a natural (and relatively simple) extension of Theorem 2. We begin by defining a requirement for an I/O CRN to properly simulate an arbitrary combinatorial circuit.

Given positive integers $n, m > 0$, we define an *n-input m-output combinatorial circuit* $C_{n,m}$ to be a directed acyclic graph where each node is a two-input one-output NAND gate. The circuit $C_{n,m}$ also has n incoming edges for *inputs* and m outgoing edges for *outputs*. The *depth* of a circuit $C_{n,m}$ is the longest path from an input to an output. Each circuit $C_{n,m}$ can also be regarded as a function $C_{n,m} : \{0,1\}^n \to \{0,1\}^m$ defined in the obvious way of passing the values of the inputs into the circuit to compute the outputs.

For a circuit $C_{n,m}$, we define the set of input species as

$$U = \{X_i, \overline{X}_i \mid 0 \leq i < n\}. \tag{27}$$

We can now define the requirement $\Phi(C_{n,m}, \tau) = (\phi, \alpha)$ where α is defined by

$$\alpha(\boldsymbol{u}, V, h) \equiv \left[V = \{Y_i, \overline{Y}_i \mid 0 \leq i < m\} \text{ and } h = h_0\right]. \tag{28}$$

To state the I/O requirement ϕ, we need a bit more terminology.

For a string $w = a_1 a_2 \cdots a_n \in \{0,1\}^n$, we define the *compliment* of w to be $\overline{w} = \overline{a}_1 \overline{a}_2 \cdots \overline{a}_n$ where $\overline{a}_i = 1 - a_i$. For a string $w \in \{0,1\}^n$ and input $\boldsymbol{u} \in C[U]$, we use the notation $\boldsymbol{u}(t) = w$ to denote that $\boldsymbol{u}(t)(X_i) = w[i]$ and $\boldsymbol{u}(t)(\overline{X}_i) = \overline{w}[i]$ for each $0 \leq i < n$. We also define the predicates

$$\phi_w(I) \equiv (\forall t \in I)\left[\boldsymbol{u}(t) = w\right]$$
$$\psi_w(I) \equiv (\forall t \in I)\left[\boldsymbol{v}(t) = w\right].$$

We now can define the I/O requirement ϕ as

$$\phi(\boldsymbol{u}, \boldsymbol{v}) \equiv (\forall I \in \boldsymbol{I}(\tau))(\forall w \in \{0,1\}^n)\left[\phi_w(I) \implies \psi_{C_{n,m}(w)}(I_\tau)\right]. \tag{29}$$

Construction 5. Given a combinatorial circuit $C_{n,m}$ with G gates and depth d along with constants $\boldsymbol{\delta} = (\delta_1, \delta_2, \delta_3, \delta_4)$, and τ, define the CRN $N(C_{n,m}, \boldsymbol{\delta}, \tau)$ by joining G copies of the I/O CRN $N\left(\boldsymbol{\delta}, \frac{\tau}{d}\right)$ from Construction 1 in the obvious way.

Theorem 6. *If $C_{n,m}$ is a combinatorial circuit, the constants $\boldsymbol{\delta} = (\delta_1, \delta_2, \delta_3, \delta_4) \in (0, \infty)^4$ and $\tau > 0$ satisfy $\delta_2 + \delta_3 < \delta_1 < \frac{1}{25}$, $\delta_2 + \delta_3 < \frac{1}{100}$, and $N = N(C_{n,m}, \boldsymbol{\delta}, \tau)$ is constructed according to Construction 5, then $N \models_{\delta_1}^{\delta} \Phi(C_{n,m}, \tau)$.*

Proof. This theorem immediately follows from the fact that each NAND gate that N is composed of is also robust. Therefore the outputs of every NAND gate within $\frac{\tau}{d}$ time will produce an output signal that is δ_1-close to its output. Since d is the length of the longest path in the circuit, the propagation delay for the combinatorial circuit is τ. $\qquad\square$

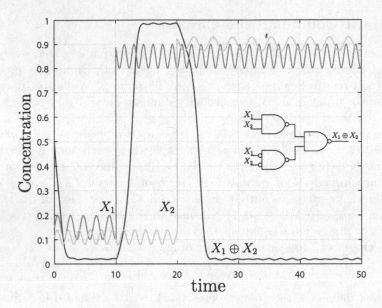

Fig. 1. XOR circuit with noise.

Simulations show gates and circuits are far more robust than the theorems predict. This is due to the loose bounding arguments used in the theorems, and shows that it may be possible to significantly tighten these bounds in the proofs. For example, Fig. 1 shows three NAND gates connected to form an exclusive OR circuit. The simulation shows inputs that transition from low to high at different times, different levels, and different noise amplitudes.

Acknowledgments. We thank Jack Lutz and the Laboratory of Molecular Programming at Iowa State University for useful discussions.

References

1. Aris, R.: Prolegomena to the rational analysis of systems of chemical reactions. Arch. Ration. Mech. Anal. **19**(2), 81–99 (1965)
2. Boemo, M.A., Lucas, A.E., Turberfield, A.J., Cardelli, L.: The formal language and design principles of autonomous DNA walker circuits. ACS Synth. Biol. **5**(8), 878–884 (2016)
3. Boruah, K., Dutta, J.C.: Development of a DNA computing model for Boolean circuit. In: Proceedings of the 2nd International Conference on Advances in Electrical, Electronics, Information, Communication and Bio-Informatics, pp. 301–304, February 2016
4. Cardelli, L.: Two-domain DNA strand displacement. Math. Struct. Comput. Sci. **23**(2), 247–271 (2013)
5. Chen, Y.J., Dalchau, N., Srinivas, N., Phillips, A., Cardelli, L., Soloveichik, D., Seelig, G.: Programmable chemical controllers made from DNA. Nat. Nanotechnol. **8**(10), 755–762 (2013)

6. Dannenberg, F., Kwiatkowska, M., Thachuk, C., Turberfield, A.J.: DNA walker circuits: computational potential, design, and verification. In: Soloveichik, D., Yurke, B. (eds.) DNA 2013. LNCS, vol. 8141, pp. 31–45. Springer, Cham (2013). https://doi.org/10.1007/978-3-319-01928-4_3

7. Douglas, S.M., Bachelet, I., Church, G.M.: A logic-gated nanorobot for targeted transport of molecular payloads. Science 335(6070), 831–834 (2012)

8. Ellis, S.J., Henderson, E.R., Klinge, T.H., Lathrop, J.I., Lutz, J.H., Lutz, R.R., Mathur, D., Miner, A.S.: Automated requirements analysis for a molecular watchdog timer. In: Proceedings of the 29th International Conference on Automated Software Engineering, pp. 767–778. ACM (2014)

9. Ge, L., Zhong, Z., Wen, D., You, X., Zhang, C.: A formal combinational logic synthesis with chemical reaction networks. IEEE Trans. Mol. Biol. Multi-Scale Commun. 3(1), 33–47 (2017)

10. Hjelmfelt, A., Weinberger, E.D., Ross, J.: Chemical implementation of neural networks and Turing machines. Proc. Natl. Acad. Sci. 88(24), 10983–10987 (1991)

11. Klinge, T.H.: Robust and modular computation with chemical reaction networks. Ph.D. thesis, Iowa State University (2016)

12. Klinge, T.H.: Robust signal restoration in chemical reaction networks. In: Proceedings of the 3rd International Conference on Nanoscale Computing and Communication, pp. 6:1–6:6. ACM (2016)

13. Klinge, T.H., Lathrop, J.I., Lutz, J.H.: Robust biomolecular finite automata. Technical report 1505.03931, arXiv.org e-Print archive (2015)

14. Klinge, T.H., Lathrop, J.I., Lutz, J.H.: (2016), Work initially introduced in [11] and will appear in a forthcoming extension of [13]

15. Lutz, R.R., Lutz, J.H., Lathrop, J.I., Klinge, T.H., Mathur, D., Stull, D.M., Bergquist, T.G., Henderson, E.R.: Requirements analysis for a product family of DNA nanodevices. In: Proceedings of the 20th International Conference on Requirements Engineering, pp. 211–220. IEEE (2012)

16. Ogihara, M., Ray, A.: Simulating Boolean circuits on a DNA computer. In: Proceedings of the First Annual International Conference on Computational Molecular Biology, RECOMB 1997, pp. 226–231. ACM, New York (1997)

17. Qian, L., Winfree, E.: Scaling up digital circuit computation with DNA strand displacement cascades. Science 332(6034), 1196–1201 (2011)

18. Soloveichik, D., Cook, M., Winfree, E., Bruck, J.: Computation with finite stochastic chemical reaction networks. Nat. Comput. 7(4), 615–633 (2008)

19. Soloveichik, D., Seelig, G., Winfree, E.: DNA as a universal substrate for chemical kinetics. Proc. Natl. Acad. Sci. 107(12), 5393–5398 (2010)

20. Song, X., Eshra, A., Dwyer, C., Reif, J.: Renewable DNA seesaw logic circuits enabled by photoregulation of toehold-mediated strand displacement. RSC Adv. 7, 28130–28144 (2017)

21. Thubagere, A.J., Thachuk, C., Berleant, J., Johnson, R.F., Ardelean, D.A., Cherry, K.M., Qian, L.: Compiler-aided systematic construction of large-scale DNA strand displacement circuits using unpurified components. Nat. Commun. 8 (2017). article number 14373

Watson-Crick Partial Words

Manasi S. Kulkarni[1(✉)], Kalpana Mahalingam[1], and Ananda Chandra Nayak[2]

[1] Department of Mathematics, Indian Institute of Technology Madras,
Chennai 600036, India
ma16ipf01@smail.iitm.ac.in, kmahalingam@iitm.ac.in
[2] Department of Mathematics, Indian Institute of Technology Guwahati,
Guwahati 781039, India
n.ananda@iitg.ernet.in

Abstract. In DNA computing experiments, it is important that the strands involved in the computation do not interact in an undesirable fashion. The mathematical formalization of the DNA WK-complementarity as an antimorphic involution, has motivated the generalization of various concepts in combinatorics of words to ones that involve pseudo-identity functions. Mismatches occurring in not so perfect WK-complement strands has motivated the study of partial words for DNA strands. In this paper, we aim to combine the concept of partial words with pseudo-identity functions, and study the basic notions such as primitivity, conjugacy, commutativity and borderedness property for partial words under morphic and antimorphic involutions.

Keywords: Computing with DNA · Partial words · Primitivity
Conjugacy · Commutativity · Bordered words · Morphic involution
Antimorphic involution

1 Introduction

Synthesizing artificial DNA strands for computation purposes require designing of these strands in such a way that only the desired computations and interactions will take place while all other undesired computations and interactions are avoided. The main obstacle in most of the DNA computing experiments is the design of DNA strands that do not interact with themselves or with other stands in an undesirable manner forming unwanted secondary structures. This problem has been theoretically addressed in the literature by various means, such as ensuring large Hamming distance between the strands [6], extending several classical concepts from combinatorics on words to incorporate Watson-Crick(WK) complementarity of DNA strands, [5,7–9,12], etc. (Recall that, a single strand of DNA can be considered as a word over the DNA alphabet $\{A, G, C, T\}$ where A is a WK-complement of T and vice versa, and G is a WK-complement of C and vice versa. This WK-complementarity of the DNA strands is mathematically formalized as an antimorphic involution.)

© Springer International Publishing AG 2017
C. Martín-Vide et al. (Eds.): TPNC 2017, LNCS 10687, pp. 190–202, 2017.
https://doi.org/10.1007/978-3-319-71069-3_15

In general, the theoretical design of the DNA strands is based on the assumption that the hybridization occurs between two perfect WK-complement strands. However, in experimental computations, the hybridization can still occur even if there are few mismatches between the two strands. Thus, these mismatches can be disregarded and can be accounted for holes, treating these strands as partial words. In [13], Peter Leupold proposed the idea of partial words to be used to find good encodings for DNA computing purposes, as the compatibility of partial words automatically brings the Hamming distance concept in. The author then extends the concepts of involution-compliance and involution-freeness [7] for partial words.

In this paper we continue this line of research by initiating the study of some of the basic notions in combinatorics on partial words in order to incorporate the involution mapping. The definition of pseudo-primitive partial words is motivated by the information equivalence between two complementary strands of DNA. In addition, pseudo-primitive partial words account for repetition-free words upto involution. The notions of conjugacy, commutativity and borderedness extended to their involution counterparts are known to have a strong link with the unwanted secondary structures formed in DNA computing experiments, [9,10]. Note that, by extending these concepts to involution partial words, for example, that of pseudo-unbordered partial words, we can ensure that, some of the self-hybridized secondary structures can be avoided even when the hybridized substrands are not perfect WK-complements.

This paper is organized as follows. In Sect. 2, we give some basic definitions and notations used throughout the paper. In Sect. 3, we define θ-primitive partial words for (anti)morphic involution[1] and discuss some basic properties of it. Section 4 defines the concept of θ-conjugacy and θ-commutativity for partial words and, provides the characterization of partial words such that one is a θ-conjugate of the other and one θ-commutes with the other. In Sect. 5, we define θ-bordered and θ-unbordered partial words with concluding remarks in Sect. 6. Note that, although from theoretical point of view, it is natural to extend the properties of words to partial words under involution mapping, not all results hold trivially for partial words as can be seen from this paper.

2   Preliminaries

Let Σ be a finite alphabet consisting of nonempty set of symbols known as letters. A word is a sequence of letters from the alphabet Σ. A total word $w = a_1 a_2 \cdots a_n$ is a total function $w : \{1, 2, \ldots, n\} \mapsto \Sigma$ where $a_i \in \Sigma$ for $i = 1, 2, \ldots, n$. The length of a word $w \in \Sigma^*$ (i.e., the number of symbols in a word) is denoted by $|w|$. The empty string λ does not contain any symbol and hence $|\lambda| = 0$. The set of all words including λ is denoted by Σ^* and $\Sigma^+ = \Sigma^* \setminus \{\lambda\}$. By $w(i)$, we denote the letter at the i-th position. Any subset L of Σ^* is called a language and the cardinality of L is denoted by $|L|$.

---

[1] By (anti)morphic involution, we mean either a morphic or an antimorphic involution.

An *involution* is a mapping $\theta : \Sigma \mapsto \Sigma$ such that θ^2 is the identity function, i.e., $\theta(\theta(x)) = x$ for all $x \in \Sigma^*$. A mapping θ is said to be a *morphism* if $\theta(xy) = \theta(x)\theta(y)$ and an *antimorphism* if $\theta(xy) = \theta(y)\theta(x)$ for all $x, y \in \Sigma^*$.

A *partial word* $w = a_1 a_2 \cdots a_n$ over an alphabet Σ can be seen as a partial function $w : \{1, 2, \ldots, n\} \mapsto \Sigma$. The partial word may have some undefined positions along with the symbols from the alphabet. These unknown positions are known as "do not know" symbols or "holes" which are denoted by $\Diamond$, and they can be replaced by any symbol from the alphabet, [3]. A length of a partial word w is the number of holes and non-holes symbol in it. For a partial word $w = a_1 a_2 \cdots a_n$, if $w(i)$ is defined then we say that $i \in D(w)$, otherwise we say that $i \in H(w)$ where $D(w)$ and $H(w)$ are the domain and the set of holes of w respectively and $1 \leq i \leq n$. A (total) word is a partial word with an empty set of holes. A partial word can be seen as a total word over an extended alphabet $\Sigma_\Diamond = \Sigma \cup \{\Diamond\}$. A language of partial words L over the alphabet Σ is a subset of $\Sigma_\Diamond^*$. Moreover, for $\Diamond$ the mapping θ is defined as $\theta(\Diamond) = \Diamond$. For example, $u = ab\Diamond b\Diamond a$ is a partial word of length 6 over an alphabet $\Sigma = \{a, b\}$ where $D(u) = \{1, 2, 4, 6\}$ and $H(u) = \{3, 5\}$.

Since a partial word can be seen as a total word over the enlarged alphabet $\Sigma_\Diamond$, the concepts of prefix, suffix and factor of a partial word can be defined similarly as that of a total word. For a partial word $w = xyz$, y is called a central factor of w if $x \neq \lambda$ and $z \neq \lambda$.

Definition 1 [3]. *Let u and v be two partial words of equal length, then*

1. *u is said be contained in v, denoted by $u \subset v$, if all elements of $D(u)$ are also in $D(v)$ and $u(i) = v(i)$ for all $i \in D(u)$;*
2. *u and v are said to be compatible, denoted by $u \uparrow v$, if there exists a partial word w such that both $u \subset w$ and $v \subset w$;*

For $w \in \Sigma_\Diamond^*$ and $u \in \Sigma^*$, $u \leq_{cp} w$ (respectively, $u \leq_{cs} w$) if and only if $w \subset uv$ (respectively, $w \subset vu$) for $v \in \Sigma^*$. Similarly, $\mathrm{CPref}(w) = \{u \in \Sigma^+ : \exists v \in \Sigma^*, w \subset uv\}$ (respectively, $\mathrm{CSuff}(w) = \{u \in \Sigma^+ : \exists v \in \Sigma^*, w \subset vu\}$) and $\mathrm{PCPref}(w) = \{u \in \Sigma^+ : \exists v \in \Sigma^+, w \subset uv\}$ (respectively, $\mathrm{PCSuff}(w) = \{u \in \Sigma^+ : \exists v \in \Sigma^+, w \subset vu\}$).

Recall that a word is said to be a palindrome if it is equal to its mirror image. Similarly, a word u is said to be a θ-palindrome if $u = \theta(u)$ for (anti)morphic involution θ. On similar lines, a partial word u is said to be a θ-palindrome if $u \uparrow \theta(u)$ for (anti)morphic involution θ.

By $u \vee v$, we denote the least upper bound of u and v, i.e., a partial word such that $u, v \subset u \vee v$ and $D(u \vee v) = D(u) \cup D(v)$. A partial word w is said to be *primitive* if there does not exist a word v such that $w \subset v^n$ with $n \geq 2$, [2]. The language of primitive partial words is denoted by Q_p, [14]. If a partial word u is primitive and $u \subset v$ then v is also primitive.

3 θ-Primitive Partial Words

The notions of primitivity and periodicity are regarded as the most basic notions in combinatorics on words. Recall that, a word is said to be primitive if it is not power of any shorter word. Similarly, a partial word is said to be primitive if it is not contained in the power of a shorter word, i.e., if there does not exist a word v such that $w \subset v^n$ with $n \geq 2$, [2]. In this section, we extend the concept of primitivity to accommodate partial words under involution mappings. We first extend the notion of a period to θ-strong and θ-weak period of a partial word where θ is (anti)morphic involution.

Definition 2. *Let θ be (anti) morphic involution and u be a partial word over Σ.*

1. *A θ-(strong) period of a partial word u is a positive integer p such that $u(i) = u(j)$ or $u(i) = \theta(u(j))$ whenever $i, j \in D(u)$ and $i \equiv j \mod p$. In such a case, we call u to be θ-p-periodic.*
2. *A θ-weak period of u is a positive integer p such that $u(i) = u(i + p)$ or $u(i) = \theta(u(i + p))$ whenever $i, i + p \in D(u)$. In such a case, we call u to be weakly θ-p-periodic.*

If a word is θ-p-periodic then it is weakly θ-p-periodic as well, but converse does not hold always. Let us illustrate the above definitions with the help of a following example.

Example 3. Let $\Sigma = \{A, C, G, T\}$ and let θ be (anti)morphic involution such that $\theta(A) = T$, $\theta(T) = A$, $\theta(G) = C$, $\theta(C) = G$ and $\theta(\Diamond) = \Diamond$. Let $u = A\Diamond\Diamond TC\Diamond TGA$, then u is θ-3,5,6,8-periodic. Similarly, $v = A\Diamond\Diamond TG\Diamond\Diamond CTG$ is weakly θ-2,3,5,8-periodic. However v is not θ-2-periodic.

Let θ be (anti)morphic involution. A partial word $w = u_1 u_2 \cdots u_n$ is said to be contained in θ-power of a word u if $u_1 \subset u$ and, either $u_i \subset u$ or $u_i \subset \theta(u)$ for all $i \in \{2, \ldots, n\}$. More specifically, a partial word $w \in \Sigma^+$ is said to be contained in pseudo-power of a nonempty word u relative to θ, if $w \subset u\{u, \theta(u)\}^*$. Furthermore, a partial word w is said to be θ-primitive if there exists no nonempty word u such that $w \subset u\{u, \theta(u)\}^+$. By Q_{p_θ} we denote the set of all θ-primitive partial words. If $w \subset u\{u, \theta(u)\}^*$ and u is a shortest such word, then u is said to be θ-primitive root of w. Formally,

$$\rho_{\theta,\Diamond}(w) = \{x : x \text{ is a } \theta\text{-primitive (total) word and } w \subset x\{x, \theta(x)\}^n, \ n \geq 0\}.$$

It is known that every non-empty word has an unique primitive root, and also an unique θ-primitive root for a morphic as well as an antimorphic involution θ, [5]. However, in case of partial words, the primitive root of a partial word need not be unique, [2]. Similarly, the θ-primitive root of a partial word need not be unique as shown by the following example.

Example 4. Let $\Sigma = \{A, T, C, G\}$ and θ be an antimorphic involution such that $\theta(A) = T, \theta(T) = A, \theta(C) = G, \theta(G) = C, \theta(\Diamond) = \Diamond$. Let $w = A\Diamond CG\Diamond T$. It can be observed that $w \subset ATC\theta(ATC)$, $w \subset ACC\theta(ACC)$, $w \subset AGC\theta(AGC)$ and $w \subset AAC\theta(AAC)$.

Proposition 5. *If a partial word $w \in \Sigma_\Diamond^+$ is θ-primitive then it is also primitive.*

Proof. Let w be a θ-primitive partial word. Suppose w is not primitive. Then there exists a word $u \in \Sigma^+$ such that $w \subset u^k$ with $k \geq 2$. Hence w is also contained in θ-power of u which is a contradiction. Thus w is a primitive partial word. □

The converse of the above proposition need not be true as illustrated by the following example.

Example 6. Let $\Sigma = \{a, b\}$ and θ be an antimorphic involution such that $\theta(a) = b, \theta(b) = a$ and $\theta(\Diamond) = \Diamond$. Let $w = abb\Diamond \in Q_p$ but $w = abb\Diamond \subset a\theta(a)\theta(a)a$ and hence w is not a θ-primitive partial word.

It is known that, for a primitive word u, u cannot be a factor of u^2 in a nontrivial way, i.e., if $u^2 = xuy$ then either x or y has to be empty. On the similar lines, it has been shown in [2] that if u is a primitive partial word with at most one hole and $uu \uparrow xuy$ then either $x = \lambda$ or $y = \lambda$. The following result generalizes this fact to any arbitrary power.

Lemma 7. *Let u be a nonempty partial word with one hole. Then the following are equivalent:*

1. u is primitive;
2. u^{n-1} is not compatible to a central factor of u^n for all $n \geq 2$.

Proof. (1) $\Rightarrow$ (2) We prove it by induction on n.

Base Case: Let $n = 2$. Since u is a primitive partial word with one hole, the result holds as proved in [2].

Inductive Hypothesis: Let us assume that the result holds for $2 \leq k \leq n - 1$, i.e., u^{k-1} is not compatible to a central factor of u^k.

Inductive step: Now we prove the result for $k = n$, i.e., we prove that u^k is not compatible to a central factor of u^{k+1}. Assume that u^k is compatible to a central factor of u^{k+1}. Thus, $u^{k+1} = tvs$ such that $v \uparrow u^k$ for some nonempty partial words t, s with $|u| = |t| + |s|$ and t and s are prefix and suffix of u respectively. This implies $u = ty = zs$ for some nonempty partial words $y, z \in \Sigma_\Diamond^+$. Now, $u^{k+1} = uu^{k-1}u = tyu^{k-1}zs = tvs$. As $v \uparrow u^k$, we have $yu^{k-1}z \uparrow u^k$. Since y and z are nonempty, u^{k-1} is compatible to a central factor of u^k which is a contradiction to the inductive hypothesis.

Hence if u is a primitive partial word then u^{n-1} cannot be compatible to a central factor of u^n for all $n \geq 2$.

(2) $\Rightarrow$ (1) Assume that u is not a primitive partial word. Then there exist a nonempty word z such that $u \subset z^k$, $k \geq 2$. Now, $u^n \subset z^{nk} = zz^{k(n-1)}z^{k-1}$. Since $u^{n-1} \subset z^{k(n-1)}$ we have $u^n \uparrow zu^{n-1}z^{k-1}$, and thus u^{n-1} is compatible to a central factor of u^n, a contradiction. Thus, u is primitive. □

However Lemma 7 does not hold for the partial words with at least two holes. For example, consider a partial word $w = a\Diamond b\Diamond$ and thus $ww = a\Diamond b\Diamond a\Diamond b\Diamond$. It is easy to observe that w is primitive and w is compatible to a central factor of ww.

Since θ-primitive partial word is primitive, the above lemma applies to θ-primitive partial words as well. However, a θ-primitive partial word x with one hole can be compatible to a central factor of a word in $\{x, \theta(x)\}^2 \backslash x^2$, as demonstrated by the following example.

Example 8. Let $\Sigma = \{A, C, G, T\}$ and θ be an antimorphic involution such that $\theta(A) = T, \theta(T) = A, \theta(G) = C, \theta(C) = G$ and $\theta(\Diamond) = \Diamond$. Then for $x = A\Diamond CG$, we can see that $\theta(x)\theta(x) = CG\Diamond TCG\Diamond T \uparrow CGA\mathbf{A}\Diamond\mathbf{C}\mathbf{G}AT$. Similarly, let $\Sigma = \{a, b, c\}$ and θ be an antimorphic involution such that $\theta(a) = b$ and vice versa, and $\theta(c) = c$. Then for $x = a\Diamond c$, $x\theta(x) = a\Diamond cc\Diamond b \uparrow a\mathbf{a}\Diamond\mathbf{c}\Diamond b$.

The primitive partial word is closed under cyclic permutation. However, the class of θ-primitive partial words not necessarily closed under cyclic permutation which is illustrated by the following example.

Example 9. Consider the DNA alphabet $\Sigma = \{A, T, C, G\}$ and let θ be a morphic involution where $\theta(A) = T, \theta(T) = A, \theta(C) = G, \theta(G) = C$ and $\theta(\Diamond) = \Diamond$. Let $w = AC\Diamond GTC$ be a primitive partial word. Consider a cyclic permutation of w, $w' = CAC\Diamond GT \subset (CA)^2\theta(CA)$ which is not a θ-primitive partial word.

4 θ-Conjugacy and θ-Commutativity

In this section we define the concept of θ-conjugacy and θ-commutativity for partial words where θ is (anti)morphic involution.

Definition 10. *Let θ be either a morphic or an antimorphic involution on $\Sigma_\Diamond^*$. A partial word u is a θ-conjugate of another partial word w if there exists $v \in \Sigma_\Diamond^*$ such that $uv \uparrow \theta(v)w$.*

It is know that θ-conjugacy is a transitive relation for total words when θ is a morphic involution, [11]. However, this may not hold in case of partial words as demonstrated by the following example.

Example 11. Let $\Sigma = \{a, b, c\}$ and let θ be a morphic involution such that $\theta(a) = b, \theta(b) = a, \theta(c) = c$ and $\theta(\Diamond) = \Diamond$. Let $u = a\Diamond bc$, $w = \Diamond acb$ and $v = b\Diamond ab$. It is easy to see that for $x = acb$ and $y = c$, $u \subset xy$, $w \subset \theta(y)x$ and hence u is a θ-conjugate of w. Similarly, for $\alpha = b$ and $\beta = acb$, $w \subset \alpha\beta$ and $v \subset \theta(\beta)\alpha$ and hence w is a θ-conjugate of v. Now, if we assume that there exists $x', y' \in \Sigma_\Diamond^+$ such that $u \subset x'y'$ and $v \subset \theta(y')x'$, then it is easy to observe that x' must begin with a and $\theta(y')$ must begin with b, i.e., y' must begin with a. Hence $x' = a$ and $y' = abc$, but then $v = b\Diamond ab \not\subset \theta(y')x' = baca$. Hence θ-conjugacy relation is not transitive for a morphic involution θ.

The following result from [4] provides a characterization of partial words u, v such that x is a conjugate of y.

Theorem 12 [4]. *Let x, y, z be partial words with $x, y \in \Sigma_\Diamond^+$ and $z \in \Sigma_\Diamond^*$. If $xy \uparrow yz$ and $xy \vee yz$ is $|x|$-periodic then there exists words $u \in \Sigma^*, v \in \Sigma^+$ such that $x \subset uv$, $y \subset vu$ and $z \subset (uv)^n u$ for $n \geq 0$.*

In the following proposition, we provide a characterization of partial words x and y such that x is a θ-conjugate of y.

Theorem 13. *Let x and y be non-empty partial words and θ be a morphic involution on $\Sigma_\Diamond^*$. If there exists a partial word z such that $xz \uparrow \theta(z)y$ and $xz \vee \theta(z)y$ is $|x|$-θ-periodic, then there exist partial words u, v such that $x \subset uv$ and one of the following holds:*

1. $y \subset v\theta(u)$ *and* $z \subset (\theta(u)\theta(v)uv)^i\theta(u)$ *for some $i \geq 0$.*
2. $y \subset \theta(v)u$ *and* $z \subset (\theta(u)\theta(v)uv)^i\theta(u)\theta(v)u$ *for some $i \geq 0$.*

Proof. Let $m > 0$ be such that $m|x| > |z| > (m-1)|x|$. Let $x = x_1y_1$ and $y = y_2x_2$ where $|x_1| = |x_2| = |z| - (m-1)|x|$ and $|y_1| = |y_2|$. Let $z = x_1'y_1'x_2'y_2'\cdots x_{m-1}'y_{m-1}'x_m'$ where $|x_1'| = |x_2'| = \cdots = |x_m'| = |x_1| = |x_2|$ and $|y_1'| = |y_2'| = \cdots = |y_{m-1}'| = |y_1| = |y_2|$. Note that such m always exist. Now, since $xz \uparrow \theta(z)y$,

$$
\begin{array}{ccccccccccc}
x_1 & y_1 & x_1' & y_1' & x_2' & y_2' & \cdots & x_{m-1}' & y_{m-1}' & x_m' & \uparrow \\
\theta(x_1') & \theta(y_1') & \theta(x_2') & \theta(y_2') & \theta(x_3') & \theta(y_3') & \cdots & \theta(x_m') & y_2 & x_2 &
\end{array}
$$

By the length argument we get, $x_1 \uparrow \theta(x_1')$, $y_1 \uparrow \theta(y_1')$, $x_1' \uparrow \theta(x_2')$, $y_1' \uparrow \theta(y_2')$, $\ldots, x_{m-1}' \uparrow \theta(x_m')$, $y_{m-1}' \uparrow y_2$, $x_m' \uparrow x_2$. Here, we have two different cases. If m is odd, then

$$x_1 \uparrow \theta(x_1') \uparrow x_2' \uparrow \theta(x_3') \uparrow \cdots \uparrow \theta(x_m') \uparrow \theta(x_2)$$

and

$$y_1 \uparrow \theta(y_1') \uparrow y_2' \uparrow \theta(y_3') \uparrow \cdots \uparrow y_{m-1}' \uparrow y_2.$$

Similarly, if m is even then,

$$x_1 \uparrow \theta(x_1') \uparrow x_2' \uparrow \theta(x_3') \uparrow \cdots \uparrow x_m' \uparrow x_2$$

and

$$y_1 \uparrow \theta(y_1') \uparrow y_2' \uparrow \theta(y_3') \uparrow \cdots \uparrow \theta(y_{m-1}') \uparrow \theta(y_2).$$

Also, $xz \vee \theta(z)y$ is $|x|$-θ-periodic. For $1 \leq i \leq |x_1|$, consider the partial word

$$
\begin{array}{cccccc}
(x_1)(i) & (x_1')(i) & (x_2')(i) & \cdots & (x_{m-1}')(i) & (x_m')(i) \vee \\
(\theta(x_1'))(i) & (\theta(x_2'))(i) & (\theta(x_3'))(i) & \cdots & (\theta(x_m'))(i) & (x_2)(i)
\end{array}
$$

It is clear that the above word is 1-θ-periodic, say with letter $a_i \in \Sigma \cup \{\Diamond\}$. Similarly, for $1 \leq j \leq |y_1|$, the partial word

$$
\begin{array}{cccccc}
(y_1)(j) & (y_1')(j) & (y_2')(j) & \cdots & (y_{m-2}')(j) & (y_{m-1}')(j) \vee \\
(\theta(y_1'))(j) & (\theta(y_2'))(j) & (\theta(y_3'))(j) & \cdots & (\theta(y_{m-1}'))(j) & (y_2)(j)
\end{array}
$$

is 1-θ-periodic, say with letter $b_j \in \Sigma \cup \{\Diamond\}$. Now, let $u = a_1a_2\cdots a_{|x_1|}$ and $v = b_1b_2\cdots b_{|y_1|}$. Let m be odd, then $x_1 \subset u$, $x_2 \subset \theta(u)$, $y_1 \subset v$ and $y_2 \subset v$. Then $x = x_1y_1 \subset uv$, $y = y_2x_2 \subset v\theta(u)$ and $z = x_1'y_1'x_2'y_2'\cdots x_{m-1}'y_{m-1}'x_m' \subset (\theta(u)\theta(v)uv)\cdots(\theta(u)\theta(v)uv)\theta(u) = (\theta(u)\theta(v)uv)^{\frac{m-1}{2}}\theta(u)$. Similarly, if m is even, then $x_1 \subset u$, $x_2 \subset u$, $y_1 \subset v$ and $y_2 \subset \theta(v)$ and $z = x_1'y_1'x_2'y_2'\cdots x_{m-1}'y_{m-1}'x_m' \subset (\theta(u)\theta(v)uv)\cdots(\theta(u)\theta(v)uv)\theta(u)\theta(v)u = (\theta(u)\theta(v)uv)^{\frac{m-2}{2}}\theta(u)\theta(v)u$. $\square$

The following theorem from [3] provides a necessary and sufficient condition for two equi-length partial words to be conjugates of each other.

Theorem 14 [3]. *Let x, y, z be partial words such that $|x| = |y| > 0$. Then $xz \uparrow zy$ if and only if xzy is weakly $|x|$-periodic.*

However, in case of partial words under the involution mapping, we have only a necessary condition. The proof technique for this proof is similar to that of Theorem 13 and hence is omitted.

Theorem 15. *Let x, y and z be partial words such that $|x| = |y| > 0$. Then for a morphic involution θ, $xz \uparrow \theta(z)y$ implies xzy is weakly θ-$|x|$-periodic.*

However, the converse of the above theorem does not hold necessarily. For example, let $\Sigma = \{A, G, C, T\}$ be such that for a morphic involution θ, $\theta(A) = T, \theta(T) = A, \theta(G) = C, \theta(C) = G$ and $\theta(\Diamond) = \Diamond$. Then for $x = A\Diamond$, $y = G\Diamond$ and $z = \Diamond TG\Diamond CT$, $xzy = A\Diamond\Diamond TG\Diamond CTG\Diamond$ is weakly 2-θ-periodic but $xz = A\Diamond\Diamond TG\Diamond CT \not\uparrow \Diamond AC\Diamond GAG\Diamond = \theta(z)y$.

4.1 θ-Commutativity

Definition 16. *Let θ be either a morphic or an antimorphic involution. A partial word $u \in \Sigma^+$ is said to θ-commute with a partial word $v \in \Sigma^+$ if $uv \uparrow \theta(v)u$.*

We define the θ-commutativity order of a partial word v as $u \leq_c^{\theta_\Diamond} v$ if and only if $v \subset ux$ and $v \subset \theta(x)u$ for some $x \in \Sigma^*$. By $L_c^{\theta_\Diamond}(v) = \{u : u \in \Sigma^*, u \leq_c^{\theta_\Diamond} v\}$ we denote the set of all partial words that θ-commute with v and $\nu_c^{\theta_\Diamond}(v) = |L_c^{\theta_\Diamond}(v)|$. For a positive integer $i \geq 1$, we define $C_{\theta_\Diamond}(i) = \{v : v \in \Sigma_\Diamond^+, \nu_c^{\theta_\Diamond}(v) = i\}$.

We illustrate θ-commutative partial words in the following example.

Example 17. Consider the DNA alphabet $\Sigma = \{A, T, C, G\}$ and θ be an antimorphic involution such that $\theta(A) = T, \theta(T) = A, \theta(C) = G, \theta(G) = C$ and $\theta(\Diamond) = \Diamond$. Let $v = A\Diamond G\Diamond$ and $x = CTAGA\Diamond G\Diamond$. Now $\theta(x) = \Diamond C\Diamond TCTAG$ and $vx = A\Diamond G\Diamond \cdot CTAGA\Diamond G\Diamond \uparrow \theta(x)v = \Diamond C\Diamond TCTAG \cdot A\Diamond G\Diamond$. Hence v θ-commutes with x.

In [10], the authors have shown that for all $a \in \Sigma$ such that $a \neq \theta(a)$, $a^+ \subseteq C_\theta(1)$ whenever θ is either a morphic or an antimorphic involution. This result does not hold in case of partial words which is illustrated in the following example.

Example 18. Let $\Sigma = \{a, b\}$ and θ be an antimorphic involution such that $\theta(a) = b, \theta(b) = a$ and $\theta(\Diamond) = \Diamond$. Consider the partial word $u = a\Diamond$ and observe that $u \subset a^2$. For $v = a, x = b$, we have $u \subset vx$ and $u \subset \theta(x)v$. Hence $a \in L_c^{\theta_\Diamond}(u)$ and thus $u \notin C_{\theta_\Diamond}(1)$.

The following result provides a characterization of partial words u and v that commutes with each other.

Lemma 19 ([1]). *Let u and v be two nonempty partial words such that uv contains at most one hole. The words u and v commute if and only if they are contained in powers of the same word, i.e., $uv \uparrow vu$ if there exists a word w such that $u \subset w^m$ and $v \subset w^n$ for some $m, n \geq 1$.*

On similar lines, in the following result, we provide a characterization for partial words u and v such that u θ-commutes with v for (anti)morphic involution θ.

Theorem 20. *Let $u, v \in \Sigma_\Diamond^+$ such that u θ-commute with v, i.e., $uv \uparrow \theta(v)u$ and $uv \vee \theta(v)u$ is $|v|$-periodic.*

1. *If θ is a morphic involution then $v \subset yx$, $u \subset (xy)^i x$ as well as $v \subset \theta(x)\theta(y)$ for $i \geq 0$ and $x \in \Sigma^+, y \in \Sigma^*$.*
2. *If θ is an antimorphic involution then $v \subset yx, u \subset (xy)^i x$ for $i \geq 0$ as well as $v \subset \theta(y)\theta(x)$ where $x \in \Sigma^+, y \in \Sigma^*$.*

Proof. We prove the result only for a morphic involution as the proof for an antimorphic is similar. Let $uv \uparrow \theta(v)u$ and $uv \vee \theta(v)u$ is $|v|$-periodic. Then by Theorem 12, there exist $x \in \Sigma^+$ and $y \in \Sigma^*$ such that $\theta(v) \subset xy$, $v \subset yx$ and $u \subset (xy)^i x$ for some $i \geq 0$. Furthermore, $\theta(v) \subset xy$ implies that $v \subset \theta(xy) = \theta(x)\theta(y)$ as θ is a morphic involution. ∎

5　θ-(Un)bordered Partial Words

In this section we introduce the concept of θ-bordered and θ-unbordered partial words for (anti)morphic involution θ. Recall that, a non-empty partial word u is said to be bordered if there exists $x \in \Sigma^+$ such that $u \subset xy$ and $u \subset zx$ for $y, z \in \Sigma^+$.

Definition 21. *Let θ be either a morphic or an antimorphic involution on $\Sigma_\Diamond^*$. A partial word $u \in \Sigma_\Diamond^+$ is said to be θ-bordered if there exists $x \in \Sigma^+$ such that $u \subset xy$ and $u \subset z\theta(x)$ for $y, z \in \Sigma^+$. A partial word which is not θ-bordered is called θ-unbordered.*

For $u \in \Sigma_\Diamond^*$ and $x, y, z \in \Sigma^*$, if $u \subset xy$ and $u \subset z\theta(x)$, then x is said to be a θ-border of u and this is denoted by $x \leq_d^{\theta_\Diamond} u$. By $L_d^{\theta_\Diamond}(u)$ and $D_{\theta_\Diamond}(i)$ we denote the set of all θ-borders of a partial word u and the set of all partial words with exactly i θ-borders, respectively. Note that, the empty word λ is always considered as a trivial θ-border for all partial words. Also, let $\nu_d^{\theta_\Diamond}(u)$ denotes the cardinality of the set $L_d^{\theta_\Diamond}(u)$ for a partial word $u \in \Sigma_\Diamond^+$.

Example 22. Let $\Sigma = \{a, b\}$ and θ be an antimorphic involution such that $\theta(a) = b, \theta(b) = a$ and $\theta(\Diamond) = \Diamond$. Then for $u = a\Diamond ab$, $L_d^{\theta_\Diamond}(u) = \{\lambda, a, ab, aba\}$ and $\nu_d^{\theta_\Diamond}(u) = |L_d^{\theta_\Diamond}(u)| = 4$. Hence $u \in D_{\theta_\Diamond}(4)$.

The following observations follow directly from the definition.

Lemma 23. *Let θ be either a morphic or an antimorphic involution over the alphabet $\Sigma_\Diamond$.*

1. *A θ-bordered partial word $u \in \Sigma_\Diamond^+$ has length greater than or equal to 2.*
2. *For $u \in \Sigma_\Diamond^+$, if $u \subset \{u_1, u_2, \ldots, u_n\}$ then $\theta(u) \subset \{\theta(u_1), \theta(u_2), \ldots, \theta(u_n)\}$.*

It was shown in [9] that in the case of total words, if $\theta(a) \neq a$ for all $a \in \Sigma$ then $a^+ \subseteq D_\theta(1)$. However, this result does not necessarily hold in case of partial words, as demonstrated by the following example.

Example 24. Consider a partial word $u = a \Diamond a \Diamond \Diamond$ over an alphabet $\Sigma = \{a, b\}$ such that $\theta(a) = b$, $\theta(b) = a$ and $\theta(\Diamond) = \Diamond$ for (anti)morphic involution θ. Clearly $u \subset a^+$ but $u \notin D_{\theta_\Diamond}(1)$ as a is a θ-border of u.

The following lemma provides the characterization of partial words that are θ-bordered for an antimorphic involution θ.

Lemma 25. *Let θ be an antimorphic involution. A nonempty partial word $u \in \Sigma_\Diamond^+$ is θ-bordered if and only if $u \subset av\theta(a)$ for $a \in \Sigma$ and $v \in \Sigma^*$.*

The following result follows immediately from Lemma 25.

Theorem 26. *$D_{\theta_\Diamond}(1)$ is a regular language when θ is an antimorphic involution on $\Sigma_\Diamond^*$.*

We have seen a characterization of θ-bordered partial words in Lemma 25 when θ is an antimorphic involution. The next lemma on similar lines provides a characterization of θ-unbordered partial words for (anti)morphic involution θ, in terms of set of contained prefixes and contained suffixes. Note that, the characterization provided in Lemma 25 is stronger than the one provided in the next lemma for an antimorphic involution θ.

Lemma 27. *Let θ be (anti)morphic involution on $\Sigma_\Diamond^*$. Then for all $u \in \Sigma_\Diamond^+$ with $|u| \geq 2$, u is θ-unbordered iff $\theta(PCPref(u)) \cap PCSuff(u) = \emptyset$.*

We know from Theorem 26 that the set $D_{\theta_\Diamond}(1)$ is a regular language for an antimorphic involution θ, while Theorem 28 states that the set of all θ-bordered words is not a context-free language for a morphic involution θ.

Theorem 28. *Let θ be a morphic involution such that $\theta(a) \neq a$ for all $a \in \Sigma$. Then the language of θ-bordered partial words over Σ is not context-free.*

We have the following result from [9] which counts the number of θ-borders of a power of a θ-palindromic primitive word.

Proposition 29 [9]. *Let u be a θ-palindrome primitive word and $j \geq 1$ be an integer.*

1. For a morphic involution θ, $\nu_d^\theta(u^j) = \nu_d^\theta(u) + j - 1$.
2. For an antimorphic involution θ, $\nu_d^\theta(u^j) = |u^j| = j * |u|$.

Both of the above results need not hold in case of partial words as illustrated by the following example.

Example 30. If θ is an antimorphic involution such that $\theta(a) = b, \theta(b) = a$ and $\theta(\lozenge) = \lozenge$ then for $u = a\lozenge b$, $u \uparrow \theta(u)$ and hence u is a θ-palindrome. Let $v = u^2 = a\lozenge ba\lozenge b$. Then $L_d^{\theta\lozenge}(u) = \{\lambda, a, aa, ab\}$ and $L_d^{\theta\lozenge}(v) = \{\lambda, a, aa, ab, aab, abb, aaba, abba, aabaa, abbaa, aabab, abbab\}$ and thus $\nu_d^{\theta\lozenge}(u^2) \neq 2 * |u|$.

Moreover, we have the following result for a partial word that is both θ-palindromic and primitive for a morphic involution θ.

Proposition 31. *Let θ be a morphic involution, $|\Sigma| = k$ and $j \geq 2$. Let $u \in \Sigma_\lozenge^+$ be a θ-palindromic primitive partial word with one hole, then*

$$\nu_d^{\theta\lozenge}(u^j) = \nu_d^{\theta\lozenge}(u) + k + k^2 + \cdots + k^{j-1}.$$

Proof. Let $u = a_1 a_2 \cdots a_n$ be a primitive partial word with one hole. Since u is θ-palindrome for a morphic involution θ, $u \uparrow \theta(u)$. Thus $a_1 a_2 \cdots a_n \uparrow \theta(a_1 a_2 \cdots a_n) = \theta(a_1)\theta(a_2) \cdots \theta(a_n)$ which implies that $a_i = \theta(a_i)$ for all $i \in \{1, 2, \ldots, n\}$. Hence $\nu_d^{\theta\lozenge}(u) = \nu_d(u)$, where $\nu_d(u)$ is the number of borders of u.

For $j = 2$, $u^2 = uu$ will have exactly two holes and since u is primitive, by Proposition 7, u will not be compatible to a central factor of u^2. The borders of u^2 will include the borders of u. Moreover, u is a proper prefix and as well as proper suffix of u^2. Since u has one hole, that hole can be replaced by any of the k symbols from the alphabet Σ. Thus $\nu_d^{\theta\lozenge}(u^2) = \nu_d(u^2) = \nu_d(u) + k$.

For u^j, by Proposition 7 observe that u^{j-1} is not compatible to a proper factor of u^j. Hence, all of $u, u^2, \ldots, u^{j-1}$ are proper prefixes as well as proper suffixes of u^j. Also u^{j-1} has exactly $j - 1$ holes. Thus, $\nu_d^{\theta\lozenge}(u^j) = \nu_d^{\theta\lozenge}(u) + k + k^2 + \cdots + k^{j-1}$.

Corollary 32. *Let θ be a morphic involution and let u be a θ-palindromic primitive partial word with one hole. Then for $j \geq 2$,*

$$u^j \in D_{\theta_\lozenge}\left(i + \sum_{p=1}^{j-1} k^p\right).$$

In the following result, for an antimorphic involution θ, we count the number of θ-borders of a θ-palindromic partial word with one hole. Note that, in a partial word u, when the hole does not occur in the middle position, the holes in the prefixes of u^j does not align with the holes in the image of suffixes of u^j under an antimorphic involution θ. However, if the hole occurs exactly in the middle position of u, the holes in the prefixes and the image of suffixes under θ aligns with each other, and hence the count.

Proposition 33. *Let θ be an antimorphic involution, $|\Sigma| = k$ and $j \geq 2$. Let $u \in \Sigma_\diamond^+$ be a θ-palindromic partial word with one hole. Then*

1. *If u is a primitive partial word such that the hole occurs anywhere but in the middle position, then $\nu_d^{\theta\diamond}(u^j) = j \times |u|$.*
2. *If the hole in u occurs exactly in the middle position, then*

$$\nu_d^{\theta\diamond}(u^j) = \nu_d^{\theta\diamond}(u) + \left(\frac{|u|+1}{2}\right)k + |u|k^2 + \cdots + |u|k^{j-1} + \left(\frac{|u|-1}{2}\right)k^j.$$

6   Conclusions

Primitivity, borderedness, conjugacy, commutativity are some of the most basic notions in combinatorics on words. We have initiated the study of some of these notions for partial words under involution mappings, drawing motivation from DNA strand design. The presence of multiple copies of θ-palindromic strands in DNA based computations is known to form unwanted intermolecular hybridizations, [12]. Thus, in addition, concepts like palindromic property can be extended to partial words under involution mapping. Also, from theoretical point of view, it is interesting to study the extended Fine-Wilf's theorem, critical factorization theorem, Lyndon-Schützenberger equations, etc., with respect to (anti)morphic involutions θ.

References

1. Berstel, J., Boasson, L.: Partial words and a theorem of Fine and Wilf. Theor. Comput. Sci. **218**(1), 135–141 (1999)
2. Blanchet-Sadri, F.: Primitive partial words. Discr. Appl. Math. **148**(3), 195–213 (2005)
3. Blanchet-Sadri, F.: Algorithmic Combinatorics on Partial Words. CRC Press, Boca Raton (2007)
4. Blanchet-Sadri, F., Luhmann, D.: Conjugacy on partial words. Theor. Comput. Sci. **289**(1), 297–312 (2002)
5. Czeizler, E., Kari, L., Seki, S.: On a special class of primitive words. Theor. Comput. Sci. **411**, 617–630 (2010)
6. Deaton, R., Garzon, M., Murphy, R.C., Rose, J.A., Franceschetti, D.R., Stevens, S.E.: Reliability and efficiency of a DNA-based computation. Phys. Rev. Lett. **80**, 417–420 (1998)
7. Hussini, S., Kari, L., Konstantinidis, S.: Coding properties of DNA languages. Theor. Comput. Sci. **290**(3), 1557–1579 (2003)
8. Jonoska, N., Mahalingam, K.: Languages of DNA based code words. In: Chen, J., Reif, J. (eds.) DNA 2003. LNCS, vol. 2943, pp. 61–73. Springer, Heidelberg (2004). https://doi.org/10.1007/978-3-540-24628-2_8
9. Kari, L., Mahalingam, K.: Involutively bordered words. Int. J. Found. Comput. Sci. **18**(05), 1089–1106 (2007)
10. Kari, L., Mahalingam, K.: Watson-Crick conjugate and commutative words. In: Garzon, M.H., Yan, H. (eds.) DNA 2007. LNCS, vol. 4848, pp. 273–283. Springer, Heidelberg (2008). https://doi.org/10.1007/978-3-540-77962-9_29

11. Kari, L., Mahalingam, K.: Watson-Crick bordered words and their syntactic monoid. Int. J. Found. Comput. Sci. **19**(05), 1163–1179 (2008)
12. Kari, L., Mahalingam, K.: Watson-Crick palindromes in DNA computing. Nat. Comput. **9**(2), 297–316 (2010)
13. Leupold, P.: Partial words for DNA coding. In: Ferretti, C., Mauri, G., Zandron, C. (eds.) DNA 2004. LNCS, vol. 3384, pp. 224–234. Springer, Heidelberg (2005). https://doi.org/10.1007/11493785_20
14. Nayak, A.C., Kapoor, K.: On the language of primitive partial words. In: Dediu, A.-H., Formenti, E., Martín-Vide, C., Truthe, B. (eds.) LATA 2015. LNCS, vol. 8977, pp. 436–445. Springer, Cham (2015). https://doi.org/10.1007/978-3-319-15579-1_34

Topological Classification of RNA Structures via Intersection Graph

Michela Quadrini[✉][iD], Rosario Culmone[iD], and Emanuela Merelli[iD]

University of Camerino, via Madonna delle Carceri, Camerino, Italy
{michela.quadrini,rosario.culmone,emanuela.merelli}@unicam.it

Abstract. We introduce a new algebraic representation of RNA secondary structures as a composition of hairpins, considered as basic loops. Starting from it, we define an abstract algebraic representation and we propose a novel methodology to classify RNA structures based on two topological invariants, the genus and the crossing number. It takes advantage of the abstract representation to easily obtain two intersection graphs: one of the RNA molecule and another one of the relative shape. The edges cardinality of the former corresponds to the number of interactions among hairpins, whereas the edges cardinality of the latter is the crossing number of the shape associated to the molecule. The aforementioned crossing number together with the genus permits to define a more precise energy function than the standard one which is based on the genus only. Our methodology is validated over a subset of RNA structures extracted from Pseudobase++ database, and we classify them according to the two topological invariants.

Keywords: RNA classification · Topological invariants
RNA algebraic representation · Intersection graph

1 Introduction

Ribonucleic acid (RNA) is a single stranded molecule made of four different types of nucleotides, known as Adenine (A), Guanine (G), Cytosine (C) and Uracil (U). Such single strand, referred to as *primary structure*, folds back on itself achieving *secondary* and *tertiary structures*. During such a process, called *folding process*, each nucleotide can interact at most with another one establishing a hydrogen bond performing Watson-Crick (G-C and A-U) and wobble (G-U) base pairs. The folding process can generate many RNA secondary structures; it depends on the free energy of RNA configurations. The RNA secondary structure is composed of five basic structural elements namely *hairpins*, *internal loops*, *bulges*, *helixes* (or *stacks*) and *multi-loops*. Each one of them, generated when at least one base pair is formed, is a *loop*. Therefore, secondary structures are composed of loops. If no interaction among loops is present, the secondary structure is said to be *pseudoknots free*, as illustrated in Fig. 1(A), otherwise it is called *pseudoknotted*, as depicted in Fig. 1(B). In this work, the phosphodiester bond,

© Springer International Publishing AG 2017
C. Martín-Vide et al. (Eds.): TPNC 2017, LNCS 10687, pp. 203–215, 2017.
https://doi.org/10.1007/978-3-319-71069-3_16

a chemical bound that links two consecutive nucleotides, is referred to as a **strong interaction** and is depicted by a black line, while the base pairs created during the folding process are called **weak interactions** and are illustrated by zig zag lines.

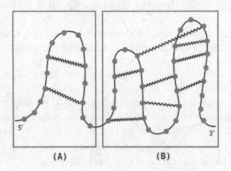

(A)   (B)

Fig. 1. RNA secondary structures

RNA molecules regulate a wide range of functions in biological systems. It has been recognized that in addition of being a carrier of genetic information, some RNA may also have enzymatic roles and may play a central part in the regulation of biological networks [5]. The pseudoknots, although it is known experimentally that they are fairly rare, usually impose some constraints on the sugar-phosphate backbone of the molecule. Their roles include forming the catalytic core of various ribozymes [13], self-splicing introns [1], and telomerase [17]. Additionally, they play critical roles in altering gene expression. For these reasons, starting from the primary structure of an RNA molecule, the prediction of the folding process is the main open problem of molecular biology [5]. Several deterministic and stochastic methods have been proposed for such prediction [2,11]. Despite great progress, their overall success is limited, especially for long RNA molecules. Part of the difficulty lies in the prediction of RNA pseudoknots, which has been identified as an NP-complete problem [8]. Bon *et al.* [4] introduced a topological classification of RNA secondary structures with pseudoknots based on a topological invariant, the *genus*. Reidys *et al.* provided relevant contributions in the research area of combinatorial topology and developed several algorithms for predicting pseudoknots [7,14]. Vernizzi *et al.* [18] added a new topological invariant, *the number of crossings*, to the aforementioned topological classification. Many different ways to represent RNA secondary structures are introduced in literature, such as the conventional diagram depicted in Fig. 2(A), arc diagram illustrated in part (B) of Fig. 2, bracket representation and many others. The arc diagram representation can be regarded as a special case of the conventional diagram, where the vertices on a straight line (backbone) represent the nucleotides and base pairs are indicated using arcs.

In this work, we introduce a multiple context-free grammar that permits to associate a unique algebraic representation for each RNA molecule, both

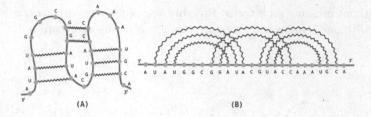

Fig. 2. Two different representations of RNA secondary structures

pseudoknot free and pseudoknotted. The main novelty of our approach, respect to the others present in the literature, is that we represent each RNA secondary structure as an algebraic composition of hairpins, considered as basic loops. Moreover, it permits to classify each RNA molecule in terms of genus and crossing number. Such crossing number and the genus, a non negative integer which depends only on the connectivity of the base pairs, are two topological invariants. They permit to improve the function for the energy calculation. Finally, a procedure, Pseudoknots Detection Procedure, is defined to identify the kind of pseudoknots of genus 1. In order to validate our methodology, we applied it to a subset of real RNA structures extracted from Pseudobase++ database, and we classified them according to their genus and crossing number.

The paper is organized as follows. In Sect. 2, we present a review of mathematical concepts necessary to understand the new proposed methodology, which is introduced in Sect. 3. The results are then commented in Sect. 4, whereas conclusions and future works are reported in Sect. 5.

2   Mathematical Background

In this Section, some basic mathematical concepts will be introduced. The interested readers can refer to [12] for a complete treatment of topological invariants and to [10] for intersection graphs.

2.1   Topological Invariants

The global properties of RNA molecule are included in topological constraints encoded at the level of secondary structure. The topological invariants provide information regarding such constraints and, roughly speaking, they do not change under continuous stretching and bending of the topological space. The *genus* of an RNA molecule measures its complexity. Its geometrical interpretation is quite simple. In fact, the genus g of an arc diagram is the minimum number of handles that a sphere must have in order that each arc of the diagram can be illustrated without any crossing. An arc diagram that does not present any crossing can be drawn on a sphere. A graphical example is given at the top of Fig. 3. The sphere has no handles, so the genus associated to the structure is equal to 0. The arc diagram illustrated at the bottom right of Fig. 3 can be drawn without crossing on a torus. Roughly speaking, the torus corresponds to a sphere with one handle and therefore the genus of the structure is 1.

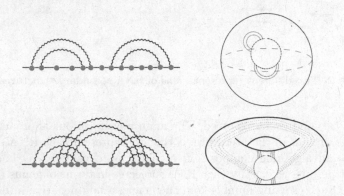

Fig. 3. Examples of the idea of genus

The genus permits to classify RNA secondary structures in equivalence classes; each class is determined by a value of genus g. In order to simplify the classification, we can observe that collapsing parallel arcs into one single arc and removing arcs which do not perform any cross, does not in fact change the genus value. This process determines the *shape* of the diagram. See Fig. 4 for an illustration of the process.

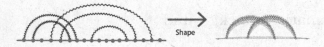

Fig. 4. The shape of a diagram

All the four types of RNA molecule with genus 1 are shown in Fig. 5.

Fig. 5. The four types of primitive pseudoknots with genus 1

A practical way for calculating the diagram genus consists in *fattening* the diagram, obtaining a double-line diagram, as illustrated in Fig. 6. Let P be the number of double lines (i.e., the number of base pairs) and let L be the number of closed loops, the genus of the diagram is the non negative integer defined by

$$g = \frac{P - L}{2} .$$

For instance, in Fig. 6 the diagram has 3 double lines and 1 closed loops.

Fig. 6. Steps to compute the genus of a structure

The genus has the property of being additive. Thus, for a structure comprised of two consecutive pseudoknots with genus g_1 and g_2 respectively, the genus of the whole structure is given by $g = g_1 + g_2$. For example, if the shape is composed of an H pseudoknot followed by a K pseudoknot, as illustrated in Fig. 7, each one has genus 1 and the genus of the whole structure is 2. In order to characterize the intrinsic complexity of a pseudoknot, the concepts of *irreducibility* and *nested* have been introduced. A shape is said to be *irreducible* if it cannot be disconnected by cutting the backbone. It is said to be *nested* if it can be removed by cutting the backbone twice, while the rest of the shape stays connected in a single component. The shape on the left of Fig. 7 is an example of a reducible one, whereas the motif on the right is irreducible.

Fig. 7. A reducible shape (left) and an irreducible one (right)

Each arc diagram with genus greater than 0 is characterized by crossing arcs. Thus, the crossing arcs indicate the presence of at least one pseudoknot. If we take into account the four shapes of genus 1, introduced in Fig. 5, we can observe that they differ by the crossing number. Moreover, such crossing number and the genus do not uniquely identify the RNA shape. A simple example of this observation is given by the eight different pseudoknots with genus 2 and crossing number $\mathcal{N}_C$ equals to 3 shown in Fig. 8.

The crossing number of a shape is a topological invariant and it has the property of being additive. In fact, if $\mathcal{D}$ is a reducible shape characterized by a sequence of two or more shapes, $\mathcal{D}_1, \mathcal{D}_2, \ldots, \mathcal{D}_n$, the crossing number, $\mathcal{N}_{\mathcal{D}}$, is given by the sum of the crossing number $\mathcal{N}_{\mathcal{D}_i}$ of each shape. Analogously, if $\mathcal{D}$

Fig. 8. The eight shapes with genus 2 and crossing number 3

can be decomposed into nested parts $\mathcal{D}_i$, the crossing number, $\mathcal{N}_\mathcal{D}$, is given by the sum of the crossing number of each nested part. Thus, it is defined as follows:

1. Given an arc diagram $\mathcal{D}$, let $\mathcal{D} = \mathcal{D}_1 + \mathcal{D}_2 + \ldots \mathcal{D}_N$ be its decomposition in irreducible or nested parts $\mathcal{D}_i$;
2. For each diagram $\mathcal{D}_i$, we consider its shape $\mathcal{D}'_i$;
3. The crossing number $\mathcal{N}_C$ of $\mathcal{D}'$ is defined as the sum of the crossing number of each $\mathcal{D}'_i$.

2.2 Intersection Graph

Intersection graphs are relevant in both theoretical and applicative perspectives. In fact, they are able to provide several types of topological information about an arc diagram. For each arc diagram, its *intersection graph* is defined as follows:

1. each vertex corresponds to a loop of the diagram;
2. each edge corresponds to an interaction between two loops of the diagram.

An example of the intersection graph of the RNA structure illustrated in Fig. 2 is shown in Fig. 9.

Fig. 9. The intersection graph of the RNA molecule shown in Fig. 2

3 Materials and Methods

The topological classification of RNA secondary structures with pseudoknots, that we propose, is based on two topological invariants, *genus* and *crossing number*, and takes advantage of a new algebraic representation and of intersection graphs. To define the new representation it is necessary to introduce an operator able to model interactions among loops; it has been introduced in Sect. 3.1. Such operator is translated into a multiple context-free grammar, in Sect. 3.2. The procedures to obtain the intersection graph of an RNA molecule and the intersection graph of the relative shape are defined in Sect. 3.3, as well as the algorithm that permits to recognize the kind of pseudoknots of genus 1.

3.1 Operator to Model Interactions Among Loops

In order to model RNA secondary structures, we define an operator *crossing*, $\bowtie_k$, able to model interactions among loops. The operator takes two arc diagrams and maps them into another one. It depends on a non integer parameter, k, which indicates that the resulting structure is obtained attaching the second arc diagram on the k–th nucleotides of the first one. According to the nature of RNA molecules, such operator is well-defined if each nucleotide of the resulting structure performs at most one weak interaction. It is also well-defined if the two structures do not share nucleotides, i.e., the first arc diagram is followed by the second one. The new structure, obtained when k is equal to 0, is a concatenation between the two structures. In order to formally define the operator $\bowtie_k$, it is necessary to introduce new symbols, $\langle\,,\,\rangle$ and $\sharp$. Algebraically, each RNA secondary structure is identified by $(a_1^s, a_N^s)\langle\alpha\rangle$, where α is the sequence of nucleotides (backbone) enclosed by the pseudoweak interaction, a fictitious weak interaction, between the first nucleotide, a_1, and the last one, a_N, identified by pair (a_1^s, a_N^s). Each nucleotide that performs a weak interaction with another one, is marked by symbol $\sharp$, while the unpaired nucleotides are marked by ϵ. Formally, let S_1 and S_2 be two structures, where $S_1 = (a_1^s, a_N^s)\langle a_2^s \ldots a_{N-1}^s\rangle$ and $S_2 = (b_1^s, b_M^s)\langle b_2^s \ldots b_{M-1}^s\rangle$, the resulting structure, $S_1 \bowtie_k S_2$, is well defined if

$$\frac{k = 0, \quad s \in \{\epsilon, \sharp\}}{S_1 \bowtie_k S_2 \to (a_1^s, b_M^s)\langle\, a_2^s \ldots a_{N-1}^s a_N^s b_1^s \ldots b_{M-1}^s\rangle}$$

$$\frac{k \leq N, s \in \{\epsilon, \sharp\}, ((b_1 = a_k) \wedge BC), ((b_2 = a_{k+1}) \wedge BC), \ldots, ((b_{n-k} = a_N) \wedge BC)}{S_1 \bowtie_k S_2 \to (a_1^s, b_M^s)\langle\, a_2^s \ldots b_1^s \ldots b_{N-k}^s b_{N-k+1}^s \ldots b_{M-1}^s\rangle}$$

where BC expresses the biological constraint that each nucleotide performs at most one weak interaction and it is formalized as follows:

$$BC : (s = \epsilon, (\bar{s} = \epsilon \vee \bar{s} = \sharp)) \vee (s = \sharp, \bar{s} = \epsilon).$$

3.2 Translating Operator into MCFG

A context-free grammar is an inadequate formalism to describe arc diagrams with pseudoknots. It can be proved applying Ogden's Lemma [6]. As a consequence, a more expressive grammar is required. An appropriate choice is the so-called *Multiple Context-Free Grammar* (MCFG), introduced in [15]. Let $\Sigma_{RNA} = \{A, U, G, C\}$ be the alphabet of RNA nucleotides, and let $\Sigma_{\overline{RNA}} = \{(A, U), (U, A), (G, C), (C, G), (G, U), (U, G)\}$ be the alphabet of weak interactions, whose elements represent Watson-Crick or wobble base pairs of nucleotides. The grammar is $G_{RNA} = (V_N, V_T, R, S, F)$, where $V_N = \{S, P, L\}$,

$V_T = \Sigma_{RNA} \cup \Sigma_{\overline{RNA}} \cup \{[,]\}$, $F = \{f_{(\bowtie,k)}\}$ is the set of partial functions and set of productions R is defined as follows:

$$
\begin{aligned}
S &::= \ \alpha P \alpha && \textit{RNA secondary structure} \\
P &::= \ f_{(\bowtie,0)}[\![P\alpha, L]\!] && \textit{Concatenation} \\
&\ \ | \ f_{(\bowtie,k)}[\![P, L]\!] && \textit{Nesting or Crossing} \\
&\ \ | \ L && \textit{Hairpin} \\
L &::= \ x[\alpha^+]
\end{aligned}
$$

where $x \in \Sigma_{\overline{RNA}}$, $\alpha \in \Sigma_{RNA}^*$ and

$$
f_{(\bowtie,k)}[\![S, L]\!] = \begin{cases} S \bowtie_k L & \text{if } \bowtie_k \text{ is defined;} \\ undefined & \text{otherwise.} \end{cases}
$$

Start symbol S represents any RNA secondary structure. The first production of the grammar formalizes the concatenation between an RNA pseudoloop P followed by a sequence of nucleotides α, eventually empty, and a loop L. Whereas the second one represents both the crossing and the nesting between a pseudoloop P and a loop L. Finally, $P \to L$ generates a hairpin. Note that a pseudoloop P is an RNA secondary structure without the head and the tail. Each loop L is a hairpin, $L \to x[\alpha^+]$, i.e., a Watson-Crick or a wobble base pair encloses a sequence of unpaired nucleotides, α^+.

Theorem 1. *Multiple context-free grammar G_{RNA}, introduced above, generates uniquely all RNA secondary structures.*

Proof. It is equivalent to prove that grammar G_{RNA} is not ambiguous. This property follows by the nature of the molecule, i.e., each nucleotide can perform at most one weak interaction and the primary structure is an ordered sequence of nucleotides. It is trivial to observe that the grammar is recursive to the right. This means that each production adds a hairpin starting from the end of the structure. Due to the biological constraint, the unambiguous property is guaranteed.

Theorem 2. *Each secondary structure can be uniquely decomposed in terms of a particular loop, i.e., hairpin.*

Proof. Each vertex which performs a weak interaction belongs to a unique hairpin. Since an unpaired nucleotide is either external or internal to a unique base pair the decomposition is unique.

3.3 From Arc Diagram to Intersection Graph

The multiple context-free grammar permits to associate a unique algebraic expression for each RNA secondary structure in terms of hairpins. Such algebraic expression contains each structural and biological information of the molecule. Obviously, two molecules having different backbones can be characterized by the same genus and same crossing number. We can observe that the two topological invariants cannot be influenced by the head and the tail of the structure, the unpaired nucleotides that characterize the loop or the number of nucleotides that two loops share. By removing the nucleotides, each weak interaction divides the backbone into three components, as illustrated in Fig. 10, which are enumerated from right to left starting from 0.

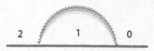

Fig. 10. Backbone components generated by an arc

For each algebraic expression

$$S = \alpha x[\alpha^+] \bowtie_k x[\alpha^+] \bowtie_k \cdots \bowtie_k x[\alpha^+]\alpha$$

the following abstract algebraic expression

$$S' = L \bowtie_t L \bowtie_t \cdots \bowtie_t L$$

is associated. Note that t is a non negative integer that represents the component of the backbone which the successive loop is attached to. Thus, operator $\bowtie_t$ is a bit different from the initial crossing operator: the initial one depends on nucleotides, whereas the second one depends on the backbone component. We decided to maintain the same symbol in order to not overload the notation. For each abstract structure, S', the intersection graph is associated by means of The Intersection Graph Procedure. It takes the input an abstract algebraic expression, that models the RNA molecule, and then returns an intersection graph as output. The core of the algorithm is based on the identification of the backbone component where the successive loop is attached on the identification of the numbers of crossing that the loop performs with the previous ones. It permits to detect the set of loops that cross each others. Another procedure, The Shape Intersection Graph Procedure, is defined over the intersection graph obtained by the previous algorithm. In fact, it takes the intersection graph of the molecule as input and returns the intersection graph of the relative shape as output, identifying and removing the edges which correspond to parallel arcs in the arc diagram. Finally, the kind of pseudoknots with genus 1 is defined by means of an additional procedure, The Pseudoknots Detection Procedure, based on edges of the shape intersection graph. The encoding of such procedures is omitted from this paper in order to not overload the readers with technicalities.

3.4   Example of Application

This methodology is applied to PKB10 molecule, extracted from Pseudobase++ database [16]. PKB10 is a tRNA-like structure 3′end pseudoknot of ononis yellow mosaic virus [9], which diagram, obtained from the database, is shown in Fig. 11. The algebraic expression of the structure is

$$S = \beta_1 x_1[\alpha_1] \Join_2 x_2[\alpha_2] \Join_1 x_3[\alpha_3] \Join_{12} x_4[\alpha_4] \Join_{11} x_5[\alpha_5] \Join_{10}$$

$$x_6[\alpha_6] \Join_9 x_7[\alpha_7] \Join_8 x_8[\alpha_8] \Join_7 x_9[\alpha_9]\beta_2$$

Fig. 11. The diagram of PKB10 obtained from Pseudobase++ database [16]

where $x_1 = x_2 = x_3 = (C, G)$, $x_4 = (A, U)$, $x_5 = (G, C)$, $x_6 = x_7 = (C, G)$, $x_8 = x_9 = (U, A)$, $\beta_1 = UGGGUUCAACUCCC$, $\alpha_1 = CUUUUCCGA$, $\alpha_2 = CCUUUUCCGAG$, $\alpha_3 = CCCUUUUCCGAGG$, $\alpha_4 = GGGUA$, $\alpha_5 = AGGGUAU$, $\alpha_6 = GAGGGUAUC$, $\alpha_7 = CGAGGGUAUCG$, $\alpha_8 = CCGAGGGUAUCGG$, $\alpha_9 = UCCGAGGGUAUCGGA$, $\beta_2 = ACC$. The abstract algebraic expression is

$$S' = L \Join_2 L \Join_2 L \Join_2\Join_3 L \Join_5 L \Join_7 L \Join_9 L \Join_{11} L$$

and the associated intersection graph, obtained applying. The Intersection Graph Procedure, is $\mathcal{G} = (V, E)$ where $V = \{L_1, L_2, L_3, L_4, L_5, L_6, L_7, L_8\}$ and $E = \{(L_1, L_4), (L_1, L_5), (L_1, L_6), (L_1, L_7), (L_1, L_8), (L_2, L_4), (L_2, L_5), (L_2, L_6), (L_2, L_7), (L_2, L_8), (L_3, L_4), (L_3, L_5), (L_3, L_6), (L_3, L_7), (L_3, L_8)\}$. Applying The Shape Intersection Graph Procedure, we obtain $G' = (V', E')$, where $V' = \{L_1, L_2\}$ and $E' = \{(L_1, L_4)\}$. Finally, using The Pseudoknots Detection Proceduce we detect that the genus of the structure is 1 and we are in the presence of an H pseudoknot, thus $\mathcal{N}_C = 1$.

4   Results and Discussion

Our methodology permits to classify each RNA molecule in terms of *genus* and *crossing number* associated to its shape. Thus, for each equivalent class determined by the genus, it is possible to define a new classification. Such classification permits to define a more accurate energy function respect to the standard one. To test the methodology, we have analyzed a subset of real molecules extracted from Pseudobase++ database [16]. The molecules of the database are classified

Table 1. Results of analysis

Molecule	Genus	Num of loops interactions	Crossing Num of Shape	Type of Pseudoknot
$PKB205$	1	16	1	$HLIn$
$PKB210$	1	63	1	$HLIn$
$PKB234$	1	63	1	$HLIn$
$PKB238$	1	80	1	$HLIn$
$PKB139$	1	24	1	LL
$PKB140$	1	68	1	LL
$PKB141$	1	27	1	LL
$PKB142$	1	35	1	LL
$PKB143$	1	35	1	LL
$PKB144$	1	32	1	LL
$PKB145$	1	30	1	LL
$PKB146$	1	25	1	LL
$PKB174$	1	112	1	LL
$PKB248$	1	18	1	LL
$PKB57$	1	28	1	LL

into groups in accord to different types of structure. We choose two groups, i.e., $HLIn$ and LL, and the results of the analysis is shown in Table 1.

The results of the analyzed molecules correspond to the expected values. In fact, the genus of each molecule is 1 as well as the crossing number of the shape. These values are in accordance with the selected molecules, since each molecule is characterized by a H pseudoknot. Note that the same result can be obtained defining a procedure that associates for each molecule its shape, and applying an algorithm similar to The Intersection Graph Procedure. We propose the first approach because we believe that starting from the intersection graph of a molecule, a new measure can be defined. Such measure will allow us to compute the distance between two RNA secondary structures in terms of interactions among loops.

5   Conclusions

In this work, a new algebraic representation of RNA secondary structures and an abstract representation have been defined. The former contains each structural and biological information of each molecule, the latter is obtained from the first one removing its primary structure. This simplification does not influence the two topological invariants, genus and crossing number, but easily allowed us to define three procedures. The Intersection Graph Procedure associates the intersection graph for each RNA molecule, while The Shape Intersection Graph

Procedure, starting from the last structure, determines the intersection graph of The shape. Over the latter structure, the kind of pseudoknot of genus 1 is determined through The Pseudoknots Detection Procedure. Such methodology permits to classify each RNA molecule in terms of genus and crossing number associated to its shape. Thus, for each equivalent class determined by the genus, it is possible to define a new classification.

We have planned to improve the developed software that implements the whole methodology presented in this paper in order to analyze efficiently two database, Worldwide Protein Data Bank [3] and Pseudobase++ [16], with the scope of carrying out a more accurate topological classification than the one obtained by Bon et al. in [4]. A statistical study will be performed to detect the relations between genus and crossing number. Finally, the challenge will be to define an algorithm for the RNA folding problem taking advantage of the classification obtained applying this proposed methodology.

References

1. Adams, P.L., Stahley, M.R., Gill, M.L., Kosen, A.B., Wang, J., Strobel, S.A.: Crystal structure of a group I intron splicing intermediate. RNA **10**(12), 1867–1887 (2004)
2. Bellaousov, S., Mathews, D.H.: Probknot: fast prediction of RNA secondary structure including pseudoknots. RNA **16**(10), 1870–1880 (2010)
3. Berman, H., Henrick, K., Nakamura, H.: Announcing the worldwide protein data bank. Nature Struct. Mol. Biol. **10**(12), 980–980 (2003)
4. Bon, M., Vernizzi, G., Orland, H., Zee, A.: Topological classification of RNA structures. J. Mol. Biol. **379**(4), 900–911 (2008)
5. Elliott, D., Ladomery, M.: Molecular Biology of RNA. Oxford University Press, Oxford (2017)
6. Harrison, M.A.: Introduction to Formal Language Theory. Addison-Wesley Longman Publishing Co., Inc., Boston (1978)
7. Huang, F.W., Reidys, C.M.: Topological language for RNA. Math. Biosci. **282**, 109–120 (2016)
8. Lyngsø, R.B., Pedersen, C.N.: RNA pseudoknot prediction in energy-based models. J. Comput. Biol. **7**(3–4), 409–427 (2000)
9. Mans, R.M., Pleij, C.W., Bosch, L.: tRNA-like structures. structure, function and evolutionary significance. Eur. J. Biochem. **201**(1), 303–324 (1991)
10. McKee, T.A., McMorris, F.R.: Topics in Intersection Graph Theory. SIAM, Philadelphia (1999)
11. Metzler, D., Nebel, M.E.: Predicting RNA secondary structures with pseudoknots by MCMC sampling. J. Math. Biol. **56**(1), 161–181 (2008)
12. Munkres, J.R.: Analysis on Manifolds. Westview Press, USA (1997)
13. Rastogi, T., Beattie, T.L., Olive, J.E., Collins, R.A.: A long-range pseudoknot is required for activity of the Neurospora VS ribozyme. EMBO J. **15**(11), 2820 (1996)
14. Reidys, C.M., Huang, F.W., Andersen, J.E., Penner, R.C., Stadler, P.F., Nebel, M.E.: Topology and prediction of RNA pseudoknots. Bioinformatics **27**(8), 1076–1085 (2011)
15. Seki, H., Matsumura, T., Fujii, M., Kasami, T.: On multiple context-free grammars. Theoret. Comput. Sci. **88**(2), 191–229 (1991)

16. Taufer, M., Licon, A., Araiza, R., Mireles, D., Van Batenburg, F., Gultyaev, A.P., Leung, M.Y.: Pseudobase++: an extension of PseudoBase for easy searching, formatting and visualization of pseudoknots. Nucleic Acids Res. **37**(suppl. 1), D127–D135 (2008)
17. Theimer, C.A., Blois, C.A., Feigon, J.: Structure of the human telomerase RNA pseudoknot reveals conserved tertiary interactions essential for function. Mol. Cell **17**(5), 671–682 (2005)
18. Vernizzi, G., Orland, H., Zee, A.: Classification and predictions of RNA pseudoknots based on topological invariants. Phys. Rev. E **94**(4), 042410 (2016)

Neural Networks

Splicing-Inspired Recognition and Composition of Musical Collectives Styles

Roberto De Prisco, Delfina Malandrino, Gianluca Zaccagnino,
Rocco Zaccagnino[✉], and Rosalba Zizza

Dipartimento di Informatica, University of Salerno, Fisciano, Italy
{robdep,delmal,zaccagnino.gianluca,zaccagnino,zizza}@dia.unisa.it

Abstract. Computer music is an emerging area for the application of computational techniques inspired by information processing in Nature. A challenging task in this area is the automatic recognition of musical styles. The style of a musician is the result of the combination of several factors such as experience, personality, preferences. In the last years, several works have been proposed for the recognition of styles for soloists performers, where the improvisation often plays an important role. The evolution of this problem, that is the recognition of multiple performers' style that collaborate over time to perform, record or compose music, know as *Musical collective*, presents many more difficulties, due to the simultaneous presence of various performers, mutually conditionable.

In this paper, we propose a new approach for both recognition and automatic composition of styles for musical collectives. Specifically, our system exploits a machine learning *recognizer*, based on one-class support vector machines and neural networks for style recognition, and a *splicing composer*, for music composition (in the style of the whole collective).

To assess the effectiveness of our system we performed several tests using transcriptions of popular jazz bands. With regard to the *recognition*, we show that our classifier is able to achieve an accuracy of 97.7%. With regard to the *composition*, we measured the quality of the generated compositions by collecting subjective perceptions from domain experts.

Keywords: Splicing-inspired recognition
Composition of musical collectives styles · Support vector machine
Neural network

1 Introduction

The interest in algorithmic music composition date back to 1950 with the development of computers, and since then both computer scientists and artists considered their use in many disciplines, such as, music information retrieval, pattern recognition, and so on. The resulting *Computer Music* field still represents an emerging research area for the application of computational intelligence techniques, such as, machine learning and bio-inspired algorithms.

In this work we focus on aspects along two directions: *(1) music information retrieval* (MIR), i.e., the science of retrieving information from music, involving

© Springer International Publishing AG 2017
C. Martín-Vide et al. (Eds.): TPNC 2017, LNCS 10687, pp. 219–231, 2017.
https://doi.org/10.1007/978-3-319-71069-3_17

activities such as content-based organization and exploration of digital music data sets, and *(2) algorithmic music composition*, i.e., how to compose music by means of a computer program with no (or minimal) human intervention. One interesting problem to solve in MIR is how to model the *musical styles*. The style of a musician stricly depends on his experience, and therefore on his personality and personal preferences, especially when the improvisation plays an important role. *Musical improvisation* is the creative activity of immediate musical composition, which combines performance with communication of emotions and instrumental technique as well as spontaneous response to other musicians, and is conditioned by the other musicians if he is part of a *Musical collective*. So we distinguish two cases: *(1)* the recognition of styles for soloists performers, and *(2)* the recognition of styles for *Musical collectives*, which presents more difficulties, due to the simultaneous presence of various performers mutually conditionable.

Several works have been proposed for the first case [7,12,23,24,26] but relatively fews for the second one. We focus on the more complex second case. An application of recognition systems can be their use in cooperation with automatic composition algorithms. In [22] several composition algorithms have been discussed, and here we investigate the use of *music splicing systems* [6]. The main contributions of our paper can be summarized as follows.

1. A new approach for automatic collectives style recognition and composition.
2. A *machine learning* technique for the *recognition* process: a one-class support vector machine classifier is defined for each performer to learn his own style, while a neural network is used to recognize the style of the collective. We define a splicing composer for each performer in the musical collective, built by using several long short-term memory networks to predict patterns in the learned style. Since the performer is influenced by his preferences as well as by the preferences of the others performers, this problem can be seen as a *multi-objective problem* in which we have to minimize the distance between the style of the generated compositions and both the stylistic *"personal"* and stylistic *"collective"* features induced by the other performers.
3. To assess our approach, we performed several tests by using transcriptions of solos from popular jazz bands. We analyzed the capability of our system in recognizing a style and we verified the stylistic coherence of the composed music. Moreover, we showed that the use of a LSTM network to predict pattern could involve better results respect to the traditional approaches.

Organization of the paper. In Sect. 2 we describe some related works. In Sect. 3 we provide the background to understand the paper. In Sects. 4, 5 and 6 we provide details about the machine learning and splicing approaches. In Sects. 7 and 8 we describe the experiment analysis and the future directions.

2   Related Work

Several works addressed the musical styles recognition problem where most of them are based on machine learning methods. In [24] the authors show how to cluster music digital libraries according to sound features of musical themes, by using self-organizing maps. A system based on neural networks and support vector machines, which is able to classify an audio fragment into a given list of artists, is described in [26]. In [25] a neural system to recognize music types from sound inputs is described. It is important to note that our approach differ from these works since they only consider the problem of recognizing the styles in terms of music genre, without considering the style of a performer or of performers in a musical collective. Furthermore, they do not face the problem of the composition of music in a specific style.

Several automatic composers, based on different approaches, exist in literature: rules and expert-systems [16], systems based on a combination of formal grammars, analysis and pattern matching techniques [5], neural networks [20]. Other automatic composers are based on meta-heuristics, and specifically on genetic algorithms [1,3,13,14,27]. Other works have been proposed for different musical genres or problems: Jazz solos [2], harmonize chords progressions [19], monophonic Jazz composition given a chord progression [3], *figured* bass problem [10], and finally, *unfigured* bass problem [13]. In [6,7] the authors define a bio-inspired approach for automatic composition, called music splicing systems. Starting from an initial set of precomposed music the system generates a language in which each word is the representation of music in the style of the chosen composer. In [12] the authors propose an approach for both recognition and automatic composition of music according to a specific performer's style. In this work we extend this approach, by considering musical collectives whose style can be view as the result of the combination of several performers' styles.

3   Background

3.1   Music Improvisation Collective

Music improvisation refers to the ability of playing music extemporaneously, without planning or preparation, by inventing variations on a melody or creating new melodies. It combines performance with communication of emotions and instrumental technique as well as spontaneous response to other musicians. This means that the style of a performer is also conditioned by the other musicians which play together, if he is part of a *Musical collective*.

In this work with the term *solo* we indicate the transcription of an improvised melody. There are musical genres in which improvisation assumes a fundamental role, and inside a musical collective, more performers could also improvise contemporaneously (for example the period of New Orleans for the Jazz music).

In our approach we are interested in modeling the style of a musical collective, which can be view as the result of the combination of several performers' styles. In each performer it is possible to found music features that characterize his specific style, and an expert ear is able to perceive such aspects. When the performer is part of a collective is also important to find the aspects of his style influenced by the presence of the other performers. Thus, given a corpus of solos, we can extract such significant features and using them to recognize his style.

As explained in [12], to extract the stylistic features is necessary to define the role that each music note assumes in the chord in which it is played. Let Ch be a music chord, usually a musician chooses a scale $S(Ch)$ (sequence of notes). In this work we assume that each scale is composed of 7 notes. Usually there are several alternativies. For example, let $Ch = D7$, a choice could be $S(D7) = (D, E, F\#, G, A, B, C)$ (mixolydian mode of Gmaj). An alternative is $S(D7) = (Ab, Cb, C, Db, Eb, F, Gb)$ (mixolydian mode in Dbmaj).

Now, let n be a note played on Ch, we indicate with $degree(n, S(Ch))$ the degree (position) of n respect to $S(Ch)$. There are 12 possible degrees, (7 degrees in $S(Ch)$ and 5 out of $S(Ch)$. For example let $Ch = Am7$ and $S(Am7) = (A, B, C, D, E, F\#, G)$ (dorian mode). Let $n = C$ then $degree(C, S(Am7)) = III$. Let $n = Bb$ then $degree(Bb, S(Am7)) = bII$. We say that the chord $D7$ has been substituted by the tritone chord $Ab7$. The process of substituting a chord with another chord is known in Jazz as *substitution* [21]. We remark that the musician's choice of $S(Ch)$ for a Ch is crucial for the definition of his style.

3.2 Splicing Systems

Splicing systems are formal models for generating sets of words [18]. It is a relatively old research topic in computer science and much early research effort has been devoted to the study of the theoretical computational power of such formal systems [8,9]. We start with an initial set of words and we apply to these words the splicing operation by using rules in a given set. The set of generated words is joined to the initial set and the process is iterated on this new set until no new word is produced. The *language generated* is the collection of all these words. Formally, a *splicing system* is a triple $\mathcal{S} = (\mathcal{A}, \mathcal{I}, \mathcal{R})$, where $\mathcal{A}$ is a finite alphabet, $\mathcal{I} \subseteq \mathcal{A}^*$ is the initial language and $\mathcal{R} \subseteq \mathcal{A}^* | \mathcal{A}^* \$ \mathcal{A}^* | \mathcal{A}^*$ is the set of rules, where $|, \$ \notin \mathcal{A}$. A splicing system $\mathcal{S}$ is finite when $\mathcal{I}$ and $\mathcal{R}$ are both finite sets. Let $L \subseteq \mathcal{A}^*$. We set $\gamma'(L) = \{w', w'' \in \mathcal{A}^* \mid (x, y) \vdash_r (w', w''), x, y \in L, r \in \mathcal{R}\}$. The definition of the splicing operation is extended to languages as follows: $\gamma^0(L) = L, \gamma^{i+1}(L) = \gamma^i(L) \cup \gamma'(\gamma^i(L))$, $i \geq 0$, and $\gamma^*(L) = \bigcup_{i \geq 0} \gamma^i(L)$. We say that $L(\mathcal{S}) = \gamma^*(\mathcal{I})$ is the a *splicing language* generated by $\mathcal{S}$.

3.3 Machine Learning Approaches to Music Problems

In this section we provide some basic notions about the machine learning classifiers used in this work, but for further information see [4].

One-class Support Vector Machine (OCSVM). A OCSVM maps input data into a high dimensional feature space and finds the maximum margin hyperplane which best separates the training data from the origin. In terms of recognition, given a melody, it verifies whether it is coherent with a music performer's style. As we will see in Sect. 4, the idea is to associate a vector of features to the melody, and to use a OCSVM for mapping the vector belonging to the training data. As we will see, in our approach, given a musical collective, for each performer in the collective we define a OCSVM to recognize his style.

Style recognition using Artificial Neural Networks (ANNs). ANNs are very useful tool also for automatic music composition [11]. One of the most commonly used neural network is the fully connected three-layer feed-forward neural network with tangent activation function, and we used it in our work. In our approach we define a ANN to recognize the style of the *whole collective*. We have one class N, where $N = 1$ indicates that the features in input correspond to the specific learned style, and $N = 0$ otherwise. The input of such network contains a value for each OCSVM corresponding to a performer in the collective. So the size of the input layer is equal to the size of the collective.

Style prediction using Long short-term memory (LSTM). LSTM are a good mechanism for learning to compose music [17] when it is necessary to store information about the past. As explained in Sect. 5, for each performer we define a LSTM to predict musical patterns that follows his style respect to *what played before*, and a LSTM for each other performer to predict musical patterns that follows his style respect to *what played at the same time by others*.

4   The Machine Learning-Based Recognition

The recognition of a musical collective's style is obtained by defining: *(1)* a OCSVM style recognizer for each performer and, *(2)* a ANN to recognize the style of the whole collective. Music features that characterize the style of a performer can be extracted from a corpus of solos. Let $\mathcal{M}$ be the corpus solos by a musical collective, for each performer X in the collective we denote with $\mathcal{M}_X$ the set of his improvised melodies. So we have a classification problem in which the melodies in $\mathcal{M}$ can belong to two possible classes: melodies coherentor not with the X's style. Obviously, the melodies in $\mathcal{M} - \mathcal{M}_X$ can be coherent with the X's style or not. The goal of the OCSVM recognizer is to classify correctly the melodies in $\mathcal{M}$ in these two classes. Let v_j be the feature vector of some melody m_j, obtained through the feature extraction model to be discussed shortly. The OCSVM recognizer will be defined to classify m_j by using v_j as input. In the following we indicate the OCSVM recognizer for X with $\mathcal{R}_X$.

4.1   Feature Model

To capture the most significant features of a melody we use the n-gram model to identify *tokens* in melodies whose importance can than be determined through some *statistical measure*. An n-gram refers to n tokens which are dependent on each other. Once obtained n-grams from the training set of melodies, we use a statistical measure to calculate their relative importance and to obtain the list of n-grams ordered according to their importance. Depending on the value of n we can have different size of such a list, so for practical reasons we fix a maximum size. Since there is no theoretical support to the style classification capability of the n-grams, we apply a *random forest* selection procedure to keep those that better contribute to the classification. As we will see in Sect. 7, we have tried several values of n but found no significant improvement beyond $n = 16$. Below, we provide details about tokens and statistical measure.

The token. A token is the set of relevant information about a music note, and one n-gram represents a sequence of n notes. A note can be described by three parameters that explain his role respect to the chord in which is played: *(1)* the *name chord* k_1, i.e., C, $C\#$, D, $D\#$, E, F, $F\#$, G, $G\#$, A, $A\#$, B; thus we have 12 possible values for k_1 (0 for C, 1 for $C\#$, 2 for D and so on). *(2)* the *type chord* k_2 that in this work is derived from the modes of the major, melodic minor and harmonic minor scales (see [21] for further details); in Table 1 we describe such type chords. *(3)* the *role* k_3 which is the position inside the scale (integer in the range from 0 to 11). So the *3-tuple* $K^i = [k_1^i, k_2^i, k_3^i]$ is the token that describes the note played at i^{th} time interval. For example $K^3 = [0, 1, 9]$ says that at the 3th time interval the note played has degree VI ($k_3 = 9$ means degree VI) in the scale corresponding to the chord $Cm7$ ($k_1 = 0$ means name chord C and $k_2 = 1$ means type chord $m7$). Thus the note played is A.

In our approach the duration of notes is relevant only for the execution of the melody and it will be established by the composer by using a specific operator.

Table 1. Modes of the major, melodic minor and harmonic minor scales.

Description $S(Ch)$	Mode	Chord type	k_2 value
Major scale			
ionic	I	maj7	0
dorian	ii	m7	1
phrygian	iii	m7b9	2
lydian	IV	maj7#11	3
mixolydian	V	7	4
aeolian	vi	m7b6	5
locrian	vii	m7b5	6
Melodic minor scale			
ipoionic	i	m(maj7)	7
dorian b2	ii	m7b9	8
augmented lydian	III	maj7#5	9
dominant lydian	IV	7#11	10
mixolydian b6	V	7b6	11
locrian #2	vi	m7b5#2	12
superlocrian	vii	7alt	13
Harmonic minor scale			
ipoionic b6	I	m(maj7)	14
locrian #6	ii	m7b5b9b13	15
augmented lydian	iii	maj7#5	16
minor lydian	iv	m7#11	17
mixolydian b2b6	V	7b9b13	18
lydian #2	VI	maj7#9#11	19
diminished superlocrian	vii	o	20

The statistical measure. In our approach the measure used to evaluate the relative importance of n-grams is the *term frequency with inverse document* *frequency* (*tfidf*). The term t, central to this measure, refers to a n-gram. We use the boolean term frequency (*tf*) measure such that $tf(t, m_j) = 1$ if $t \in m_j$ (the sequence of notes corresponding to t occurs in the melody m_j), 0 otherwise. The inverse document frequency measure (*idf*) is defined as: $idf(t, m_j, \mathcal{M}) = \log(|\mathcal{M}| / |\{ m_j \in \mathcal{M} : t \in m_j \}|)$. Finally we obtain *tf* with *idf* for each $t \in m_j$ over the corpus $\mathcal{M}$, as: $tfidf(t, m_j, \mathcal{M}) = tf(t, m_j) \cdot idf(t, m_j, \mathcal{M})$. The *tfidf* measure gives more weight to terms that are less common in $\mathcal{M}$, since such terms are more likely to make the corresponding melody stand out. It transforms our corpus $\mathcal{M}$ to the feature vector space. The feature vector corresponding to a melody m_j is denoted by v_j and $v_j[i]$ is equal to $tfidf(t_i, m_j, \mathcal{M})$.

4.2   The Recognizers

The OCSVM performer-recognizers. As explained before, let m_j be a melody we define a feature vector corresponding to m_j denoted by v_j, which contains an element for each significant feature of the melody, and the value of this element is the *tfidf* explained in Sect. 4.1. In our approach, for each performer X in the collective we use a OCSVM denoted $\mathcal{R}_X$ and named *performer-recognizer for X*, for mapping v_j. It uses the rule $f(v_j) = \langle w, v_j \rangle + b$, where $\langle w, v_j \rangle + b$ is the equation of the hyperplane, with w being the vector normal to this hyperplane and b being the intercept. If $f(v_j) \geq 0$ then m_j is considered as melody not coherent with the X's style, otherwise m_j is coherent.

The ANN collective-recognizer. In our approach we define a ANN trained to recognize the style of the whole collective. Thus we have one class N, where $N = 1$ indicates that the features in input correspond to the specific learned style, and $N = 0$ otherwise. The input of such classifier contains a value for each performer-recognizer defined. So the size of the input layer is equal to the size of the collective. We denote with $\mathcal{R}$ the *collective-recognizer*.

5   The Machine Learning-Based Prediction

For each performer X in the collective we define: *(1)* a LSTM used to predict musical patterns that follows the style of X respect to *what played before by X*, and *(2)* a LSTM for each other performer Y in the collective used to predict musical patterns that follows the style of X respect to *what played at the same time by Y*. Observe that the first network gives a temporal information of the musical behavior of X, while the second type of networks seeks to capture the musical relation between X and each other performer Y, at the same time.

We remark that we first build the performer-recognizers $\mathcal{R}_X$, for each performer X in the collective, then we build the collective-recognizer $\mathcal{R}$ as described in Sect. 4, and finally we build the predictors for X.

5.1   Temporal Predictor for X

Now we describe the LSTM used to predict musical patterns that follows the style of X respect to *what played before by X*. Let $\mathcal{M}$ be a corpus of solos for a musical collective, and $\mathcal{M}_X \subseteq \mathcal{M}$ be the set of solos performed by X. Let $\mathcal{R}_X$ be the performer-recognizer for X and n the value used for the construction of the n-grams as described in Sect. 4.1. The idea is to define a predictor $\mathcal{P}_X$ that given a n-gram at time t have to predict the n-gram at time $t + 1$. This is equivalent to say that given the sequence of n music notes at time t, $\mathcal{P}_X$ has to predict the sequence of n music notes at time $t + 1$.

The training set. We define a data set of n-grams as follows. Let $\mathcal{T}_X \subseteq \mathcal{M}$ be the training set used for the training of $\mathcal{R}_X$. For each $m_j \in \mathcal{T}_X$ such that $\mathcal{R}_X$ says that m_j is coherent with the X's style ($f(m_j) < 0$), we consider the sequence of n-grams extract by m_j. So, let $Ngrams(m_j) = (ng_1, \ldots, ng_{k_j})$ be the sequence of n-grams extract from m_j, we insert the pair (ng_i, ng_{i+1}) in the training set for $\mathcal{P}_X$, for each $1 \le i \le k_j - 1$.

The architecture. In our approach the predictor $\mathcal{P}_X$ is a LSTM and we now describe the steps and reasons for its definition.

1. We define a ANN to predict the note at time $i + 1$ given the note at time i. As described in Sect. 4, each note is a token $K^i = [k_1^i, k_2^i, k_3^i]$. Thus, input and output layers have size 3. We also use four hidden layers having size 3.
2. To add "recurrency", we take the output of each node of the hidden layer, and feed it back to itself as an additional input. Each node of the hidden layer receives both the list of inputs from the previous layer and the list of outputs of the current layer in the last time.
3. To solve the problem of shot-term memory we use LSTM nodes.
4. $\mathcal{P}_X$ has to be identical *(1)* for each step (time-invariant), and *(2)* for each note (note-invariant). We build a stack of n identical RNN, one for each token, and the overall network can be viewed as a predictor of the n-gram at time $i + 1$ given the n-gram at time i. We use a "biaxial RNN" approach: the first two recurrent layers sends recurrent connections along the *time-axis*, but are independent across notes. The last two layers sends recurrent connections along the *note-axis*, but are independent between time steps.

5.2   Temporal Predictor for (X,Y)

Now we describe the LSTM defined for each other performer Y in the collective, used to predict musical patterns that follows the style of X respect to *what played at the same time by* Y. Let $\mathcal{M}$ be a corpus of solos for a musical collective, $\mathcal{M}_X \subseteq \mathcal{M}$ be the set of solos performed by X, and $\mathcal{M}_Y \subseteq \mathcal{M}$ be the set of solos performed by Y. Let $\mathcal{R}_X$ be the performer-recognizer for X, $\mathcal{R}_Y$ be the performer-recognizer for Y and n the value used for the construction of the n-grams as described in Sect. 4.1. We remark that n is equal for each performer. Then, we define a predictor $\mathcal{P}_{X,Y}$ (having the same architecture of $\mathcal{P}_X$) that given a n-gram at time t for Y have to predict the n-gram at time t for X. This equivalent to saying that given the sequence of n music notes at time t by Y, $\mathcal{P}_{X,Y}$ has to predict the sequence of n music notes at time t by X.

The training set. We define a data set of n-grams as follows. Let $\mathcal{T}_X \subseteq \mathcal{M}$ be the training set used for the training of $\mathcal{R}_X$ and $\mathcal{T}_Y \subseteq \mathcal{M}$ be the training set used for the training of $\mathcal{R}_Y$. For each $m_j \in \mathcal{T}_X$ such that $\mathcal{R}_X$ says that m_j is coherent with the X's style ($f(m_j) < 0$), let $m'_j \in \mathcal{T}_Y$ such that $\mathcal{R}_Y$ says that m'_j is coherent with the Y's style and m_j, m'_j are played at the same time. Then, we consider the sequence of n-grams extract by m_j and n-grams extract by m'_j. So, let $Ngrams(m_j) = (ng_1, \ldots, ng_{k_j})$ be the sequence of n-grams extract from m_j, $Ngrams(m'_j) = (ng'_1, \ldots, ng'_{k_j})$ be the sequence of n-grams extract from m'_j we insert the pair (ng'_i, ng_i) in the training set for $\mathcal{P}_{X,Y}$, for each $1 \le i \le k_j - 1$.

6 The Splicing-Based Composition

For each performer X, we define a music splicing system to compose melodies coherent with the style learned by $\mathcal{R}_X$. We denote with $\mathcal{C}_X$ the performer-composer for X. We remark that, unlike the cases of the recognizers, in which we first built a single performer-recognizer for each performer in the collective and then a collective-recognizer for the whole collective, here we do not need to define a collective composer. The composition corrsponding to the collective will be the combination of the single compositions generated by the performer-composers.

First we build the performer-recognizers $\mathcal{R}_X$ for each performer X and the collective-recognizer $\mathcal{R}$ as described in Sect. 4, then we build the predictors $\mathcal{P}_X$, $\mathcal{P}_{X,Y}$ for each pair of performers X, Y as described in Sect. 5 and finally we build the performer-composers $\mathcal{C}_X$ for each performer X. Thus, let $\mathcal{M}_X \subseteq \mathcal{M}$, the idea is to build a music splicing composer which produces melodies coherent with the X's style. As explained in [6,12] to define a music splicing composer we need to define an alphabet, an initial set and a set of rules. Such a system is defined by an initial set of melodies coherent with the X's style, and a set of rules built by using $\mathcal{P}$. The language generated contains words that represent pieces of "new" melodies coherent the X's style. Formally, a music splicing system is a triple $\mathcal{S}_{\text{MSS}} = (\mathcal{A}_{\text{MSS}}, \mathcal{I}_{\text{MSS}}, \mathcal{R}_{\text{MSS}})$. Among the generated words we choose the best solution according to the evaluation function defined in Sect. 6.1.

We remark that in this work we use the same techniques of construction of the splicing system proposed in [12] except the evaluation function. In fact, unlike [12] in the musical collective context each splicing composer has to solve a multi-objective problem. Below we only provide details about such a function.

6.1 Implementation Details and Evaluation Function

Given a splicing system $\mathcal{S} = (\mathcal{A}, \mathcal{I}, \mathcal{R})$, the generated language $L(\mathcal{S})$ is an infinite set of words, and the number of iterations of the splicing operation to generate it is unbounded. Thus, we fix a number k of iterations and a maximal cardinality p_{max}. We also define k languages as follows. We set $L_0 = \mathcal{I}_{\text{MSS}} = \gamma^0(\mathcal{I}_{\text{MSS}})$. For any i, $1 \le i \le k$, we consider $L'_i = L_{i-1} \cup \gamma'(L_{i-1})$, which corresponds to enlarge L_{i-1} by an application of all the rules in $\mathcal{R}_{\text{MSS}}$ to all possible pairs of words in L_{i-1}. If $\text{Card}(L'_i) \le p_{max}$, then $L_i = L'_i$. Otherwise, L_i is obtained from L'_i by erasing the $Card(L'_i) - p_{max}$ words in L'_i that are the worst with respect to an evaluation function, i.e., the quality of the melody in terms of stylistic coherence. Therefore, to measure the quality of the compositions and to choose the better solutions we consider such a function. Finally, we define $L(k, p_{max}) = \cup_{1 \le i \le k} L_i$ as the (k, p_{max})-language generated by $\mathcal{S}_{\text{MSS}}$. We remark that $L(k, p_{max})$ is the language considered during the experiments described in Sect. 7.

We have not music rules to use for defining a function that evaluate a composition in terms of "stylistic" goodness. So we use the predictor $\mathcal{P}_X$ and the predictors $\mathcal{P}_{X,Y}$ as follows. The composition problem can be view as a multi-objective problem in which we have to minimize the distance between the style of the compositions generated by $\mathcal{C}_X$ and both (a) the features related to the personal experience and (b) the features related to the influence of the other performers. Let w be a word generated by the composer $\mathcal{S}_{\text{MSS}}$ and let $m = (n_1, \ldots, n_l)$ the melody such that $w = \mathcal{W}(m)$. Now, let $Ngrams(m) = (ng_1, \ldots, ng_{l-1})$ be the sequence of n-grams extract from m. First function f_X is defined as:

$$f_X(m) = \sum_{1 \le i \le l-1} (tfidf(ng_i, m, \mathcal{M})) + Diff(ng_{i+1}, \mathcal{P}_X(ng_i))$$

where $Diff(ng_i, \mathcal{P}_X(ng_i))$ is the *difference* between ng_{i+1} and $\mathcal{P}_X(ng_i)$ that is the n-gram predicted by $\mathcal{P}_X$ with ng_i as input. Such a difference is defined as follows: let $K^{i+1} = [k_1^{i+1}, k_2^{i+1}, k_3^{i+1}]$ be the token for ng_{i+1} and $K'^{i+1} = [k_1'^{i+1}, k_2'^{i+1}, k_3'^{i+1}]$ be the token for $\mathcal{P}(ng_i)$. Then $Diff(ng_{i+1}, \mathcal{P}(ng_i)) = |k_1^{i+1} - k_1'^{i+1}| + |k_2^{i+1} - k_2'^{i+1}| + |k_3^{i+1} - k_3'^{i+1}|$. About the second class of functions, for each other performer Y we define $f_{X,Y}$ as:

$$f_{X,Y}(m) = \sum_{1 \le i \le l} (tfidf(ng'_i, m, \mathcal{M})) + Diff(ng_i, \mathcal{P}_{X,Y}(ng'_i))$$

where $Diff(ng_i, \mathcal{P}_{X,Y}(ng'_i))$ is the *difference* between ng_i and $\mathcal{P}_{X,Y}(ng'_i)$ that is the n-gram predicted by $\mathcal{P}_{X,Y}$ with ng'_i as input. So, let m be a melody produced by $\mathcal{C}_X$, let $X_1, \ldots, X_l$ the performers of the collective (including X), we say that $f(m)_X = (e_1, \ldots, e_l)$ where $e_i = f_X(m)$ if $x_i = X$, otherwise $e_i = f_{X,X_i}(m)$. Thus the composition process of $\mathcal{C}_X$ can be view as a multi-objective problem in which we have to minimize the functions f_X and each f_{X,X_i} with $X \ne X_i$. To solve such a problem, we adopt the strategies of elitism and pareto front described in [13,15]. Now, let the sets of solutions produced by each $\mathcal{C}_i$, in order to obtain composition for the whole collective, we create each possible l-uple $m_1, \ldots, m_l$ where m_i is one of the best solutions produced by $\mathcal{C}_i$. So we consider the pareto front of l-uple as the best solutions for the collective.

7   Experimental Analysis

We report results of tests that we carried out to assess the validity of our approach. We considered several musical collectives: the Hot Five and Hot Seven by Louis Armstrong, the Creole Band by King Oliver, the Countie Basie Orchestra and the Ornette Coleman quartet (by the disc "Free Jazz: A Collective Improvisation"). For each collective we create a data set M of transcribed solos. In this section we refer to the collective by using directly the corresponding datset. The average number of transcriptions for each dataset is 23 and the average number of notes for each melody is 215. For each collective M we build the performer-recognizers and the collective-recognizer R and we compute the recognition rate. As result we obtained that the average recognition rate is 97.7%.

Recognition performances. In our experiments we used a traditional supervised two-class support vector machine as a benchmark for the performance of each R_X. For each collective M and for each R_X, we build a training set by considering the 80% of melodies in M_X (randomly chosen). For the SSVM, we build a training set by considering the 80% of melodies in $M_\mathcal{X}$ and a testing set by considering the 20% of melodies in $M_\mathcal{X}$. As we can see in Table 2 (left) best average results have been obtained with $n = 16$, and in this case two classifiers achieve very similar rates, with true positive and negative rates of up to 0.97 and false positive and negative of only 0.03. As proved for the study described in [12], also in this new study we obtain that the performance of R_X are comparable to the traditional SSVM with the advantage that it requires fewer examples.

Prediction efficacy. In our experiments we assessed the efficacy of each P_X in terms of abilities in predicting patterns that follows the X's style. As explained in Sect. 5 the accuracy of P_X is also validated and compared against a ANN and a RNN trained on the same training set. Table 2 (right) summarizes the (most significant) best average results (over the three experiments) about the prediction rate. As we can see, in a range of 150000 epochs, we have obtained the highest prediction rate using the LSTM recurrent neural network, with Back propagation training, $M = 0.4$ (momentum) and $L = 0.5$ (learning rate).

Table 2. Classifiers performances (left) and Test with average prediction rate (right)

Feature model	Classifier	M_X Yes	M_X Not	$M - M_X$ Yes	$M - M_X$ Not
$n = 12$	R_X	0.88	0.12	0.08	0.92
	SSVM	0.87	0.13	0.07	0.93
$n = 16$	R_X	0.5	0.95	0.06	0.94
	SSVM	0.5	0.95	0.06	0.94
$n = 24$	R_X	0.94	0.06	0.07	0.93
	SSVM	0.93	0.07	0.08	0.92

Representation	M	L	Prediction rate [%]
LSTM	0.4	0.5	98.1
Recurrent NN	0.3	0.6	94.3
LSTM	0.3	0.3	90.2
LSTM	0.2	0.5	88.3
ANN	0.4	0.4	87.1

Music quality. The stylistic coherence of each splicing composer has been evaluated by experts among musicians with more than 10 years of experience in the music field. For each collective we select the best 2 solutions[1] according to the evaluation function (see Sect. 6.1). We asked participants to listen and respond to the following questions: *(1) "How do you rate the quality of music?"*,

---

[1] https://goo.gl/RnVVT5.

and *(2) "How do you rate the coherence of the music with the collective's style?"* (rating on a 7-point Likert scale). Our experts rated very positively both quality and stylistic coherence (M = 6.8 and M = 6.7, respectively).

8   Conclusion

The recognition of multiple performers' style that collaborate over time to perform music, know as *Musical collective*, is a complex problem due to the simultaneous presence of various performers, mutually conditionable. We propose a new approach for both recognition and automatic composition of styles for musical collectives. Our system exploits a machine learning *recognizer* in cooperation with a *splicing composer* for music composition in the style of the whole collective. To assess the effectiveness of our system we performed tests using transcriptions of popular jazz bands. With regard to the *recognition*, we show that our classifier is able to achieve an accuracy of 97.7%. With regard to the *composition*, the quality of the produced compositions was rated positively.

References

1. Acampora, G., Cadenas, J.M., Prisco, R.D., Loia, V., Ballester, E.M., Zaccagnino, R.: A hybrid computational intelligence approach for automatic music composition. In: IEEE International Conference on Fuzzy Systems, pp. 202–209 (2011)
2. Biles, J.A.: GenJam: a genetic algorithm for generating jazz solos. In: International Computer Music Conference, pp. 131–137 (1994)
3. Biles, J.A.: GenJam in perspective: a tentative taxonomy for GA music and art systems. Leonardo **36**(1), 43–45 (2003)
4. Bishop, C.M.: Pattern Recognition and Machine Learning (Information Science and Statistics). Springer, New York (2006)
5. Cope, D.: Experiments in Musical Intelligence. Computer Music and Digital Audio Series. A-R Editions, Middleton (1996)
6. De Felice, C., De Prisco, R., Malandrino, D., Zaccagnino, G., Zaccagnino, R., Zizza, R.: Chorale music splicing system: an algorithmic music composer inspired by molecular splicing. In: Johnson, C., Carballal, A., Correia, J. (eds.) EvoMUSART 2015. LNCS, vol. 9027, pp. 50–61. Springer, Cham (2015). https://doi.org/10.1007/978-3-319-16498-4_5
7. De Felice, C., De Prisco, R., Malandrino, D., Zaccagnino, G., Zaccagnino, R., Zizza, R.: Splicing music composition. Inf. Sci. **385–386**, 196–212 (2017)
8. De Felice, C., Zaccagnino, R., Zizza, R.: Unavoidable sets and regularity of languages generated by (1, 3)-circular splicing systems. In: TPNC 2014. Proceedings, Granada, pp. 169–180, 9–11 December 2014
9. De Felice, C., Zaccagnino, R., Zizza, R.: Unavoidable sets and circular splicing languages. Theor. Comput. Sci. **658**, 148–158 (2017)
10. De Prisco, R., Zaccagnino, R.: An evolutionary music composer algorithm for bass harmonization. In: Giacobini, M., Brabazon, A., Cagnoni, S., Caro, G.A., Ekárt, A., Esparcia-Alcázar, A.I., Farooq, M., Fink, A., Machado, P. (eds.) EvoWorkshops 2009. LNCS, vol. 5484, pp. 567–572. Springer, Heidelberg (2009). https://doi.org/10.1007/978-3-642-01129-0_63

11. De Prisco, R., Eletto, A., Torre, A., Zaccagnino, R.: A neural network for bass functional harmonization. In: Di Chio, C., Brabazon, A., Di Caro, G.A., Ebner, M., Farooq, M., Fink, A., Grahl, J., Greenfield, G., Machado, P., ONeill, M., Tarantino, E., Urquhart, N. (eds.) EvoApplications 2010. LNCS, vol. 6025, pp. 351–360. Springer, Heidelberg (2010). https://doi.org/10.1007/978-3-642-12242-2_36
12. De Prisco, R., Malandrino, D., Zaccagnino, G., Zaccagnino, R., Zizza, R.: A Kind of bio-inspired learning of music style. In: Correia, J., Ciesielski, V., Liapis, A. (eds.) EvoMUSART 2017. LNCS, vol. 10198, pp. 97–113. Springer, Cham (2017). https://doi.org/10.1007/978-3-319-55750-2_7
13. De Prisco, R., Zaccagnino, G., Zaccagnino, R.: Evobasscomposer: a multi-objective genetic algorithm for 4-voice compositions. In: GECCO, pp. 817–818 (2010)
14. De Prisco, R., Zaccagnino, G., Zaccagnino, R.: A genetic algorithm for dodeca-phonic compositions. In: Chio, C., Brabazon, A., Caro, G.A., Drechsler, R., Farooq, M., Grahl, J., Greenfield, G., Prins, C., Romero, J., Squillero, G., Tarantino, E., Tettamanzi, A.G.B., Urquhart, N., Uyar, A.Ş. (eds.) EvoApplications 2011. LNCS, vol. 6625, pp. 244–253. Springer, Heidelberg (2011). https://doi.org/10.1007/978-3-642-20520-0_25
15. De Prisco, R., Zaccagnino, G., Zaccagnino, R.: A multi-objective differential evo-lution algorithm for 4-voice compositions. In: SDE, pp. 65–72 (2011)
16. Ebcioglu, K.: An expert system for harmonizing four-part chorales. In: Machine Models of Music, pp. 385–401. MIT Press, Cambridge (1992)
17. Gers, F.A., Schmidhuber, J.: Recurrent nets that time and count. In: International Joint Conference on Neural Networks, Como (2000)
18. Head, T.: Formal language theory and DNA: an analysis of the generative capacity of specific recombinant behaviours. Bull. Math. Biol. **49**, 737–759 (1987)
19. Horner, A., Ayers, L.: Harmonization of musical progression with genetic algo-rithms. In: International Computer Music Conference, pp. 483–484 (1995)
20. Lehmann, D.: Harmonizing melodies in real-time: the connectionist approach. In: Proceedings of the International Computer Music Association, pp. 27–31 (1997)
21. Levine, M.: The Jazz Theory Book. Curci (2009)
22. Miranda, E.: Composing Music with Computers. Focal Press (2001)
23. Pachet, F., Westermann, G., Laigre, D.: Musical data mining for electronic music distribution. In: WEB Delivering of Music (WEDELMUSIC), pp. 101–106 (2001)
24. Pampalk, E., Dixon, S., Widmer, G.: Exploring music collections by browsing dif-ferent views. In: Music Information Retrieval (2003)
25. Soltau, H., Schultz, T., Westphal, M., Waibel, A.: Recognition of music types. In: International Conference on Acoustics, Speech, and Signal Processing (1998)
26. Whitman, B., Flake, G., Lawrence, S.: Artist detection in music with minnow-match. In: Neural Networks for Signal Processing XI, pp. 559–568 (2001)
27. Wiggins, G., Papadopoulos, G., Amnuaisuk, S., Tuson, A.: Evolutionary methods for musical composition. In: CASYS1998 (1998)

Regularized Stacked Auto-Encoder Based Pre-training for Generalization of Multi-layer Perceptron

Prasenjit Dey, Abhijit Ghosh, and Tandra Pal[✉]

Department of Computer Science and Engineering,
National Institute of Technology, Durgapur,
Durgapur 713209, West Bengal, India
prasenjitdey13@gmail.com, mailabhijit93@gmail.com,
tandra.pal@gmail.com

Abstract. Generalization capability of multi-layer perceptron (MLP) depends on the initialization of its weights. If the weights of an MLP are not initialized properly, it may fail to achieve good generalization. In this article, we propose a weight initialization technique for MLP to improve its generalization. This is achieved by a regularized stacked auto-encoder based pre-training method. During pre-training, the weights between each adjacent layers of an MLP, upto the penultimate layer, are trained layer wise by an auto-encoder. To train the auto-encoder, we use weighted sum of two terms: (i) mean squared error (MSE) and (ii) sum of squares of the first order derivatives of the outputs with respect to inputs. Here, the second term acts as a regularizer. It is used to penalize the training of auto-encoder during pre-training to generate better initial values of the weights for each successive layers of MLP. To compare the proposed initialization technique with random weight initialization, we have considered ten standard classification data sets. Empirical results show that the proposed initialization technique improves the generalization of MLP.

Keywords: Auto-encoder · Initialization · Multi-layer perceptron
Pre-training · Regularization

1 Introduction

In multi-layer perceptron (MLP), while dealing with large number of hidden layers, random weight initialization technique may not work well [7], due to the problem called vanishing gradient. In this scenario, the weights associated with the layers closer to the input layer could not be updated significantly during back propagation of the error from the output layer. To deal with this scenario, various methods related to pre-training of the weights have been used in the literature of MLP and deep neural network (DNN) [16,17]. Note that, an MLP with more than one hidden layer can be considered as DNN. Layer wise stacked auto-encoder based weight initialization is one of them. An auto-encoder

© Springer International Publishing AG 2017
C. Martín-Vide et al. (Eds.): TPNC 2017, LNCS 10687, pp. 232–242, 2017.
https://doi.org/10.1007/978-3-319-71069-3_18

is a computational model with an encoding function $f(\cdot)$ and a decoding function $g(\cdot)$, where, for any input $x \in R^n$, $g(f(x)) \approx x$. In auto-encoder based learning, the weights between each of the adjacent layers of MLP are trained layer wise starting from the input layer to the penultimate layer.

Hinton et al., in [8], performed unsupervised pre-training by stacking restricted boltzmann machines (RBM) for proper initialization of weights of the DNNs. DNNs mainly use learning techniques with multiple levels of representation [11]. Traditional machine learning approaches involve features, extracting explicitly from a data set and then feed it to a neural network for training. Although such approaches are still effective for small problems, but for real world problems, it becomes increasingly difficult to hand engineer features from huge data sets. In DNNs, the data is directly fed into the network. It is the job of the network to extract the features from the data using non-linear modules that transform the representation at one level (starting form the raw input) into a representation at a higher and slightly more abstract level, and learn the mapping between the input to the required output. DNNs perform layer wise unsupervised pre-training to obtain the higher level of abstraction from data sets followed by conventional supervised training of the network [8].

In the proposed work, we use regularized stacked auto-encoders to achieve the higher level abstraction of the original data set at each hidden layer. The auto-encoders are trained layer wise using gradient descent based back propagation technique. For training the auto-encoder, we use a weighted sum of the two terms: (i) mean squared error (MSE) and (ii) sum of squares of the first order derivatives of the outputs with respect to inputs. During pre-training, the regularizers in auto-encoders make the deviations in the hidden representation less with respect to the inputs. The proposed method have been tested for generalization using ten classification data sets. The empirical results show that the proposed initialization method gives better generalization capability of MLP when compared to initialization by auto-encoders without regularizer and random weight initialization methods.

This article is organised into five sections. In Sect. 2, we review the works, existing in the literature, similar to the proposed model, i.e., pre-training based initialization of weights. The proposed model is discussed, in detail, in Sect. 3. In Sect. 4, we provide experimental results. Finally, we conclude in Sect. 5.

2   Literature Review

Over the years, various researchers have worked towards improving the generalization capability of MLP using various regularization techniques. Some of them have used early stopping [18], curvature-driven smoothing [5] or weight decay [9]. Early stopping involves stopping the training process depending on validation error. In curvature-driven smoothing, we penalize the mappings with large curvature by adding a curvature smoothing term [3,4]. Weight decay involves additional terms, added to the cost function in order to penalize high values of weights and biases, thereby reducing classifier complexity. There are various such additional terms discussed in [5]. In [13], the authors have introduced a new regularization scheme termed as eigenvalue decay. The cost function that they use in their work is given as follows

$$E^{**} = E + \kappa(\lambda_{min} + \lambda_{max}). \qquad (1)$$

Here, E is the mean squared error, κ is the regularization coefficient, λ_{min} is the smallest eigenvalue of square of $(\mathbf{W}^H)(\mathbf{W}^H)^T$, and λ_{max} is the biggest eigenvalue of $(\mathbf{W}^H)(\mathbf{W}^H)^T$. With the introduction to pre-training, it has become possible to train deeper networks. The starting parameters that we get after pre-training is robust with respect to random initialization. It ensures better generalization [7]. In [2], Bengio et al. have used stacked RBMs for pre-training the DNN in a greedy layer wise unsupervised manner. To improve the performance further, they have suggested that the idea of greedy layer wise unsupervised training can also be extended to auto associators to get a better representation in higher layers, which reflects the capability to generate higher level of abstractions from the raw data. Erhan et al. [6] have demonstrated through their experiments that supervised learning of the parameters generated through unsupervised pre-training produces better results compared to randomly generated parameters in MLP. For justifying their work philosophically they have stated that while the network learns one hidden representation at a time, the weights tend to reach near the global minima. Thus, once the entire network is pre-trained, all the parameters are already in the neighbourhood of the global minima.

Larochelle et al. [10] have shown the results on MNIST data set using both the stacked RBMs and the auto-encoders. The authors have validated that in order to achieve better generalization capability of deep architectures, it is important to perform local unsupervised pre-training each layer at a time. Each layer produces a higher layer representation from the lower level representation output by the previous layer by altering the parameters between them. A key difference between an auto-encoder based pre-training and a restricted boltzmann machine (RBM) based pre-training is that the weights used by RBMs to generate the data is same as those used to infer from the data. This is not the case in auto-encoder, which is basically a special type of neural network, where hidden activations are the new representations of the input that has been learnt by back-propagating the reconstruction error. It is not compulsory to use the same weights for inference and reconstruction. It is, however, suggested that care must be taken while training the auto encoder network to prevent any trivial and uninteresting mapping that can be learnt [10]. In [10,14,15], the authors have tied both the weights together, i.e., $(W^I)^T = W^H$, where W^I and W^H represent the input-hidden and hidden-output weights of the auto-encoder respectively. However, they have suggestted that use of weight decay as a regularizer with error function during training can also be useful.

To achieve a good hidden representation, Rifai et al. [15] have proposed to use the sum of square of first order derivative of the hidden representation with respect to inputs as a regularizer, penalizing the standard loss function of an auto encoder. Such auto-encoders are called contractive auto-encoders (CAEs).

The cost function $C(\theta)$, the authors [15] have used is

$$C_{CAE}(\theta) = \sum_{x \epsilon D_n} (L(x;\theta) + \lambda||J_f(x)||_F^2), \qquad (2)$$

where θ is the set of weights and biases of the input-hidden and the hidden-output layer, and x is a training sample from the training set D_n. $L(x;\theta)$ is the mean squared error of the input and the output for the sample x. $||J_f(x)||_F^2$ is the term for regularization given as follows,

$$||J_f(x)||_F^2 = \sum_{ij} (\frac{\partial h_j(x)}{\partial x_i})^2, \qquad (3)$$

where $h_j(x)$ is the hidden representation of the input x at the jth hidden node. In [14], Rifai et al. have proposed a higher order contractive auto-encoder by introducing the second order derivative of the representations with respect to the inputs as the penalising term. Thus, their cost function becomes as follows in (4).

$$C_{CAE+H}(\theta) = C_{CAE} + \gamma E[||J_f(x) - J_f(x + \epsilon)||^2] \qquad (4)$$

Here C_{CAE} is the same as Eq. (2). λ and γ respectively in Eqs. (2) and (4) are non negative hyperparameters. These regularised auto-encoders have then been stacked to obtain deep networks and tested on various standard data sets. However, in [15] and [14], the authors have not considered the fact that the hidden representation is achieved by virtue of weights and biases learnt by minimizing the mean squared difference or loss between the achieved output/reconstruction and the target output (which is actually the input). M.B. Ali, in his dissertation [1], has done an elaborate comparison on the effects of standard $l1$ and $l2$ regularizers as well as dropouts in pre-training of the auto-encoders. The author has also proposed the k-lowest dropout auto-encoder and fine-tuning, in which k number of hidden nodes having the lowest outputs were switched off. The outputs from the rest were only forwarded to the next layer.

3   Proposed Model

In the proposed model, we have used regularized stacked auto-encoders to train the weights between each adjacent layers except those between penultimate and output layers. Reconstruction error of an auto-encoder is the deviation of the output of the decoding function from the input of the encoder. We have used an MLP as auto-encoder with the hidden layer activation function as the encoder and the output layer activation function as the decoder. The cost function of the MLP is the reconstruction error which is minimized with respect to the weights of the network during pre-training.

As auto-encoders are used to train the weights between each of the adjacent layers one at a time, we need the hidden representation to retain information of input as much as possible. The hidden representation is used to obtain higher abstraction of the input which is finally mapped with the target output. In the proposed model, we use untied weights, i.e., $(W^I)^T \neq W^H$, where W^I and W^H are respectively the input-hidden weights and hidden-output weights of the auto-encoder. It makes sure that the network does not learn any trivial identity function. We also introduce a new penalty term as a regularizer along with the reconstruction error in the cost function. The regularizer, used in the model, is the first order derivative of the output with respect to the input of the auto-encoder. Weight updation restricts the outputs of the auto-encoders to reconstruct the inputs faithfully and not deviate much from the desired value. It ensures that the inputs that are comparatively similar have similar hidden representations, resulting better generalization. The new cost function is then minimized using gradient descent to obtain the weight updates. Note that, the regularizer is used only in the pre-training phase when the weights of successive layers are trained one at a time.

Once the weights of the hidden layer of the auto-encoder is trained, the weights of the output layer of the auto-encoder is discarded. The encoding parameters, i.e., the input-hidden weights are frozen and the output of the hidden layer is then used as the input to the next auto-encoder, which is stacked on top of it to generate the next level of representation. It is continued upto the penultimate layer. The pre-trained parameters of the encoder part of all the stacked auto-encoders, i.e., the input-hidden weights including the bias of the auto-encoder, are the initial weights for the training of the MLP. The proposed method is explained below in detail.

3.1   Pre-training

Let us consider a data set $\mathbf{D}$ of size P, $\mathbf{D} = \{(x_1, t_1), (x_2, t_2), \cdots, (x_P, t_P)\}$, where the input $\mathbf{x}_i \in \mathbb{R}^n$ and the corresponding output $\mathbf{t}_i \in [0, 1]^j$. In pre-training, the auto-encoders are used to generate a hidden representation of the input. The input $\mathbf{x}_i$ is fed to the auto-encoder having a single hidden layer with h hidden nodes. An auto-encoder reconstructs its input by altering the weighted connections in between the successive layers. The output of the hidden layer is as follows in (5).

$$s_i(\mathbf{z}) = \frac{1}{1 + \exp^{-\mathbf{z}}}, \qquad \mathbf{z} = \mathbf{W}^I \mathbf{x}_i + \mathbf{b}_h. \tag{5}$$

Here, $\mathbf{W}^I$ is the input-hidden weight matrix. $\mathbf{b}_h$ is the weight between the bias node of the input layer and the hth hidden node.

The function of the output layer of the auto-encoder is

$$s_i(\mathbf{y}) = \frac{1}{1 + \exp^{-\mathbf{y}}}, \qquad \mathbf{y} = \mathbf{W}^H s_i(\mathbf{z}) + \mathbf{b}_o. \tag{6}$$

Here, $\mathbf{W}^H$ is the hidden-output weight matrix and $\mathbf{b}_o$ is the weight between the bias node of the hidden layer and the oth output node.

We use the bias as a special node in the preceding layer increasing the dimension of vector $\mathbf{x}_i$ by 1, i.e., $(n+1)$. Thus, $\mathbf{x}_i = (x_i^1, x_i^3, x_i^3, \cdots, x_i^{n+1})$, where $x_i^1 = 1$. $W_{1h}^I = b_h$ represents the connection between the bias node and the hth hidden layer node. Similarly, a node is added in the hidden layer as the bias node of output layer.

As an auto-encoder approximates its input, the cost function can be written as follows in (7).

$$e_i = \frac{1}{2} \sum_{k=1}^{n} (x_i^k - s_i(y^k))^2, \tag{7}$$

where e_i is the error corresponding to the ith sample and y^k is the input of kth node of the output layer.

For updation of weights, we compute the first order derivative of the cost function with respect to the weights $\mathbf{W}^I$ and $\mathbf{W}^H$ as given below.

$$\Delta \mathbf{W}^I = -\eta_1 \frac{\partial e_i}{\partial \mathbf{W}^I} \qquad \Delta \mathbf{W}^H = -\eta_1 \frac{\partial e_i}{\partial \mathbf{W}^H} \tag{8}$$

In our work, the cost function of the auto-encoder, given in (7), is penalized using a regularization function, which is the first order derivative of the output representation with respect to the input. Therefore, the cost function in (7) is replaced by (9) as follows.

$$e_i^{new} = e_i + \lambda R, \qquad R = \frac{\partial s_i(\mathbf{y})}{\partial \mathbf{x}_i}, \tag{9}$$

where λ is the regularization parameter and R is the regularization function. From (9), we derive

$$R = \sum_{j=1}^{n} \sum_{k=1}^{n+1} (\partial s_i(y^j) \sum_{l=2}^{h+1} (W_{lj}^H \partial s_i(z^l) W_{k(l-1)}^I)). \tag{10}$$

The corresponding updation of weights $\mathbf{W}^I$ and $\mathbf{W}^H$ are respectively given below in (11) and (12).

$$\Delta \mathbf{W}^I = -\eta_1 (\frac{\partial e_i}{\partial \mathbf{W}^I} + \lambda \frac{\partial R}{\partial \mathbf{W}^I}) \tag{11}$$

$$\Delta \mathbf{W}^H = -\eta_1 (\frac{\partial e_i}{\partial \mathbf{W}^H} + \lambda \frac{\partial R}{\partial \mathbf{W}^H}) \tag{12}$$

As the learning is done in batch mode, we have

$$\frac{\partial e_i}{\partial W_{pq}^I} = \frac{1}{P} \sum_{i=1}^{P} \sum_{j=1}^{n} (-e_i^j \partial s_i(y^j) W_{qj}^H) \partial s_i(z^q) s_i(x^p), \tag{13}$$

$$\frac{\partial R}{\partial W_{pq}^I} = \frac{1}{P} \sum_{i=1}^{P} (\partial s_i(z^{q+1}) \sum_{j=1}^{n} (\partial s_i(y^j) W_{(q+1)j}^H)) \tag{14}$$

and

$$\frac{\partial e_i}{\partial W_{qr}^H} = \frac{1}{P} \sum_{i=1}^{P} -e_i^r \partial s_i(y^r) s_i(z^q) \tag{15}$$

$$\frac{\partial R}{\partial W_{qr}^H} = \frac{1}{P} \sum_{i=1}^{P} (\partial s_i(y^r) \partial s_i(z^q) \sum_{k=1}^{n+1} (W_{k(q-1)}^I)) \tag{16}$$

Substituting (13) and (14) in (11), and (15) and (16) in (12), we finally get the updates for the weights and biases of the auto-encoder. We obtain a hidden representation of the input $\mathbf{x}_i$ in the form of $s_i(\mathbf{z})$ by virtue of the trained input-hidden weight $\mathbf{W}^I$. We therefore retain $\mathbf{W}^I$ as the pre-trained weight.

3.2   Training of the Pre-trained Weights

The weights, already pre-trained, are then trained in MLP in batch mode. The size of the batch is equal to the number of samples present in the training data set. For the given data set, we perform the following operation for the output of the hidden layer.

$$s_i(\mathbf{z}) = f(W^I \mathbf{x}_i) \tag{17}$$

Here $f(.)$ is the sigmoid transfer function, W^I is the pre-trained weight between the input and hidden layers with W_{1h}^I as weight between the bias node of input layer and h^{th} hidden node, and $\mathbf{x}_i$ is the ith input sample. In our study, we have used a single hidden layer in MLP. So, $s_i(\mathbf{z})$ is used as the input to the output layer. The output of the final layer is given in (18).

$$s_i(\mathbf{y}) = f(W^{class} s_i(\mathbf{z})) \tag{18}$$

Here, W^{class} is the weight between the pre-final and the final layers with W_{1o}^{class} as weight between the bias node of hidden layer and o^{th} output node. $s_i(y)$ represents the actual output, which is compared with the target output t_i to give the loss function of the whole network as given below.

$$e_i = \frac{1}{2} \sum_{k=1}^{c} (t_i^k - s_i(y^k))^2 \tag{19}$$

The loss function is then optimized using gradient descent based back propagation to train the network for its set of parameters, W^{class} and W^I.

4   Experimentation

4.1   Experimental Settings

For experimentation, we have used ten standard classification data sets, taken from [12]. The information of all the data sets and their class wise distribution is shown in Table 1. The simulations are performed in MATLAB

(Version 8.1). We have compared the proposed model with two different approaches: (i) an MLP with random weight initialization and (ii) stacked auto-encoder with unsupervised pre-training without regularizer. We have first performed z-score normalization on the training data set and found the mean and standard deviation. The mean and standard deviation have been used to obtain the z-score normalization of the test data set. All the models, that we have used for our experiment, have a single hidden layer with 5 hidden nodes except for *Tae* data set. For *Tae* data set, we have taken 4 hidden nodes. As *Tae* data set has 5 input features, if we take 5 hidden nodes during pre-training, the auto-encoder shall have five input, five hidden and five output nodes. This configuration will adjust the weights in such a way that the input will be simply memorized to the hidden layer.

Table 1. Summary of the classification data sets

Data sets	# features	# classes	Size and class wise distribution
Bands	19	2	365(135,230)
Cleveland	13	5	297(160,54,35,35,13)
Glass	9	6	214(70,76,17,13,9,29)
Ionosphere	34	2	351(225,126)
Satimage	36	6	6435(1533,703,1358,626,707,1508)
Sonar	60	2	208(97,111)
Spectfheart	44	2	267(212,55)
Tae	5	3	151(49,50,52)
Vowel	10	11	990(90 X 11)
Yeast	8	10	1484(224,429,463,44,51,163,35,30,20,5)

Conventional MLP has comparatively less number of hyperparameters, e.g., the number of hidden nodes and the learning rate. But in the stacked auto-encoder with regularizer, we have an additional learning rate and the regularization coefficient corresponding to the pre-training. For all the data sets, we use $\eta_1 = 0.5$ and $\eta_2 = 0.3$, where η_1 and η_2 are respectively the learning rates for pre-training and final training. For the selection of the initial learning rate (η_1), we have performed cross validation method with different values of learning rate and observed that for the most of the data sets system best performance is best $\eta_1 = 0.5$. With this primitive experimentation, we decide to choose the value of learning rate as 0.5. We have performed batch mode learning with 10000 epochs for both of the pre-training and final training of the MLP. Here, the size of the batch is equal to the number of samples present in the training data set. In conventional MLP, weights are initialized randomly within $[-0.5, +0.5]$.

The learning rate η_1 during pre-training is kept at a higher value than the learning rate during final training η_2, i.e., $\eta_1 > \eta_2$, because during pre-training the auto-encoder searches for the global minima over the whole solution space of parameters. If the step size is small, then it might take a lot of time to reach in the vicinity of the global minima. Therefore, it is kept relatively large, so that it can cover the search space and avoid getting stuck in local minima. After the pre-training, the parameters correspond to the vicinity of the optimum. So, during training, the learning rate is kept low so that it does not surpass the area of the global minimum and thus properly searches the area for the best possible solution.

4.2   Results and Discussion

The detailed result of the experiment is given in Table 2. The bold faced entries in the table signify the best classification accuracy for the respective data sets. We have performed ten fold cross validation for all the data sets with ten different initialization of the seed to obtain the above results. Column 2 of Table 2 shows the classification accuracy of the data sets obtained by conventional MLP, i.e., MLP with random initialization of weights. In Table 2, column 3 shows the classification accuracy of the data sets obtained by MLP with non-regularized unsupervised pre-training based initialization of weight. Note that, in column 3, $\lambda = 0$ signifies that the regularizer is absent which is equivalent to unsupervised pre-training without regularizer. Column 4 to column 6 in Table 2 shows the accuracies of the data sets obtained by MLP with regularized unsupervised pre-training of auto-encoders for different values of regularization coefficient (λ). In this experiment, we vary the value of λ from 0.01 to 0.03 as shown in Table 2, which shows that the proposed initialization scheme provides better classification accuracy for six out of ten data sets when compared with the column 2, i.e., conventional MLP. Thus, the proposed model has more generalization capa-

Table 2. Table showing the classification accuracy for MLP with random weight initialization and proposed method with pre-initialized weights for different λ.

Data sets	MLP with random weight initialization	Proposed method with pre-initialized weights			
		Without regularization	With regularization		
		$\lambda = 0.00$	$\lambda = 0.01$	$\lambda = 0.02$	$\lambda = 0.03$
Bands	64.48 ± 1.52	63.20 ± 2.01	$\mathbf{65.19 \pm 1.83}$	63.73 ± 1.93	63.97 ± 2.53
Cleveland	56.36 ± 1.30	56.04 ± 1.13	55.71 ± 0.86	56.45 ± 1.22	$\mathbf{56.72 \pm 0.97}$
Glass	62.86 ± 1.56	62.90 ± 2.52	62.94 ± 1.50	62.71 ± 1.31	$\mathbf{63.11 \pm 2.18}$
Ionosphere	$\mathbf{90.87 \pm 0.73}$	90.46 ± 1.07	89.81 ± 1.07	88.44 ± 1.74	85.23 ± 1.97
Satimage	83.56 ± 0.32	85.61 ± 0.58	$\mathbf{85.82 \pm 0.42}$	85.66 ± 0.32	85.07 ± 0.79
Sonar	79.78 ± 1.91	$\mathbf{80.42 \pm 2.43}$	77.02 ± 2.82	73.93 ± 2.38	70.56 ± 2.96
Spectfheart	76.41 ± 1.51	77.61 ± 1.10	77.59 ± 1.46	$\mathbf{77.85 \pm 1.21}$	77.36 ± 1.56
Tae	53.98 ± 2.16	$\mathbf{55.00 \pm 1.17}$	53.68 ± 0.92	53.23 ± 1.56	54.82 ± 1.83
Vowel	58.87 ± 2.38	58.69 ± 2.24	$\mathbf{59.42 \pm 1.83}$	57.71 ± 2.64	51.87 ± 3.73
Yeast	56.80 ± 0.65	$\mathbf{57.55 \pm 0.43}$	57.27 ± 0.49	57.26 ± 0.48	57.00 ± 0.64

bility than the conventional MLP. For Ionosphere data set, randomly initialized MLP yields better result than MLP with pre-trained parameters. While comparing with the column 3, i.e., unsupervised auto-encoder based training without regularizer, we observe that the proposed initialization scheme has higher classification accuracy. Hence, our empirical results show that the proposed model of pre-training enhances the generalizaion of MLP. It shows the importance of the proposed pre-initialization technique for generalization. Optimal value of the regularization coefficient (λ) depends on the data set. Proper empirical analysis may fix it.

5   Conclusion

In this study, we present a model that generates better values for initialization of weights by pre-training the network using regularized auto-encoders. It provides better classification accuracy than conventional MLP, i.e., better generalization of MLP. The empirical experimentation shows that the proposed model performs better than a network whose weights are initialized by an auto-encoder without any regularizer as well as random weight initialization. The purpose of such pre-training technique is the same as any other pre-training methodology, i.e., to have a better starting point for the gradient descent learning. The use of the regularizer in unsupervised pre-training ensures that the inputs that are comparatively similar have similar hidden representations. This is done by restricting the outputs of the auto-encoders, used during pre-training, to reconstruct the inputs correctly and not to deviate much because of weight updates. The main motive of this work is to use the regularizer in the greedy unsupervised layer wise pre-training framework using auto-encoders to produce good initialization of weights as compared to random initialization. The hyperparameters and regularization coefficient are required to be chosen judiciously to obtain the optimal classification accuracy. In future, we will study the selection mechanism of these hyperparameters and regularization coefficient. Furthermore, the proposed model having a single hidden layer can be extended for more than one hidden layer.

References

1. Ali, M.B.: Use of dropouts and sparsity for regularization of autoencoders in deep neural networks. Ph.D. thesis, bilkent university (2015)
2. Bengio, Y., Lamblin, P., Popovici, D., Larochelle, H., et al.: Greedy layer-wise training of deep networks. Adv. Neural Inform. Process. Syst. **19**, 153 (2007)
3. Bishop, C.M.: Curvature-driven smoothing in back-propagation neural networks. Theory Appl. Neural Networks **2**, 139–148 (1990)
4. Bishop, C.M.: Curvature-driven smoothing: a learning algorithm for feedforward networks. IEEE Trans. Neural Networks **4**(5), 882–884 (1993)
5. Bishop, C.M.: Pattern Recognition and Machine Learning. Springer, New York (2006)

6. Erhan, D., Bengio, Y., Courville, A., Manzagol, P.A., Vincent, P., Bengio, S.: Why does unsupervised pre-training help deep learning? J. Mach. Learn. Res. **11**, 625–660 (2010)
7. Erhan, D., Manzagol, P.A., Bengio, Y., Bengio, S., Vincent, P.: The difficulty of training deep architectures and the effect of unsupervised pre-training. In: AISTATS, vol. 5, pp. 153–160 (2009)
8. Hinton, G.E., Osindero, S., Teh, Y.W.: A fast learning algorithm for deep belief nets. Neural Comput. **18**(7), 1527–1554 (2006)
9. Jin, Y., Okabe, T., Sendhoff, B.: Neural network regularization and ensembling using multi-objective evolutionary algorithms. In: IEEE Congress on Evolutionary Computation, CEC 2004, vol. 1, pp. 1–8. IEEE (2004)
10. Larochelle, H., Bengio, Y., Louradour, J., Lamblin, P.: Exploring strategies for training deep neural networks. J. Mach. Learn. Res. **10**, 1–40 (2009)
11. LeCun, Y., Bengio, Y., Hinton, G.: Deep learning. Nature **521**(7553), 436–444 (2015)
12. Lichman, M.: UCI machine learning repository (2013). http://archive.ics.uci.edu/ml
13. Ludwig, O., Nunes, U., Araujo, R.: Eigenvalue decay: a new method for neural network regularization. Neurocomputing **124**, 33–42 (2014)
14. Rifai, S., Mesnil, G., Vincent, P., Muller, X., Bengio, Y., Dauphin, Y., Glorot, X.: Higher order contractive auto-encoder. In: Gunopulos, D., Hofmann, T., Malerba, D., Vazirgiannis, M. (eds.) ECML PKDD 2011. LNCS (LNAI), vol. 6912, pp. 645–660. Springer, Heidelberg (2011). https://doi.org/10.1007/978-3-642-23783-6_41
15. Rifai, S., Vincent, P., Muller, X., Glorot, X., Bengio, Y.: Contractive auto-encoders: explicit invariance during feature extraction. In: Proceedings of the 28th International Conference on Machine Learning (ICML 2011), pp. 833–840 (2011)
16. Santara, A., Maji, D., Tejas, D., Mitra, P., Gupta, A.: Faster learning of deep stacked autoencoders on multi-core systems using synchronized layer-wise pre-training. arXiv preprint arXiv:1603.02836 (2016)
17. Seyyedsalehi, S.Z., Seyyedsalehi, S.A.: A fast and efficient pre-training method based on layer-by-layer maximum discrimination for deep neural networks. Neurocomputing **168**, 669–680 (2015)
18. Treadgold, N.K., Gedeon, T.D.: Exploring constructive cascade networks. IEEE Trans. Neural Networks **10**(6), 1335–1350 (1999)

Historical Markings in Neuroevolution of Augmenting Topologies Revisited

Lukas Pastorek[✉] and Michael O'Neill

UCD Natural Computing Research & Applications Group,
University College Dublin, Dublin, Ireland
{lukas.pastorek,m.oneill}@ucd.ie

Abstract. Historical markings in the NEAT algorithm provides a powerful feature for easy genetic alignment of any networks in the population, and allows speciation to protect networks with novelties. The original approach incorporated in NEAT always generates a new record for a connection with a unique ID when the connection is proposed in a generation. However, because of this mechanism, identical novelties developed in different generations are associated with different IDs and are not recognized as matching connections between networks. Despite popularity of the NEAT algorithm, there has been no existing study, which empirically investigates impact of this encoding on behavioral dynamics. The aim of this study is: firstly, to theoretically discuss generation context-dependent and generation context-free definitions for innovations (GC vs. GC-F); secondly, experimentally compare them on an XOR experiment under different speciation scenarios.

Our analyses suggest that the GC-F approach produces 40–50% less innovation records than the GC approach. Moreover, the GC algorithm exploits more innovation records from the register. However, the assumption about a higher number of species for the GC approach is observed to be true only for the first 30 generations. The difference represents a maximum of 10% decline of GC-F rates when compared to GC. The analysis of migratory patterns shows, that GC-F leads to higher migration to older species. However, differences in migration to younger species were minimal. In conclusion, the exuberant number of innovation records in the register in NEAT does not lead to critical behavioral differences.

Keywords: NEAT · XOR · Historical markings · Bloat
Context-free encoding

1 Introduction

Neuroevolution of Augmenting Topologies (NEAT), see [12], is a popular evolutionary algorithm for evolution of artificial neural networks – their topologies and synaptic weights. It can be seen as the alternative to training of neural networks through classic backpropagation. This algorithm and its principles became part of the highly-cited studies in the field of neural and evolutionary computations

© Springer International Publishing AG 2017
C. Martín-Vide et al. (Eds.): TPNC 2017, LNCS 10687, pp. 243–254, 2017.
https://doi.org/10.1007/978-3-319-71069-3_19

[3, 9, 11], artificial life [13] or detection and classification [15]. However, the most eminent fields of application and development represent reinforcement learning tasks, robotics and video games [1, 4, 6, 10, 14, 17].

This paper attempts to address one of the intrinsic and originally proposed NEAT features, whose effect has only been the subject of hypothesis and speculation. The simple, but powerful concept of global innovation numbers dependent on the generational context were accepted by the community with no more need for further investigation. The behavioral effect of this idea has not been reported in the literature. Although, the existence of multiple IDs of identical novelties can be the source of very complex patterns. Moreover, the dynamics of various behavioral and genetic attributes is beyond the reach of human intuition. In this paper, we try to describe data patterns in the particular case of the XOR problem and compare with results of a generation context-free encoding of innovation numbers.

The remainder of the paper is structured as follows. Section 2 describes the original algorithmic implementation of historical markings. In Sect. 3, we theoretically discuss conceptual nature of different definitions of innovations. Section 4 contains a description of the testing problem and settings of algorithm. In Sect. 5, we present and discuss experimental results. Finally, Sect. 6 summarizes our study.

2   Tracking Genes Through Historical Markings

Historical markings, in the form of innovation numbers, were originally proposed to simplify genetic alignment (line up) of any two networks in the population in a metaphorical mating procedure (called recombination or crossover) [12]. As a result, inheritance of genes from parents to the offspring is clear, straightforward and computationally not expensive.

Each individual (neural network) can be constructed based on its set of connections (list of pairs of neuron IDs). So, each individual is defined by the set of neuron IDs and set of connections between these neurons. A connection is understood as a gene and the set of connections in an individual as a genome. At initialization a *register of innovations* (array) is created including the list of connections, which is shared by all networks. At the start of evolution, all networks have the same connections – the identical topology (minimal structure). Each gene in the innovation register is also linked with the unique ID called an *innovation number*. These unique innovation numbers are also adopted from the register of innovations by all networks. Thus, the definition of the individual in NEAT is expanded to the set of connections with their unique innovation numbers (innovation number is the integral part of each connection). At the beginning, all networks have identical connections and neurons. However, they differ in connection weights. Weights are assigned to the individual's connections at the initialization of the networks before evolution.

The innovation numbers can be understood as historical markings of genes and enable the tracking of the evolutionary origins of genes (connections).

A new connection in the individual's genome can rise through two types of mutations. Firstly, when two previously unconnected neurons in the individual are linked. The new connection is created. And secondly, when a new neuron is inserted into the existing connection. Consequently, two new connections are initialized (connection from the existing node to the new node and from the new node to the other existing node).

Always, when a new, previously unseen connection in population arises, the proposed new connection is recorded in the register of innovations and associated with a new unique innovation number. Consequently, this connection with a newly assigned innovation number is inserted into the genome of the given individual. As innovation numbers in the genome of individuals are never changed, they can be also inherited by offspring during recombination. They are an integral part of inherited connections.

By using this technique, it is easy to line up genomes of any two individuals and compare, which genes match up with which (share the same innovation number).

Moreover, this encoding approach provides another powerful new capability. This tracking mechanism allows speciation to isolate networks with novel connections, which have arisen due to mutation and serve to protect these novelties. Using this method, the algorithm promotes survival and reproduction of uncommon individuals through reduced competition in separate niches (species).

3 Generation Context-Dependent Versus Generation Context-Free Encoding

Despite the technical nature of innovations in the original algorithm, it represents the implementation of an important conceptual idea. However, the concept of generation-dependent innovation numbers was not theoretically discussed by the authors in [12]. Nor, was its presumed advantageous nature empirically justified in other publications.

Nevertheless, this novel concept can be compared with the older and more conventional perspective, which does not consider generation context.

3.1 Generation Context-Dependent Definition of the Innovation

One of the important features, which is specific for the original NEAT implementation is dependence of the connection encoding on a generational context.

According to the original rule, a new innovation record in the innovation register is initialized only in the situation when a new innovation is proposed for the first time *in the given generation*. For the other cases Stanley stated "*When the same structure arises more than once through independent mutations in the same generation, each identical mutation is assigned the same innovation number.*" [12].

However, this generation context-dependent procedure (GC) does not prevent the assignment of a new incremented innovation number to the identical structure in future generations. The term "innovation" can be misleading in this case, as its general meaning is associated with something absolutely "new". In the original implementation, innovations are also called identical structures, which are not new in the true sense (when the entire length of evolution is considered). They are considered new because the algorithm considers a single generation as temporal context (they can appear for the first time in the given generation). So, an additional innovation record in the register is always established when known structural innovations emerge again in any subsequent generation. Identical innovations from the previous generations are not taken into account, as if they were forgotten. Due to the repeated onset of innovations at different times (generations), the innovation register includes multiple clones of connections with different innovation numbers. This implementation does not consider structures, which originated in different generations, as related despite their apparent architectural equality. As they arose under different circumstances, they are considered as different.

3.2   Generation Context-Free Definition of the Innovation

In this paper, we challenge this generation-dependent interpretation of innovation with the classic, generation context-free implementation (GC-F). This traditional approach inhibits the described multiplicity by assigning the same innovation numbers to the same innovations regardless of their generational onset.

Under this approach, the innovation number is generated in the innovation register only once, when the innovation is introduced for the first time. Afterwards, when mutation introduces the already seen innovation for insertion into the genome, the gene is associated with the known, already initialized innovation number from the register. So the algorithm considers the context of the entire evolutionary history.

However, this approach leads to a potential exception. A potential advantage for the occasional multiplicity of apparently identical structures is the capability of the network to create parallel paths. The random nature of mutations allows the insertion of new nodes to identical connections more often in history (connections can become subjects of mutation repeatedly). If a connection is being mutated the second time and no other network in history experienced such a scenario for a given innovation, two new connections with new incremented innovation numbers are created in the innovation register and associated with the individual's genome (inserted into the genome).

The maximum number of repetitions of the architecturally equal connections in the innovation register means, that in the population there existed the network, which experienced as many mutations of the identical structure, as there are clones of the given innovation. Accordingly, if any network is mutated, the algorithm checks if the given network includes all copies of matching innovations from the register. Only if the network owns all of them, will a new record with a new innovation number be initialized in the register and inserted into the individuals genome. Otherwise, the missing copy of innovation is adopted from the register. The presented mechanism inspects matching connections in the register from the oldest to the youngest records.

4 Experiments and Settings

Following [16], where authors adjusted JNEAT parameters to limit network growth, we compare our approaches on the classic XOR problem with the algorithmic settings described in this section. The XOR problem was addressed in the original paper by Stanley and its modifications are still spread in publications concerning the issue of modularity of complex networks, see [2,5,8].

Despite the known minimal neural architecture capable to solve this problem, the existence of this topology does not imply the limit for other architectures to deal with this task. This problem can illustrate evolution of more complex structures too. It is true especially for the situation when the algorithm prefers solutions of bigger size. We applied a linear algebra-based NEAT implementation by Mayr [7] (available officially through Miikkulainen's Neural Networks Research Group), which promotes network growth at the expense of very small structures on this problem. This implementation was migrated to the Python language.

The neuroevolutionary algorithm for each approach was run 1000 times and all measured features in each generation were averaged. The population included 150 individuals, which were allowed to evolve for a maximum 100 generations. Networks were initialized with minimal architecture (sigmoid slope parameter in model was 4.9). Coefficients for measuring compatibility were $c1 = 1.0$, $c2 = 1.0$, and $c3 = 0.4$. Evolutionary behavior was investigated for 5 different speciation scenarios: speciation threshold $\delta = \{1, 2, 3, 4, 5\}$. The speciation procedure inspected compatibility of the individual always starting with compatibility distance to the representative of the oldest living species (species centroid). In case of incompatibility (computed distance exceeded the threshold), a new distance from the representative of the second oldest living species was calculated. Otherwise, the individual was assigned to the compatible species (computed distance was less than threshold). If an individual was assigned to the existing species, the other younger species were not investigated. If the individual was not compatible with any species, the individual initialized a new species with itself as the representative.

The elite individual of each species with more than 5 individuals was copied into the population for following generation with no change. Each generation 20% of each species was eliminated (if species had more than 5 individuals). After the elimination step the new representative (centroid) for each species was randomly chosen from left individuals in given species.

For the purpose of evaluation of stagnation, the champion (individual with the best fitness value) was identified for each living species and for each generation. Stagnation of species was declared if the computed differences between the best fitness values for a given species in the last 15 generations and the arithmetic mean calculated from these values did not exceed the threshold 0.01 in all 15 generations. The state of freezing evolution was tested each generation too. If the best species (which includes the top champion) stagnated for the last 20 generations. If true, then only the top two living species for given generation were allowed to exist (two species with champions with the highest fitness values among species).

Individuals' fitness values were transformed through a linear ranking method (selection pressure $s = 2$) and stochastic universal sampling was implemented as the selection scheme for reproduction. Each generation, 80% of offspring (excluding elites) in each species were produced using recombination of parents. The others were left as copies. In a recombination step, an offspring inherited all connections from the superior parent with higher fitness. Excess or disjoint connections from the less successful parent were never inherited. In the case of matching connections between parents there was 0.6 probability that the inherited gene is the arithmetic mean of weights from both parents. Otherwise, weights were inherited randomly from parents. There was zero probability of interspecies mating.

Each connection, which was disabled in the genome had 25% probability to be enabled. Each connection had 90% probability that its weight was mutated. Each weight could be shifted by another value from the uniform distribution $\langle -2.5, 2.5 \rangle$. However, weights were restricted by caps to be inside the interval $\langle -8, 8 \rangle$. Each individual had 5% probability of adding a new connection between unconnected nodes and 3% probability of splitting the existing connection into two new connections by insertion of a new node. The network could not experience both mutations in the same generation.

5   Results and Discussion

The basic assumption behind the GC approach to innovation numbers compared to GC-F is that there is a larger number of innovation numbers generated in the innovation register. Our observations confirm this under all speciation scenarios, see Fig. 1a. Curves representing the GC approach (upper non-dotted curves) reaches average levels of 600–800 innovations records in the 50-th generation and 1300–1500 records after 100 generations. To uncover the relative dynamics, we divided the GC-F rates (dotted curves) by corresponding GC values in each generation. As a consequence Fig. 1b exposes the behavioral convergence to the linear trend in production of innovation records after the 25-th generation. The figure shows that the GC-F approach produces 40–50% less innovation records than the GC approach.

Additionally, we explored how many of the initialized innovation records from the register were actually present in the population (how many of them were present at least in one individual). The results in Fig. 1c reveals the higher absolute frequency of innovations in the GC approach. More informative results can be obtained from Fig. 1d where the GC-F rates are divided by GC values from Fig. 1c. This figure demonstrates divergence between approaches in the initial generations leading to extreme situations with the speciation threshold

2. Under this scenario, the population in the GC approach absorbs nearly twice as many unique innovations as in the GC-F approach. This relative difference corresponds approximately to 80–110 innovation records. For comparison, the minimal maximum difference under the scenario of threshold 5 (25%) is induced by 5 innovation records. Interestingly, the initial relative divergence is gradually reduced under all scenarios.

Another assumption about the GC approach is that a higher number of species are present in the population due to the larger number of innovations. The observations in Fig. 1e shows that this assumption is correct in the first 30 generations. However, the difference is not as clear as it might be hypothesized. After exceeding this generational limit, differences between approaches are minor. Better insight is provided in Fig. 1f. When we compared values of the GC approach with rates of the GC-F approach from Fig. 1e for the first 50 generations, we uncovered approximately a 10% decline of rates in the GC-F approach in the initial stage of evolution.

Furthermore, we investigated the effect of different codings on the speciation procedure. One of the strongly demanded effects of the diversity maintaining techniques is protection of the innovations in newly established species. However, the presented relocation mechanism includes also the migration of the individuals between existing species. Surprisingly, results in Fig. 2a (upper curves) show that migration is encouraged more by the GC-F approach. This approach is associated with a smaller number of non-migrating individuals. These migrants are heading predominantly to the older species (lower curves and higher rates for GC-F approach). This fact is consistent with the idea that it is more difficult for the algorithm with the GC-F approach to establish new species.

We can conclude from our observations that most of the time migration to younger species involves less than 5% of individuals in the first 20 generations. Afterwards, this type of migration dropped to even lower levels. Only under speciation threshold 1, rates exceeded by as little 10% in the first 20 generations. Differences in migration of individuals to younger species between GC and GC-F approaches were minimal (maximum difference ±1 individual). These findings combined with results in Fig. 1e suggests the hypothesis that the GC approach leads to somewhat less similar species. Speciation with the GC approach may produce slightly higher numbers of new species. These new species are founded by individuals included in the category of migrants heading to younger species. Further, it is less likely that migrants to younger species in the GC-F approach establish new species. It is due to the higher chance of their assignment to any other existing species, which is younger than their original one.

On the other hand, the side effect of algorithmic migration is also the potential extinction of species (all individuals can leave an existing species and become members of any different species). The results in Fig. 2b exhibits higher rates for the GC-F approach, which is consistent with the previous findings of the higher similarity between individuals.

To sufficiently identify factors responsible for differences in the number of species, we calculated the average relative frequency of individuals of different

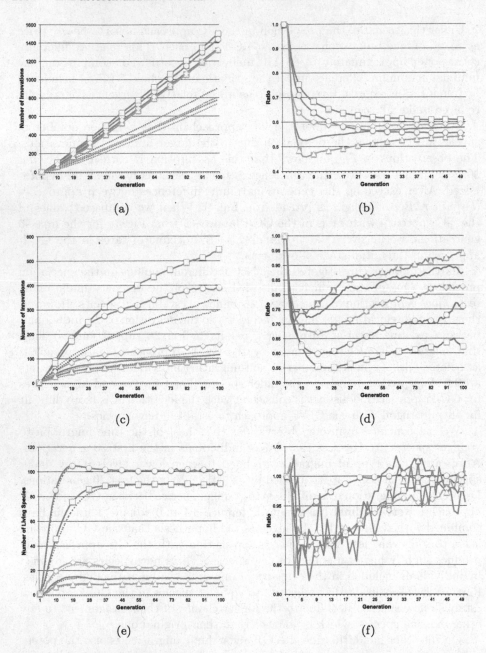

Fig. 1. (a, c, e) Solid lines: rates for GC, dotted: GC-F approach. (a–f) Speciation thresholds: $\delta_1 = 1$ (blue, $\bigcirc$), $\delta_2 = 2$ (red, $\square$), $\delta_3 = 3$ (green, $\diamond$), $\delta_4 = 4$ (purple, no marker), $\delta_5 = 5$ (cyan, $\triangle$). (a) Number of innovations in register. (b) Num. of innovations in register: GC-F rates/GC rates. (c) Number of unique innovations in population. (d) Num. of unique innovations in population: GC-F rates/GC rates. (e) Number of living species in population. (f) Num. of living species in population: GC-F rates/GC rates. (Color figure online)

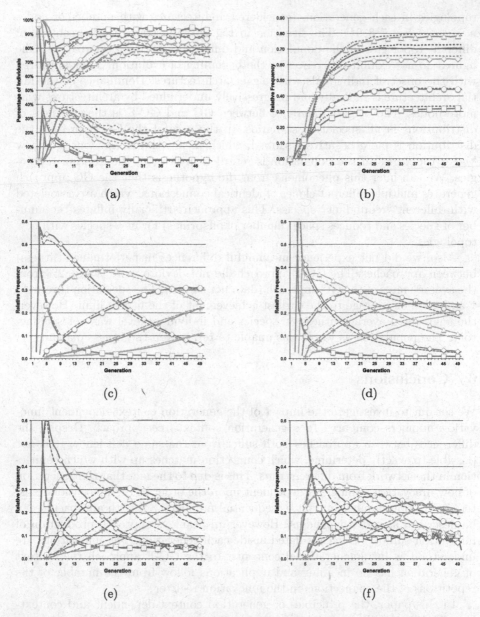

Fig. 2. (a–e) Solid lines: rates for GC, dotted: GC-F approach. (a, b) Speciation thresholds: $\delta_1 = 1$ (blue, $\bigcirc$), $\delta_2 = 2$ (red, $\square$), $\delta_3 = 3$ (green, $\diamondsuit$), $\delta_4 = 4$ (purple, no marker), $\delta_5 = 5$ (cyan, $\triangle$). (a) Migration of individuals: num. of individuals, which did not migrate (upper part of figure), num. of individuals, which migrated to older species (lower part). (b) Portion of species in species register, which became extinct due to exodus of individuals. (c–f) Distribution of networks with given topology (number of nodes) in population: 4 nodes (blue, $\square$), 5 (red, $\diamondsuit$), 6 (green, $\triangle$), 7 (purple, $\bigcirc$), 8 (cyan, $+$), 9 (orange, no marker). (Color figure online)

topologies in each generation. (considered architectures with number of nodes n; $n = \{4, 5, 6, 7, 8, 9\}$). The situation in Fig. 2c–f illustrates the percentage of different topologies in the population and differences between approaches. The figures do not exhibit differences at the beginning of evolution. They appeared with the onset of individuals with bigger architectures. Dominance of the initial architecture is radically and progressively undermined by architectures with more nodes. The biggest difference between GC and GC-F is the skewness of distributions in all speciation scenarios. In the case of the GC approach, the distribution is more negatively skewed, which means that major onset of new bigger topologies in the population is retarded in favor of the existing topologies. We can infer this phenomena from the hypothesis that the GC approach generates multiple different clones of identical connections, which are associated with different "redundant" species. This approach artificially inflates the number of species and reduces space (number of offsprings) for new species with new topologies.

Also, we did not experience meaningful differences in performance (fitness) between approaches. The GC-F approach did not deviate more than $\pm 2\%$ from the average rates of the GC approach (data not shown). The speciation threshold 1 and 2 led on average to the earliest achievement of the fitness limit. However, the aggregated average fitness on species and individual level was not satisfactory. The population as whole was unable to reach even the fitness plateau.

6   Conclusions

We set out to investigate the impact of the generation context-dependent innovation numbers compared to a generation context-free approach. Despite the differences between approaches both suffer from the same deficiency. It is not possible to exactly determine, which connection matches up with which connection in the network from different runs. This is due to the fact that the generation of new innovation numbers is dependent upon the order in the innovation register (innovation number, in fact, is sequential number). So, both approaches can be described as order-dependent. However, in Stanleys approach production of innovation numbers is encapsulated inside each generation. The innovations are understood as intra-generational concepts. In the GC-F approach the context of generation has no meaning and implications follow from the number of the repetitions of the connections in the innovation register.

In this paper, the principles of generation context-dependent and context-free (GC vs. GC-F) encodings for innovation numbers have been empirically investigated on the XOR problem under different speciation scenarios.

It can be concluded that the GC approach leads to bloat of innovation records in the innovation register. We hypothesize, that the GC encoding is an active mechanism primarily in the initial stage of evolution. In this stage, there are only a few connections that can be the subject of mutation. As only a small number of connections can be mutated, identical connections are mutated repeatably in different generations. This situation leads to an initial structural multiplicity in the register and the population. On the contrary, the production of multiple architectural clones and their acceptance by the population gradually decreases the probability that certain innovations are mutated repeatably in different generations. The probability is additionally reduced by a number of copies of identical structures in the register and their share in the population. We speculate that the initial multiplicity in the register is mostly responsible for the exuberant generation of innovation records in later stages of evolution. This dependence and growth resembles the theoretical mechanism of the butterfly effect.

We have uncovered the behavioral convergence of the production of innovation records between approaches to a linear trend after the 25-th generation. We can deduce that the GC-F approach produces 40–50% less innovation records than GC under given settings.

Also, our analysis confirms that the algorithm with the GC approach incorporates more innovation records from the register into the population. In extreme situations the population under the GC strategy exploits nearly twice as many unique innovations from the register when compared to the GC-F rates.

Moreover, the assumption about a higher number of species when adopting the GC approach is observed to be true only in the first 30 generations. The difference represents a maximum of 10% decline of GC-F rates when compared to the GC coding.

Analysis of migratory patterns have not revealed differences in the number of individuals migrating into younger species. However, it is observed that GC-F encourages more frequent migration to older species. It leads us to the suggestion that GC generates a larger number of new species due to a slightly higher dissimilarity between individuals in new and older species.

The investigation of the onset of new topologies and their relative representation in the population have uncovered more negatively skewed distributions for the GC approach. They may be outcomes of multiplicity of connections as these clones are linked with extra and redundant species. Consequently, this phenomena inflates the number of species and reduces space for offpring of new species of bigger architectures.

Our data has also revealed uncommon behavioral patterns under speciation scenario 2, which may be due to coupling of the speciation procedure with the other complementary mechanisms. As the observations in the current study are valid for the XOR problem and given settings, investigation on different problems could enhance the generalization power of any conclusions.

In conclusion, the exuberant number of innovation records in the register in NEAT does not lead to critical behavioral differences with the observed behaviour being comparable with the generation context-free approach on the XOR problem. On the other hand, the original GC approach complicates and makes less clear lineage in the population.

Acknowledgments. This research is based upon works supported by Science Foundation Ireland under grant 13/RC/2094 which is co-funded under the European Regional Development Fund through the Southern & Eastern Regional Operational Programme to Lero - the Irish Software Research Centre (www.lero.ie).

References

1. Clune, J., Beckmann, B.E., Ofria, C., Pennock, R.T.: Evolving coordinated quadruped gaits with the hyperneat generative encoding. In: IEEE Congress on Evolutionary Computation, CEC 2009, pp. 2764–2771. IEEE (2009)
2. Clune, J., Mouret, J.B., Lipson, H.: The evolutionary origins of modularity. Proc. R. Soc. B. **280**, 2012–2863 (2013). The Royal Society
3. Gauci, J., Stanley, K.O.: Autonomous evolution of topographic regularities in artificial neural networks. Neural Comput. **22**(7), 1860–1898 (2010)
4. Hastings, E.J., Guha, R.K., Stanley, K.O.: Evolving content in the galactic arms race video game. In: IEEE Symposium on Computational Intelligence and Games, CIG 2009, pp. 241–248. IEEE (2009)
5. Kashtan, N., Alon, U.: Spontaneous evolution of modularity and network motifs. Proc. Natl. Acad. Sci. U.S.A. **102**(39), 13773–13778 (2005)
6. Lehman, J., Stanley, K.O.: Evolving a diversity of virtual creatures through novelty search and local competition. In: Proceedings of the 13th Annual Conference on Genetic and Evolutionary Computation, pp. 211–218. ACM (2011)
7. Mayr, C.: Neat matlab. Last accessed (2017)
8. Mengistu, H., Huizinga, J., Mouret, J.B., Clune, J.: The evolutionary origins of hierarchy. PLoS Comput. Biol. **12**(6), e1004829 (2016)
9. Stanley, K.O., Bryant, B.D., Miikkulainen, R.: Evolving adaptive neural networks with and without adaptive synapses. In: The 2003 Congress on Evolutionary Computation, CEC 2003, vol. 4, pp. 2557–2564. IEEE (2003)
10. Stanley, K.O., Bryant, B.D., Miikkulainen, R.: Real-time neuroevolution in the nero video game. IEEE Trans. Evol. Comput. **9**(6), 653–668 (2005)
11. Stanley, K.O., D'Ambrosio, D.B., Gauci, J.: A hypercube-based encoding for evolving large-scale neural networks. Artif. Life **15**(2), 185–212 (2009)
12. Stanley, K.O., Miikkulainen, R.: Evolving neural networks through augmenting topologies. Evol. Comput. **10**(2), 99–127 (2002)
13. Stanley, K.O., Miikkulainen, R.: A taxonomy for artificial embryogeny. Artif. Life **9**(2), 93–130 (2003)
14. Stanley, K.O., Miikkulainen, R.: Competitive coevolution through evolutionary complexification (2004)
15. Tan, M., Deklerck, R., Jansen, B., Bister, M., Cornelis, J.: A novel computer-aided lung nodule detection system for ct images. Med. Phys. **38**(10), 5630–5645 (2011)
16. Trujillo, L., Muñoz, L., Naredo, E., Martínez, Y.: NEAT, there's no bloat. In: Nicolau, M., Krawiec, K., Heywood, M.I., Castelli, M., García-Sánchez, P., Merelo, J.J., Rivas Santos, V.M., Sim, K. (eds.) EuroGP 2014. LNCS, vol. 8599, pp. 174–185. Springer, Heidelberg (2014). https://doi.org/10.1007/978-3-662-44303-3_15
17. Whiteson, S., Stone, P.: Evolutionary function approximation for reinforcement learning. J. Mach. Learn. Res. **7**, 877–917 (2006)

Long-Short Term Memory Network for RNA Structure Profiling Super-Resolution

Pak-Kan Wong[1]([⊠]) [iD], Man-Leung Wong[2] [iD], and Kwong-Sak Leung[1] [iD]

[1] The Chinese University of Hong Kong, Sha Tin, Hong Kong
{pkwong,ksleung}@cse.cuhk.edu.hk
[2] Lingnan University, Tuen Mun, Hong Kong
mlwong@ln.edu.hk

Abstract. Profiling of RNAs improves understanding of cellular mechanisms, which can be essential to cure various diseases. It is estimated to take years to fully characterize the three-dimensional structure of around 200,000 RNAs in human using the mutate-and-map strategy. In order to speed up the profiling process, we propose a solution based on super-resolution. We applied five machine learning regression methods to perform RNA structure profiling super-resolution, i.e. to recover the whole data sets using self-similarity in low-resolution (undersampled) data sets. In particular, our novel Interaction Encoded Long-Short Term Memory (IELSTM) network can handle multiple distant interactions in the RNA sequences. When compared with ridge regression, LASSO regression, multilayer perceptron regression, and random forest regression, IELSTM network can reduce the mean squared error and the median absolute error by at least 33% and 31% respectively in three RNA structure profiling data sets.

Keywords: Long-short term memory · RNA structure
Machine learning regression methods

1 Introduction

The goal of super-resolution is to generate high-resolution signals based on the low-resolution signals. For example, high-resolution enlargements of pixel-based images can be reconstructed from lower resolution images via super-resolution algorithms. Super-resolution is popular in computer vision, medical imaging, and compiling images from space probes. Figure 1 shows an example of super-resolution using an image of a flower with raindrops. The rightmost image is the original image taken by us. The leftmost image is the low-resolution image by magnifying the original image. The edges of the petals of the flower are blurred in the magnified image due to undersampling. Besides, the raindrops on the flower almost disappear. The middle image is obtained by applying image super-resolution using the low-resolution image as input. The fine details of the complex structure of the edges are sharpened. The raindrops on the flower also become more visible.

© Springer International Publishing AG 2017
C. Martín-Vide et al. (Eds.): TPNC 2017, LNCS 10687, pp. 255–266, 2017.
https://doi.org/10.1007/978-3-319-71069-3_20

Fig. 1. Images demonstrating the concept of super-resolution. Left to right: the magnified image, the super-resolution image, and the original image. The original image was taken by us. The super-resolution image was generated from the magnified image using the algorithm in [6].

Apart from image processing, super-resolution techniques are effective information processing techniques for other data types, including audio data, tracking data, and genomic data. This paper studies the super-resolution problem on the Sequence Series Data (SSD) resembling time series data. The 'time' variable in the SSD are sequences which can be ordered naturally. Each sequence ('time point') is associated with at least one response variable. SSD can be found in sentiment analysis and physiological measurement. In this paper, we focus on the application of SSD super-resolution to accelerate RNA structure profiling.

Cellular activities are controlled by around 200,000 RNAs [12]. RNAs in human are highly specialized and their functions are closely related to the folding structure [4]. Structure profiling experiments provide quantitative single-nucleotide information (i.e. a reactivity value) about RNAs using chemical probing techniques. The data obtained from RNA structure profiling experiments is a form of SSD data. A sequence in the SSD is an RNA sequence. They can be naturally ordered by their mutation positions. At each position in the RNA sequence, a reactivity value measured from the experiment is associated to it.

The time spent on profiling the wild-type and the variants of 71-nucleotide adenine-sensing *add* ribòswitch from *V. vulnificus* is reported to be a single afternoon (about five and eight hours) [18]. The profiling rate is about three to six RNAs per day. However, there are about 27,720 long non-coding RNA loci transcripts (excluding other types of RNAs) in human as reported by GENCODE (ver. 26) [12]. Therefore, performing SHAPE experiments in lower resolution (i.e. skipping the measurements of some RNA variants) can be helpful in the preliminary stage of RNA study. After that, super-resolution data are reconstructed from the low-resolution data via SSD super-resolution methods. The artificial data set is an approximation of the high-resolution data set. In addition, because of many successes of machine learning techniques for image super-resolution, machine learning regression techniques are focused in this paper. The contributions of this study are as follows:

1. We present RNA structure profiling super-resolution methods based on several machine learning regression algorithms, such as ridge regression [15], LASSO regression [26], multilayer perceptron regression [22,23], and random forest regression [2,20].

2. We present our Long-Short Term Memory (LSTM) network to capture long range interactions across multiple positions in the RNA sequences.
3. We demonstrate our super-resolution methods on RNA structure profiling data.

The rest of the paper is organized as follows. Section 2 presents the related works about our methods. The super-resolution problem is introduced in Sect. 3. Section 4 presents classical approaches and our Interaction Encoded Long-Short Term Memory (IELSTM) network-based approach. In Sect. 5, the data sets for evaluation are described. Section 6 compares the performance of different approaches using multiple criteria. Lastly, we conclude the paper and discuss the future works.

2   Related Works

In this section, a brief summary of the related works on image super-resolution and LSTM are presented.

2.1   Image Super-Resolution

Recent methods become more data-driven and apply machine learning techniques to match existing high-resolution image(s) of the low-resolution image. Substantial improvements are achieved using data-driven approaches. The super-resolution problem is reformulated as a machine learning problem which is to find the best high-resolution image(s) given the low-resolution image. Pairs of high-resolution image patches and the low-resolution image patches are served as training data. Modern image super-resolution algorithms can be categorized by how training image patches are prepared [17]. There are three categories: external database driven approach, internal database driven approach, and generalized database driven approach. Only internal database driven approach is reviewed because our super-resolution approach belongs to this category.

The internal database driven approach analyzes the given low resolution image and finds out self-similarity, which includes patch recurrence within the spatial neighborhood in an image across multiple scales [9]. Generative adversarial network [10] and residual network [13] allow us to infer photo-realistic natural images for 4x upscaling factors under mean-opinion-score test [19].

2.2   Long-Short Term Memory Network

LSTM network is a type of recurrent neural network [14,16] (and a forget gate was introduced later [8]). LSTM network is popular and very suitable for modeling many temporal data and sequence data available nowadays. Bidirectional LSTM networks [11] have succeeded in solving problems in acoustic modeling, such as phoneme recognition [24] and non-verbal signal detection [3]. LSTM network in tree-structured network topologies are proposed to measure the semantic similarity of two sentences for sentiment analysis [25]. LSTM is a practical solution when researchers develop new language parsers. For example, transition-based dependency parser can be implemented using stack LSTM, which supports both reading (pushing) and forgetting (popping) inputs [7].

3   RNA Structure Profiling Super-Resolution Problem

This paper focuses on the RNA structure profiling data sets generated using a two-dimensional mutate-and-map methodology [18]. Each data set studies a wild-type sequence. Two-dimensional mutate-and-map method is applied to measure the reactivity at every position of the RNA sequence. Apart from the reactivity measurement on the wild-type sequence, the reactivities of a set of mutated sequences of the wild-type sequence are measured. In the experiment, a mutated sequence differs from the wild-type sequence at exactly one position.

An example of RNA structure profiling data has been depicted in Fig. 2. The table on the leftmost in the figure shows six RNA sequences: CUGAU, GUGAU, CAGAU, CUCAU, CUGUU, and CUGAA, which are denoted by $s^{(0)}$, $s^{(1)}$, $s^{(2)}$, $s^{(3)}$, $s^{(4)}$, and $s^{(5)}$ respectively. Sequence CUGAU is the wild-type sequence and the remaining sequences are the mutated sequences. In this paper, we assume two-dimensional mutate-and-map experiments are performed on all sequences. Their measured reactivity values are shown in the table in the middle of Fig. 2. For example, the measured reactivity values of each position in the sequence $s^{(1)}$ (i.e. GUGAU) are 16, 12, 10, 37, and 45 respectively.

To speed up the RNA structure profiling process, we apply downsampling during measurement. This means that we only select and measure a subset of the mutated sequences in the two-dimensional mutate-and-map experiments. In other words, the original high-resolution RNA structure profiling data set is downsampled to obtain a low-resolution data set (the rightmost table in Fig. 2). The measured reactivity values (shaded rows, i.e. $m^{(1)}$, $m^{(2)}$, $m^{(4)}$, and $m^{(5)}$) of four sequences (i.e. $s^{(1)}$, $s^{(2)}$, $s^{(4)}$, and $s^{(5)}$) are not available.

The objective of our super-resolution task is to reconstruct all measured values (shaded rows) in the low-resolution RNA structure profiling data (i.e. the rightmost table in Fig. 2) so that it is (approximately) the same as the ground truth high-resolution profiling data (i.e. the table in the middle in Fig. 2). Machine learning-based RNA structure profiling super-resolution methods extract patterns from the low-resolution data set to perform reconstruction.

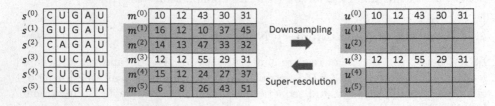

Fig. 2. An example of RNA structure profiling data and the super-resolution problem.

4 Super-Resolution Methods

In this section, we describe two kinds of methods to perform machine learning-based RNA structure profiling super-resolution. The first kind of methods adopts classical machine learning regression approaches, including LASSO regression and random forest regression. Very often, they are designed to forecast a single variable at a time. In order to extend these approaches, the low-resolution data are split into smaller sub-data set by position of the measured values (see Fig. 3) and then regression models are learnt for each position using the position-separated tables. The predictions made by the regression models on each sub-data set are aggregated to produce the overall prediction.

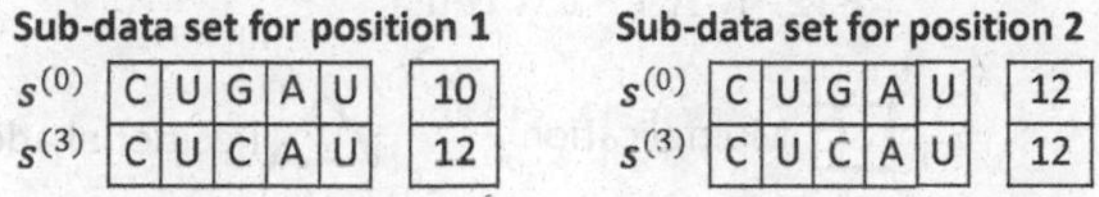

Sub-data set for position 1

| $s^{(0)}$ | C | U | G | A | U | 10 |
| $s^{(3)}$ | C | U | C | A | U | 12 |

Sub-data set for position 2

| $s^{(0)}$ | C | U | G | A | U | 12 |
| $s^{(3)}$ | C | U | C | A | U | 12 |

...

Fig. 3. Sub-data sets of the low-resolution data in Fig. 2.

4.1 Limitations of LSTM Network

LSTM network is a type of recurrent neural network and is formed by connecting multiple LSTM cells in a chain structure [14]. Each cell may emit a prediction and predictions from multiple cells can be concatenated to form an output sequence. The behaviors of a LSTM cell are governed by the following composite function:

$$f_i^{(0)} = q(W^{(0)}[h_{i-1}; s_i] + b^{(0)}) \tag{1}$$

$$f_i^{(1)} = \sigma(W^{(1)}[h_{i-1}; s_i] + b^{(1)}) \tag{2}$$

$$f_i^{(2)} = tanh(W^{(2)}[h_{i-1}; s_i] + b^{(2)}) \tag{3}$$

$$f_i^{(3)} = \sigma(W^{(3)}[h_{i-1}; s_i] + b^{(3)}) \tag{4}$$

$$c_i = c_{i-1}f_i^{(0)} + f_i^{(1)}f_i^{(2)} \tag{5}$$

$$h_i = \sigma(c_{i-1})f_i^{(3)} \tag{6}$$

The corresponding graphical representation is shown in Fig. 4. The meaning of each internal building block can be found in Fig. 5. There are three inputs: the input value at position s_i, the previous cell state c_{i-1}, and the previous hidden state h_{i-1}. Besides, there are three gates in the cell: input gate, output gate, and forget gate. They are implemented using sigmoid functions which determine how much information to retain or discard. Finally, h_i and c_{i-1} store the result and a new cell state respectively.

This model has to be adapted because of the following issues. Firstly, the output h_i cannot be larger than 1. Besides, future input information cannot be

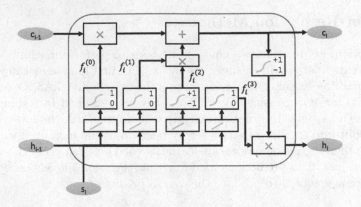

Fig. 4. A LSTM cell.

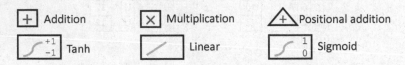

Fig. 5. Building blocks in the LSTM cell and IELSTM cell.

accessed from the current state. For instance, suppose the measured values of the first and the last RNA sequences are positively correlated, the measured values of the first RNA sequence can be better estimated given the measured values of the last RNA sequence. Therefore, we propose using a new type of LSTM cell, namely Interaction Encoded Long-Short Term Memory (IELSTM) cell.

4.2 Interaction Encoding LSTM Network

IELSTM network is a type of LSTM network. The graphical representation is depicted in Fig. 6. A IELSTM cell at position i is defined by the following composite function:

$$f_i^{(0)} = IE_{1,2}(s_0 s_1 ... s_{N-1}, i) \tag{7}$$

$$f_i^{(1)} = c_{i-1} + f_i^{(0)} \tag{8}$$

$$f_i^{(2)} = \tanh(W^{(0)} s_i + b^{(0)}) \tag{9}$$

$$c_i = tanh(W^{(1)}[c_{i-1}; f_i^{(0)}] + b^{(1)}) \tag{10}$$

$$h_i = f_i^{(1)} f_i^{(2)} \tag{11}$$

There are four inputs and two outputs in the i-th IELSTM cell. The whole input sequence $s_0 s_1 ... s_{N-1}$ s_i is the item at i th position of the input sequence. The cell state c_{i-1} of the i-th cell is connected to the output c_{i-1} of the previous

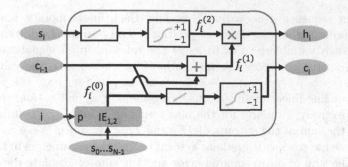

Fig. 6. The architecture of IELSTM.

IELSTM cell. The outputs of the cell depend on the information from the short-term memory stored in the cell state. The predicted output at the i-th position is denoted by h_i.

Interaction encoder $IE_{1,2}$ is a main component in a IELSTM cell. It analyzes the whole input sequence and captures the global information. As shown in Fig. 7, the interaction encoder constitutes a first order interaction encoder IE_1 and a second order interaction encoder IE_2. Using Fig. 7 as an example, IE_1 transforms characters s_0, s_1, and s_3 in the input sequence using a linear module. The positional addition module is controlled by variable p so as to select the relevant input signals. Suppose the value of p is 1, the value of $g^{(1)}$ is $w_1 s_1 + b_1$, where w_1 and b_1 are the weight and the bias term respectively. Similarly, in order to extract information from second order interactions among the characters in the input sequence, every linear module combines a pair of input signals linearly in IE_2. Refer to Fig. 7, IE_2 transforms characters s_0, s_1, and s_3

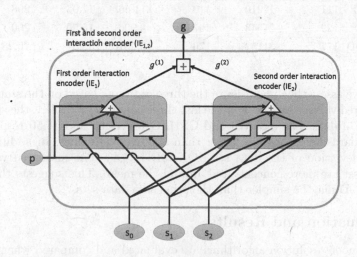

Fig. 7. The architecture of a first and second order interaction encoder.

in the input sequence using a linear module. Each linear module handles one possible interaction among different positions. The positional addition module is controlled by variable p so as to select the relevant input signals connecting the input signal s_p. Suppose the value of p of IE_2 is set to 1, the value of $g^{(2)}$ is $w_{0,1}[s_0; s_1] + b_{0,1} + w_{1,2}[s_1; s_2] + b_{1,2}$, where $w_{0,1}$ and $w_{1,2}$ are the weights of the corresponding linear modules connecting the pair s_0 and s_1, and the pair s_1 and s_2 respectively; similarly for the bias terms $b_{0,1}$ and $b_{1,2}$. The final output of $IE_{1,2}$ is the sum of the outputs of IE_1 and IE_2, i.e. $g = g^{(1)} + g^{(2)}$.

Lastly, we use stochastic gradient descent to find the parameters in the neural network. The sum of mean squared error and the sum of absolute deviations is used as the loss function in neural network training.

5   Data Sets

Three data sets were collected from the RNA Mapping Database [5], which use 1-methyl-7-nitroisatoic anhydride reagent in the experiments. A summary of the three data sets is presented in Table 1. The first column gives the names of the data sets, which are 16SFWJ, CL1LIG, and HOXA9D, and their RMDB_IDs are 16SFWJ_1M7_0001, CL1LIG_1M7_0001, and HOXA9D_1M7_0001 respectively. Data set 16SFWJ has the least amount of sequences and the least amount of data points. It has only 111 sequences and 12,210 data points. Data set HOXA9D is the largest and has 31,152 data points. The sequences in data set HOXA9D are the longest.

Table 1. Data sets.

Data set	# of sequences	# of data points	Sequence length	Average	Standard deviation	Maximum value
16SFWJ	111	12210	110	11.46	17.05	298
CL1LIG	129	21543	167	8.996	15.50	200
HOXA9D	177	31152	176	5.2816	4.43	75.28

Next, we assess the difficulties of the three data sets based on the statistics of the measured values. As shown in the last three columns in Table 1, the standard deviations of data sets 16SFWJ and CL1LIG are 17.05 and 15.50 respectively Both standard deviations are larger than the average values. In addition, the standard deviation of the data set HOXA9D is 4.43. The measured values in this data set are more concentrated around the mean. This suggests that data set HOXA9D may be simpler than the other two data sets.

6   Evaluation and Results

Different super-resolution algorithms are evaluated and compared when solving the RNA structure profiling super-resolution problem. We adopted four state-of-the-art machine learning algorithms in the framework of classical approaches:

ridge regression, LASSO regression, multilayer perceptron regression, and random forest regression, which are respectively labeled as *Ridge*, *LASSO*, *MLP*, and *RFR*. They were implemented using Scikit-learn machine learning library version 0.18.1 [21] and the default parameters in the library are kept unchanged. PyTorch [1] is a deep learning framework released by Facebook AI Research and was chosen to implement the IELSTM network.

Besides, training subsets were created via downsampling by a factor of three from the original data sets. This means that one-third of the data points were used to reconstruct the remaining two-third of the data points in every data set. As such, three testing subsets (indexed by 0, 1, and 2) were created by selecting different portions of data points for training and testing.

In the evaluation, mean squared error and median absolute error were selected to compare the performance across different approaches. A better reconstruction algorithm should produce a smaller error value in the reconstructed data set. The average performance in different data sets is also provided for each metric.

Table 2. Mean squared error results for all data sets.

Data set	Algorithm	Training subset 0	Training subset 1	Training subset 2	Average
16SFWJ	Ridge	209.47	206.75	169.87	195.36
	LASSO	274.80	278.45	237.05	263.43
	MLP	186.95	186.01	147.62	173.53
	RFR	186.58	186.31	146.52	173.14
	IELSTM	**131.34**	**127.82**	**85.88**	**115.01**
CL1LIG	Ridge	102.97	102.84	103.29	103.03
	LASSO	240.12	240.14	237.30	239.19
	MLP	54.87	54.69	56.59	55.38
	RFR	54.50	54.80	58.25	55.85
	IELSTM	**15.34**	**14.78**	**17.66**	**15.93**
HOXA9D	Ridge	10.98	10.92	11.97	11.29
	LASSO	19.47	19.45	20.40	19.77
	MLP	9.57	9.51	10.38	9.82
	RFR	9.64	9.48	10.35	9.82
	IELSTM	**7.06**	**6.08**	**6.13**	**6.42**

Mean Squared Error. The mean squared error measures the discrepancy between the original data and the reconstructed data. It penalizes large errors heavily and maximizes the signal-to-noise ratio. Refer to Table 2, IELSTM always attained the lowest mean squared error, which are in bold, among the others. The mean squared errors of IELSTM were 115.01, 15.93, and 6.42 in data sets 16SFWJ, CL1LIG, and HOXA9D respectively. LASSO was the worst among all methods. Besides, MLP and RFR performed similarly and were the second best approaches. However, IELSTM outperformed them by a large margin and was able to reduce the average mean squared error by at least 33%.

Median Absolute Error. Median absolute error is defined as the median of all absolute differences between the target values and the predicted values. It measures the robustness of a method to the variability in the samples. In data set 16SFWJ, IELSTM attained 2.18 median absolute error on average. The second best algorithm was RFR, which attained 3.17 median absolute error on average. IELSTM attained 0.70 median absolute error on average and was 0.48 less than the second best result obtained by RFR in data set CL1LIG. Lastly, in data set HOXA9D, IELSTM attained 0.90 median absolute error on average and was 0.57 less than the second best result obtained by RFR. The results suggested that IELSTM was a more robust method to variability in the samples (Table 3).

Table 3. Median absolute error results for all data sets.

Data set	Algorithm	Training subset 0	Training subset 1	Training subset 2	Average
16SFWJ	Ridge	4.67	4.48	4.40	4.52
	LASSO	6.86	7.12	6.66	6.88
	MLP	3.02	3.43	3.22	3.22
	RFR	2.94	3.40	3.18	3.17
	IELSTM	**1.97**	**2.42**	**2.14**	**2.18**
CL1LIG	Ridge	3.87	3.65	3.70	3.74
	LASSO	7.54	7.43	7.55	7.51
	MLP	1.33	1.31	1.11	1.25
	RFR	1.19	1.22	1.12	1.18
	IELSTM	**0.72**	**0.69**	**0.68**	**0.70**
HOXA9D	Ridge	1.90	1.81	1.78	1.83
	LASSO	3.11	3.21	2.70	3.01
	MLP	1.52	1.54	1.38	1.48
	RFR	1.53	1.51	1.38	1.47
	IELSTM	**1.03**	**0.90**	**0.77**	**0.90**

In summary, we concluded that IELSTM is the most suitable method for our super-resolution task based on the two metrics.

7   Conclusions and Future Works

This paper addressed the problem in structure profiling of a large amount of RNAs in cells. We formulated the RNA structure profiling problem into a super-resolution problem which was then solved via machine learning-based super-resolution algorithms. Three mutate-and-map data sets using 1-methyl-7-nitroisatoic anhydride reagent in the experiments were selected in the evaluation. Our novel IELSTM network was demonstrated to be the best algorithm among other classical approaches across the data sets based on two metrics.

In the future, our IELSTM network will be extended to unify several super-resolution models learnt from different data sets and perform super-resolution on data sets at a lower resolution. The major challenge will be how to align the data sets when the lengths of the target RNA sequences are not the same. In addition, we will also deploy the network to other SSD sets, for instance, sentiment analysis data sets to predict the changes in mood.

Acknowledgments. This research is supported by General Research Fund (LU310111 and 414413) from the Research Grant Council of the Hong Kong Special Administrative Region and the Lingnan University Direct Grant (DR16A7).

References

1. PyTorch. http://pytorch.org/. Accessed 30 Jan 2017
2. Breiman, L.: Random forests. Mach. Learn. **45**(1), 5–32 (2001)
3. Brueckner, R., Schulter, B.: Social signal classification using deep BLSTM recurrent neural networks. In: Proceedings of IEEE International Conference on Acoustics, Speech and Signal Processing, pp. 4823–4827. IEEE (2014)
4. Choudhary, K., Deng, F., Aviran, S.: Comparative and integrative analysis of RNA structural profiling data: current practices and emerging questions. Quantit. Biol. **5**, 1–22 (2017)
5. Cordero, P., Lucks, J.B., Das, R.: An RNA mapping database for curating RNA structure mapping experiments. Bioinformatics **28**(22), 3006–3008 (2012)
6. Dong, C., Loy, C.C., He, K., Tang, X.: Image super-resolution using deep convolutional networks. IEEE Trans. Pattern Anal. Mach. Intell. **38**(2), 295–307 (2016)
7. Dyer, C., Ballesteros, M., Ling, W., Matthews, A., Smith, N.A.: Transition-based dependency parsing with stack long short-term memory. arXiv preprint arXiv:1505.08075 (2015)
8. Gers, F.A., Schmidhuber, J., Cummins, F.: Learning to forget: continual prediction with LSTM. Neural Comput. **12**(10), 2451–2471 (2000)
9. Glasner, D., Bagon, S., Irani, M.: Super-resolution from a single image. In: Proceedings of the IEEE International Conference on Computer Vision, pp. 349–356. IEEE (2009)
10. Goodfellow, I., Pouget-Abadie, J., Mirza, M., Xu, B., Warde-Farley, D., Ozair, S., Courville, A., Bengio, Y.: Generative adversarial nets. In: Advances in Neural Information Processing Systems, pp. 2672–2680 (2014)
11. Graves, A., Schmidhuber, J.: Framewise phoneme classification with bidirectional LSTM and other neural network architectures. Neural Networks **18**(5), 602–610 (2005)
12. Harrow, J., Frankish, A., Gonzalez, J.M., Tapanari, E., Diekhans, M., Kokocinski, F., Aken, B.L., Barrell, D., Zadissa, A., Searle, S., et al.: GENCODE: the reference human genome annotation for the encode project. Genome Res. **22**(9), 1760–1774 (2012)
13. He, K., Zhang, X., Ren, S., Sun, J.: Deep residual learning for image recognition. In: Proceedings of the IEEE Conference on Computer Vision and Pattern Recognition, pp. 770–778 (2016)
14. Hochreiter, S., Schmidhuber, J.: Long short-term memory. Neural Comput. **9**(8), 1735–1780 (1997)

15. Hoerl, A.E., Kennard, R.W.: Ridge regression: biased estimation for nonorthogonal problems. Technometrics **12**(1), 55–67 (1970)
16. Hopfield, J.J.: Neural networks and physical systems with emergent collective computational abilities. Proc. Natl. Acad. Sci. **79**(8), 2554–2558 (1982)
17. Huang, J.B., Singh, A., Ahuja, N.: Single image super-resolution from transformed self-exemplars. In: Proceedings of the IEEE Conference on Computer Vision and Pattern Recognition, pp. 5197–5206 (2015)
18. Kladwang, W., VanLang, C.C., Cordero, P., Das, R.: A two-dimensional mutate-and-map strategy for non-coding RNA structure. Nat. Chem. **3**(12), 954–962 (2011)
19. Ledig, C., Theis, L., Huszár, F., Caballero, J., Cunningham, A., Acosta, A., Aitken, A., Tejani, A., Totz, J., Wang, Z., et al.: Photo-realistic single image super-resolution using a generative adversarial network. arXiv preprint arXiv:1609.04802 (2016)
20. Liaw, A., Wiener, M., et al.: Classification and regression by random forest. R News **2**(3), 18–22 (2002)
21. Pedregosa, F., Varoquaux, G., Gramfort, A., Michel, V., Thirion, B., Grisel, O., Blondel, M., Prettenhofer, P., Weiss, R., Dubourg, V., Vanderplas, J., Passos, A., Cournapeau, D., Brucher, M., Perrot, M., Duchesnay, E.: Scikit-learn: machine learning in Python. J. Mach. Learn. Res. **12**, 2825–2830 (2011)
22. Rosenblatt, F.: Principles of Neurodynamics: Perceptrons and the Theory of Brain Mechanisms. Spartan Books, Washington (1962)
23. Rumelhart, D.E., Hinton, G.E., Williams, R.J.: Parallel distributed processing: explorations in the microstructure of cognition. In: Learning Internal Representations by Error Propagation, vol. 1, pp. 318–362. MIT Press, Cambridge (1986)
24. Sak, H., Senior, A., Beaufays, F.: Long short-term memory recurrent neural network architectures for large scale acoustic modeling. In: Proceedings of the Fifteenth Annual Conference of the International Speech Communication Association (2014)
25. Tai, K.S., Socher, R., Manning, C.D.: Improved semantic representations from tree-structured long short-term memory networks. arXiv preprint arXiv:1503.00075 (2015)
26. Tibshirani, R.: Regression shrinkage and selection via the LASSO. J. Roy. Stat. Soc. Ser. B (Methodol.) **58**(1), 267–288 (1966)

Quantum Computing

Hamming Distance Kernelisation via Topological Quantum Computation

Alessandra Di Pierro[1(✉)], Riccardo Mengoni[1], Rajagopal Nagarajan[2], and David Windridge[2]

[1] Dipartimento di Informatica, Università di Verona, Verona, Italy
alessandra.dipierro@univr.it
[2] Department of Computer Science, Middlesex University, London, UK

Abstract. We present a novel approach to computing Hamming distance and its kernelisation within Topological Quantum Computation. This approach is based on an encoding of two binary strings into a topological Hilbert space, whose inner product yields a natural Hamming distance kernel on the two strings. Kernelisation forges a link with the field of Machine Learning, particularly in relation to binary classifiers such as the Support Vector Machine (SVM). This makes our approach of potential interest to the quantum machine learning community.

Keywords: Quantum computing · Topology · Kernel function

1 Introduction

The Hamming distance of two strings is defined as the number of positions in which the strings are different. It was introduced in the context of error detecting and error correcting codes [8]. The concept is widely applicable to diverse areas such as information theory, coding theory, cryptography and telecommunication. As well as its use throughout computer science, the Hamming distance is interesting from the perspectives of statistical data analysis and machine learning in that it constitutes a simple (in fact the simplest) instance of a *kernel distance*. Kernel distances are built from kernel functions via the metric relation $D(x, y) = K(x, x) + K(y, y) - 2K(x, y)$. Critically, from our perspective, kernel functions can be shown to be equivalent to an inner product within a space produced via the kernel function's implicit feature mapping, thereby enabling e.g. linear learning algorithms to learn highly non-linear decision boundaries. In many applications where data classification is based on dissimilarity measures (e.g. string matching for pattern recognition), kernels provide a method for classification and regression in the absence of obvious features.

R. Nagarajan—Partially supported by EU ICT COST Action IC1405 "Reversible Computation Extending Horizons of Computing".
D. Windridge—Supported by EU Horizon 2020 research project No. 731593 "Dreamlike simulation abilities for automated cars (DREAMS4CARS)".

C. Martín-Vide et al. (Eds.): TPNC 2017, LNCS 10687, pp. 269–280, 2017.
https://doi.org/10.1007/978-3-319-71069-3_21

In this paper we show that there is a strong relationship between Hamming distance and Topology and we use it to define a quantum algorithm that computes a Hamming distance based kernel. Topology is the branch of Mathematics in which two objects are identified whenever one can continuously be deformed into the other. It has been used in physics to define a very particular class of quantum field theories, namely the Topological Quantum Field Theories (TQFTs), modelling phenomena such as the fractional quantum Hall effect. Quantum computers can benefit from the use of topological properties in as far as they can guarantee a form of robustness [14]. This is possible because in a *topological quantum computer* information is encoded in the collective states of many quasi-particles, so-called *anyons*, which are naturally protected from decoherence by their braiding behaviour.

Topological Quantum Computation (TQC) is equivalent in computational power to other standard models of quantum computation such as the quantum circuit model and the quantum Turing machine model. However, certain algorithms are more naturally implementable on a topological quantum computer. A well known example of such an algorithm is the one for evaluating a knot invariant called the Jones polynomial [2,7]. The quantum algorithm we present is essentially the application of the Jones polynomial algorithm after an appropriate problem reduction. This is obtained by an encoding of binary strings as some special braiding in TQC and deriving their Hamming distance as the Jones polynomial of a particular link. We can then exploit the computational features of TQC for comparing two strings and obtain an estimation of the Hamming distance between them. Moreover, the encoding function corresponds to the feature map of a kernel defined as the dot product in the Hilbert space of the topological quantum algorithm (i.e. the feature space). This demonstrates the suitability of TQC for defining kernel methods in a natural way.

2   Preliminaries

In this section we briefly review the main concepts in Topology that are relevant for the work presented in this paper, namely those of knots/links, braiding and related results.

Knot theory [1,12] studies the topological properties of mathematical knots and links. A knot is an embedding of a circle in the 3-dimensional Euclidean space $\mathbb{R}^3$, up to continuous deformations, and a link is a collection a knots that may be linked or knotted together. A fundamental question in knot theory is whether two knot diagrams, i.e. projections of knots on the plane, represent the same knot or rather they are distinct. The Reidemeister theorem [16] says that two links can be continuously deformed into each other if and only if any diagram of one can be transformed into a diagram of the other by a sequence of moves called Reidemeister moves [17]. If there exists such a transformation the two links are said to be isotopic.

The Reidemeister moves can be of three types, as depicted in Fig. 1. Move I undoes a twist of a single strand, move II separates two unbraided strands and

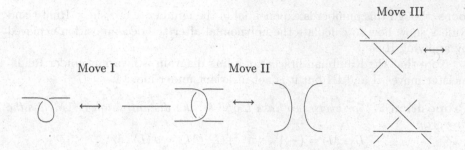

Fig. 1. The Reidemeister moves

finally move III slides a strand under a crossing. A powerful knot invariant is the Jones polynomial $V_L(A)$ [9] which is a Laurent polynomial in the variable A with integer coefficients. Given two links L_1 and L_2 and their respective Jones polynomials $V_{L_1}(A)$ and $V_{L_2}(A)$, the following relation holds true:

$$L_1 = L_2 \Rightarrow V_{L_1}(A) = V_{L_2}(A) \text{ or, equivalently, } V_{L_1}(A) \neq V_{L_2}(A) \Rightarrow L_1 \neq L_2.$$

A useful formulation of this polynomial due to Kauffman [10,11] is given in terms of the so-called bracket polynomial or Kauffman bracket, defined in the following section. Crucial for our work is that such a polynomial can be efficiently computed in TQC [2].

2.1 Kauffman Bracket

Definition 1. *The Kauffman bracket of any (unoriented) link diagram D, denoted $\langle L \rangle$, is a Laurent polynomial in the variable A, characterized by the three rules:*

1. *$\langle \bigcirc \rangle = 1$, where $\bigcirc$ is the standard diagram of the loop*
2. *$\langle D \sqcup \bigcirc \rangle = (-A^2 - A^{-2})\langle D \rangle = d\langle D \rangle$, where $\sqcup$ denotes the distant union[1] and $(-A^2 - A^{-2}) = d$.*
3. *$\langle \times \rangle = A \langle \asymp \rangle + A^{-1} \langle)(\rangle$*

where $\times$ and $)($ represent some regions of link diagrams where they differ as shown.

Rule 3 expresses the *skein relation*: it takes in input a crossing r_i and dissolves it generating two new links that are equal to the original link except for r_i, and therefore with a smaller number of crossings. By applying it recursively to a link we obtain at the end a number of links with no crossings but only simple

---

[1] The distant union of two arbitrary links L and M, denoted by $L \sqcup M$ is obtained by first moving L and M so that they are separated by a plane, and then taking the union.

loops, though this number is exponential in the number of crossings. Rule 1 and Rule 2 show how to calculate the polynomial after the decomposition achieved by applying Rule 3.

Note that the Kauffman bracket of a link diagram is invariant under Reidemeister moves II and III but it is not invariant under move I.

Proposition 2. *For every two links L and M, the distant union $L \sqcup M$ has the property:*

$$\langle L \sqcup M \rangle = (-A^2 - A^{-2}) \langle L \rangle \langle M \rangle = d \langle L \rangle \langle M \rangle$$

The Kauffman Bracket of the Hopf Link. We show here the calculation of the Kauffman bracket for the simplest non-trivial link with more than one component, i.e. the Hopf link depicted below [15].

By applying Rule 3 of Definition 1 to the upper crossing we get

Now we use also Rules 1 and 2 of Definition 1 to compute the new two brackets separately:

Finally we get

It is worth noting that the Hopf link calculated here and the one obtained by reversing all the crossings have the same Kauffman brackets, i.e.

2.2 Braids and Links

A braid can be visualised as an intertwining of some number of strands, i.e. strings attached to top and bottom bars such that each string never turns back.

Given n strands, the operator σ_i performs a crossing between the ith strand and the $(i+1)^{th}$, keeping the former above the latter. In a similar way, the operator σ_i^{-1} denotes a crossing of the ith strand below the $(i+1)^{th}$. A generic braid B on n strings is obtained by iteratively applying the σ_i and σ_i^{-1} operators in order to form a braid-word, e.g. $\sigma_1\sigma_2\sigma_1^{-1}\sigma_4$. It is well-know that the operators σ_i and σ_i^{-1} on n strands define a group B_n called *braid group* [18].

Definition 3 *(Markov trace)*. *Given a braid B, its Markov trace is the closure obtained connecting opposite endpoints of B together, as shown below.*

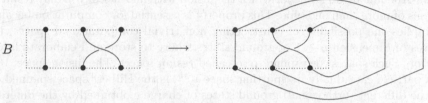

The relation between links and open ended strands is defined by two important theorems [3,4].

Theorem 4 (Alexander's theorem). *Every link (or knot) can be obtained as the closure of a braid.*

The result of the Markov closure of a braid B is a link that we will denote by $L = (B)^{Markov}$.

Theorem 5 (Markov's theorem). *The closure of two braids B_1 and B_2 gives the same link (or knot) if and only if it is possible to transforms one braid into the other by successive applications of the Markov moves:*

(1) conjugation: $B = \sigma_i B \sigma_i^{-1} = \sigma_i^{-1} B \sigma_i$, where $B \in B_n$
(2) stabilization: $B = B\sigma_n^{-1} = B\sigma_n$, where σ_n, $B\sigma_n$ and $B\sigma_n^{-1} \in B_{n+1}$.

3 Topological Quantum Computation

Topological Quantum Computation (TQC) [6,13,14] is related to the presumable existence of some special particles, called *anyons*, whose statistics substantially differ from the more common physical particles observed in nature. They were discovered at the end of the 1970's when Leinaas and Myrheim observed that these particles could not be identified neither with bosons nor with fermions; in fact their behaviour could be described by the statistics generated by the exchanging of one particle with another. This exchange rotates the system quantum state and produces non trivial phases [19].

In the following we give a quick explanation of the basic features of the TQC computational paradigm, which we will use for defining our algorithm for the Hamming distance and its kernelisation.

In order to perform a topological quantum computation we need to fix an *anyon system*, i.e. a system with a fixed number anyons for which we specify: (1) the type, i.e. the anyon physical charge, (2) the fusion rules N_{ab}^c (i.e. the laws of interaction), (3) the F-matrices, and (4) the R-matrices. The role of these latter will be made clear in the following.

The *fusion rules*, give the charge of a composite particle in terms of its constituents. The fusion rule $a \otimes b = N_{ab}^c c$ indicates the different ways of fusing a and b into c; these are exactly N_{ab}^c. Dually, we can look at these rules as *splitting rules* giving the constituent charges of a composite particle.

An anyon type a for which $\sum_c N_{ab}^c > 1$ is called *non-Abelian*. In other words, a non-Abelian anyon is one for which the fusion with another anyon may result in anyons of more than one type. This property is essential for computation because it implies the possibility of constructing non trivial computational spaces, i.e. spaces of dimension $n \geq 1$ of ground states where to store and elaborate information. Such spaces correspond to so-called *fusion spaces*. The fusion space, V_{ab}^c, of a particle c, or dually its splitting space V_c^{ab}, is the Hilbert space spanned by all the different (orthogonal) ground states of charge c obtained by the different fusion channels. The dimension of such a space is called the *quantum dimension* of c; clearly this is 1 for Abelian anyons.

Considering the dual splitting process, a non-Abelian anyon can therefore have more than one splitting rule that applies to it, e.g. $a \otimes b = c$ and $e \otimes b = c$. Given an anyon of type c we can split it into two new anyons a, b and obtain a tree with root c and a, b as leaves. By applying another rule to a, say $a = c \otimes d$, we will obtain a tree with leaf anyons c, d, b and root c. The same result can also be obtained by splitting the original anyon c into e, b and, supposing that there exists a fusion rule of the form $c \otimes d = e$, we can again split e into the leaves c and d. The two resulting, which have leaf anyons and root anyon of same type and differ only for the internal anyons a, e, represent two orthogonal vectors of the Hilbert space V_c^{cdb}.

Applying the fusion rules in different order generates other (non orthogonal) trees which have different shapes but contain the same information. This is because the total charge is conserved by locally exchanging two anyons, a property that deserves the 'topological' attribute to anyon systems and that determines the fault-tolerance of the quantum computational paradigm based on them.

3.1 Computing with Anyons

The idea behind the use of anyons for performing computation is to exploit the properties of their statistical behavior; this essentially means to look at the exchanges of the anyons of the system as a process evolving in time, i.e., looking at an anyon system as a $2 + 1$ dimensional space. This corresponds to *braiding* the threads (a.k.a. world-lines) starting from each anyon of the system. Particle trajectories are braided according to rules specifying how pairs (or bipartite subsystems) behave under exchange. The braiding process causes non-trivial unitary rotations of the fusion space resulting in a *computation*. Equivalently, a topological quantum computation can be seen as a splitting process (creating the initial configuration) followed by a braiding process (the unitary transformation) followed by a fusion process (measuring the final state). The latter essentially consists in checking whether the initial anyons fuse back to the vacuum from which they were created by splitting.

3.2 Calculation of the Kauffman Bracket via TQC

Consider n pairs of anyons created (via splitting) from the vacuum. Each anyonic pair is in the vacuum fusion channel with initial state denoted by $|\psi\rangle$. The final state $\langle\psi|$ corresponds to a fusion of these anyons back into the vacuum [15].

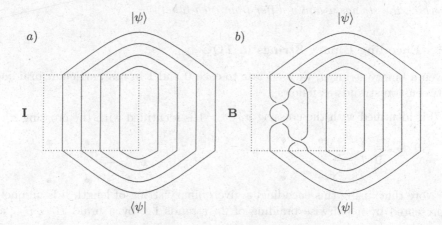

Fig. 2. Two anyonic quantum evolutions. In both cases pairs of anyons are created from the vacuum and then fused back into it. In (a) no braiding, i.e. the identity operator, is performed, in (b) some braiding operator is applied.

As shown in Fig. 2 part a, if no braiding is performed on the anyons (**I** stands for the identity), then the probability that they fuse back to the vacuum in the same pairwise order is trivially given by

$$\langle\psi|\,\mathbf{I}\,|\psi\rangle = \langle\psi|\psi\rangle = 1.$$

Consider instead the situation represented in Fig. 2 part b, where, after creating $n = 8$ anyons in pairs from the vacuum, we braid half of them with each other to produce the anyonic unitary evolution represented by the operator **B**. In this case, the probability amplitude of fusing the anyons in the same pairwise order to obtain the vacuum state is given by

$$\langle\psi|\,\mathbf{B}\,|\psi\rangle = \frac{\langle (B)^{Markov}\rangle}{d^{n-1}}, \quad \text{where} \quad d = (-A^2 - A^{-2}). \tag{1}$$

This equation expresses the relation between the probability amplitude of obtaining the vacuum state after the braiding given by the operator $\mathbf{B}$ and the Kauffman bracket of the link obtained from the Markov trace of braid B, i.e. $(B)^{Markov}$.

4 Topological Quantum Calculation of Hamming Distance Between Binary Strings

In this section we define a topological quantum algorithm for the approximation of the Hamming distance between two binary strings. This will be the base for the definition of a distance based kernel.

Definition 6 (*Hamming distance*). *Given two binary strings u and v of length n, the Hamming distance $d_H(u,v)$ is the number of components (bits) by which the strings u and v differ from each other.*

4.1 Encoding Binary Strings in TQC

Given a binary string u, we associate to each 0 and 1 in u a particular braiding between two strands as follows:

- 0 is identified with the crossing σ_i - 1 is identified with the crossing $\sigma_i^\dagger$

$$0 \longrightarrow \quad\quad\quad\quad\quad\quad 1 \longrightarrow$$

Note that, using this encoding, a given binary string of length n is uniquely represented by a pairwise braiding of $2n$ strands i.e. by a braid $B \in B_{2n}$ as shown below.

$$010... \longrightarrow$$

4.2 Hamming Distance Calculation: Base Case

Given two binary strings of length one ($n = 1$), u and v, we consider the braiding operators, $\mathbf{B}_u$ and $\mathbf{B}_v$, associated to u and v, respectively. Then we construct the composite braiding operator $\mathbf{B}_u \mathbf{B}_v^\dagger$ and apply the Markov trace, obtaining a link. Our aim is to calculate the Hamming distance $d_H(u,v)$ by exploiting the properties of the Kauffman brackets associated to these links. All the possible cases are shown below.

As we can see from Fig. 3,

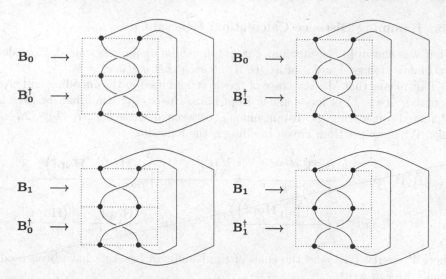

Fig. 3. Links associated to the Hamming distance between two single-digit binary strings.

– $d_H(0,0)$ and $d_H(1,1)$ can be continuously transformed in two loops (using the Reidemeister moves of Sect. 2) with Kauffman brackets (using rules in Sect. 2.2)

$$\langle \bigcirc \sqcup \bigcirc \rangle = (-A^2 - A^{-2})\langle \bigcirc \rangle = d\langle \bigcirc \rangle = d$$

– $d_H(1,0)$ and $d_H(0,1)$ are both represented by the Hopf link with Kauffman brackets (calculated as in Sect. 2.1)

$$\langle \mathbf{Hopf} \rangle = (-A^4 - A^{-4})$$

If we could perform the calculation of such Kauffman brackets using anyons, as discussed in Sect. 3.2, we would get:

– for $d_H(0,0)$ and $d_H(1,1)$

$$\langle \psi | \, \mathbf{B}_u \mathbf{B}_v^{\dagger} \, | \psi \rangle = \frac{\left\langle (\mathbf{B}_u \mathbf{B}_v^{\dagger})^{Markov} \right\rangle}{d^{2n-1}} = \frac{\langle \bigcirc \sqcup \bigcirc \rangle}{d^{2-1}} = \frac{d}{d} = 1$$

– for $d_H(1,0)$ and $d_H(0,1)$

$$\langle \psi | \, \mathbf{B}_u \mathbf{B}_v^{\dagger} \, | \psi \rangle = \frac{\left\langle (\mathbf{B}_u \mathbf{B}_v^{\dagger})^{Markov} \right\rangle}{d^{2n-1}} = \frac{\langle \mathbf{Hopf} \rangle}{d}$$

This means that, when the Hamming distance is zero (i.e. in the cases $d_H(0,0)$ and $d_H(1,1)$), the probability of the anyons fusing back into the vacuum is 1. When the hamming distance is 1 instead (i.e. in both cases $d_H(0,1)$ and $d_H(1,0)$), this probability reduces to $\left| \dfrac{\langle \mathbf{Hopf} \rangle}{d} \right|^2$.

4.3   Hamming Distance Calculation: General Case

What was shown in the previous paragraph can be easily generalised. Consider two binary strings u and v of length $n > 0$ such that $d_H(u, v) = k$.

This means that Markov trace of the $2n$ strand used in the encoding will give a number $2(n - k)$ of loops and k Hopf links. Hence, the Kauffman bracket is calculated considering the distant union $\sqcup$ between all these $k + 2(n - k) = 2n - k$ links. What we get from anyon braiding is the following:

$$\langle\psi|\,\mathbf{B}_u\mathbf{B}_v^\dagger\,|\psi\rangle = \frac{\left\langle (\mathbf{B}_u\mathbf{B}_v^\dagger)^{Markov} \right\rangle}{d^{2n-1}} = \frac{\left\langle \left(\bigsqcup_{i=1}^{2(n-k)} \bigcirc\right) \sqcup \left(\bigsqcup_{j=1}^{k} \mathbf{Hopf}\right) \right\rangle}{d^{2n-1}} =$$

$$= d^{2(n-k)} \frac{\left\langle \left(\bigsqcup_{j=1}^{k} \mathbf{Hopf}\right) \right\rangle}{d^{2n-1}} = d^{2(n-k)} d^{k-1} \frac{\langle \mathbf{Hopf}\rangle^k}{d^{2n-1}} = \frac{\langle \mathbf{Hopf}\rangle^k}{d^k}$$

where Property 1.1.1 and the rules of the Kauffman brackets have been used. Finally we can write

$$\langle\psi|\,\mathbf{B}_u\mathbf{B}_v^\dagger\,|\psi\rangle = \left(\frac{\langle \mathbf{Hopf}\rangle}{d}\right)^{d_H(u,v)} \tag{2}$$

which means that, given two arbitrary binary string u and v, of length n, their associated braiding $\mathbf{B}_u$ and $\mathbf{B}_v$ are such that the probability amplitude of $2n$ anyons fusing back into the vacuum after a braid $\mathbf{B}_u\mathbf{B}_v^\dagger$ is given by a constant $\frac{\langle \mathbf{Hopf}\rangle}{d}$ multiplied by itself a number of times equal to the Hamming distance between the two strings $d_H(u, v)$.

From Eq. 2 we can calculate an approximation to the Hamming distance $d_H(u, v)$ as follows (note that like in the case of the evaluation of the Jones polynomials, the result is probabilistic):

$$d_H(u, v) = \log_{\frac{\langle \mathbf{Hopf}\rangle}{d}} \langle\psi|\,\mathbf{B}_u\mathbf{B}_v^\dagger\,|\psi\rangle .$$

5   Kernel Functions

Kernel functions are generalised inner products that profoundly extend the capabilities of any mathematical optimisation that can be written in terms of a *Gram matrix* of discrete vectors (for example, a Gram matrix of vectors over training examples in machine-learning or samples requiring interpolation in regression). In particular, the Gram matrix $(\mathbf{x}_i^T\mathbf{x}_j)$ may be freely replaced by any kernel function $K(\mathbf{x}_i, \mathbf{x}_j)$ that satisfies the Mercer condition, i.e. a condition guaranteeing positive semi-definiteness. Many optimisation problems fall into this category (e.g. the dual form of the support vector machine training problem [5]). The Mercer space is given in terms of the input space x via $\phi(\mathbf{x})$, where $K(\mathbf{x}_i, \mathbf{x}_j) \equiv \phi(\mathbf{x}_i)^T(\phi(\mathbf{x}_j)$; the Mercer condition guarantees the existence of ϕ, but the kernel itself may be calculated based on any similarity function that gives rise to a legitimate kernel matrix. A kernel enforces a *feature mapping* of the input objects into a Hilbert space; however, the feature mapping does not need at any stage to be directly computed in itself; the kernel matrix alone is sufficient. This can, for example, enable machine learning to apply in areas in which there is not a readily apparent real vector space of feature measures (a motivating example is genomics, for which it is much more straightforward to compute a similarity measure between pairs of DNA strands than it is to embed each strand individually into a vector space of feature measurements). More generally, the very large choice of kernels available effectively infinitely extends the capabilities of kernelisable regression and machine-learning algorithms, allowing them to apply to essentially arbitrary domains.

In the next we show how a kernel can be naturally defined using TQC. To this purpose we use the Hamming distance as a demonstrative example of an approach to the definition of kernel methods that may involve more complex distance notions (note that the Hamming distance is essentially the simplest case of an edit distance, which excludes edit operations such as insertion, deletion and substitution; these clearly provide a more general and accurate measure of sequence dissimilarities).

5.1 Hamming Distance Based Kernel

The topological quantum computation of the Hamming distance shown in Sect. 4 can be used to define a kernel function. In fact, the encoding of binary strings as vectors $\mathbf{B}\,|\psi\rangle$ in the anyonic space allows us to define an embedding ϕ into the Hilbert space $\mathcal{H}$ defined by the fusion space of the anyonic configurations, i.e. for each string u, the mapping $\phi(u)$ is such that $\phi(u) = \mathbf{B}_u\,|\psi\rangle \in \mathcal{H}$. With this, using Eq. 2 we can define a string kernel by

$$K(u,v) \equiv \langle\psi|\,\mathbf{B}_u\mathbf{B}_v^\dagger\,|\psi\rangle = \left(\frac{\langle\mathbf{Hopf}\rangle}{d}\right)^{d_H(u,v)} = \left(\frac{A^4 + A^{-4}}{A^2 + A^{-2}}\right)^{d_H(u,v)}$$

If we work with so-called Fibonacci anyons, we have that $A = e^{\pi i/10}$ and the resulting kernel matrix is semi-definite positive. Thus it satisfies the Mercer condition for a valid kernel. Moreover, we can show that the Euclidean distance in the Mercer space, i.e. the fusion space $\mathcal{H}$, can be defined in terms of $\frac{\langle\mathbf{Hopf}\rangle}{d}$. In fact, we have, using the fact that vectors in $\mathcal{H}$ are normailized to unity,

$$\|\phi(u) - \phi(v)\|^2_{\mathcal{H}} = \|\phi(u)\|^2_{\mathcal{H}} + \|\phi(v)\|^2_{\mathcal{H}} - 2\phi(u)^T\phi(v) = 2 - 2K(u,v).$$

6 Conclusions

We have presented an encoding of the Hamming distance problem into a link invariant problem and we have shown how to solve it by means of topological quantum computation. We have also shown that the anyonic encoding of the string data and their braiding evolution naturally define a kernel function. The choice of a simple distance such as the Hamming distance allowed us to focus on the description of the approach rather than on the technicalities of the encodings of more complex distance notions.

We are not aware of other approaches that similarly to ours associate some topological properties to a given problem with no intrinsic topology, in order to exploit TQC. Our aim is to further investigate the potential offered by topological quantum algorithmic techniques for Machine Learning. It will be the subject of future work to extend the range of applicability of topological quantum computation to kernel methods.

References

1. Adams, C.: The Knot Book. W.H. Freeman, New York (1994)
2. Aharonov, D., Jones, V., Landau, Z.: A polynomial quantum algorithm for approximating the Jones polynomial. In: Proceedings of the 38th Annual ACM Symposium on Theory of Computing, Seattle, WA, USA, 21–23 May 2006, pp. 427–436 (2006)
3. Alexander, J.W.: A lemma on systems of knotted curves. Proc. Natl. Acad. Sci. U.S.A. 9(3), 93–95 (1923)
4. Markoff, A.: Uber die freie äquivalenz der geschlossenen zöpfe. Rec. Math. [Mat. Sbornik] N.S. (1936)
5. Cortes, C., Vapnik, V.: Support-vector networks. Mach. Learn. 20(3), 273–297 (1995)
6. Freedman, M.H.: P/NP, and the quantum field computer. Proc. Natl. Acad. Sci. 95(1), 98–101 (1998)
7. Freedman, M.H., Kitaev, A., Wang, Z.: Simulation of topological field theories by quantum computers. Commun. Math. Phys. 227, 587–603 (2002)
8. Hamming, R.W.: Error detecting and error correcting codes. Bell System Tech J. 29, 147–160 (1950)
9. Jones, V.F.R.: A polynomial invariant for knots via von Neumann algebras. Bull. Amer. Math. Soc. (N.S.) 12(1), 103–111 (1985)
10. Kauffman, L.H.: State models and the Jones polynomial. Topology 26(3), 395–407 (1987)
11. Kauffman, L.H.: New invariants in the theory of knots. Am. Math. Monthly 95(3), 195–242 (1988)
12. Kauffman, L.H.: Knots and Physics. Series on Knots and Everything, 4th edn. World Scientific, Singapore (2013)
13. Kitaev, A., Preskill, J.: Topological entanglement entropy. Phys. Rev. Lett. 96, 110404 (2006)
14. Kitaev, A.: Fault-tolerant quantum computation by anyons. Ann. Phys. 303(1), 2–30 (2003)
15. Pachos, J.K.: Introduction to Topological Quantum Computation. Cambridge University Press, New York (2012)
16. Reidemeister, K.: Knoten und Gruppen. Springer, Heidelberg (1932). https://doi.org/10.1007/978-3-642-65616-3
17. Reidemeister, K.: Elementare begründung der knotentheorie. Abhandlungen aus dem Mathematischen Seminar der Universität Hamburg 5(1), 24–32 (1927)
18. Satō, H.: Algebraic Topology: An Intuitive Approach. Iwanami Series in Modern Mathematics. American Mathematical Society, Providence (1999)
19. Wilczek, F.: Quantum mechanics of fractional-spin particles. Phys. Rev. Lett. 49, 957–959 (1982)

Typing Quantum Superpositions
and Measurement

Alejandro Díaz-Caro[1](✉) ⓘD and Gilles Dowek[2]

[1] Universidad Nacional de Quilmes and CONICET,
Roque Sáenz Peña 352, B1876BXD Bernal, Buenos Aires, Argentina
alejandro.diaz-caro@unq.edu.ar
[2] Inria, LSV, ENS Paris-Saclay,
61, avenue du Président Wilson, 94235 Cachan Cedex, France
gilles.dowek@ens-paris-saclay.fr

Abstract. We propose a way to unify two approaches of non-cloning in quantum lambda-calculi. The first approach is to forbid duplicating variables, while the second is to consider all lambda-terms as algebraic-linear functions. We illustrate this idea by defining a quantum extension of first-order simply-typed lambda-calculus, where the type is linear on superposition, while allows cloning base vectors. In addition, we provide an interpretation of the calculus where superposed types are interpreted as vector spaces and non-superposed types as their basis.

Keywords: Quantum computing · Lambda-calculus
Algebraic linearity · Linear logic · Measurement

1 Introduction

In λ-calculus, applying the term $\lambda x\ (x \otimes x)$, that expresses a non-linear function for some convenient definition of $\otimes$, to a term u yields the term $(\lambda x\ (x \otimes x))u$, that reduces to $u \otimes u$. But "cloning" this vector u is forbidden in quantum computing. Various quantum λ-calculi address this problem in different ways.

One way is to forbid the construction of the term $\lambda x\ (x \otimes x)$ using a typing system inspired from linear logic [1,9], leading to logic-linear calculi [2,10,11, 13,14]. Another is to consider all λ-terms expressing linear functions. The term $\lambda x\ (x \otimes x)$, for instance, expresses the linear function that maps $|0\rangle$ to $|0\rangle \otimes |0\rangle$ and $|1\rangle$ to $|1\rangle \otimes |1\rangle$[1]. This leads to restrict beta-reduction to the case where u is a base vector (in the computational basis) and to add the linearity rule $f(u + v) \longrightarrow (fu + fv)$, leading to algebraic-linear calculi [3–6,8].

Each solution has its advantages and drawbacks. For example, let $t?u\cdot v$ be the conditional statement on $|0\rangle$ and $|1\rangle$. Interpreting λ-terms as algebraic-linear functions permits to reduce the term $(\lambda x\ x?|0\rangle\cdot|1\rangle)(\alpha.|0\rangle + \beta.|1\rangle)$ to

---

Partially funded by the STIC-AmSud Project FoQCoSS and PICT-PRH 2015-1208.

[1] Where $|x\rangle$ is the Dirac notation for vectors, with $|0\rangle = \left(\begin{smallmatrix} 1 \\ 0 \end{smallmatrix}\right) \in \mathbb{C}^2$ and $|1\rangle = \left(\begin{smallmatrix} 0 \\ 1 \end{smallmatrix}\right) \in \mathbb{C}^2$, so $\{|0\rangle, |1\rangle\}$ is an orthonormal basis of $\mathbb{C}^2$, called here the "computational basis".

© Springer International Publishing AG 2017
C. Martín-Vide et al. (Eds.): TPNC 2017, LNCS 10687, pp. 281–293, 2017.
https://doi.org/10.1007/978-3-319-71069-3_22

$(\alpha.(\lambda x\ x?|0\rangle\cdot|1\rangle)|0\rangle + \beta.(\lambda x\ x?|0\rangle\cdot|1\rangle)|1\rangle)$ then to $(\alpha.|1\rangle + \beta.|0\rangle)$, instead of reducing it to the term $(\alpha.|0\rangle + \beta.|1\rangle)?|0\rangle\cdot|1\rangle$ that would be blocked. This explains that this linearity rule, that is systematic in the algebraic-linear languages cited above, is also present for the condition in [2] (the so-called **if°** operator).

However, interpreting all λ-terms as linear functions forbids to extend the calculus with non-linear operators, such as measurement. For instance, the term $(\lambda x\ \pi x)(|0\rangle + |1\rangle)$, where π represents a measurement in the computational basis, would reduce to $((\lambda x\ \pi x)|0\rangle + (\lambda x\ \pi x)|1\rangle)$, while it should reduce to $|0\rangle$ with probability $\frac{1}{2}$ and to $|1\rangle$ with probability $\frac{1}{2}$.

In this paper, we propose a way to unify the two approaches, distinguishing duplicable and non-duplicable data by their type, like in the logic-linear calculi; and interpreting λ-terms as linear functions, like in the algebraic-linear calculi, when they expect duplicable data. We illustrate this idea with an example of such a calculus.

In this calculus, a qubit has type $\mathbb{B}$ when it is in the computational basis, hence duplicable (a non-linear term in the sense of linear logic), and $S(\mathbb{B})$ when it is a superposition, hence non-duplicable (a linear term in the sense of linear logic). Hence, the term $|0\rangle \otimes (|0\rangle + |1\rangle)$ has type $\mathbb{B} \otimes S(\mathbb{B})$. Giving this type to this term and the type $S(\mathbb{B}\otimes\mathbb{B})$ to the term $(|0\rangle \otimes |0\rangle + |0\rangle \otimes |1\rangle)$ however jeopardizes the subject reduction property as, using the bilinearity of the product, the former should develop to the latter. This dilemma is not specific to quantum computing as computing is often a non-reversible process where some information is lost. For instance, if we express, in its type, that the term $(X-1)(X-2)$ is a product of two polynomials, developing it to $X^2 - 3X + 2$ does not preserve this type. A solution is to introduce, in the language, an explicit cast. For example, from the type of tensor products to the type of arbitrary vectors. The term $|0\rangle \otimes (|0\rangle + |1\rangle)$ then has type $\mathbb{B} \otimes S(\mathbb{B})$ and it cannot be reduced. But the term $\Uparrow (|0\rangle \otimes (|0\rangle + |1\rangle))$ has type $S(\mathbb{B} \otimes \mathbb{B})$ and can be developed to $(|0\rangle \otimes |0\rangle + |0\rangle \otimes |1\rangle)$.

This language permits expressing quantum algorithms with a very precise information about the nature of the data processed by these algorithms.

Outline of the Paper. In Sect. 2 we introduce the calculus, without tensor. In Sect. 3 we extend the language with a tensor operator for multiple-qubits systems, and state the Subject Reduction property of the resulting system. In Sect. 4 we provide a straightforward interpretation of the calculus considering base types as sets of vectors, and types $S(\cdot)$ as vector spaces. Finally, in Sect. 5 we express a non-trivial example in our calculus: the Teleportation algorithm, demonstrating the expressivity of the proposed language. A long version of this paper (51 pages) with all the detailed proofs is available at arXiv:1601.04294.

2   No-Cloning, Superpositions and Measurement

The grammar of types and terms is defined as follows, with $\alpha \in \mathbb{C}$.

$$
\begin{aligned}
\Psi &:= \mathbb{B} \mid S(\Psi) & \text{Qubit types } (\mathcal{Q}) \\
A &:= \Psi \mid \Psi \Rightarrow A \mid S(A) & \text{Types } (\mathcal{T}) \\
b &:= x \mid \lambda x : \Psi\, t \mid |0\rangle \mid |1\rangle & \text{Base terms } (\mathcal{B}) \\
v &:= b \mid (v+v) \mid \vec{0}_{S(A)} \mid \alpha.v & \text{Values } (\mathcal{V}) \\
t &:= v \mid tt \mid (t+t) \mid \pi t \mid ?{\cdot} \mid \alpha.t & \text{Terms } (\Lambda)
\end{aligned}
$$

Terms are variables, abstractions, applications, two constants for base qubits ($|0\rangle$ and $|1\rangle$), linear combinations of terms (built with addition and product by a scalar, addition being commutative and associative), a family of constants for the null vectors, one for each type of the form $S(A)$, ($\vec{0}_{S(A)}$), and an if-then-else construction ($?{\cdot}$) deciding on base vectors. We also include a symbol π for measurement in the computational basis.

The set of free variables of a term t is defined as usual in λ-calculus and denoted by $FV(t)$. We use $[\alpha.]t$ as a notation to refer indistinctly to $\alpha.t$ and to t. We use $-t$ as a shorthand notation for $-1.t$, and $(t-r)$ as a shorthand notation for $(t+(-r))$. The term $(t-t)$ has type $S(A)$, and reduces to $\vec{0}_{S(A)}$, which is not a base term.

An important property of this calculus is that types $S(\cdot)$ are linear types. Indeed, those correspond to superpositions, and so no duplication is allowed on them. Instead, at this tensor-free stage, a type without an $S(\cdot)$ on head position is a non-linear type, such as $\mathbb{B}$, which correspond to base terms, i.e. terms that can be cloned. A non-linear function is allowed to be applied to a linear argument, for example, $\lambda x : \mathbb{B}\ (fxx)$ can be applied to $(\frac{1}{\sqrt{2}}.|0\rangle + \frac{1}{\sqrt{2}}.|1\rangle)$, however, it distributes in the following way: $(\lambda x : \mathbb{B}\ (fxx))\ (\frac{1}{\sqrt{2}}.|0\rangle + \frac{1}{\sqrt{2}}.|1\rangle) \longrightarrow (\frac{1}{\sqrt{2}}.(\lambda x : \mathbb{B}\ (fxx))|0\rangle + \frac{1}{\sqrt{2}}.(\lambda x : \mathbb{B}\ (fxx))|1\rangle) \longrightarrow (\frac{1}{\sqrt{2}}.(f|0\rangle|0\rangle) + \frac{1}{\sqrt{2}}.(f|1\rangle|1\rangle))$.

Hence, the beta reduction occurs only when the type of the argument is the same as the type expected by the abstraction. Thus, the rewrite system depends on types. For this reason, we describe first the type system, and only then the rewrite system.

A type A will be interpreted as a set of vectors and $S(A)$ as the vector space generated by the span of such a set (cf. Sect. 4). Hence, we naturally have $A \subseteq S(A)$ and $S(S(A)) = S(A)$. Therefore, we also define a subtyping relation on types. The type system and the subtyping relation are given below, where contexts Γ and Δ have a disjoint support.

$$\frac{}{A \preceq S(A)} \qquad \frac{}{S(S(A)) \preceq S(A)} \qquad \frac{A \preceq B}{\Psi \Rightarrow A \preceq \Psi \Rightarrow B} \qquad \frac{A \preceq B}{S(A) \preceq S(B)}$$

$$\frac{}{x : \Psi \vdash x : \Psi} \; Ax \qquad \frac{}{\vdash \vec{0}_{S(A)} : S(A)} \; Ax_{\vec{0}} \qquad \frac{}{\vdash |0\rangle : \mathbb{B}} \; Ax_{|0\rangle} \qquad \frac{}{\vdash |1\rangle : \mathbb{B}} \; Ax_{|1\rangle}$$

$$\frac{\Gamma \vdash t : A}{\Gamma \vdash \alpha.t : S(A)} \; S_I^\alpha \qquad \frac{\Gamma \vdash t : A \quad \Delta \vdash u : A}{\Gamma, \Delta \vdash (t + u) : S(A)} \; S_I^+ \qquad \frac{\Gamma \vdash t : S(\mathbb{B})}{\Gamma \vdash \pi t : \mathbb{B}} \; S_E$$

$$\frac{\Gamma \vdash t : A \; (A \preceq B)}{\Gamma \vdash t : B} \; \preceq \qquad \frac{}{\vdash \; ? \cdot : \mathbb{B} \Rightarrow \mathbb{B} \Rightarrow \mathbb{B} \Rightarrow \mathbb{B}} \; If \qquad \frac{\Gamma, x : \Psi \vdash t : A}{\Gamma \vdash \lambda x : \Psi \; t : \Psi \Rightarrow A} \Rightarrow_I$$

$$\frac{\Gamma \vdash t : \Psi \Rightarrow A \quad \Delta \vdash u : \Psi}{\Gamma, \Delta \vdash tu : A} \Rightarrow_E \qquad \frac{\Gamma \vdash t : S(\Psi \Rightarrow A) \quad \Delta \vdash u : S(\Psi)}{\Gamma, \Delta \vdash tu : S(A)} \Rightarrow_{ES}$$

$$\frac{\Gamma \vdash t : A}{\Gamma, x : \mathbb{B} \vdash t : A} \; W \qquad \frac{\Gamma, x : \mathbb{B}, y : \mathbb{B} \vdash t : A}{\Gamma, x : \mathbb{B} \vdash (x/y)t : A} \; C$$

Remarks: Rule Ax allows typing variables only with qubit types. Hence, the system is first-order and only qubits can be passed as arguments (more when the rewrite system is presented). Rule $Ax_{\vec{0}}$ types the null vector as a non-base term, because the null vector cannot belong to the base of any vector space.

Thanks to rule $\preceq$ the term $|0\rangle$ has type $\mathbb{B}$ and also the more general type $S(\mathbb{B})$. Note that $((|0\rangle + |0\rangle) - |0\rangle)$ has type $S(\mathbb{B})$ and reduces to $|0\rangle$ that has the same type $S(\mathbb{B})$. Reducing this term to $|0\rangle$ of type $\mathbb{B}$ would not preserve its type. Moreover, this type would contain information impossible to compute, because the value $|0\rangle$ is not the result of a measurement, but of an interference.

Rule S_I^α states that a term multiplied by a scalar is not a base term. Even if the scalar is just a phase, we must type the term with an $S(\cdot)$ type, because our measurement operator removes the scalars, so having the scalar means that it has not been measured yet. Rule S_I^+ is the analog for sums to the previous rule. Rule S_E is the elimination of the superposition, which is achieved by measuring (using the π operator).

We use $r?s \cdot t$ as a notation for $(? \cdot) rst$. Notice that it is typed as a non-linear function by rule If, and so, the if-then-else linearly distributes over superpositions.

Rule $\Rightarrow_{ES}$ is the elimination for superpositions, corresponding to the linear distribution. Notice that the type of the argument is a superposition of the argument expected by the abstraction ($S(\Psi)$ vs. Ψ). Also, the abstraction is allowed to be a superposition. If, for example, we want to apply the sum of functions $(f + g)$ to the base argument $|0\rangle$, we would obtain the superposition $(f|0\rangle + g|0\rangle)$. The typing is as follows:

$$\frac{\frac{\vdash f : \mathbb{B} \Rightarrow A \quad \vdash g : \mathbb{B} \Rightarrow A}{\vdash (f + g) : S(\mathbb{B} \Rightarrow A)} \; S_I^+ \quad \frac{\frac{\vdash |0\rangle : \mathbb{B}}{\vdash |0\rangle : S(\mathbb{B})} \; Ax_{|0\rangle}}{\vdash |0\rangle : S(\mathbb{B})} \; \preceq}{\vdash (f + g)|0\rangle : S(A)} \Rightarrow_{ES} \longrightarrow \frac{\frac{\vdash f : \mathbb{B} \Rightarrow A \quad \vdash |0\rangle : \mathbb{B}}{\vdash f|0\rangle : A} \; Ax_{|0\rangle}}{\vdash f|0\rangle : A} \Rightarrow_E \quad \frac{\vdash g : \mathbb{B} \Rightarrow A \quad \vdash |0\rangle : \mathbb{B}}{\vdash g|0\rangle : A} \; Ax_{|0\rangle} \Rightarrow_E}{\vdash (f|0\rangle + g|0\rangle) : S(A)} \; S_I^+$$

Similarly, a linear function ($\vdash f : \mathbb{B} \Rightarrow A$) applied to a superposition ($|0\rangle + |1\rangle$) reduces to a superposition ($f|0\rangle + f|1\rangle$).

Finally, Rules W and C correspond to weakening and contraction on variables with base types. The rationale is that base terms can be cloned.

The rewrite system is given bellow, where, in rule (proj), $\forall i$, $b_i = |0\rangle$ or $b_i = |1\rangle$, $\sum_{i=1}^{n} \alpha_i.b_i$ is normal (so $1 \leq n \leq 2$), if an α_k is absent, $|\alpha_k|^2 = 1$, and $1 \leq k \leq n$.

Beta

If b has type $\mathbb{B}$ and $b \in \mathcal{B}$, then
$$(\lambda x : \mathbb{B}\ t)b \longrightarrow_{(1)} (b/x)t \qquad (\beta_b)$$
If u has type $S(\Psi)$, then
$$(\lambda x : S(\Psi)\ t)u \longrightarrow_{(1)} (u/x)t \qquad (\beta_n)$$

If

$$|1\rangle?u\cdot v \longrightarrow_{(1)} u \qquad (\mathsf{if}_1)$$
$$|0\rangle?u\cdot v \longrightarrow_{(1)} v \qquad (\mathsf{if}_0)$$

Linear distribution

If t has type $\mathbb{B} \Rightarrow A$, then
$$t(u+v) \longrightarrow_{(1)} (tu + tv) \qquad (\mathsf{lin}_r^+)$$
If t has type $\mathbb{B} \Rightarrow A$ then
$$t(\alpha.u) \longrightarrow_{(1)} \alpha.tu \qquad (\mathsf{lin}_r^\alpha)$$
If t has type $\mathbb{B} \Rightarrow A$, then
$$t\vec{0}_{S(\mathbb{B})} \longrightarrow_{(1)} \vec{0}_{S(A)} \qquad (\mathsf{lin}_r^0)$$
$$(t + u)v \longrightarrow_{(1)} (tv + uv) \qquad (\mathsf{lin}_l^+)$$
$$(\alpha.t)u \longrightarrow_{(1)} \alpha.tu \qquad (\mathsf{lin}_l^\alpha)$$
$$\vec{0}_{S(\mathbb{B} \Rightarrow A)}t \longrightarrow_{(1)} \vec{0}_{S(A)} \qquad (\mathsf{lin}_l^0)$$

Vector space axioms

$$(\vec{0}_{S(A)} + t) \longrightarrow_{(1)} t \qquad \text{(neutral)}$$
$$1.t \longrightarrow_{(1)} t \qquad \text{(unit)}$$
If t has type A, then
$$0.t \longrightarrow_{(1)} \vec{0}_{S(A)} \qquad (\mathsf{zero}_\alpha)$$
$$\alpha.\vec{0}_{S(A)} \longrightarrow_{(1)} \vec{0}_{S(A)} \qquad \text{(zero)}$$
$$\alpha.(\beta.t) \longrightarrow_{(1)} (\alpha \times \beta).t \qquad \text{(prod)}$$
$$\alpha.(t + u) \longrightarrow_{(1)} (\alpha.t + \alpha.u) \qquad (\alpha\mathsf{dist})$$
$$(\alpha.t + \beta.t) \longrightarrow_{(1)} (\alpha + \beta).t \qquad \text{(fact)}$$
$$(\alpha.t + t) \longrightarrow_{(1)} (\alpha + 1).t \qquad (\mathsf{fact}^1)$$
$$(t + t) \longrightarrow_{(1)} 2.t \qquad (\mathsf{fact}^2)$$

=

$$(u + v) =_{AC} (v + u) \qquad \text{(comm)}$$
$$((u + v) + w) =_{AC} (u + (v + w)) \qquad \text{(assoc)}$$

Project.

$$\pi\left(\sum_{i=1}^{n}[\alpha_i.]b_i\right) \longrightarrow_{(p)} b_k \qquad \text{(proj)}$$
$$\text{with } p = \frac{|\alpha_k|^2}{\sum_{i=1}^{n}|\alpha_i|^2}$$

$$\frac{t \longrightarrow_{(p)} u}{tv \longrightarrow_{(p)} uv} \qquad \frac{t \longrightarrow_{(p)} u}{(\lambda x : \mathbb{B}\ v)t \longrightarrow_{(p)} (\lambda x : \mathbb{B}\ v)u}$$

$$\frac{t \longrightarrow_{(p)} u}{t + v \longrightarrow_{(p)} u + v} \qquad \frac{t \longrightarrow_{(p)} u}{\alpha.t \longrightarrow_{(p)} \alpha u} \qquad \frac{t \longrightarrow_{(p)} u}{\pi t \longrightarrow_{(p)} \pi u}$$

The relation $\longrightarrow_{(p)}$ is a probabilistic relation where p is the probability of occurrence. Every rewrite rule has a probability 1 of occurrence, except for the projection ((proj) rule).

There are two beta rules. Rule (β_b) acts only when the argument is a base term, and the type expected by the abstraction is a base type. Hence, rule (β_b) is "call-by-base" (base terms coincides with values of λ-calculus, while values on this calculus also includes superpositions of base terms and the null vector). Instead, (β_n) is the usual call-by-name beta rule. They are distinguished by the type of the argument. Rule (β_b) acts on non-linear functions while (β_n) is for linear functions. The test on the type of the argument is due to the type system that allows an argument with a type not matching with the type expected by the abstraction (in such a case, one of the linear distribution rules applies).

The group If-then-else contains the tests over the base qubits $|0\rangle$ and $|1\rangle$.

The first three of the linear distribution rules (those marked with subindex r), are the rules that are used when a non-linear abstraction is applied to a linear argument (that is, when an abstraction expecting a base term is given a superposition). In these cases the beta reductions cannot be used since the side conditions on types are not met. Hence, these distributivity rules apply instead. The remaining rules in this group deal with a superposition of functions. For example, rule (lin_l^+) is the sum of functions: A superposition is a sum, therefore, if an argument is given to a sum of functions, it needs to be given to each function in the sum. We use a weak reduction strategy (i.e. reduction occurs only on closed terms), hence the argument v on this rule is closed, otherwise, it could not be typed. For example $x : S(\mathbb{B}), t : \mathbb{B} \Rightarrow \mathbb{B}, u : \mathbb{B} \Rightarrow \mathbb{B} \vdash (t + u)x : S(\mathbb{B})$ is derivable, but $x : S(\mathbb{B}), t : \mathbb{B} \Rightarrow \mathbb{B}, u : \mathbb{B} \Rightarrow \mathbb{B} \vdash (tx + ux) : S(\mathbb{B})$ is not.

The vector space axioms rules are the directed axioms of vector spaces [5,6]. The Modulo AC rules are not proper rewrite rules, but express that we consider the symbol $+$ to be associative and commutative, and hence our rewrite system is *rewrite modulo AC* [12].

Finally, rule (proj) is the projection over weighted associative pairs, that is, the projection over a generalization of multisets where the multiplicities are given by complex numbers. This reduction rule is the only one with a probability different from 1, and it is given by the square of the modulus of the weights[2], implementing this way the quantum measurement over the computational basis.

3   Multi-qubit Systems: Tensor Products

A multi-qubit system is represented with the tensor product between single-qubit Hilbert spaces. The tensor product of base terms can be seen as an ordered list. Hence, we represent the tensor product as a conjunction-like operator. The distributivity of linear combinations over tensor products is not trivially tracked in the type system, and so an explicit cast between types is also added.

Each level in the term grammar (base terms, values and general terms) is extended with the tensor of the terms in such a level. The primitives *head* and *tail* are added to the general terms. The projector π is generalized to π_j, where the subindex j stands for the number of qubits to be measured, which are those in the first j positions. Notice that it is always possible to do a swap between qubits and so place the qubits to be measured at the beginning. For instance, $\lambda x : \mathbb{B} \otimes \mathbb{B} \ (tail \ x \otimes head \ x)$.

An explicit type cast of a term t $(\Uparrow_{S(A)}^{S(B \otimes C)} t)$ is included in the general terms. It is only allowed to cast a superposed type into a superposed tensor product. We also add the tensor between types, and, as a consequence, a new level.

$B := \mathbb{B} \mid B \otimes B$	Base qubit types $(\mathcal{B})$
$\Psi := B \mid S(\Psi) \mid \Psi \otimes \Psi$	Qubit types $(\mathcal{Q})$
$A := \Psi \mid \Psi \Rightarrow A \mid S(A) \mid A \otimes A$	Types $(\mathcal{T})$
$b := x \mid \lambda x : \Psi \ t \mid \left|0\right\rangle \mid \left|1\right\rangle \mid b \otimes b$	Base terms $(\mathcal{B})$
$v := b \mid (v + v) \mid \vec{0}_{S(A)} \mid \alpha.v \mid v \otimes v$	Values $(\mathcal{V})$
$t := v \mid tt \mid (t + t) \mid \pi_j t \mid ?\cdot \mid \alpha.t \mid t \otimes t \mid head \ t \mid tail \ t \mid \Uparrow_{S(A)}^{S(B \otimes C)} t$	Terms (Λ)

The type system includes all the typing rules given in the previous section, plus the rules for tensor, for cast, and an updated rule S_E, for which we introduce the following notation:

---

[2] We speak about weights and not amplitudes, since the vector may not have norm 1. The projection rule normalizes the vector while reducing.

Let $S \subseteq \{1, \cdots, n\}$. We define Q_n^S inductively by:

$$Q_n^S = \begin{cases} A_{n-1}^S(\mathbb{B}) & \text{if } n \notin S \\ A_{n-1}^{S \setminus \{n\}}(S(\mathbb{B})) & \text{if } n \in S \end{cases}$$

$$A_0^\emptyset(B) = B$$

$$A_{k+1}^S(\mathbb{B}) = \begin{cases} A_k^S(\mathbb{B}) \otimes \mathbb{B} & \text{if } k+1 \notin S \\ A_k^{S \setminus \{k+1\}}(S(\mathbb{B})) \otimes \mathbb{B} & \text{if } k+1 \in S \end{cases}$$

$$A_{k+1}^S(S(B)) = \begin{cases} A_k^S(\mathbb{B}) \otimes S(B) & \text{if } k+1 \notin S \\ A_k^{S \setminus \{k+1\}}(S(\mathbb{B} \otimes B)) & \text{if } k+1 \in S \end{cases}$$

where B is any type.

In simple words, notation Q_n^S stands for a tensor of n qubits, where those indexed by the set S are superposed and typed with the most general type, for example $Q_3^{\{1,2\}}$ stands for $S(\mathbb{B} \otimes \mathbb{B}) \otimes \mathbb{B}$ and not for $S(\mathbb{B}) \otimes S(\mathbb{B}) \otimes \mathbb{B}$. The following example may be clarifying. $Q_5^{\{1,2,4\}} = A_4^{\{1,2,4\}}(\mathbb{B}) = A_3^{\{1,2\}}(S(\mathbb{B})) \otimes \mathbb{B} = A_2^{\{1,2\}}(\mathbb{B}) \otimes S(\mathbb{B}) \otimes \mathbb{B} = A_1^{\{1\}}(S(\mathbb{B})) \otimes \mathbb{B} \otimes S(\mathbb{B}) \otimes \mathbb{B} = A_0^\emptyset(S(\mathbb{B} \otimes \mathbb{B})) \otimes \mathbb{B} \otimes S(\mathbb{B}) \otimes \mathbb{B} = S(\mathbb{B} \otimes \mathbb{B}) \otimes \mathbb{B} \otimes S(\mathbb{B}) \otimes \mathbb{B}$.

In addition, we update the subtyping relation adding the following two rules.

$$\frac{A \preceq B}{A \otimes C \preceq B \otimes C} \quad \text{and} \quad \frac{A \preceq B}{C \otimes A \preceq C \otimes B}.$$

The updated type system is given below.

$$\frac{}{x : \Psi \vdash x : \Psi} Ax \qquad \frac{}{\vdash \vec{0}_{S(A)} : S(A)} Ax_{\vec{0}} \qquad \frac{}{\vdash |0\rangle : \mathbb{B}} Ax_{|0\rangle} \qquad \frac{}{\vdash |1\rangle : \mathbb{B}} Ax_{|1\rangle}$$

$$\frac{\Gamma \vdash t : A}{\Gamma \vdash \alpha.t : S(A)} S_I^\alpha \qquad \frac{\Gamma \vdash t : A \quad \Delta \vdash u : A}{\Gamma, \Delta \vdash (t + u) : S(A)} S_I^+ \qquad \frac{\Gamma \vdash t : Q_n^S}{\Gamma \vdash \pi_j t : Q_n^{S \setminus \{1,\dots,j\}}} S_E \; {\scriptstyle (\frac{S \subseteq \mathbb{N}^{\leq n}}{j \leq n})}$$

$$\frac{\Gamma \vdash t : A \; (A \preceq B)}{\Gamma \vdash t : B} \preceq \qquad \frac{}{\vdash ?. : \mathbb{B} \Rightarrow \mathbb{B} \Rightarrow \mathbb{B} \Rightarrow \mathbb{B}} If \qquad \frac{\Gamma, x : \Psi \vdash t : A}{\Gamma \vdash \lambda x : \Psi\, t : \Psi \Rightarrow A} \Rightarrow_I$$

$$\frac{\Gamma \vdash t : \Psi \Rightarrow A \quad \Delta \vdash u : \Psi}{\Gamma, \Delta \vdash tu : A} \Rightarrow_E \qquad \frac{\Gamma \vdash t : S(\Psi \Rightarrow A) \quad \Delta \vdash u : S(\Psi)}{\Gamma, \Delta \vdash tu : S(A)} \Rightarrow_{ES}$$

$$\frac{\Gamma \vdash t : A}{\Gamma, x : B \vdash t : A} W \qquad \frac{\Gamma, x : B, y : B \vdash t : A}{\Gamma, x : B \vdash (x/y)t : A} C$$

$$\frac{\Gamma \vdash t : A \quad \Delta \vdash u : B}{\Gamma, \Delta \vdash t \otimes u : A \otimes B} \otimes_I \qquad \frac{\Gamma \vdash t : \mathbb{B} \otimes B}{\Gamma \vdash \text{head}\, t : \mathbb{B}} \otimes_{Er} \qquad \frac{\Gamma \vdash t : \mathbb{B} \otimes B}{\Gamma \vdash \text{tail}\, t : B} \otimes_{El}$$

$$\frac{\Gamma \vdash t : S(S(A) \otimes B)}{\Gamma \vdash \Uparrow_{S(S(A) \otimes B)}^{S(A \otimes B)} t : S(A \otimes B)} \Uparrow_r \qquad \frac{\Gamma \vdash t : S(A \otimes S(B))}{\Gamma \vdash \Uparrow_{S(A \otimes S(B))}^{S(A \otimes B)} t : S(A \otimes B)} \Uparrow_l$$

$$\frac{\Gamma \vdash \Uparrow_{S(B)}^{S(A)} t : S(A)}{\Gamma \vdash \Uparrow_{S(B)}^{S(A)} \alpha.t : S(A)} \Uparrow^\alpha \qquad \frac{\Gamma \vdash \Uparrow_{S(B)}^{S(A)} t : S(A) \quad \Delta \vdash \Uparrow_{S(B)}^{S(A)} r : S(A)}{\Gamma, \Delta \vdash \Uparrow_{S(B)}^{S(A)} (t + r) : S(A)} \Uparrow^+$$

The new rule S_E types the generalized projection: we force the term to be measured to be typed with a type of the form Q_n^S, and then, after measuring the first j qubits, the new type becomes $Q_n^{S \setminus \{1,\dots,j\}}$, that is, we remove the superposition mark $S(\cdot)$ from the first j types in the tensor product.

The added rules $\otimes_I$, $\otimes_{Er}$, $\otimes_{El}$ are the standard introduction and eliminations for lists. Rules $\Uparrow_r$ and $\Uparrow_l$ type the castings. The only valid casts are $S(S(A) \otimes B)$

and $S(A \otimes S(B))$ into $S(A \otimes B)$. Rules $\Uparrow^\alpha$ and $\Uparrow^+$ allow for compositional reasoning. Indeed, casting a linear combination of terms will rewrite to casting each term in the combination.

The rewrite system is given below. It includes all the rules from the previous section plus the rules for tensors: (head) and (tail) to deal with lists, and the typing casts rules, which normalize superpositions to sums of base terms, while update the types.

In the rule (proj), $j \leq m$, $k \leq n$, $\forall i \leq n$, $\forall h \leq m$, $b_{hi} = |0\rangle$ or $b_{ih} = |1\rangle$, if an α_i is absent, it is taken as 1, $\sum_{i=1}^{n}[\alpha_i].(b_{1i} \otimes \cdots \otimes b_{mi})$ is in normal form (hence, $1 \leq n \leq 2^m$), and $P \subseteq \mathbb{N}^{\leq n}$, such that $\forall i \in P$, $\forall h \leq j$, $b_{hi} = b_{hk}$.

Beta	If b has type B and $b \in \mathcal{B}$, then $(\lambda x : B\ t)b \longrightarrow_{(1)} (b/x)t$ (β_b)	$(\vec{0}_{S(A)} + t) \longrightarrow_{(1)} t$	(neutral)	
		$1.t \longrightarrow_{(1)} t$	(unit)	
	If u has type $S(\Psi)$, then $(\lambda x : S(\Psi)\ t)u \longrightarrow_{(1)} (u/x)t$ (β_n)	If t has type A, then		**Vector space axioms**
If	$|1\rangle?u\cdot v \longrightarrow_{(1)} u$ (if_1)	$0.t \longrightarrow_{(1)} \vec{0}_{S(A)}$	(zero$_\alpha$)	
	$|0\rangle?u\cdot v \longrightarrow_{(1)} v$ (if_0)	$\alpha.\vec{0}_{S(A)} \longrightarrow_{(1)} \vec{0}_{S(A)}$	(zero)	
Linear distribution	If t has type $B \Rightarrow A$, then $t(u+v) \longrightarrow_{(1)} (tu + tv)$ (lin_r^+)	$\alpha.(\beta.t) \longrightarrow_{(1)} (\alpha \times \beta).t$	(prod)	
		$\alpha.(t+u) \longrightarrow_{(1)} (\alpha.t + \alpha.u)$	(αdist)	
	If t has type $B \Rightarrow A$ then $t(\alpha.u) \longrightarrow_{(1)} \alpha.tu$ (lin_r^α)	$(\alpha.t + \beta.t) \longrightarrow_{(1)} (\alpha + \beta).t$	(fact)	
		$(\alpha.t + t) \longrightarrow_{(1)} (\alpha + 1).t$	(fact^1)	
	If t has type $B \Rightarrow A$, then $t\vec{0}_{S(\mathbb{B})} \longrightarrow_{(1)} \vec{0}_{S(A)}$ (lin_r^0)	$(t+t) \longrightarrow_{(1)} 2.t$	(fact^2)	
	$(t+u)v \longrightarrow_{(1)} (tv + uv)$ (lin_l^+)	$(u+v) =_{AC} (v+u)$	(comm)	$\parallel$
	$(\alpha.t)u \longrightarrow_{(1)} \alpha.tu$ (lin_l^α)	$((u+v)+w) =_{AC} (u+(v+w))$	(assoc)	
	$\vec{0}_{S(\mathbb{B}\Rightarrow A)}t \longrightarrow_{(1)} \vec{0}_{S(A)}$ (lin_l^0)	If $h \neq u \otimes v$ and $h \in \mathcal{B}$, then $head\ (h \otimes t) \longrightarrow_{(1)} h$	(head)	**Lists**
		If $h \neq u \otimes v$ and $h \in \mathcal{B}$, then $tail\ (h \otimes t) \longrightarrow_{(1)} t$	(tail)	
Typing casts	$\Uparrow_{S(S(A)\otimes B)}^{S(A\otimes B)} ((r+s) \otimes u) \longrightarrow_{(1)} (\Uparrow_{S(S(A)\otimes B)}^{S(A\otimes B)} (r \otimes u) + \Uparrow_{S(S(A)\otimes B)}^{S(A\otimes B)} (s \otimes u))$		(dist$_r^+$)	
	$\Uparrow_{S(B\otimes S(A))}^{S(B\otimes A)} (u \otimes (r+s)) \longrightarrow_{(1)} (\Uparrow_{S(B\otimes S(A))}^{S(B\otimes A)} (u \otimes r) + \Uparrow_{S(B\otimes S(A))}^{S(B\otimes A)} (u \otimes s))$		(dist$_l^+$)	
	$\Uparrow_{S(S(A)\otimes B)}^{S(A\otimes B)} ((\alpha.r) \otimes u) \longrightarrow_{(1)} \alpha. \Uparrow_{S(S(A)\otimes B)}^{S(A\otimes B)} (r \otimes u)$		(dist$_r^\alpha$)	
	$\Uparrow_{S(B\otimes S(A))}^{S(B\otimes A)} (u \otimes (\alpha.r)) \longrightarrow_{(1)} \alpha. \Uparrow_{S(B\otimes S(A))}^{S(B\otimes A)} (u \otimes r)$		(dist$_l^\alpha$)	
	$\Uparrow_{S(S(A)\otimes B)}^{S(A\otimes B)} (\vec{0}_{S(A)} \otimes u) \longrightarrow_{(1)} \vec{0}_{S(A\otimes B)}$		(dist$_r^0$)	
	$\Uparrow_{S(B\otimes S(A))}^{S(B\otimes A)} (u \otimes \vec{0}_{S(A)}) \longrightarrow_{(1)} \vec{0}_{S(B\otimes A)}$		(dist$_l^0$)	
	$\Uparrow_{S(A)}^{S(B\otimes C)} (t+u) \longrightarrow_{(1)} (\Uparrow_{S(A)}^{S(B\otimes C)} t + \Uparrow_{S(A)}^{S(B\otimes C)} u)$		(dist$_\Uparrow^+$)	
	$\Uparrow_{S(A)}^{S(B\otimes C)} (\alpha.t) \longrightarrow_{(1)} \alpha. \Uparrow_{S(A)}^{S(B\otimes C)} t$		(dist$_\Uparrow^\alpha$)	
	If $u \in \mathcal{B}$, then, $\Uparrow_{S(S(A)\otimes B)}^{S(A\otimes B)} (u \otimes v) \longrightarrow_{(1)} u \otimes v$		(neut$_r^\Uparrow$)	
	If $u \in \mathcal{B}$, then, $\Uparrow_{S(A\otimes S(B))}^{S(A\otimes B)} (v \otimes u) \longrightarrow_{(1)} v \otimes u$		(neut$_l^\Uparrow$)	
Project.	$\pi_j(\sum_{i=1}^{n}[\alpha_i].(b_{1i} \otimes \cdots \otimes b_{mi}))$ $\longrightarrow_{(p)} \bigotimes_{h=1}^{j} b_{hk} \otimes \sum_{i \in P} \left(\frac{\alpha_i}{\sqrt{\sum_{i \in P} |\alpha_i|^2}} \right).(b_{j+1,i} \otimes \cdots \otimes b_{mi})$ with $p = \sum_{i \in P} \left(\frac{|\alpha_i|^2}{\sum_{i=1}^{n} |\alpha_i|^2} \right)$		(proj)	

$$\dfrac{t \longrightarrow_{(p)} u}{tv \longrightarrow_{(p)} uv} \qquad \dfrac{t \longrightarrow_{(p)} u}{(\lambda x : B\ v)t \longrightarrow_{(p)} (\lambda x : B\ v)u}$$

$$\dfrac{t \longrightarrow_{(p)} u}{t+v \longrightarrow_{(p)} u+v} \qquad \dfrac{t \longrightarrow_{(p)} u}{\alpha.t \longrightarrow_{(p)} \alpha u} \qquad \dfrac{t \longrightarrow_{(p)} u}{\pi_j t \longrightarrow_{(p)} \pi_j u} \qquad \dfrac{t \longrightarrow_{(p)} u}{t \otimes v \longrightarrow_{(p)} u \otimes v}$$

$$\dfrac{t \longrightarrow_{(p)} u}{head\ t \longrightarrow_{(p)} head\ u} \qquad \dfrac{t \longrightarrow_{(p)} u}{tail\ t \longrightarrow_{(p)} tail\ u} \qquad \dfrac{t \longrightarrow_{(p)} u}{\Uparrow_{S(A)}^{S(B)} t \longrightarrow_{(p)} \Uparrow_{S(A)}^{S(B)} u}$$

The rule (proj) has been updated to account for multiple qubits systems. It normalizes (as in norm 1) the scalars on the obtained term.

The first six rules in the group typing casts—(dist$_r^+$), (dist$_r^\alpha$), and (dist$_r^0$), and their analogous (dist$_l^+$), (dist$_l^\alpha$), and (dist$_l^0$)—deal with the distributivity of sums, scalar product and null vector respectively. If we ignore the type cast $\Uparrow_{S(A)}^{S(B)}$ on each rule, these rules are just distributivity rules. For example, rule (dist$_r^+$) acts on the term $(r + s) \otimes u$, distributing the sum with respect to the tensor product, producing $(r \otimes u + s \otimes u)$ (distribution to the right). However, the term $(r + s) \otimes u$ may have type $S(A) \otimes B$, $S(A) \otimes S(B)$ or $S(A \otimes B)$, while, among those, the term $(r \otimes u + s \otimes u)$ can only have type $S(A \otimes B)$. Hence, we cannot reduce the first term to the second without losing subject reduction. Instead, we need to cast the term explicitly to the valid type in order to reduce. Notice that in the previous example it would have been enough to use $\Uparrow_{S(A) \otimes B}^{S(A \otimes B)}$. Indeed, the term $(r + s) \otimes u$ can be typed with $S(A) \otimes B$. However, we prefer the more general $S(S(A) \otimes B)$ and hence to use the same rule when, for example, a sum is given.

The next two rules, (dist$_\Uparrow^+$) and (dist$_\Uparrow^\alpha$), distribute the cast over sums and scalars. For example $\Uparrow_{S(S(B) \otimes B)}^{S(B \otimes B)} ((\alpha.|1\rangle) \otimes |0\rangle + (\beta.|0\rangle) \otimes |1\rangle)$ reduces by rule (dist$_\Uparrow^+$) to $(\Uparrow_{S(S(B) \otimes B)}^{S(B \otimes B)} (\alpha.|1\rangle) \otimes |0\rangle + \Uparrow_{S(S(B) \otimes B)}^{S(B \otimes B)} (\beta.|0\rangle) \otimes |1\rangle)$, and hence, the distributivity rule can act. The last two rules in the group, (neut$_r^\Uparrow$) and (neut$_l^\Uparrow$), remove the cast when it is not needed anymore. For example $\Uparrow_{S(S(B) \otimes B)}^{S(B \otimes B)} (\alpha.\beta.|0\rangle) \otimes |1\rangle \xrightarrow{\text{(dist}_r^\alpha)}_{(1)} \alpha. \ \Uparrow_{S(S(B) \otimes B)}^{S(B \otimes B)} (\beta.|0\rangle) \otimes |1\rangle \xrightarrow{\text{(dist}_r^\alpha)}_{(1)} \alpha.\beta. \ \Uparrow_{S(S(B) \otimes B)}^{S(B \otimes B)} |0\rangle \otimes |1\rangle \xrightarrow{\text{(neut}_l^\Uparrow)}_{(1)} \alpha.\beta.|0\rangle \otimes |1\rangle$.

The measurement rule (proj) is updated to measure the first j qubits. Hence, a n-qubits in normal form (that is, a sum of tensors of qubits with or without a scalar in front), for example, the term $((2.(|0\rangle \otimes |1\rangle \otimes |1\rangle)) + |0\rangle \otimes |1\rangle \otimes |0\rangle) + 3.(|1\rangle \otimes |1\rangle \otimes |1\rangle))$ can be measured and will produce a n-qubits where the first j qubits are the same and the remaining are untouched, with its scalars changed to have norm 1. In this 3-qubits example, measuring the first two can produce either $|0\rangle \otimes |1\rangle \otimes (\frac{2}{\sqrt{5}}.|1\rangle + \frac{1}{\sqrt{5}}.|0\rangle)$ or $|1\rangle \otimes |1\rangle \otimes (1.|1\rangle)$. The probability of producing the first is $\frac{|2|^2}{(|2|^2+|1|^2+|3|^2)} + \frac{|1|^2}{(|2|^2+|1|^2+|3|^2)} = \frac{5}{14}$ and the probability of producing the second is $\frac{|3|^2}{(|2|^2+|1|^2+|3|^2)} = \frac{9}{14}$.

Remark, to conclude, that since the calculus presented in this paper is call-by-base for the functions expecting a non-linear argument, it avoids a well-known problem in others λ-calculi with a linear logic type system including modalities. To illustrate this problem, consider the following typing judgement: $y : S(\mathbb{B}) \vdash (\lambda x : \mathbb{B} \ (x \otimes x))(\pi y) : S(\mathbb{B}) \otimes S(\mathbb{B})$. If we allow to β-reduce this term, we would obtain $(\pi y) \otimes (\pi y)$ which is not typable in the context $y : S(\mathbb{B})$. A standard solution to this problem is illustrated in [7], where the terms that can be cloned are distinguished by a mark, and used in a *let* construction, while non-clonable terms are used in λ abstractions.

Thanks to the explicit casts, the resulting system has the Subject Reduction property (Theorem 2), that is, the typing is preserved by weak-reduction (i.e. reduction on closed terms). The proof of this theorem is not trivial, specially due to the complexity of the system itself. The detailed proof is given in a seven-page long appendix in a preprint submitted to arXiv:1601.04294.

Lemma 1 (Substitution lemma). *Let $FV(u) = \emptyset$, then if $\Gamma, x : \Psi \vdash t : A$, $\Delta \vdash u : \Psi$, where if $\Psi = B$ then $u \in \mathcal{B}$, we have $\Gamma, \Delta \vdash (u/x)t : A$.*

Theorem 2 (Subject reduction on closed terms). *For any closed terms t and u and type A, if $t \longrightarrow_{(p)} u$ and $\vdash t : A$, then $\vdash u : A$.*

4   Interpretation

We consider vector spaces equipped with a canonical base, and subsets of such spaces.

Let E and F be two vector spaces with canonical bases $B = \{\vec{b_i} \mid i \in I\}$ and $C = \{\vec{c_j} \mid j \in J\}$. The tensor product $E \otimes F$ of E and F is the vector space of canonical base $\{\vec{b_i} \otimes \vec{c_j} \mid i \in I \text{ and } j \in J\}$, where $\vec{b_i} \otimes \vec{c_j}$ is the ordered pair formed with the vector $\vec{b_i}$ and the vector $\vec{c_j}$. The operation $\otimes$ is extended to the vectors of E and F bilinearly: $(\sum_i \alpha_i \vec{b_i}) \otimes (\sum_j \beta_j \vec{c_j}) = \sum_{ij} \alpha_i \beta_j (\vec{b_i} \otimes \vec{c_j})$.

Let E and F be two vector spaces equipped with bases B and C, and S and T be two subsets of E and F respectively, we define the set $S \times T$, subset of the vector space $E \otimes F$, as follows: $S \times T = \{\vec{u} \otimes \vec{v} \mid \vec{u} \in S, \vec{v} \in T\}$.

Remark that $E \times F$ differs from $E \otimes F$. For instance, if E and F are $\mathbb{C}^2$ equipped with the base $\{\vec{i}, \vec{j}\}$, then $E \times F$ contains $\vec{i} \otimes \vec{i}$ and $\vec{j} \otimes \vec{j}$ but not $\vec{i} \otimes \vec{i} + \vec{j} \otimes \vec{j}$, that is not a tensor product of two vectors of $\mathbb{C}^2$.

Let E be a vector space equipped with a base B, and S a subset of E. We write $\mathcal{S}(S)$ for the vector space over $\mathbb{C}$ generated by the span of S, that is, containing all the linear combinations of elements of S.

Hence, if E and F are two vector spaces of bases B and C then $E \otimes F = \mathcal{S}(B \times C) = \mathcal{S}(E \times F)$.

Let S and T be two sets. We write $S \to T$ for the vector space of formal linear combination of functions from S to T. The set $S \Rightarrow T$ of the functions from S to T is a subset—and even a basis—of this vector space.

Note that if S and T are two sets, then $S \to T = \mathcal{S}(S \Rightarrow T)$.

To each type we associate the subset of some vector space

$$[\![\mathbb{B}]\!] = \{\left(\begin{smallmatrix}1\\0\end{smallmatrix}\right), \left(\begin{smallmatrix}0\\1\end{smallmatrix}\right)\}, \text{a subset of } \mathbb{C}^2$$
$$[\![S(A)]\!] = \mathcal{S}[\![A]\!]$$
$$[\![\Psi \Rightarrow A]\!] = [\![\Psi]\!] \Rightarrow [\![A]\!]$$
$$[\![A \otimes B]\!] = [\![A]\!] \times [\![B]\!]$$

Remark that $[\![S(A \otimes B)]\!] = \mathcal{S}([\![A]\!] \times [\![B]\!]) = [\![A]\!] \otimes [\![B]\!]$.

If $\Gamma = x_1 : \Psi_1, ..., x_n : \Psi_n$ is a context, then a Γ-valuation is a function ϕ mapping each x_i to $[\![\Psi_i]\!]$. Notation: $\phi \vDash \Gamma$.

We now would associate to each term t of type A an element $[\![t]\!]$ of $[\![A]\!]$. But as our calculus is probabilistic, due to the presence of a measurement operator, we must associate to each term a set of elements of $[\![A]\!]$.

Let $\Gamma \vdash t : A$ and $\phi \vDash \Gamma$. We define the interpretation of t, $[\![t]\!]_\phi$ as follows.

$[\![x]\!]_\phi = \phi x$

$[\![\lambda x : \Psi.t]\!]_\phi = \{f \mid \forall a \in [\![\Psi]\!], fa \in [\![t]\!]_{\phi, x \mapsto [\![\Psi]\!]}\}$

$[\![|0\rangle]\!]_\phi = \{\left(\begin{smallmatrix}1\\0\end{smallmatrix}\right)\} \qquad ; \qquad [\![|1\rangle]\!]_\phi = \{\left(\begin{smallmatrix}0\\1\end{smallmatrix}\right)\}$

$[\![t \otimes u]\!]_\phi = [\![t]\!]_\phi \times [\![u]\!]_\phi$

$[\![(t+u)]\!]_\phi = \{a + b \mid a \in [\![t]\!]_\phi \text{ and } b \in [\![u]\!]_\phi\}$

$[\![\alpha.t]\!]_\phi = \{\alpha a \mid a \in [\![t]\!]_\phi\}$

$[\![\vec{0}_{S(B)}]\!]_\phi = \{\vec{0}\}$, the null vector of the vector space $[\![S(B)]\!]$

$$[\![tu]\!]_\phi = \begin{cases} \{\sum_{i \in I} \alpha_i g_i(a) \mid \sum_{i \in I} \alpha_i g_i \in [\![t]\!]_\phi, a \in [\![u]\!]_\phi & \text{If } \Gamma \vdash t : \Psi \Rightarrow A \\ \{\sum_{i \in I, j \in J} \alpha_i \beta_j g_j(c_j) \mid \sum_{i \in I} \alpha_i g_i \in [\![t]\!]_\phi, \sum_{j \in J} \beta_j c_j \in [\![u]\!]_\phi\} & \text{If } \Gamma \vdash t : S(\Psi \Rightarrow A) \end{cases}$$

$[\![\pi_j t]\!]_\phi = \{\bigotimes_{h=1}^{j} b_{hk} \otimes \sum_{i \in P} (\frac{\alpha_i}{\sqrt{\sum_{i \in P} |\alpha_i|^2}})(b_{j+1,i} \otimes \cdots \otimes b_{mi}) \mid \forall i \in P, \forall h, b_{hi} = b_{hk}\}$

where $[\![t]\!]_\phi = \{\sum_{i=1}^{n} \alpha_i (b_{1i} \otimes \cdots \otimes b_{mi})\}$ with $b_{ih} = \left(\begin{smallmatrix}0\\1\end{smallmatrix}\right)$ or $\left(\begin{smallmatrix}1\\0\end{smallmatrix}\right)$

$[\![?.]\!]_\phi = \{f \mid \forall a, b, c \in [\![\mathbb{B}]\!], fabc = b \text{ if } a = \left(\begin{smallmatrix}0\\1\end{smallmatrix}\right) \text{ and } fabc = c \text{ if } a = \left(\begin{smallmatrix}1\\0\end{smallmatrix}\right)\}$

$[\![head\ t]\!]_\phi = \{a_1 \mid a_1 \otimes \cdots \otimes a_n \in [\![t]\!]_\phi, a_1 \in [\![\mathbb{B}]\!]\}$

$[\![tail\ t]\!]_\phi = \{a_2 \otimes \cdots \otimes a_n \mid a_1 \otimes \cdots \otimes a_n \in [\![t]\!]_\phi, a_1 \in [\![\mathbb{B}]\!]\}$

$[\![\Uparrow_{S(A)}^{S(B \otimes C)} t]\!]_\phi = [\![t]\!]_\phi$

Lemma 3. *If $A \preceq B$, then $[\![A]\!] \subseteq [\![B]\!]$.*

Lemma 4. *If $\Gamma \vdash t : A$ and $\phi, x \mapsto S, y \mapsto S \vDash \Gamma$ then $[\![t]\!]_{\phi, x \mapsto S, y \mapsto S} = [\![(x/y)t]\!]_{\phi, x \mapsto S}$.*

Theorem 5. *If $\Gamma \vdash t : A$, and $\phi \vDash \Gamma$ then $[\![t]\!]_\phi \subseteq [\![A]\!]$.*

Theorem 6. *If $\Gamma \vdash t : A$, $\phi \vDash \Gamma$, and $t \longrightarrow_{(p_i)} r_i$, with $\sum_i p_i = 1$, then $[\![t]\!]_\phi = \bigcup_i [\![r_i]\!]_\phi$.*

5   Example: The Teleportation Algorithm

In this section we show that our language is expressive enough to express the Teleportation algorithm. The circuit for this algorithm is given in Fig. 1. The Hadamard gate (H) produces $\frac{1}{\sqrt{2}}.(|0\rangle + |1\rangle)$ when applied to $|0\rangle$ and $\frac{1}{\sqrt{2}}.(|0\rangle - |1\rangle)$ when applied to $|1\rangle$. Hence, it can be implemented with the if-then-else construction: $\mathsf{H} = \lambda x : \mathbb{B} \frac{1}{\sqrt{2}}.(|0\rangle + (x?(-|1\rangle).|1\rangle))$. Notice that the

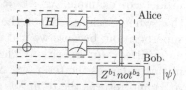

Fig. 1. Teleportation circuit

abstracted variable has a base type (i.e. non-linear). Hence, if H is applied to a superposition, say $(\alpha.|0\rangle + \beta.|1\rangle)$, it reduces, as expected, in the following way: $\mathsf{H}(\alpha.|0\rangle + \beta.|1\rangle) \xrightarrow{(\mathsf{lin}_r^+)}_{(1)} (\mathsf{H}\alpha.|0\rangle + \mathsf{H}\beta.|1\rangle) \xrightarrow{(\mathsf{lin}_r^\alpha)^2}_{(1)} (\alpha.\mathsf{H}|0\rangle + \beta.\mathsf{H}|1\rangle)$, and then is applied to the base terms. The *cnot* gate, which applies *not* to the second qubit only when the first qubit is $|1\rangle$, can be implemented with an if-then-else construction as follows: $\mathsf{cnot} = \lambda x : \mathbb{B} \otimes \mathbb{B} ((head\ x) \otimes ((head\ x)?(\mathsf{not}\ (tail\ x)).(tail\ x)))$. We define H_1^3 to apply H to the first qubit of a three-qubit system. $\mathsf{H}_1^3 = \lambda x :$

$\mathbb{B} \otimes \mathbb{B} \otimes \mathbb{B}$ ((H (head x)) $\otimes$ (tail x)). In addition, we need to apply cnot to the two first qubits, so we define cnot^3_{12} as $\mathsf{cnot}^3_{12} = \lambda x : \mathbb{B} \otimes \mathbb{B} \otimes \mathbb{B}$ ((cnot (head x $\otimes$ (head tail x)))$\otimes$(tail tail x)). The Z gate returns $|0\rangle$ when it receives $|0\rangle$, and $-|1\rangle$ when it receives $|1\rangle$. Hence, it can be implemented by: $\mathsf{Z} = \lambda x : \mathbb{B}$ $(x?(-|1\rangle)\cdot|0\rangle)$. The Bob side of the algorithm will apply Z and/or *not* according to the bits it receives from Alice. Hence, for any $\vdash \mathsf{U} : \mathbb{B} \Rightarrow S(\mathbb{B})$ or $\vdash \mathsf{U} : \mathbb{B} \Rightarrow \mathbb{B}$, we define $\mathsf{U}^{(b)}$ to be the function which depending on the value of a base qubit b applies the U gate or not: $\mathsf{U}^{(b)} = (\lambda x : \mathbb{B} \; \lambda y : \mathbb{B} \; (x?\mathsf{U}y\cdot y)) \; b$. Alice and Bob parts of the algorithm are defined separately. $\mathsf{Alice} = \lambda x : S(\mathbb{B}) \otimes S(\mathbb{B} \otimes \mathbb{B})(\pi_2(\Uparrow^{S(\mathbb{B} \otimes \mathbb{B} \otimes \mathbb{B})}_{S(S(\mathbb{B}) \otimes \mathbb{B} \otimes \mathbb{B})}$ $\mathsf{H}^3_1 \; (\mathsf{cnot}^3_{12} \; \Uparrow^{S(\mathbb{B} \otimes \mathbb{B} \otimes \mathbb{B})}_{S(\mathbb{B} \otimes S(\mathbb{B} \otimes \mathbb{B}))} \Uparrow^{S(\mathbb{B} \otimes S(\mathbb{B} \otimes \mathbb{B}))}_{S(S(\mathbb{B}) \otimes \mathbb{B} \otimes S(\mathbb{B} \otimes \mathbb{B}))} \; x)))$. Notice that before passing to cnot^3_{12} the parameter of type $S(\mathbb{B}) \otimes S(\mathbb{B} \otimes \mathbb{B})$, we need to fully develop the term using the two casts, and again, after the Hadamard gate. Bob side is implemented by $\mathsf{Bob} = \lambda x : \mathbb{B} \otimes \mathbb{B} \otimes \mathbb{B}$ ($\mathsf{Z}^{(head \; x)}(\mathsf{not}^{(head \; tail \; x)} \; (tail \; tail \; x)))$.

The teleportation is applied to an arbitrary qubit and to the following Bell state $\beta_{00} = (\frac{1}{\sqrt{2}}.|0\rangle \otimes |0\rangle + \frac{1}{\sqrt{2}}.|1\rangle \otimes |1\rangle)$ and it is defined by $\mathsf{Teleportation} = \lambda q : S(\mathbb{B})$ $(\mathsf{Bob}(\Uparrow^{S(\mathbb{B} \otimes \mathbb{B} \otimes \mathbb{B})}_{S(\mathbb{B} \otimes \mathbb{B} \otimes S(\mathbb{B}))} \; \mathsf{Alice} \; (q \otimes \beta_{00})))$.

This term is typed, as expected, by: $\vdash \mathsf{Teleportation} : S(\mathbb{B}) \Rightarrow S(\mathbb{B})$ and applying the teleportation to any superposition $(\alpha.|0\rangle + \beta.|1\rangle)$ will reduce, as expected, to $(\alpha.|0\rangle + \beta.|1\rangle)$.

6   Conclusion

In this paper we have proposed a way to unify logic-linear and algebraic-linear quantum λ-calculi, by interpreting λ-terms as linear functions when they expect duplicable data and as non-linear ones when they do not, and illustrated this idea with the definition of a calculus.

This calculus is first-order in the sense that variables do not have functional types. In a higher-order version we should expect abstractions to be clonable. But, allowing cloning abstractions allows cloning superpositions, by hiding them inside. For example, $\lambda x : \mathbb{B} \Rightarrow \mathbb{B}$ $(\frac{1}{\sqrt{2}}.|0\rangle + \frac{1}{\sqrt{2}}.|1\rangle)$. It has been argued [4,5] that what is cloned is not the superposition but a function that creates the superposition, because we had no way there to create such an abstraction from an arbitrary superposition. The situation is different in the calculus presented in this paper as the term $\lambda x : S(\mathbb{B}) \; \lambda y : \mathbb{B} \; x$ precisely takes any term t of type $S(\mathbb{B})$ and returns the term $\lambda y : \mathbb{B} \; t$. So, a cloning machine could be constructed by encapsulating any superposition t under a lambda, which transform it into a basis term, so a clonable term. Extending this calculus to the higher-order will require characterizing precisely the abstractions that can be taken as arguments, not allowing to duplicate functions creating superpositions.

Acknowledgements. We would like to thank Eduardo Bonelli, Luca Paolini, Simona Ronchi della Rocca and Luca Roversi for interesting comments and suggestions.

References

1. Abramsky, S.: Computational interpretations of linear logic. Theor. Comput. Sci. **111**(1), 3–57 (1993)
2. Altenkirch, T., Grattage, J.: A functional quantum programming language. In: Proceedings of LICS 2005, pp. 249–258. IEEE (2005)
3. Arrighi, P., Díaz-Caro, A.: A system F accounting for scalars. Logical Methods in Computer Science 8(1:11) (2012)
4. Arrighi, P., Díaz-Caro, A., Valiron, B.: The vectorial lambda-calculus. Inf. Comput. **254**(1), 105–139 (2017)
5. Arrighi, P., Dowek, G.: Lineal: a linear-algebraic lambda-calculus. Logical Methods in Computer Science 13(1:8) (2017)
6. Assaf, A., Díaz-Caro, A., Perdrix, S., Tasson, C., Valiron, B.: Call-by-value, call-by-name and the vectorial behaviour of the algebraic λ-calculus. Logical Methods in Computer Science 10(4:8) (2014)
7. Barber, A.: Dual intuitionistic linear logic. Technical report ECS-LFCS-96-347, The Laboratory for Foundations of Computer Science, University of Edinburgh (1996)
8. Díaz-Caro, A., Petit, B.: Linearity in the non-deterministic call-by-value setting. In: Ong, L., de Queiroz, R. (eds.) WoLLIC 2012. LNCS, vol. 7456, pp. 216–231. Springer, Heidelberg (2012). https://doi.org/10.1007/978-3-642-32621-9_16
9. Girard, J.Y.: Linear logic. Theor. Comput. Sci. **50**, 1–102 (1987)
10. Green, A.S., Lumsdaine, P.L., Ross, N.J., Selinger, P., Valiron, B.: Quipper: a scalable quantum programming language. In: ACM SIGPLAN Notices (PLDI 2013), vol. 48, no. 6, pp. 333–342 (2013)
11. Pagani, M., Selinger, P., Valiron, B.: Applying quantitative semantics to higher-order quantum computing. In: ACM SIGPLAN Notices (POPL 2014), vol. 49, no. 1, pp. 647–658 (2014)
12. Peterson, G.E., Stickel, M.E.: Complete sets of reductions for some equational theories. J. ACM **28**(2), 233–264 (1981)
13. Selinger, P., Valiron, B.: Quantum lambda calculus. In: Gay, S., Mackie, I. (eds.) Semantic Techniques in Quantum Computation, pp. 135–172. Cambridge University Press, Cambridge (2009). Chapter 9
14. Zorzi, M.: On quantum lambda calculi: a foundational perspective. Math. Struct. Comput. Sci. **26**(7), 1107–1195 (2016)

Heat-Bath Algorithmic Cooling
with Correlated-Qubits Relaxation

Raymond Laflamme[1,2,3,4] (iD), Tal Mor[5] (iD),
Nayeli A. Rodríguez-Briones[1,2,3] (iD), and Yossi Weinstein[5(✉)] (iD)

[1] Institute for Quantum Computing, University of Waterloo,
Waterloo, ON N2L 3G1, Canada
[2] Department of Physics and Astronomy, University of Waterloo,
Waterloo, ON N2L 3G1, Canada
[3] Perimeter Institute for Theoretical Physics,
31 Caroline Street North, Waterloo, ON N2L 2Y5, Canada
narodrig@uwaterloo.ca
[4] Canadian Institute for Advanced Research,
Toronto, ON M5G 1Z8, Canada
laflamme@uwaterloo.ca
[5] Computer Science Department, Technion – Israel Institute of Technology,
3200003 Haifa, Israel
talmo@cs.technion.ac.il, yossiv@cs.technion.ac.il

Abstract. Pure states are needed for many quantum algorithms and
in particular for quantum error correction. Algorithmic cooling has been
shown to purify qubits by a controlled redistribution of entropy and multiple contact with a heat-bath. In previous heat-bath algorithmic cooling work, it was assumed that each qubit undergoes thermal relaxation
independently. In this paper we remove this constraint, and introduce an
additional tool for cooling algorithms which we call "state-reset". State-
reset can occur when the coupling to the environment is generalized from
individual-qubits relaxation to correlated-qubits relaxation. We present
several improved cooling algorithms which lead to an increase of polarization beyond the ones all previous work believed to be optimal, and we
relate our results to an effect in chemical physics, known as the Nuclear
Overhauser Effect.

Keywords: Algorithmic cooling · Nuclear Overhauser Effect
Fault-tolerant quantum computing

1 Introduction

Quantum information processing brought novel ways for cooling physical systems by manipulating entropy in an algorithmic way [3,11,26,27]. Understanding these *algorithmic cooling* processes and their cooling limits can elucidate
fundamental theoretical properties of thermodynamics and lead to new experimental possibilities. In particular, these processes have important applications

C. Martín-Vide et al. (Eds.): TPNC 2017, LNCS 10687, pp. 294–304, 2017.
https://doi.org/10.1007/978-3-319-71069-3_23

in quantum computing as they provide a potential solution to the problem of preparing quantum systems with sufficient purity in ensemble implementations [1,2,4,5,9,12,18,19,24]. Algorithmic cooling is mainly useful in ensemble quantum computing implementations. However, it could also be used to increase the purity of initial states up to the fault-tolerance threshold [26] for other technologies. First, for technologies with strong but imperfect projective measurements; and second, for technologies in which purification through contact with the bath does not lead to sufficiently pure qubits. Controlled preparation of nearly pure quantum states is at the core of many quantum algorithms and is essential for a reliable supply of ancilla qubits in quantum error correction. Another potential use of algorithmic cooling is for improving signal to noise ratio in NMR and MRI applications [15] (but see also the limitations analyzed in [6]).

Sørensen [28] was the first to observe the constraint of unitary dynamics to increase the polarization $\epsilon = Tr[\rho Z]$, for the density matrix ρ, and the Pauli operator Z, of a subset of qubits (e.g. spins), at the expense of decreasing the polarization of the complementary spins. In the context of quantum information, Schulman and Vazirani proposed cooling algorithms and used the term "quantum mechanical heat engine" [27], which was inspired by Peres's recursive algorithm [20] of von Neumann's extraction of fair coin flips from a sequence of biased ones [29]. This heat engine carries out a reversible entropy compression process in which an input of energy to the system results in a separation of cold and hot regions. Furthermore, an explicit way to implement entropy compression in ensemble quantum computers (such as in NMR) was given by Schulman and Vazirani [27]. They showed that it is possible to reach polarization of order unity using only a number of qubits that scales as $1/\epsilon_b^2$ for initial polarization $\epsilon_b \ll 1$.

This scheme was generalized by Boykin, Mor, Roychowdhury, Vatan, and Vrijen, by adding contact with a heat bath to cool the qubits that were heated during the process [3]. They termed the generalized process "algorithmic cooling" (AC). To distinguish the two processes, they named the reversible process of Schulman-Vazirani "reversible algorithmic cooling", and the more general process (that may contain many irreversible steps) — "heat-bath algorithmic cooling" (HBAC). Fernandez, Lloyd, Mor and Roychowdhury [11] then showed that for $\epsilon_b \ll 1$ and a relatively small number of qubits (e.g., $n \ll 1/\epsilon_b^2$), the ratio between the final polarization bias and the initial polarization bias may grow exponentially with the number of qubits used during the process, if HBAC is applied, while reversible AC may only improve it by $\sqrt{n}$. Based on those ideas, many algorithms have been designed to purify a set of qubits by removing entropy of a subset of them at the expense of increasing the entropy of others [6,8,10,13,16,25,26]. Beyond the theoretical interest, experiments have demonstrated proof-of-principle of the reversible algorithmic cooling [7] and the heat-bath algorithmic cooling [1,2,18,24], and showed improvement in polarization for a few qubits.

The ultimate cooling limits of HBAC have been studied using a specific algorithm, the Partner Pairing Algorithm (PPA), which was introduced by Schulman, Mor and Weinstein (SMW) [25], and believed to be optimal among all possible reversible AC and HBAC in [26]. For simplicity, the case of n qubits had been analyzed, assuming the ideal case in which just one qubit is strongly coupled with the environment and hence reaches thermal equilibrium rapidly (henceforth "reset qubit"), while the others are hardly influenced by the environment (henceforth "computing qubits"). SMW claimed in the above two papers that the PPA gives the optimal physical cooling in terms of entropy extraction. In particular, this claim means that for just two spins, one computer spin and one reset spin, with identical equilibrium polarization, there is no way to improve the polarization of the computer spin beyond its equilibrium polarization (see also [21,22]), no matter how many reversible steps and re-thermalization steps (henceforth REFRESH steps) one applies. SMW, as well as all HBAC literature, implicitly assume that the reset qubit can only be refreshed independently of the other qubits.

In the original PPA, a reversible entropy compression operation on a string of n qubits always makes a descending ordering (SORT) of the diagonal elements of the system's density matrix. That is, the probabilities of states starting with 0 ($0\ldots00$, $0\ldots01$, etc.) will receive the biggest values of the diagonal elements, while that of states starting with 1 will receive the smallest ones. A sequence of repeated SORT steps, each followed by a REFRESH of the reset spin, increases the polarization of the qubits, leading to the maximal polarization on the first qubit of the string, where the last qubit is the reset qubit. The algorithm always converges to a steady state. The compression can no longer improve the polarization of the first qubit, or any other qubit for that matter, if the diagonal elements of the system's density matrix are already in descending order before the entropy compression step. Hence, there is a range of initial polarizations that cannot be improved by any step of PPA — a range of steady states of PPA [26]. Within that range, an exact steady state of the cooling limit of PPA was recently found and presented in [21,22].

In this work, we present algorithms which lead to an increase in polarization beyond the achievable cooling for the original PPA, thus presenting a different and more powerful HBAC than the PPA. In the original PPA (as well as in all papers discussing and analyzing AC), it was assumed that the reset mechanism can only re-thermalize qubits individually, implying that this mechanism was the *most general possible*. Under this restriction, the qubit-reset is the optimal refresh operation in terms of entropy extraction. In our model we remove this restriction and include correlations between qubits *as they reset*, a mechanism that we call "state-reset". We relate our new HBAC method, which we call *state-reset HBAC*, to the Nuclear Overhauser Effect (NOE) [17]. By comparing NOE on two spins to algorithmic cooling we identified that NOE may be "simulated" if we add two additional mechanisms:

1. reset to the completely mixed state (we call this operation "CMS-reset").
2. state-reset as described below.

The algorithms that we present here combine four "tools": unitary evolution (only SORT is needed here), qubit-reset (REFRESH of individual spins), CMS-reset and state-reset. We name this type of HBAC state-reset-HBAC. We analytically calculate the achievable polarization for the state-reset process combined with SORT as in the original PPA, as a function of the number of qubits, n, and the heat-bath polarization, $\epsilon_b = \tanh\frac{\Delta E}{2k_B T}$, where ΔE is the energy gap between the two states of a qubit, T is the temperature of the heat-bath, and k_B is the Bolzman constant. We present the polarization evolution as a function of the number of algorithm-iterations and we compare these new results with the corresponding ones of the original PPA. We give explicit examples for two, three, and n qubits, with analytical and numerical solutions for low and general bath polarization. Thus, we prove that our generalized PPA algorithm, in which SORT is combined with generalized reset, surpasses the original PPA.

2 PPA versus NOE

The original PPA, using only one reset qubit and a total of n qubits, gives [22] the first qubit an asymptotic polarization of

$$\epsilon_{max} = \frac{(1 + \epsilon_b)^{2^{n-2}} - (1 - \epsilon_b)^{2^{n-2}}}{(1 + \epsilon_b)^{2^{n-2}} + (1 - \epsilon_b)^{2^{n-2}}} \tag{1}$$

where ϵ_b is the thermal equilibrium polarization of each of the spins (the reset spin and the computer spins). Hence it may be regarded as the polarization of the bath. This asymptotic steady state holds for the wide range of initial states in which the polarization bias of each qubit is smaller than $\epsilon_{max} - \delta$, for a very small δ [22]. For example, the completely mixed state is in this range, and was used as the initial state in [26]. For two ($n = 2$ above) qubits (one qubit which is going to be cooled, and one reset qubit), starting in the maximally mixed state, the original PPA gives a steady state with the qubits at the bath temperature and no polarization gain (beyond that of the bath) is observed.

In a recent paper [14], Li et al. studied the efficiency of polarization transfer in the presence of a bath using *vector of coherence representation*. They presented a numerical solution and an experiment that showed polarization enhancement above the bath polarization for two qubits, thus bypassing the optimal cooling allowed by the original PPA. The surprising improvement turns out to be related to the NOE discovered in 1953 [17]: It appears that in the presence of cross-relaxation, the polarization of one qubit can be boosted beyond the original PPA limit. The boost of the polarization (of the computer qubit) appears when the second one (the reset qubit) is saturated, i.e. rotated rapidly so that over relevant timescale its polarization averages to zero. This can be predicted by the Solomon equation, see a preliminary extended version of this paper in [23]. The effect relies on cross-relaxation (see Γ_2 in Fig. 1) and cannot be understood as a simple swap of the polarization of the hot qubits with the polarization of the bath (the most general relaxation mechanism allowed in the original PPA).

Understanding this effect from quantum information processing point of view seems vital, as this observation seems to contradict the optimality proof of SMW. Analyzing this effect also allows merging NOE into HBAC, thus yielding a stronger PPA, potentially improving over both the original PPA and the two-spins NOE. The way to understand the process from an algorithmic point of view

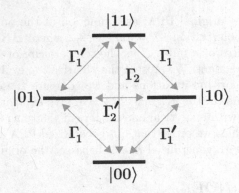

Fig. 1. Relaxation diagram for a two qubit system. The various Γ are the population-exchange rates between the corresponding states. The process illustrated as Γ_2 ($|00\rangle \leftrightarrow |11\rangle$) cannot be described as a qubit-reset with the bath as in the PPA, and results in the boost of polarization of one qubit when the other is saturated.

is to realize that the cross-relaxation effectively provides a new form of relaxation that had not been taken into account in [25, 26] and in other theoretical analysis of HBAC. For a system of two spins, such state-relaxation ("state-reset") means re-thermalization between $|00\rangle$ and $|11\rangle$, while leaving other states intact for some time. To achieve this, the state-reset, and algorithms which utilize it, are limited to case where Γ_2 is much larger than the other relaxation rate. In NMR this is termed "double-quantum transition", instead of a "qubit-reset" as in the PPA. We now show, using the language of quantum information processing, that this form of state-reset, accompanied by a "reset to the completely-mixed-state" (that we abbreviate as "CMS-reset") of the second qubit (the reset spin) can boost the polarization of the first qubit. This boost, not predicted by the original PPA, is thus beyond what would be obtained solely by unitary transformations (simply named here "rotations") and qubit-reset. Therefore the PPA, already for two qubits, does not give the maximum polarization achievable for HBAC.

It is also possible to generalize this idea to increase the polarization of a qubit in a larger n–qubit system, by an n–qubit designated algorithm — generalizing the PPA to contain, in addition to SORT steps and qubit-reset, also state-reset and CMS-reset steps.

3   Two-Qubit Analysis — Cooling Beyond the Original PPA

Here we show that we can represent the NOE process solely via the iteration of two operations, with no additional unitary transformation: the CMS operation (i.e. CMS-reset) that simulates the saturation of the second (reset) qubit, and Γ_2 for the state-reset of the system between the states $|00\rangle$ and $|11\rangle$, see Fig. 2. For simplicity, consider a system of two homonuclear spins. Let the system start in thermal equilibrium with polarization ϵ_b, hence, the initial state is $\rho_0^{\otimes 2} = \frac{1}{2}\begin{bmatrix} 1+\epsilon_b & 0 \\ 0 & 1-\epsilon_b \end{bmatrix}^{\otimes 2}$. This state can be represented by the diagonal of its density matrix, $diag\left(\rho_0^{\otimes 2}\right)$. For low polarization $\epsilon_b \ll 1$, this diagonal is approximately $\frac{1}{4}(1+2\epsilon_b, 1, 1, 1-2\epsilon_b)$. This state will evolve as follows, under two iterations of the two mentioned steps (see Fig. 2 and [23]):

$$
\begin{aligned}
diag\left(\rho_0^{\otimes 2}\right) &= \frac{1}{4}\left(1 + 2\epsilon_b, 1, 1, 1 - 2\epsilon_b\right) \\
&\xrightarrow{CMS(2)} \frac{1}{2}\left(1 + \epsilon_b, 1 - \epsilon_b\right) \otimes \frac{1}{2}(1, 1) \\
&= \frac{1}{4}\left(1 + \epsilon_b, 1 + \epsilon_b, 1 - \epsilon_b, 1 - \epsilon_b\right) \\
&\xrightarrow{\Gamma_2} \frac{1}{4}\left(1 + 2\epsilon_b, 1 + \epsilon_b, 1 - \epsilon_b, 1 - 2\epsilon_b\right) \\
&\xrightarrow{CMS(2)} \frac{1}{4}\left(1 + \frac{3}{2}\epsilon_b, 1 - \frac{3}{2}\epsilon_b\right) \otimes \frac{1}{2}(1, 1) \\
&= \frac{1}{4}\left(1 + \frac{3}{2}\epsilon_b, 1 + \frac{3}{2}\epsilon_b, 1 - \frac{3}{2}\epsilon_b, 1 - \frac{3}{2}\epsilon_b\right) \\
&\xrightarrow{\Gamma_2} \frac{1}{4}\left(1 + 2\epsilon_b, 1 + \frac{3}{2}\epsilon_b, 1 - \frac{3}{2}\epsilon_b, 1 - 2\epsilon_b\right),
\end{aligned}
\tag{2}
$$

where $CMS(2)$ stands for the saturation process of the second qubit, and Γ_2 resets the ratio of the probabilities of the states $|00\rangle$ and $|11\rangle$ from $\frac{1+x}{1-x}$ to their thermal equilibrium ratio $\frac{1+2\epsilon_b}{1-2\epsilon_b}$.

From Eq. (2), we can see that the polarization of the first qubit has an enhancement of $3/2$ after the first round, and of $7/4$ after the second round, and so on. This enhancement grows asymptotically to a fixed point, corresponding to the polarization ϵ_{NOE}^∞. I.e., in the limit of the algorithm, after applying an iteration,

$$
\begin{aligned}
&\frac{1}{2}\left(1 + \epsilon_{NOE}^\infty, 1 - \epsilon_{NOE}^\infty\right) \otimes \frac{1}{2}(1, 1) \\
&\xrightarrow{\Gamma_2} \frac{1}{4}\left(1 + 2\epsilon_b, 1 + \epsilon_{NOE}^\infty, 1 - \epsilon_{NOE}^\infty, 1 - 2\epsilon_b\right) \\
&\xrightarrow{CMS} \frac{1}{2}\left(1 + \frac{2\epsilon_b + \epsilon_{NOE}^\infty}{2}, 1 - \frac{2\epsilon_b + \epsilon_{NOE}^\infty}{2}\right) \otimes \frac{1}{2}(1, 1)
\end{aligned}
\tag{3}
$$

the polarization of the first qubit should remain the same. Thus, $\epsilon_{NOE}^\infty = \frac{2\epsilon_b + \epsilon_{NOE}^\infty}{2}$, in $\epsilon_{NOE}^\infty = 2\epsilon_b$, yielding exactly the same enhancement as obtained from the Solomon equations [23].

See Fig. 2 for the NOE-process yielding polarization of $2\epsilon_b$. If combined with a final step of relaxation of the reset spin then the process is described in Fig. 3. We name this simple algorithm "2-qubit-state-reset HBAC" and it will be used as a subroutine when cooling a string of more qubits. For the string of (two) qubits, where the reset spin is the rightmost bit, the obtained probabilities for each spin to be in state $|0\rangle$ are $\{(1 + 2\epsilon_b)/2, (1 + \epsilon_b)/2\}$ representing a diagonal matrix $\rho_{(\mathrm{Final-NOE})}$, that can be denoted more simply using the shifted-and-scaled diagonal terms $\{2, 1\}$ in units of ϵ_b, for the string of (two) qubits.

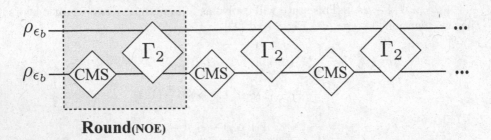

Round(NOE)

Fig. 2. Circuit of the NOE process on two qubits, presented via quantum information processing terminology. Γ_2 is the state-reset operation on two qubits, and CMS is the "reset to a completely mixed state" of the reset spin, respectively. The part inside the dotted box represents a single round, and the entire circuit is just the repetition of that round. The entire circuit, when repeated a sufficient number of times, represents the NOE process in which the cross relaxation is effective during the saturation process applied onto the reset spin.

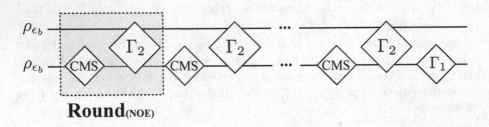

Round(NOE)

Fig. 3. Circuit of the NOE process followed by a reset (Γ_1) step on the reset spin, as the final step of this two-qubit cooling algorithm which we name "2-qubit state-reset HBAC".

4   Precise Calculation for the NOE Process

We now generalize our calculation to initial polarizations of any size between 0 and 1. For any $0 < \epsilon_b < 1$, let $\epsilon_b = \tanh(\xi)$. The operation Γ_2, applied to an initial density-matrix diagonal of a 2-qubit-system, produces

$$[A_1, A_2, A_3, A_4]$$
$$\xrightarrow{\Gamma_2} [(A_1 + A_4)p_2, A_2, A_3, (A_1 + A_4)(1 - p_2)], \tag{4}$$

where $p_2 = \frac{e^{2\xi}}{2\cosh 2\xi}$ is the population of state $|00\rangle$ at thermal equilibrium with the heat bath ($e^{2\xi}/N$), normalized by the sum of thermal populations of both states $|00\rangle$ and $|11\rangle$ (i.e. $N = e^{2\xi} + e^{2\xi} = 2\cosh 2\xi$); and so $1 - p_2$ is the complementary population of $|11\rangle$ at thermal equilibrium. For the initial diagonal of Eq. 3,

$$\frac{1}{2}\left(1 + \epsilon_{NOE}^{\infty}, 1 - \epsilon_{NOE}^{\infty}\right) \otimes \frac{1}{2}(1,1)$$

$$\xrightarrow{\Gamma_2} \frac{1}{4}\left(2p_2, 1 + \epsilon_{NOE}^{\infty}, 1 - \epsilon_{NOE}^{\infty}, 2(1 - p_2)\right) \tag{5}$$

$$\xrightarrow{CMS} \frac{1}{2}\left(\frac{1 + 2p_2 + \epsilon_{NOE}^{\infty}}{2}, \frac{3 - 2p_2 - \epsilon_{NOE}^{\infty}}{2}\right) \otimes \frac{1}{2}(1,1).$$

The assymptotic polarization should hence obey

$$2p_2 = \frac{1 + 2p_2 + \epsilon_{NOE}^{\infty}}{2}$$

$$\Rightarrow \epsilon_{NOE}^{\infty} = 2p_2 - 1 = \tanh 2\xi \tag{6}$$

5   The 3 Qubit Case

For the case of small initial polarizations it is trivial to show that the subroutine 2-qubit-state-reset-HBAC may be used to cool a three qubit string, where the rightmost bit is the reset spin, to $\{3, 2, 1\}$ in units of ϵ_b. When starting from thermal equilibrium $\{1, 1, 1\}$, this is done by using the 2-qubit-state-reset-HBAC subroutine onto the two rightmost bits (yielding $\{1, 2, 1\}$), followed by a SORT step (in this case of just three qubits — known as 3-bit-compression), to cool the leftmost bit to 2, then another 2-qubit-state-reset-HBAC (yielding $\{2, 2, 1\}$). Repeating these two steps once more yields $\{2.5, 2, 1\}$, and another repetition yields $\{2.75, 2, 1\}$.

We can see that the polarization of the first qubit has an enhancement of 2 after the first round, of 2.5 after the second round, of 2.75 after the third round, and so on. This enhancement grows asymptotically to a fixed point, corresponding to the polarization ϵ^{∞} for the rightmost bit when there are 3 qubits. I.e., in the limit of the algorithm, after applying an iteration,

$$\frac{1}{2}\left(1 + \epsilon^{\infty}, 1 - \epsilon^{\infty}\right) \otimes \rho_{(\text{Final} - \text{NOE})}$$

$$\xrightarrow{2 - \text{qubit} - \text{state} - \text{reset} - \text{HBAC}} \tag{7}$$

$$\frac{1}{2}\left(1 + \frac{3\epsilon_b + \epsilon^{\infty}}{2}, 1 - \frac{3\epsilon_b + \epsilon^{\infty}}{2}\right) \otimes \rho_{(\text{Final} - \text{NOE})}$$

the polarization of the coldest qubit should remain the same. Thus, $\epsilon^{\infty} = \frac{3\epsilon_b + \epsilon^{\infty}}{2}$, in $\epsilon^{\infty} = 3\epsilon_b$, yielding the final string polarization $\{3, 2, 1\}$.

6 The n Qubit Case

Using the same process as above, and with 3-bit-compression, it is easy to obtain a Fibonacci-like series — $\{...13, 8, 5, 3, 2, 1\}$; note the only advantage over the SMW-Fibonacci result [8, 26] is that the above is somewhat better than $\{...8, 5, 3, 2, 1, 1\}$ with the same number of qubits.

Finally, we show how to get the limit — yielding $\{...24, 12, 6, 3, 2, 1\}$; and again, the above is somewhat better than the original PPA, namely $\{...16, 8, 4, 2, 1, 1\}$. This is done by using a SORT rather than 3-bit-compression, as in the original PPA [8, 26].

7 Conclusion

In conclusion, we have presented a new HBAC technique and a new PPA-and-NOE based algorithm, that can have a better polarization enhancement than the achievable cooling for the original PPA, for any number of qubits, bypassing what was believed to be the optimal cooling. That enhancement is achievable when the coupling to the environment is not limited to qubit-resets, but could also include correlations between the qubits during thermalization. We called that "state-reset". We calculated the maximum polarization for this new method as a function of the number of qubits, n, and as a function of the polarization in the equilibrium, ϵ_b. Also, we presented the polarization evolution as a function of the number of algorithm-iterations and we made a comparison between these new results, and the corresponding ones of the original PPA.

In the full paper [23] we show that, unlike the original PPA, SORT combined with generalized reset is also not optimal once one allows to replace the SORT by a different entropy-redistribution operation.

Acknowledgments. The authors would like to thank Jun Li, Xinhua Peng, Xian Ma, Aharon Brodutch, Osama Moussa, Daniel Park, David Cory, Om Patange, and David Layden for insightful discussions. N.A. R.-B. is supported by CONACYT-COZCYT and the Mike and Ophelia Lazaridis Fellowship program. R. L. is supported by Industry Canada, the government of Ontario, CIFAR and the U.S. Army Research Laboratory. R. L., T. M. and Y. M. thank the Schwartz/Reisman Foundation.

References

1. Atia, Y., Elias, Y., Mor, T., Weinstein, Y.: Algorithmic cooling in liquid-state nuclear magnetic resonance. Phys. Rev. A **93**, 012325 (2016)
2. Baugh, J., Moussa, O., Ryan, C.A., Nayak, A., Laflamme, R.: Experimental implementation of heat-bath algorithmic cooling using solid-state nuclear magnetic resonance. Nature **438**(7067), 470–473 (2005)
3. Boykin, P.O., Mor, T., Roychowdhury, V., Vatan, F., Vrijen, R.: Algorithmic cooling and scalable NMR quantum computers. Proc. Natl. Acad. Sci. **99**(6), 3388–3393 (2002)

4. Brassard, G., Elias, Y., Fernandez, J.M., Gilboa, H., Jones, J.A., Mor, T., Weinstein, Y., Xiao, L.: Experimental heat-bath cooling of spins. arXiv preprint quant-ph/0511156 (2005)
5. Brassard, G., Elias, Y., Fernandez, J.M., Gilboa, H., Jones, J.A., Mor, T., Weinstein, Y., Xiao, L.: Experimental heat-bath cooling of spins. Eur. Phys. J. Plus **129**, 266 (2014)
6. Brassard, G., Elias, Y., Mor, T., Weinstein, Y.: Prospects and limitations of algorithmic cooling. Eur. Phys. J. Plus **129**(11), 1–16 (2014)
7. Chang, D., Vandersypen, L., Steffen, M.: NMR implementation of a building block for scalable quantum computation. Chem. Phys. Lett. **338**(4–6), 337 (2001)
8. Elias, Y., Fernandez, J.M., Mor, T., Weinstein, Y.: Optimal algorithmic cooling of spins. In: Akl, S.G., Calude, C.S., Dinneen, M.J., Rozenberg, G., Wareham, H.T. (eds.) UC 2007. LNCS, vol. 4618, pp. 2–26. Springer, Heidelberg (2007). https://doi.org/10.1007/978-3-540-73554-0_2
9. Elias, Y., Gilboa, H., Mor, T., Weinstein, Y.: Heat-bath cooling of spins in two amino acids. Chem. Phys. Lett. **517**(4), 126–131 (2011)
10. Elias, Y., Mor, T., Weinstein, Y.: Semioptimal practicable algorithmic cooling. Phys. Rev. A **83**(4), 042340 (2011)
11. Fernandez, J.M., Lloyd, S., Mor, T., Roychowdhury, V.: Algorithmic cooling of spins: a practicable method for increasing polarization. Int. J. Quantum Inf. **2**(04), 461–477 (2004)
12. Fernandez, J.M., Mor, T., Weinstein, Y.: Paramagnetic materials and practical algorithmic cooling for NMR quantum computing. Int. J. Quantum Inf. **3**(1), 281–285 (2005)
13. Kaye, P.: Cooling algorithms based on the 3-bit majority. Quantum Inf. Process. **6**(4), 295–322 (2007)
14. Li, J., Lu, D., Luo, Z., Laflamme, R., Peng, X., Du, J.: Maximally accessible purity in coherently controlled open quantum systems: application to quantum state engineering. Phys. Rev. A **94**(3), 032316 (2016)
15. Mor, T., Fernandez, J.M., Lloyd, S., Mor, T., Roychowdhury, V., Weinstein, Y.: Algorithmic cooling. USA PATENT (US6873154 B2) (2005)
16. Moussa, O.: On heat-bath algorithmic cooling and its implementation in solid-state NMR. Master of Science in Physics thesis, University of Waterloo (2005)
17. Overhauser, A.W.: Paramagnetic relaxation in metals. Phys. Rev. **89**(4), 689 (1953)
18. Park, D.K., Feng, G., Rahimi, R., Labruyere, S., Shibata, T., Nakazawa, S., Sato, K., Takui, T., Laflamme, R., Baugh, J.: Hyperfine spin qubits in irradiated malonic acid: heat-bath algorithmic cooling. Quantum Inf. Process. **14**(7), 2435–2461 (2015)
19. Park, D.K., Rodriguez-Briones, N.A., Feng, G., Rahimi, R., Baugh, J., Laflamme, R.: Heat bath algorithmic cooling with spins: review and prospects. In: Takui, T., Berliner, L., Hanson, G. (eds.) Electron Spin Resonance (ESR) Based Quantum Computing. BMR, vol. 31, pp. 227–255. Springer, New York (2016). https://doi.org/10.1007/978-1-4939-3658-8_8
20. Peres, Y.: Iterating von Neumann's procedure for extracting random bits. Ann. Statist. **20**(1), 590–597 (1992)
21. Raeisi, S., Mosca, M.: Asymptotic bound for heat-bath algorithmic cooling. Phys. Rev. Lett. **114**(10), 100404 (2015)
22. Rodríguez-Briones, N.A., Laflamme, R.: Achievable polarization for heat-bath algorithmic cooling. Phys. Rev. Lett. **116**, 170501 (2016)

23. Rodriguez-Briones, N.A., Li, J., Peng, X., Mor, T., Weinstein, Y., Laflamme, R.: Heat-bath algorithmic cooling with correlated qubit-environment interactions. To appear in New Journal of Physics (2017). arXiv preprint arXiv:1703.02999 [quant-ph]
24. Ryan, C.A., Moussa, O., Baugh, J., Laflamme, R.: Spin based heat engine: demonstration of multiple rounds of algorithmic cooling. Phys. Rev. Lett. **100**(14), 140501 (2008)
25. Schulman, L.J., Mor, T., Weinstein, Y.: Physical limits of heat-bath algorithmic cooling. Phys. Rev. Lett. **94**(12), 120501 (2005)
26. Schulman, L.J., Mor, T., Weinstein, Y.: Physical limits of heat-bath algorithmic cooling. SIAM J. Comput. **36**(6), 1729–1747 (2007)
27. Schulman, L.J., Vazirani, U.V.: Molecular scale heat engines and scalable quantum computation. In: Proceedings of the 31st Annual ACM Symposium on Theory of Computing (STOC), pp. 322–329. ACM (1999)
28. Sørensen, O.W.: The entropy bound as a limiting case of the universal bound on spin dynamics. polarization transfer in $I_N S_M$ spin systems. J. Magn. Resonance (1969) **93**(3), 648–652 (1991)
29. Von Neumann, J.: Various techniques used in connection with random digits. Natl. Bur. Stand. Appl. Math. Ser. **12**, 36–38 (1951)

Time-Space Complexity Advantages
for Quantum Computing

Shenggen Zheng[1], Daowen Qiu[1(✉)], and Jozef Gruska[2]

[1] School of Data and Computer Science, Institute of Computer Science Theory,
Sun Yat-sen University, Guangzhou 510006, China
zhengshg@mail2.sysu.edu.cn, issqdw@mail.sysu.edu.cn
[2] Faculty of Informatics, Masaryk University, 602 00 Brno, Czech Republic
gruska@fi.muni.cz

Abstract. It has been proved that quantum computing has advantages in query complexity, communication complexity and also other computing models. However, it is hard to prove strictly that quantum computing has advantage in the Turing machine models in time complexity. For example, we do not know how to prove that Shor's algorithm is strictly better than any classical algorithm, since we do not know the lower bound of time complexity of the factoring problem in Turing machine. In this paper, we consider the *time-space complexity* and prove strictly that quantum computing has advantages compared to their classical counterparts. We prove: (1) a time-space upper bound for recognition of the languages $L_{INT}(n)$ on *two-way finite automata with quantum and classical states* (2QCFA): $TS = \mathbf{O}(n^{3/2} \log n)$, whereas a lower bound on probabilistic Turing machine is $TS = \mathbf{\Omega}(n^2)$; (2) a time-space upper bound for recognition of the languages $L_{NE}(n)$ on exact 2QCFA: $TS = \mathbf{O}(n^{1.87} \log n)$, whereas a lower bound on probabilistic Turing machine is $TS = \mathbf{\Omega}(n^2)$.

It has been proved (Klauck, STOC'00) that the exact one-way quantum finite automata have no advantage comparing to classical finite automata in recognizing languages. However, the result (2) shows that the exact 2QCFA do have an advantage in comparison with their classical counterparts, which is the first example showing that the exact quantum computing has advantage in time-space complexity comparing to classical computing.

Keywords: Quantum computing · Time-space complexity

This work was supported by the National Natural Science Foundation of China (Nos. 61572532, 61272058, 61602532), the Fundamental Research Funds for the Central Universities of China (Nos. 17lgjc24, 161gpy43, 17lgzd29) and the National Natural Science Foundation of Guangdong Province of China (Nos. 2017B030311011, 2017A030313378) and Qiu is partially funded by FCT project UID/EEA/50008/2013.

C. Martín-Vide et al. (Eds.): TPNC 2017, LNCS 10687, pp. 305–317, 2017.
https://doi.org/10.1007/978-3-319-71069-3_24

1 Introduction

Time-space complexity is a natural and interesting research topics for computation and communication, see for example [9, 10, 20, 21] with respect to various computing models. Since it is hard to prove that quantum computing have advantage in time complexity, we try to show the advantage in time-space complexity. We start our proof from the model of finite automata, which is a very restricted model of Turing machine. In the case of two-way finite automata, there is not previous work on their time-space complexity as far as we know. Mostly only their time complexity or state complexity (space complexity) has been investigated.

One way to present insights obtained this way is to consider language recognition and time and space as related to the length of input. In this paper we take another approach and demonstrate that it can provide also interesting and important results. Namely, time and space are here related to the parameter n in the language specification. It is clear that it can be transformed into the length of the input is $O(n)$ in the corresponding Turing machine. The space used by the automaton refers to the number of (qu)bits required to represent an arbitrary automaton state [5].

When just time complexity or state complexity (space complexity) of two-way finite automata to recognize some special languages (such as the languages we defined in this paper) are considered, it seems that quantum finite automata have no advantages at all compared to their classical counterparts. However, quite surprisingly, when time-space complexity is considered, then advantages of quantum variations of the classical models can be demonstrated as shown in this paper.

Time-space complexity considered in this paper will be closely related to the communication complexity. Indeed, in this paper we will use communication complexity results to derive time-space upper-bounds for two-way finite automata. We prove that the time-space complexity for recognizing some languages in two-way finite automata with quantum and classical states (2QCFA) [4] are better than in probabilistic Turing machine (PTM). We prove also that probabilistic two-way quantum finite automata (2PFA) [13] are better than deterministic Turing machine (DTM) in time-space complexity in recognizing some special languages.

Since Yao [26] introduced the topic of communication complexity, it has been studied very intensively in various settings [22]. The most basic one, used also here, is the following one. One party, say Alice, gets an $x \in \{0,1\}^n$, the second party, say Bob, gets another string, say $y \in \{0,1\}^n$ and they have to compute value of a given Boolean function $f : \{0,1\}^n \times \{0,1\}^n \to \{0,1\}$ using local computations and communications using as small number of (qu)bits as possible. In this setting local computations are considered as free, but communications as expensive and have to be minimized.

Two of the most basic and most often explored communication problems are that of equality and intersection [22]. They are defined as follows: (1) **Equality**: $EQ(x, y) = 1$ if $x = y$ and 0 otherwise. (2) **Intersection**: $INT(x, y) = 1$ if there is an index i such that $x_i = y_i = 1$ and 0 otherwise.

We describe main results of the paper here. Their full proofs will be given in the section afterwards.

Let us consider the following language over the alphabet $\Sigma = \{0, 1, \#\}$:

$$L_{EQ}(n) = \{x\#^n y \mid x, y \in \{0, 1\}^n, EQ(x, y) = 1\}.$$

It is clear that 2DFA (therefore also 2PFA) can recognize $L_{EQ}(n)$. The time complexity of 2DFA recognizing this language is $O(n)$. The state complexity of 2DFA recognizing the language is $O(n^2)$-that is the space used is $O(\log n)$. The time complexity and also the space used of 2PFA recognizing the same language is almost the same. However, when we consider time-space complexity for the language $L_{EQ}(n)$, the situation is very different.

To prove the following theorem we will use a 2PFA to simulate the probabilistic communication protocol from Chap. 1 of [18] for the problem EQ and get an upper bound for the time-space complexity for 2PFA.

Theorem 1. *There is a 2PFA that accepts the language $L_{EQ}(n)$ in the time T using the space S such that $TS = O(n \log n)$.*

Using communication complexity lower bound proof method [22], we can get the following lower bound for time-space complexity for DTM.

Theorem 2. *Let $\mathcal{A}$ be a deterministic Turing machine that accepts the language $L_{EQ}(n)$ in time T using space S. Then, $TS = \Omega(n^2)$.*

In order to prove the time-space complexity advantages of 2QCFA compared to 2PFA, let us consider the following language over the alphabet $\Sigma = \{0, 1, \#\}$:

$$L_{INT}(n) = \{x\#^n y \mid x, y \in \{0, 1\}^n, INT(x, y) = 1\}.$$

In order to prove the next result we use a 2QCFA to simulate the quantum communication protocol from [11] for the problem INT and get an upper bound for the time-space complexity for PTM.

Theorem 3. *There is a 2QCFA that accepts the language $L_{INT}(n)$ in time T using space S such that $TS = O(n^{3/2} \log n)$.*

In order to prove our last main result we will make use of the fact that Buhrman et al. [11] reduced certain quantum communication tasks to computation problems, which is essentially a way to transform quantum query algorithms to quantum communication protocols. More exactly, they showed that if there is a t-query quantum algorithm computing an n-bit Boolean function f with an error ε, then there is a communication protocol with $O(t \log n)$ communication for the function $f(x \wedge y)$ with the same error ε.

The main idea in the proofs of our main results is to transform quantum query algorithms and quantum communication protocols to algorithms for 2QCFA.

In particular, using one of communication complexity lower bound proof methods, we can get the following lower bound for the time-space complexity for the language $L_{INT}(n)$ on 2PFA.

Theorem 4. *Let $\mathcal{A}$ be a probabilistic Turing machine that accepts the language $L_{INT}(n)$ in time T using space S. Then, $TS = \Omega(n^2)$.*

Concerning the exact computing mode, Klauck [19] proved, for any regular language L, that the state complexity of the exact one-way quantum finite automata (1QFA) for L is not less than the state complexity of an equivalent one-way deterministic finite automata (DFA). That means that the exact 1QFA have no advantage in recognizing regular languages. It is therefore of interest to consider the case of two-way finite automata. We still do not know whether there is time complexity or state complexity advantages for two-way quantum finite automata in recognition of languages. However, we prove that exact 2QCFA do have time-space complexity advantages for recognizing some special languages. In order to do that, let us consider a special sequence of functions introduced and studied in [6].

Let us consider the sequence of functions studied in [6]. Let us first define the function $NE(x_1, x_2, x_3)$ as follows: $NE(x_1, x_2, x_3) = 0$ if $x_1 = x_2 = x_3$ and $NE(x_1, x_2, x_3) = 1$ otherwise. Now we can define a sequence of functions NE^d as follows: (1) $NE^0(x_1) = x_1$ and (2) $NE^d(x_1, \ldots, x_{3^d}) = NE(NE^{d-1}(x_1, \ldots, x_{3^{d-1}}), NE^{d-1}(x_{3^{d-1}+1}, \ldots, x_{2 \cdot 3^{d-1}}), NE^{d-1}(x_{2 \cdot 3^{d-1}+1}, \ldots, x_{3^d}))$ for all $d > 0$.

Let $n = 3^d$, we now define the function $RNE(x, y) = NE^d(x_1 \wedge y_1, \ldots, x_n \wedge y_n)$, where $x, y \in \{0, 1\}^n$, and let us consider the following language

$$L_{NE}(n) = \{x \#^n y \mid x, y \in \{0, 1\}^n, RNE(x, y) = 1\}.$$

In order to prove the last two main theorems, we will use a 2QCFA to simulate the quantum communication protocol from [6] for the problem RNE and get an upper bound for the time-space complexity for 2QCFA.

Theorem 5. *There is an exact 2QCFA that accepts the language $L_{NE}(n)$ in time T using space S such that $TS = O(n^{1.87} \log n)$.*

Theorem 6. *Let $\mathcal{A}$ be be a probabilistic Turing machine that accepts the language $L_{NE}(n)$ in time T using space S. Then, $TS = \Omega(n^2)$.*

2   Preliminaries

2.1   Quantum Query Algorithm

In the following let input $x = x_1 \cdots x_n \in \{0, 1\}^n$ for some fixed n. We will consider a Hilbert space $\mathcal{H}$ with basis states $|i, j\rangle$ for $i \in \{0, 1, \ldots, n\}$ and $j \in \{1, \cdots, m\}$ (where m can be chosen arbitrarily). A query O_x to an input $x \in \{0, 1\}^n$ will be formulated as the following unitary transformation:

- $O_x|0, j\rangle = |0, j\rangle$;
- $O_x|i, j\rangle = (-1)^{x_i}|i, j\rangle$ for $i \in \{1, 2, \cdots, n\}$.

A quantum query algorithm $\mathcal{A}$ which uses t queries for an input x consists of a sequence of unitary operators $U_0, O_x, U_1, \ldots, O_x, U_t$, where U_i's do not depend on the input x and the query O_x does. The algorithm will start in a fixed starting state $|\psi_s\rangle$ of $\mathcal{H}$ and will perform the above sequence of operations. This leads to the final state

$$|\psi_f\rangle = U_t O_x U_{t-1} \cdots U_1 O_x U_0 |\psi_s\rangle. \tag{1}$$

The final state is then measured with a measurement $\{M_0, M_1\}$. For an input $x \in \{0, 1\}^n$, we denote $\mathcal{A}(x)$ the output of the quantum query algorithm $\mathcal{A}$. Obviously, $Pr[\mathcal{A}(x) = 0] = \|M_0|\psi_f\rangle\|^2$ and $Pr[\mathcal{A}(x) = 1] = \|M_1|\psi_f\rangle\|^2 = 1 - Pr[\mathcal{A}(x) = 0]$. We say that the quantum query algorithm $\mathcal{A}$ computes f within an error ε if for every input $x \in \{0, 1\}^n$ it holds that $Pr[\mathcal{A}(x) = f(x)] \geq 1 - \varepsilon$. If $\varepsilon = 0$, we says that the quantum algorithm is an exact quantum algorithm. For more details on the definition of quantum query complexity see [6, 12, 16].

2.2   Communication Complexity

We will use the following standard model of communication complexity. Two parties Alice and Bob compute a function f on distributed inputs x and y. A deterministic communication protocol $\mathcal{P}$ will compute a function f, if for every input pair $(x, y) \in X \times Y$ the protocol terminates with the value $f(x, y)$ as its output at a well specified party. In a probabilistic protocol, Alice and Bob may also flip coins during the protocol execution and proceed according to outcomes of the coins. Moreover, the protocol can have an erroneous output with a small probability. In a quantum protocol, Alice and Bob may use also quantum resources for communication. Let $\mathcal{P}(x, y)$ denote the output of the protocol $\mathcal{P}$. We will consider two kinds of protocols for computing a function f:

- An exact protocol $\mathcal{P}$ such that $Pr(\mathcal{P}(x, y) = f(x, y)) = 1$.
- A bounded error protocol $\mathcal{P}$ such that $Pr(\mathcal{P}(x, y) = f(x, y)) \geq \frac{2}{3}$.

The communication complexity of a protocol $\mathcal{P}$ is the number of (qu)bits exchanged in the worst case. The communication complexity of f is, which respect to the communication mode used, the complexity of an optimal protocol for f. We will use $D(f)$ and $R(f)$ to denote the deterministic communication complexity and the bounded error probabilistic communication complexity of the function f, respectively. Similarly, we use notations $Q_E(f)$ and $Q(f)$ for the exact and bounded error quantum communication complexity of a function f. For more details on the definition of communication complexity see [22].

Some communication complexity results that we will use in this paper are:

1. $D(\text{EQ}) = \mathbf{\Omega}(n)$, $R(\text{EQ}) = \mathbf{O}(\log n)$ [22].
2. $R(\text{INT}) = \mathbf{\Omega}(n)$ [25], $Q(\text{INT}) = \mathbf{O}(\sqrt{n} \log n)$ [11].
3. $R(\text{RNE}) = \mathbf{\Omega}(n)$, $Q_E(\text{RNE}) = \mathbf{O}(n^{0.87} \log n)$ [6].

2.3   Two-Way Finite Automata

We assume familiarity with the models of finite automata introduced in [3,4,13, 24]. We denote the input alphabet by Σ, which does not include symbols ¢ (the left end-marker) and \$ (the right end-marker). A two-way finite automaton that we will use in this paper halts when it enters an accepting or a rejecting state.

2QCFA were introduced by Ambainis and Watrous [4] and further studied by Zheng *et al.* [17,23,27–29]. Informally, a 2QCFA can be seen as a 2DFA with an access to a quantum memory for states of a fixed Hilbert space upon which at each step either a unitary operation is performed or a projective measurement and the outcomes of which then probabilistically determine the next move of the underlying 2DFA.

A 2QCFA $\mathcal{M}$ is specified by a 9-tuple $\mathcal{M} = (Q, S, \Sigma, \Theta, \delta, |q_0\rangle, s_0, S_{acc}, S_{rej})$ where: (1) Q is a finite set of orthonormal quantum basis states. (2) S is a finite set of classical states. (3) Σ is a finite alphabet of input symbols and let $\Sigma' = \Sigma \cup \{¢, \$\}$, where ¢ will be used as the left end-marker and \$ as the right end-marker. (4) $|q_0\rangle \in Q$ is the initial quantum state. (5) s_0 is the initial classical state. (6) $S_{acc} \subset S$ and $S_{rej} \subset S$, where $S_{acc} \cap S_{rej} = \emptyset$ are sets of the classical accepting and rejecting states, respectively. (7) Θ is a quantum transition function $\Theta : S \setminus (S_{acc} \cup S_{rej}) \times \Sigma' \rightarrow U(H(Q)) \cup O(H(Q))$, where $U(H(Q))$ and $O(H(Q))$ are sets of unitary operations and measurements on the Hilbert space generated by quantum states from Q. (8) δ is a classical transition function. If the automaton $\mathcal{M}$ is in the classical state s and in the quantum state $|\psi\rangle$, its tape head is scanning a symbol σ, then $\mathcal{M}$ performs quantum and classical transitions as follows. (a) If $\Theta(s, \sigma) \in U(H(Q))$, then the unitary operation $\Theta(s, \sigma)$ is applied on the current quantum state $|\psi\rangle$ to produce a new quantum state. The automaton then performs, in addition, the following classical transition function $\delta : S \setminus (S_{acc} \cup S_{rej}) \times \Sigma' \rightarrow S \times \{-1, 0, 1\}$. If $\delta(s, \sigma) = (s', d)$, then the new classical state of the automaton will be s' and its head moves in the direction d. (b) If $\Theta(s, \sigma) \in O(H(Q))$, then the measurement operation $\Theta(s, \sigma)$ is applied on the current state $|\psi\rangle$. Suppose the measurement $\Theta(s, \sigma)$ is specified by operators $\{P_1, \ldots, P_m\}$ and its corresponding classical outcome is from the set $N_{\Theta(s,\sigma)} = \{1, 2, \cdots, m\}$. The classical transition function δ can be then specified as follow $\delta : S \setminus (S_{acc} \cup S_{rej}) \times \Sigma' \times N_{\Theta(s,\sigma)} \rightarrow S \times \{-1, 0, 1\}$. In such a case, if i is the classical outcome of the measurement, then the current quantum state $|\psi\rangle$ is changed to the state $P_i|\psi\rangle/\|P_i|\psi\rangle\|$. Moreover, if $\delta(s, \sigma)(i) = (s', d)$, then the new classical state of the automaton is s' and its head moves in the direction d.

The automaton halts and accepts (rejects) the input when it enters a classical accepting (rejecting) state (from $S_{acc}(S_{rej})$).

The computation of a 2QCFA $\mathcal{M} = (Q, S, \Sigma, \Theta, \delta, |q_0\rangle, s_0, S_{acc}, S_{rej})$ on an input $w \in \Sigma^*$ starts with the string ¢x\$ on the input tape. At the start, the tape head of the automation is positioned on the left end-marker and the automaton begins the computation in the classical initial state s_0 and in the initial quantum state $|q_0\rangle$. After that, in each step, if its classical state is s, its tape head reads a symbol σ and its quantum state is $|\psi\rangle$, then the automaton changes its states and makes its head movement following the steps described in the definition.

Let $0 \leq \varepsilon < \frac{1}{3}$. A finite automaton $\mathcal{M}$ recognizes L with bounded error ε if, for $w \in \Sigma^*$,

1. $\forall w \in L$, $Pr[\mathcal{M}$ accepts $w] \geq 1 - \varepsilon$, and
2. $\forall w \notin L$, $Pr[\mathcal{M}$ rejects $w] \geq 1 - \varepsilon$.

If $\varepsilon = 0$, we say the finite automaton $\mathcal{M}$ is an exact finite automaton.

3   Main Proofs

Proof (**Proof of Theorem** 1). At first we describe a 2PFA $\mathcal{A}$ to accept the language $L_{EQ}(n)$. The automaton will use states $s_{q,k,l}$ where $0 \leq q, k, l \leq n^2$.

First of all, the automaton will start $\mathcal{A}$, using $O(n)$ states, to check that the input is in the form $x\#^n y$, where $|x| = |y| = n$. If the length of the input $|w| > 3n$, then the automaton halts and rejects the input in $O(n)$ time. After that $\mathcal{A}$ starts an addition computation in the state $s_{0,0,0}$. After reading the left-end marker, the automaton changes its state randomly to $s_{p,0,0}$, where $p \leq n^2$ is a prime. When the 2PFA $\mathcal{A}$ finishes reading the "x-region" of the input, it changes its state from $s_{p,0,0}$ to $s_{p,s,0}$, where $s = Num(x) \bmod p$. ($Num(x)$ is the natural number whose binary representation is the string x). It is clear that such computation can be done by a 2PFA. When $\mathcal{A}$ reads the "$\#$-region", it keeps its state unchanged. When $\mathcal{A}$ finishes reading the "y-region", it changes its state from $s_{p,s,0}$ to $s_{p,s,t}$, where $t = Num(y) \bmod p$. The automaton reaches the right end-marker in a state $s_{p,s,t}$. If $s = t$, then the input is accepted. If $s \neq t$, the input is rejected.

The automaton $\mathcal{A}$ simulates the communication protocol [18] for the problem EQ. If the input $w \in L_{EQ}(n)$, $\mathcal{A}$ will accept it for certainty.

Let us now say that a prime $2 < p < n^2$ is bad for a pair (x,y) such that $x \neq y$, if the above 2PFA for such an input pair (x,y) and such a choice of prime yields a wrong answer. It is clear that there are at most $n-1$ bad primes. Let $Prime(m)$ be the number of primes smaller than m. By the Prime number theorem, $Prime(n^2) > \frac{n^2}{2\ln n}$.

If the input $x\#^n y \notin L_{EQ}(n)$, $\mathcal{A}$ accepts the input only with the probability

$$\frac{\text{number of bad primes}}{Prime(n^2)} < \frac{n-1}{n^2/2\ln n} < \frac{2\ln n}{n}. \tag{2}$$

Obviously, the space used by $\mathcal{A}$ is $S = \mathbf{O}(\log n^6) = \mathbf{O}(\log n)$ and the time is $T = \mathbf{O}(n)$. Therefore, $TS = \mathbf{O}(n \log n)$.

Proof (**Proof of Theorem** 2). Let $\mathcal{A}$ be a Turing machine that recognizes the language $L_{EQ}(n)$ in time T using space S. We describe now a deterministic communication protocol for Alice and Bob that solves the problem EQ.

For an input $(x,y) \in \{0,1\}^n \times \{0,1\}^n$, Alice and Bob simulate $\mathcal{A}$ with the input $x\#^n y$, where $x, y \in \{0,1\}^n$. It is obvious that $x\#^n y \in L_{EQ}(n)$ iff $EQ(x,y) = 1$. Alice starts to simulate $\mathcal{A}$'s computation as long as the tape head of $\mathcal{A}$ is either in "x-region" of the input or in the "#-region" of the input. When the tape head of $\mathcal{A}$ moves to the "y-region", then Bob simulates $\mathcal{A}$'s computation as long as the tape head of $\mathcal{A}$ is either in the "y-region" of the input or in the "#-region" of the input. When the tape head of $\mathcal{A}$ moves to the "x-region" of the input, Alice simulates $\mathcal{A}$'s computation again. The idea is that each player is responsible for the simulation in regions where he knows the input bits. In any step in which the tape goes from "x-region" and "#-region" to "y-region" (from "y-region" and "#-region" to "x-region"), Alice (Bob) sends the current configuration of $\mathcal{A}$ to Bob (Alice).

In each time, the information which is required to send to the other party is not more than S. Since move from the "x-region" to the "y-region" and vice versa takes at least n steps (at least the size of "#-region"), the number of times Alice and Bob send information to each other is at most T/n. All together the amount of communicating information in the protocol is not more than $S \cdot T/n$. Since $D(\text{EQ}) = \Omega(n)$ [22], we have $S \cdot T/n = \Omega(n)$ and therefore $TS = \Omega(n^2)$.

Before we prove Theorem 3, we present a main proof technique of this paper. Namely, that every quantum query algorithm can be efficiently simulated by a 2QCFA. Some similar proof method can be found in the lines of [30].

Theorem 7. *The computation of a quantum query algorithm $\mathcal{A}$ for a Boolean function $f : \{0,1\}^n \to \{0,1\}$ can be simulated by a 2QCFA $\mathcal{M}$. Moreover, if the quantum query algorithm $\mathcal{A}$ uses t queries and l quantum basis states, then the 2QCFA $\mathcal{M}$ uses $O(l)$ quantum basis states, $O(n^2)$ classical states, and $O(t \cdot n)$ time.*

Proof. Suppose that we have a quantum query algorithm $\mathcal{A}$ which use t queries is defined as in Subsect. 2.1. The input of the 2QCFA $\mathcal{M}$ is the same as the input of the quantum query algorithm $\mathcal{A}$, which is $\mathcal{c}x\$$ on its tape. The main idea of the simulation goes as follows: We consider now a 2QCFA $\mathcal{M}$ with quantum basis states $|0\rangle$ and $|i,j\rangle$ for $i \in \{0,1,\ldots,n\}$ and $j \in \{1,\cdots,m\}$. $\mathcal{M}$ starts its computation in the initial quantum state $|0\rangle$ and the initial classical state s_0. The first time when $\mathcal{M}$ reads the left-end marker $\mathcal{c}$, $\mathcal{M}$ applies $\Theta(s_0, \mathcal{c})$ to the quantum state such that $\Theta(s_0, \mathcal{c})|0\rangle = U_0|\psi_s\rangle$.

The k-th time when $\mathcal{M}$ reads the right-end marker $\$$, $\mathcal{M}$ applies U_k to the quantum state, where $1 \le k \le t$. $\mathcal{M}$ simulates the query O_x every time when it reads the input $x = x_1 \cdots x_n$ from left to right. The automaton proceeds precisely as in Fig. 1, where

$$\Theta(s_{k,i}, \sigma)|0\rangle = |0\rangle, \Theta(s_{k,i}, \sigma)|i,j\rangle = (-1)^\sigma |i,j\rangle \text{ and } \Theta(s_{k,i}, \sigma)|u,j\rangle = |u,j\rangle \text{ for } u \ne i. \tag{3}$$

It is easy to verify that the unitary operators preformed in Step 2.1 are

$$\Theta(s_{k,n}, x_n)\Theta(s_{k,n-1}, x_{n-1}) \ldots \Theta(s_{k,1}, x_1) = O_x. \tag{4}$$

It is clear that for any input x, $Pr[\mathcal{A}(x) = 1] = Pr[\mathcal{M} \text{ accepts } x]$ and $Pr[\mathcal{A}(x) = 0] = Pr[\mathcal{M} \text{ rejects } x]$. From the above simulation, we can see that if the quantum query algorithm $\mathcal{A}$ uses l quantum basis states and t queries,

Check that the input x is of the form of $\{0,1\}^n$. Repeat the following ad infinity:
1. Read the left end-marker ¢, perform $\Theta(s_0, ¢)$ on the initial quantum state $|0\rangle$, change its classical state to $\delta(s_0, ¢) = s_{1,1}$, and move the tape head one cell to the right.
2. While the current classical state is not $s_{t+1,1}$, do the following
   2.1 While the currently scanned symbol σ is not the right end marker \$, do the following:
      2.1.1 Apply $\Theta(s_{k,i}, \sigma)$ to the current quantum state.
      2.1.2 Change the classical state $s_{k,i}$ to $s_{k,i+1}$ and move the tape head one cell to the right.
   2.2 When the right end-marker \$ is reached, perform $\Theta(s_{k,n+1}, \$) = U_k$ on the current quantum state. Change the classical state $s_{k,n+1}$ to $s_{k+1,1}$ and move the tape head to the symbol of x.
3. Measure the current quantum state with the measurement $\{M_0, M_1\}$.
   If the outcome is 1, the input is accepted. Otherwise, the input is rejected.

Fig. 1. Description of the behavior of 2QCFA $\mathcal{M}$ when simulating the quantum algorithm $\mathcal{A}$.

then the 2QCFA $\mathcal{M}$ uses $\mathbf{O}(l)$ quantum basis states, $\mathbf{O}(n^2)$ classical states, and $\mathbf{O}(t \cdot n)$ time.

We have proved that 2QCFA can simulate quantum query algorithms. Now what about the quantum communication protocol for the INT problem? According to [11], we need to simulate the following unitary map:

$$O_z : |i\rangle \mapsto (-1)^{z_i}|i\rangle, \tag{5}$$

where $z = x \wedge y$ is a bit-wise AND of x and y, since $z_i = 1$ whenever both $x_i = 1$ and $y_i = 1$.

In the following prove of Theorem we will use the following result:

Lemma 8. *Let $w = x\#^n y$, where $x, y \in \{0,1\}^n$, be the input of a 2QCFA $\mathcal{M}$. Then, the unitary map: $O_z : |i\rangle \mapsto (-1)^{z_i}|i\rangle$, where $z = x \wedge y$, can be simulated by $\mathcal{M}$. Moreover, $\mathcal{M}$ uses one additional auxiliary qubit and $\mathbf{O}(n)$ classical states and its running time is $\mathbf{O}(n)$.*

Proof. Assume that Alice wants to apply O_z to a quantum state $|\phi\rangle = \sum_{i=1}^n \alpha_i |i\rangle$. $\mathcal{M}$ will use quantum states $\{|i\rangle|0\rangle, |i\rangle|1\rangle\}_{i=1}^n$ and classical states $\{s_i\}_{i=0}^{2n+1}$. $\mathcal{M}$ will start with the quantum state $|\phi\rangle|0\rangle$. The procedure to simulate the unitary map O_z is as in Fig. 2, where

$$U_{i,\sigma}|j\rangle|b\rangle = |j\rangle|b \oplus \sigma\rangle \text{ if } j = i, \text{ otherwise } U_{i,\sigma}|j\rangle|b\rangle = |j\rangle|b\rangle; \tag{6}$$

$$V_{i,\sigma}|j\rangle|1\rangle = (-1)^{\sigma}|j\rangle|1\rangle \text{ if } j = i, \text{ otherwise } V_{i,\sigma}|j\rangle|b\rangle = |j\rangle|b\rangle. \tag{7}$$

It is easy to verify that $U_{i,\sigma}$ and $V_{i,\sigma}$ are unitary. After Step 2, the quantum state changes to

$$U_{n,x_n} \cdots U_{1,x_1} \sum_{i=1}^n \alpha_i |i\rangle|0\rangle = \sum_{i=1}^n \alpha_i |i\rangle|x_i\rangle. \tag{8}$$

After Step 4, the quantum state changes to

$$V_{n,y_n} \cdots V_{1,y_1} \sum_{i=1}^{n} \alpha_i |i\rangle |x_i\rangle = \sum_{i=1}^{n} \alpha_i \cdot (-1)^{x_i \wedge y_i} |i\rangle |x_i\rangle. \tag{9}$$

After Step 6, the quantum state changes to

$$U_{n,x_n} \cdots U_{1,x_1} \sum_{i=1}^{n} \alpha_i \cdot (-1)^{x_i \wedge y_i} |i\rangle |x_i\rangle = \sum_{i=1}^{n} \alpha_i \cdot (-1)^{x_i \wedge y_i} |i\rangle |0\rangle = O_z |\phi\rangle |0\rangle. \tag{10}$$

---

1. Move the tape head to the first symbol of x, set its classical state to s_1.
2. While the currently scanned symbol σ is not $\#$, do the following:
   2.1 Apply $\Theta(s_i, \sigma) = U_{i,\sigma}$ to the current quantum state.
   2.2 Change the classical state s_i to s_{i+1} and move the tape head one cell to the right.
3. Move the tape head to the first symbol of y.
4. While the currently scanned symbol σ is not \$, do the following:
   4.1 Apply $\Theta(s_{n+i}, \sigma) = V_{i,\sigma}$ to the current quantum state.
   4.2 Change the classical state s_{n+i} to s_{n+i+1} and move the tape head one cell to the right.
5. Change the classical state s_{2n+1} to s_1 and move the tape head to the first symbol of x.
6. While the currently scanned symbol σ is not $\#$, do the following:
   6.1 Apply $\Theta(s_i, \sigma) = U_{i,\sigma}$ to the current quantum state.
   6.2 Change the classical state s_i to s_{i+1} and move the tape head one cell to the right.

Fig. 2. Description of the behavior of 2QCFA when simulating the unitary map O_z.

Proof (**Proof of Theorem 3**). Combining the simulation techniques from Theorem 7 and Lemma 8, we can use a 2QCFA to simulate a Grover search [16] on the input $z \in \{0,1\}^n$, where $z_i = x_i \wedge y_i$. Therefore it is clear that there is a 2QCFA recognizing the language $L_{INT}(n)$. Since the Grover's algorithm requires $\mathbf{O}(\sqrt{n})$ queries and uses $\mathbf{O}(n)$ quantum basis states, the time used by the 2QCFA is $T = \mathbf{O}(\sqrt{n} \cdot n) \doteq \mathbf{O}(n^{3/2})$. The number of quantum states used by the 2QCFA is $\mathbf{O}(n)$ and the number of classical states is $\mathbf{O}(n^2)$. Therefore, the space used by the 2QCFA is $S = \mathbf{O}(\log n + \log n^2) = \mathbf{O}(\log n)$. Hence, $TS = \mathbf{O}(n^{3/2} \log n)$.

Proof (**Proof of Theorem 4**). The proof is similar to the proof of Theorem 2 except that probabilistic computation is used instead of deterministic one. The result is based on $R(\text{INT}) = \mathbf{\Omega}(n)$ [25].

Proof (**Proof of Theorem 5**). By combining the simulation techniques from Theorem 7 and Lemma 8, we can use a 2QCFA to simulate Ambainis' exact query algorithm in [6] on the input $z \in \{0,1\}^n$, where $z_i = x_i \wedge y_i$. Therefore, there is an exact 2QCFA recognizing the language $L_{NE}(n)$. Since the exact algorithm requires $\mathbf{O}(n^{0.87})$ queries and uses $\mathbf{O}(n)$ quantum basis states, the time used by the exact 2QCFA is $T = \mathbf{O}(n^{0.87} \cdot n) = \mathbf{O}(n^{1.87})$. The space used is $S = \mathbf{O}(\log n)$. Hence, $TS = \mathbf{O}(n^{1.87} \log n)$.

Proof (**Proof of Theorem 6**). The proof is similar to that of Theorem 2 except that probabilistic computation is used instead of deterministic one. The final result is then based on $R(\text{RNE}) = \mathbf{\Omega}(n)$ [6].

4   Conclusion and Open Problems

Query complexity and communication complexity are related to each other. By using a simulation technique that transforms quantum query algorithms to quantum communication protocols, Buhrman et al. [11] obtained new quantum communication protocols and showed the first exponential gap between quantum and classical communication complexity.

In this paper, we have developed the connection among 2QCFA, quantum communication protocols and quantum query algorithms. We have constructed 2QCFA to simulate quantum query algorithms. Using known quantum query algorithms and quantum communication protocols, this simulation enabled us to prove several time-space complexity results for 2QCFA.

Some problems for future research:

1. The quantum communication complexity tight bound $Q(\text{DISJ}) = \Theta(\sqrt{n})$ [1]. Does there exists a 2QCFA that accepts the language $L_{INT}(n)$ in time T using space S such that $TS = \mathbf{O}(n^{3/2})$?
2. Recently, there have appeared recently several papers on new separations for query/communication complexity [2,7,8,14,15], can we use those results to improve our separations in this paper?
3. We have proved that the exact 2QCFA have superlinear advantage in time-space complexity. Can we prove that exact 2QCFA have superlinear advantage in time complexity or space complexity in recognizing languages comparing to 2DFA or 2PFA?

Acknowledgements. The authors are thankful to anonymous referees for their comments and suggestions that greatly help to improve the quality of the manuscript. Zheng would like to thanks A. Ambainis for his suggestion and hospitality in Riga, C. Mereghetti and B. Palano for their discussions and hospitality in Milan, L. Li for his helpful discussions.

References

1. Aaronson, S., Ambainis, A.: Quantum search of spatial regions. In: Proceedings of the 44th FOCS, pp. 200–209 (2003)
2. Aaronson, S., Ben-David, S., Kothari, R.: Separations in query complexity using cheat sheets. In: Proceedings of the 48th STOC, pp. 863–876 (2016)
3. Ambainis, A., Freivalds, R.: One-way quantum finite automata: strengths, weaknesses and generalizations. In: Proceedings of the 39th FOCS, pp. 332–341 (1998)
4. Ambainis, A., Watrous, J.: Two-way finite automata with quantum and classical states. TCS **287**, 299–311 (2002)
5. Ambainis, A., Nayak, A., Ta-Shma, A., Vazirani, U.: Dense quantum coding and quantum finite automata. J. ACM **49**, 496–511 (2002)
6. Ambainis, A.: Superlinear advantage for exact quantum algorithms. In: Proceedings of the 45th STOC, pp. 891–900 (2013)
7. Ambainis, A., Balodis, K., Belovs, A., Lee, T., Santha, M., Smotrovs, J.: Separations in query complexity based on pointer functions. In: Proceedings of the 48th STOC, pp. 800–813 (2016)

8. Ambainis, A., Kokainis, M., Kothari, R.: Nearly optimal separations between communication (or query) complexity and partitions. In: Proceedings of the 31st CCC, pp. 4:1–4:14 (2016)
9. Borodin, A., Cook, S.: A time-space tradeoff for sorting on a general sequential model of computation. SIAM J. Comput. **11**, 287–297 (1982)
10. Babai, L., Nisan, N., Szegedy, M.: Multiparty protocols, pseudorandom generators for logspace, and time-space trade-offs. JCSS **45**, 204–232 (1992)
11. Buhrman, H., Cleve, R., Wigderson, A.: Quantum vs. classical communication and computation. In: Proceedings of the 30th STOC, pp. 63–68 (1998)
12. Buhrman, H., de Wolf, R.: Complexity measures and decision tree complexity: a survey. TCS **288**, 21–43 (2002)
13. Freivalds, R.: Probabilistic two-way machines. In: Gruska, J., Chytil, M. (eds.) MFCS 1981. LNCS, vol. 118, pp. 33–45. Springer, Heidelberg (1981). https://doi.org/10.1007/3-540-10856-4_72
14. Goos, M., Pitassi, T., Watson, T.: Deterministic communication vs. partition number. In: Proceedings of the 56th FOCS, pp. 1077–1088 (2015)
15. Goos, M., Pitassi, T., Watson, T.: Randomized communication vs. partition number. In: Proceedings of the 44th ICALP, pp. 52:1–52:15 (2017)
16. Grover, L.: A fast quantum mechanical algorithm for database search. In: Proceedings of the 28th STOC, pp. 212–219 (1996)
17. Gruska, J., Qiu, D.W., Zheng, S.G.: Generalizations of the distributed Deutsch-Jozsa promise problem. Math. Struct. Comput. Sci. **27**, 311–331 (2017). arXiv:1402.7254
18. Hromkovič, J.: Design and Analysis of Randomized Algorithms. Springer, Cham (2005). https://doi.org/10.1007/3-540-27903-2
19. Klauck, H.: On quantum and probabilistic communication: Las Vegas and one-way protocols. In: Proceedings of the 32th STOC, pp. 644–651 (2000)
20. Klauck, H.: Quantum time-space tradeoffs for sorting. In: Proceedings of the 35th STOC, pp. 69–76 (2003)
21. Klauck, H., Špalek, R., de Wolf, R.: Quantum and classical strong direct product theorems and optimal time-space tradeoffs. SIAM J. Comput. **36**, 1472–1493 (2007)
22. Kushilevitz, E., Nisan, N.: Communication Complexity. Cambridge University Press, New York (1997)
23. Li, L.Z., Feng, Y.: On hybrid models of quantum finite automata. J. Comput. Syst. Sci. **81**, 1144–1158 (2015). arXiv:1206.2131
24. Qiu, D.W., Li, L.Z., Mateus, P., Gruska, J.: Quantum finite automata. In: Wang, J. (ed.) Handbook on Finite State Based Models and Applications, pp. 113–141. CRC Press, Boca Raton (2012)
25. Razborov, A.: On the distributional complexity of disjointness. TCS **106**, 385–390 (1992)
26. Yao, A.C.: Some complexity questions related to distributed computing. In: Proceedings of 11th STOC, pp. 209–213 (1979)
27. Yakaryılmaz, A., Say, A.C.C.: Succinctness of two-way probabilistic and quantum finite automata. Discrete Math. Theor. Comput. Sci. **12**, 19–40 (2010)
28. Zheng, S., Qiu, D., Li, L., Gruska, J.: One-way finite automata with quantum and classical states. In: Bordihn, H., Kutrib, M., Truthe, B. (eds.) Languages Alive. LNCS, vol. 7300, pp. 273–290. Springer, Heidelberg (2012). https://doi.org/10.1007/978-3-642-31644-9_19

29. Zheng, S.G., Gruska, J., Qiu, D.W.: On the state complexity of semi-quantum finite automata. RAIRO-Theor. Inform. Appl. **48**, 187–207 (2014). Earlier version in LATA 2014. arXiv:1307.2499
30. Zheng, S., Qiu, D.: From quantum query complexity to state complexity. In: Calude, C.S., Freivalds, R., Kazuo, I. (eds.) Computing with New Resources. LNCS, vol. 8808, pp. 231–245. Springer, Cham (2014). https://doi.org/10.1007/978-3-319-13350-8_18

Author Index

Printed in the United States
By Bookmasters